Education–Health for Life

Education and Medicine working together for healthy development

Michaela Glöckler
Stefan Langhammer
Christof Wiechert

Medical and Pedagogical Sections at the Goetheanum

WALDORF EARLY CHILDHOOD
ASSOCIATION OF NORTH AMERICA

Education–Health for Life
Education and Medicine working together for healthy development

Michaela Glöckler
Stefan Langhammer
Christof Wiechert

Education – Health for Life
Education and medicine working together for healthy development

© 2019 Waldorf Early Childhood Association of North America

ISBN: **978-1-936849-47-5**

Editors: **Michaela Glöckler, Stefan Langhammer, Christof Wiechert**
Copy Editors: Susan Bruck, Donna Miele, Astrid Schmitt-Stegmann
Production Editor: Donna Miele
Graphic Design: Amy Thesing

Published in the United States by the Waldorf Early Childhood Association of North America,
285 Hungry Hollow Road, Spring Valley, NY 10977
www.waldorfearlychildhood.org
Visit our online store at ***store.waldorfearlychildhood.org***

Second English edition

First English edition published by the Medical and Pedagogical Sections of the Goetheanum,
School of Spiritual Science, Rüttiweg 45, 4143 Dornach, Switzerland

This publication is made possible through a grant from the Waldorf Curriculum Fund.

All rights reserved. No part of this book may be reproduced without the written permission of the publisher, except for brief quotations embodied in critical reviews and articles.

CONTENTS

Preface 9

1. Education: A Pathway of Silent Healing 11
   Michaela Glöckler

2. Pictures of the Development of Physiology 29
   Michaela Glöckler

3. Healthy Timetabling: Everything Has Its Time 37
   Michaela Glöckler

4. Salutogenic Approach to Education in Early Childhood 41
   Peter Lang

5. Questions from Waldorf Educators 55
   Michaela Glöckler

6. The Nature of the Human Being 79
   Astrid Schmitt-Stegmann

7. The Curriculum Physiology: Age-Specific Subjects and Therapeutic Pedagogy 87
   Christof Wiechert

8. Projective Geometry: A Holistic Understanding of Space 103
   Georg Glöckler

9. Professional Ethics and a Spiritual Approach in the Teaching Profession 139
   Michaela Glöckler

10. Meditation and Community Building 145
    Christof Wiechert

11. Two Meditations for Teachers 153
    Christof Wiechert

12. The Seven Virtues of the Art of Teaching 157
    Christof Wiechert

13. What Helps in Daily Practice? 161
    Christof Wiechert

14. How Long to Work with a Class as a Class Teacher? 165
    Christof Wiechert

15. Perspectives on Pedagogic-Medical Diagnostics and Therapies 169
    The Task of the School Doctor – *Michaela Glöckler* • Child Study – *Christof Wiechert* • Children with Special Gifts – *Michaela Glöckler* • The Schubert Remedial Class – *Reinoud Engelsman* • Examples for Remedial Support – *Ingrid Ruhrman* • Educational and Medical Assessment and Therapy – *Bernd Ruf* • EOS Experiential Education – *Michael Birnthaler*

16. Examples of Spirituality in Science, Art, and Religion.. 209
    The Heart Does Not Drive the Blood, but the Blood Drives the Heart – *Eugen Kolisko* • Experiences with Modeling, Speech, Eurythmy, and Methodology – *Helle Loewe* • Speech – *Barbara Deanjean-von Stryk* • Eurhythmy – *Ulrike Wendt, Helga Daniel* • Methodology – *Rudolf Steiner* • Religious Qualities in Education – *Elisabeth von Kügelgen*

17. Questions of Today:
    Media, Technology, and Approaches to Sex Education 239
    The Child and Technology – *Michaela Glöckler* • The Child and Television, Computer Games, and Comics – *Michaela Glöckler* • The Child and Drugs – *Michaela Glöckler* • Educational Tasks for Adolescents – *Christof Wiechert* • Questions Relating to Sexuality and Sex Education – *Michaela Glöckler*

18. Areas of Collaboration with Parents and Pupils 267
    Stefan Langhammer

19. The College of Teachers as a Working Group Responsible for School Management 279
    Michaela Glöckler

20. The Life and Work of Karl Schubert 285
    Elisabeth von Kügelgen

21. The Life and Work of Eugen Kolisko... 293
    Peter Selg

Chapter Notes 305

Appendix I – Promoting Health Through Education 320

Appendix II – Research Provides Evidence of Steiner Education's Salutogenic Effects..... 329

Appendix III – Research in Rhythm: Two Examples 336

Appendix IV – The Color Scheme in Steiner Waldorf Schools 338

Appendix V – Addresses and References... 340

Appendix VI – "The Poor Words" by Rainer Maria Rilke 345

Appendix VII – Medical and Pedagogical Sections at the Goetheanum 346

Appendix VIII – Why Life Oscillates:
From a Topographical Towards a Functional Chronobiology 347

About the Kolisko Conferences 359

This book is dedicated to parents, teachers, and doctors
who promote the health of children in education.

PREFACE

In the face of the escalation in bullying and violence in schools, the need to forge cultural understanding that surmounts ethical and religious boundaries, increasing concentration difficulties amongst children and adolescents, multiple learning difficulties and developmental crises, we need to address the burning question of how home and school can best meet these challenges. The Kolisko conferences aim to offer a discussion forum where perspectives can unfold and approaches to daily educational practice can be developed. Dr. Eugen Kolisko was the first physician to endorse the concept of Waldorf education, and to see education and daily school life itself as a means of prevention and health promotion. From 1920 onwards he was involved in developing the first Waldorf (Steiner) school in Stuttgart, Germany.

Since then around 900 schools and 1,600 kindergartens have been established in over fifty countries. Furthermore, in countless public (state) and private schools, Waldorf education has provided stimulus for an education that consistently bases its approach on developmental conditions in childhood. Its founder, Rudolf Steiner, repeatedly stressed that educational perspectives must *arise from the nature of the growing child himself.*

To what does Waldorf education owe its name and origin? Directly after the First World War, Emil Molt, director of the Waldorf Astoria cigarette factory, invited the Goethe scholar and anthroposophist Rudolf Steiner to set up a school for the children of his staff. Steiner took this as an opportunity to develop an educational concept fully based on promoting health. It was not just that children after the war were suffering from many illnesses, including war-related malnutrition, but that Steiner was concerned with the fundamental question of how education can serve to foster development and nurture health. Establishing a full-time post of "doctor at the Waldorf School" followed naturally from this. Kolisko, invited to take up this post, took it upon himself to meet the challenge.

Steiner said of him: "I consider it a very special piece of good fortune for the Waldorf School that our school doctor is part of the faculty of teachers, that he takes part in faculty meetings. Dr. Kolisko, who is a medical doctor by profession, and deeply involved in health issues, also participates fully in the faculty, in a teaching context. In this way everything relating to the children's physical health can be undertaken in full harmony with all that is taught, all educational measures. And this is…what is needed: our teacher training must develop in such a way that it integrates all that relates to health and illness in the child."[1]

The postwar problems in Germany in 1919 find their counterpart today in the consequences of overeating and lack of exercise or movement in the western world, and in grave problems of malnutrition and infectious diseases on an epidemic scale in the under-privileged regions of Africa, South America, and the Pacific Basin. First and foremost among these are HIV infections, which for example affect 12.5 percent of teachers in South Africa. This is compounded by environmental stress and, in the psychological realm, unmistakable damage arising from trauma in childhood and adolescence due to violence, being misunderstood or neglected, sexual abuse, or also sensory bombardment from internet and mass media, and repercussions from excessive computer games. Irrespective of which of these problems affect a child, the same question repeatedly surfaces: How can school be used to give children and adolescents maximum healing and strengthening forces? How can teachers, therapists, doctors, and parents work together to ensure that children feel fully accepted and acknowledged, and are supported in their age-appropriate needs? How can their psychological and spiritual development receive just as much attention as their intellectual and physical growth?

We need to develop concepts and educational approaches that do justice to the most varied developmental needs and conditions in different countries. In other words, a form of education is needed that, just as much as promoting goal-oriented motivation and intelligence, contributes to the development of joy in life, courage, responsibility, and the so-called soft skills of social competence. To contribute constructively here is the great concern of Waldorf and Rudolf Steiner education. Rudolf Steiner says succinctly: *The social question is an educational question and the education question is a medical question.*[2] Developing healthy thinking about individual, cultural, social, and economic issues, and drawing the appropriate conclusions, is just as necessary as an education that builds on values such as truthfulness, loving interest, and respect for the child's dignity.

The articles compiled in this conference companion aim not only to address these often-posed questions, but also to identify possible solutions and perspectives for work. Special emphasis is given to projective geometry in the article relating to this subject, since it is as yet little known but represents a field which is of utmost service in developing awareness of oneself and the world. We would like to warmly thank Peter Selg and Elisabeth von Kügelgen for allowing us to include their abbreviated biographical studies of the first Waldorf school doctor, Eugen Kolisko, and the Waldorf remedial teacher Karl Schubert.

Our heartfelt thanks go to the authors and others who made this conference companion possible, including: Barbara Illemann (compiling and initial editing), Sue Scott (English editing), Martin Pieris (cover design and formatting), Astrid Schmitt-Stegmann (English proofreading), together with translators Margot Saar, Christian von Arnim, Matthew Barton, and Daniel Maslen.

It is our hope that perspectives presented here can provide stimulus and motivation for the parents, teachers and doctors involved in educational work.

Dornach, March 30, 2006
Medical and Pedagogical Sections at the Goetheanum
Michaela Glöckler
Stefan Langhammer
Christof Wiechert

CHAPTER 1

Education: A Pathway of Silent Healing

Michaela Glöckler

> *In olden times*
> *There lived in the souls of initiates*
> *Powerfully the thought*
> *That by nature*
> *Every person is ill.*
> *And education was seen*
> *As a healing process*
> *Which gave the child, as he matured*
> *The health to be a true human being.*
>
> — RUDOLF STEINER[1]

Fundamentals

Research by Robert Plomin and Judy Dunn[2] has clearly shown that three factors determine physical maturation and development in human beings:

1. Genetics
2. Upbringing and social environment
3. The quality of human relationships that the child experiences during his formative years.

Education and medicine must be always orientated in regard to these three factors.

Since it was discovered, however, that genes do not at all function as reliably and consistently as was assumed in the nineteenth and much of the twentieth centuries, scientists were surprised at the extent to which the quality of genetic material can be influenced positively as well as negatively with regard to what is passed on to the next generation. It is now commonly known that factors such as maternal alcohol and paternal nicotine consumption can accelerate the degeneration of genetic material.[3] A healthy environment, good nutrition, and loving care, on the other hand, have a positive and stabilizing effect on the child. It only became evident, however, as a result of extensive research into bonding and education, that the quality of human relationships was the decisive factor that tipped the scales of positive and negative influences, and this applied to all relationships—parents, neighbors, acquaintances, educators, teachers, doctors, or clergy. What is important is that the child feel accepted and understood for herself. If that is the case, then everything else tends to fall more or less into place.[4]

How is this relevant for educators? One must carry this understanding consciously! Whatever we do with children and adolescents through all the developmental stages they go through, we have to ask ourselves: How will this activity influence the child's physical development? Will it enhance or hinder the growth and maturation processes that belong to his particular age?

In order to answer these questions, we need to have an overview of physical development.

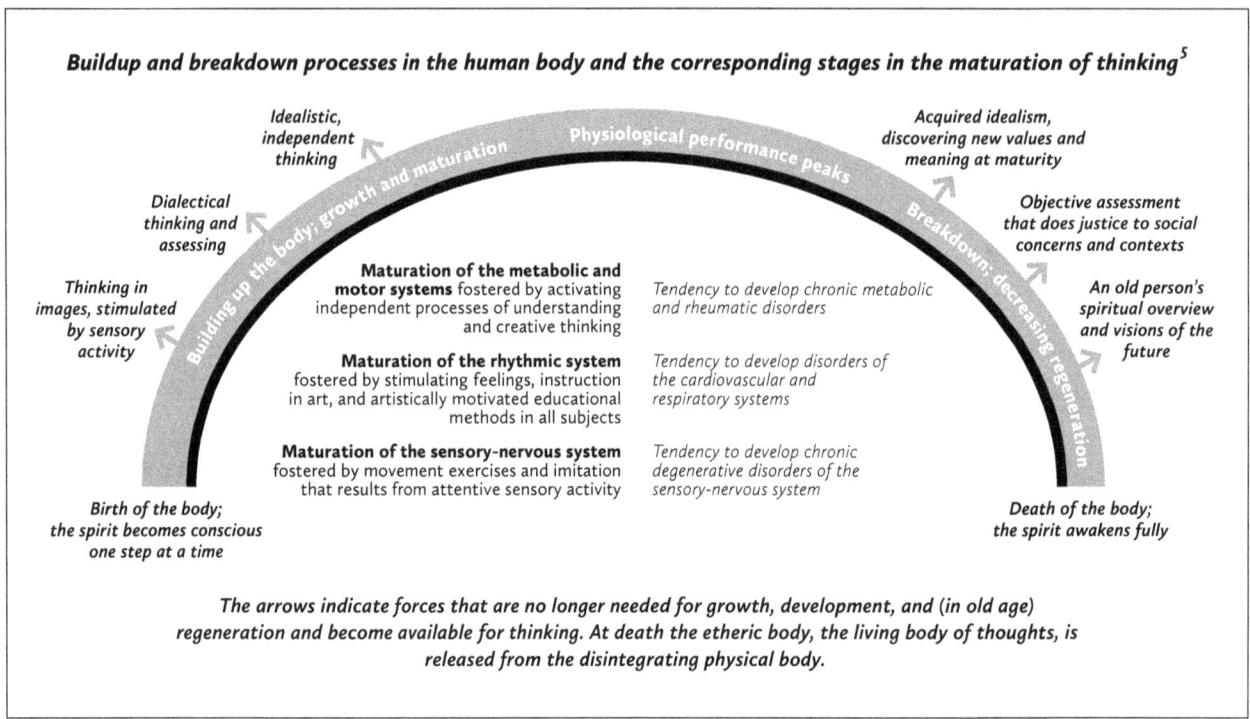

This diagram shows the most important phases of anatomic-physiological maturation in the human body in parallel to the development of thinking. The other aspect of the diagram shows the phases of involution and the changes in the last third of life. After birth, the development of the nervous system is most active, then come the organs of the rhythmic system and finally the maturation of the skeleton and the metabolic organs.

1. Maturation of the senses and of approximately 90 percent of the central nervous system occurs during the first nine years of life.

2. Development and stabilization of biological rhythms, including the ratio between breathing and heartbeat, takes place up to age 15 or 16.

3. Maturation of the skeleton, metabolic processes, and hormone regulation continues up to age 20 to 23.

It is interesting to note that these three systems degenerate in reverse order in later life:

1. Menopause sets in between age 40 and 50. According to statistics, signs of rheumatic deforming and metabolic disorders such as type 2 diabetes show their highest incidence at this time.

2. Between the age of 50 and 60 high blood pressure, cardiac arrhythmia, and chronic lung diseases have the highest incidence.

3. Between age 60 and 70 comes degeneration of the sense organs and central nervous system.

Thus, human development is not linear; it mirrors developmental phases of life, leading to the disconcerting question: Could the quality of development through childhood and adolescence determine the extent of chronic complaints in later life? Might primary prevention depend on a person's childhood quality of life? This is what Rudolf Steiner meant when he said that the educational question is a medical question.

Consequences for educational and medical practice in relation to children

...up to age nine

The differentiated maturation of the nervous system and the sensory-motor coordination (i.e. linking of sensory function and physical activity) comes from physical coordinated movement and joy in the discovery of the sense world, with the help of all the senses; therefore, children know instinctively that it is good for them. Created spaces are needed for children to move in, to play and be active in, making use of the dexterity and ability that goes with their age.

The Waldorf curriculum for children up to nine years of age is true to this principle. An element of movement forms an integral part of each lesson, not just the so-called movement lessons, which are of particular sensory-motor value. All movement—child-appropriate games lessons included—is at this age closely connected with sense experiences, especially those that arise out of the musical-rhythmical realm through singing and through language and movement games. Through this the child also learns to listen, which is a good preparation for the development of social awareness later on in life.

It is also in support of physiological and psychological development that Waldorf education is strictly against the use of computers and screens by kindergarten- and primary-school-age children. What is now propagated worldwide, with strong scientific backing, is the "one laptop per child" slogan, and in particular for third-world children to be brought into the digital world—a good idea, but at the wrong time for the child. This is not only because of a more urgent need for developing countries to have access to clean water, medical care, and adequate schooling, but because every hour a child sits in front of a screen makes it more difficult for her to have an un-manipulated inner life; her very movement development is held back. The brain function will not be fully activated, and the sensory motor integration will be disturbed independent of the particular program content, and there will be an increased inability to problem-solve.

Recommendations for this age:

- Stimulating initiative through one's own deeds and role modelling
- Toys that encourage the child to be active: simple objects and materials that leave the child free to develop and practice his own imagination
- Activating and nurturing the senses through appropriate play areas
- Establishing good habits with the help of a regular rhythm, little rituals in the mornings, evenings, at meal times, and when going to bed
- Rhythmical organization of the day, the week, the months, and the year
- Times when the child gets undivided attention, for example when getting up or going to bed and intermittently during the day where there can be real moments of meeting
- A predominantly nonverbal approach; not the word but rather the method which acts as a role model to be experienced in a way that leaves the child free to respond out of his/her own accord
- Opportunities to encounter nature
- Avoiding multi-media exposure and technical toys
- Bearing the child in one's consciousness, even on a stressful day, and holding him in one's thoughts when separated from him. This kind of "inner activity" ensures that the outer contact is quickly re-established on meeting again. What is important is the nearness and truthfulness in the relationship, independent of school achievements and approved behaviors
- Displaying cheerfulness and gratitude
- Set clear boundaries and "live." This gives certainty and orientation

...to the fourteenth and fifteenth years

What is now paramount is schooling that stimulates the rhythmical functions, emotions and feelings. We never breathe in as deeply as when we feel good, a child's heart never beats in a healthier way than when he is happy or fully engaged with a task. Between age 9 and 15 or 16, the overall pedagogical emphasis is on artistic processes and aesthetic awareness, in all subjects. In sports it can be a perfectly performed sequence of motions that needs practice. In history it lives in conversations and questions, which allow students to look at events from different points of view, so that a kind of balance or aesthetic situation arises through which they learn to understand and come to terms with even problematic events. In science it is provided in the experiments which the students observe with a sense of wonder. They discover the underlying laws of nature and, by describing and illustrating them in their own way, they learn to understand and apply them. There is something aesthetic also about mathematical laws, because they are true and constituent, not only in science and technology but also in human culture and life. In this way students also become familiar with the peculiarities and reliability of numbers.

It is also recommended, to age 14 or 15, that screen time be restrained. One should really only delegate to machines that which one has learned to govern and can understand—calculations, plays, music, dancing, life experience, and discoveries need to be explored. Learning through life needs to be nurtured. What is often brought into the house as a concession, by way of multimedia, needs to be balanced out in the school by motivating students to find life and reality instead of only technology and virtual worlds.

Sometimes this simple realization can help parents and students: the inventors of computers and multimedia themselves did not have these elements in their own childhoods. To develop the new, one needs creativity, not conditioning.[6]

Recommendations for this age:

- Cultivate conversation—let the child take part in interesting conversations between adults
- Live with inner questions such as:
    - When did we last talk?
    - When did I have time, show interest?
    - Do I show enough acknowledgment? Do I praise enough or do I tend to express only dissatisfaction?
    - Modern leadership structures focus on a "blame culture," however, those who learn from their mistakes can develop—this can strengthen teamwork. The question is, how do I deal with mistakes and bad behavior? How can I help the child be positive about learning from mistakes rather than to just find them awful?
- Clear guidance with regard to basic daily routine; inclusion of the child's wishes—keeping promises and making clear agreements as to how the child will be supervised.
- Artistic activities, especially learning to play a musical instrument.
- Controlled multimedia consumption; where possible, experiences should be worked through in conversations.

...to the twenty-first and twenty-second years

Between the ages of 13 to 15 and 18 to 22 the question arises as to how education can support the physiological development that happens at this time, i.e., maturation of the skeleton, hormonal changes, and maturation of the intermediary metabolism post-puberty. We usually assume that the metabolism and skeleton primarily need movement. This is true, of course, but it is not all. There are other things that continuously, from the inside so to speak, warm and stimulate the human being, and bring uprightness and fulfilment: these are objectives, interests, points of view, and motivation, which enthuse and inspire the young person. A glance at gait and movements of adolescents, at their posture and facial expression will suffice to establish whether they have uplifting and stimulating thoughts or whether mental emptiness makes them feel unmotivated and disinterested. The wisdom of language becomes apparent in the double meaning of the word "uprightness": honesty and truthfulness on the one hand and physical straightness and uprightness on the other.

In the upper school the educational focus shifts from imitation and modeling, from harmony and beauty, to meaning and significance. Now the focus is on the development of conscience, truth and freedom.

When a lesson does not succeed, then teachers must ask: how can I teach so that the young person comes to the right, meaningful, loved insights in my particular subject? It is not a matter of expecting the students to regurgitate thoughts which the teacher developed in front of them, but of supplying points of view, relating conditions, which help them to find their own answer to a given question.

Recommendations for this age:

- Encourage questions, thinking "for oneself"
- Be a friend and companion, show interest in what interests them
- Respect the growing need for freedom and independence, putting your own expectations aside
- Hold a "family council," make arrangements together, analyze how successful or not they were and discuss further steps together
- Learn to be happy about what is "totally different" in the other, wish to understand that which moves the adolescent
- Have the courage to trust risks and give the signal: I am on your side, no matter what happens and I am looking forward to seeing what your life will bring to you.

The lesson as a process of finding oneself, education at all levels as self-education—this is what we have to come to if we want our education to be in tune with the physiological development of the child. After all, the child is the one who is developing. The child should have the experience: I observed this myself; I saw it and I learned it myself. "Doing it myself" brings so much more joy, even for the young child, than having it done by somebody else who is "better" at it. An education that observes the realities of developmental physiology will motivate the child to become active and will conceive the task of education as Rudolf Steiner characterized it in the lecture course he gave to teachers in Basel.

> Education is always self-education, and as teachers and educators we are merely the environment in which the child is educating himself. We need to place the child in such an environment so that she herself can draw upon as many experiences as possible to develop the will.[7]

The person who develops accordingly, is inwardly active enough to not suffer from boredom, or become addicted to drugs, relationships, and multimedia. He can then also in later life use technology in a meaningful way, without becoming unproductive, dissatisfied, and disinterested. He has the chance to live in a way true to himself.

Sense activity, self-experience, self-awareness, spiritual experience

As it has become accepted that not only the healthy development of self-experience and self-awareness, but also certain intellectual achievements strongly depend on the differentiation and coordination of the sensory functions, an interest in possibilities for fostering the senses has been increasing. Many new therapies (sensory integration therapy, neurophysiological movement training, ergotherapeutic treatment, Rota therapy) try to balance, through intensive training, the results of former neglect in this field of sensory-motor development. The child of preschool age in particular absorbs and responds to all sensory experiences with his whole being: he will skip for joy whenever he sees something beautiful, wriggle with delight when something tastes good or shiver when discovering an unpleasant smell. As well as affecting the sense organs, the whole body responds to such experiences with much greater intensity than in later life and—as Rudolf Steiner points out again and again—becomes wholly sense organ. As a consequence the body, especially in early childhood, is extremely vulnerable and becomes irritable when exposed to pointless or harmful influences. This is why in pedagogical terms the nurturing of the senses is—in the true sense of the word—of constitutional significance, not only for the development of feeling and the forming of mental pictures, but above all for physical development—"to feel well in one's skin."

The following list, which is based on Rudolf Steiner's insights,[8] describes the twelve senses, how they work, and how we can nurture them and protect them from harmful influences.

Senses that relate to the physical and bring self-experience

Main development period: first year to preschool age

SENSE OF TOUCH

Organ	• Tactile corpuscles and free nerve endings
Conveys	• Self-experience at the periphery of the body through touch • Feeling secure because of physical contact • Existential trust

Nurturing influences especially for babies and toddlers	• Change between being alone and feeling held, gentle body contact and peacefully being left to himself; letting go is as important as embracing. • Creates spaces where the child can touch, explore and discover
Harmful influences	• Outer provision without a real inner acceptance of the child • Too much holding or too much leaving alone • Touching that serves more the satisfaction of the adult's own needs rather than respecting the body-soul integration of the child.

SENSE OF LIFE

Organ	• Vegetative nervous system • Experience of comfort, harmony • The feeling that "all's well with the world"
Nurturing influences	• Regular daily rhythm • A generally positive mood • Experience of the right measure and the right time, i.e. of order and harmony • Joyful mealtimes
Harmful influences	• Conflict, violence, intimidation • Stress, shock • Dissatisfaction • Indulgence • Nervousness • Lack of coherence in outer events

SENSE OF MOVEMENT

Organ	• Neuromuscular spindles
Conveys	• Perception of own movemen • Experience of freedom and self-control because of the ability to control movements
Nurturing influences	• Encourage child to become active
	• Arrange children's room so that everything can be touched and free play is possible • Movement sequences that make sense
Harmful influences	• Following children around and constantly forbidding certain things • Lack of stimulation due to passivity and absence of examples • Immobility in front of TV or other screen • Automatic toys which turn children into mere observers

SENSE OF BALANCE

Organ	• Semicircular canal of the inner ear
Conveys	• Experience of balance, equilibrium, resting points, self-confidence
Nurturing influences	• Movement games, see-saw experiences, jumping, running, turning, etc. • Adult's calm assurance when dealing with the child • Adult's striving for inner balance
Harmful influences	• Lack of movement • Inner restlessness • Depression, resignation, suicidal thoughts • Agitation, indecision

Senses that relate primarily to the feeling life

SENSE OF SMELL

Organ	• Olfactory mucosa at the root of the nose
Conveys	• A feeling of being connected with the aroma
Nurturing influences	• Providing different scent experiences in plants, food, in town and in the country
Harmful influences	• Stuffy rooms • Bad smells • Disgusting impressions and behavior

SENSE OF TASTE

Organ	• Taste buds in the mucous membrane of the tongue
Conveys	• Experience of sweet, sour, salty, or bitter tastes • Differentiated taste experiences (together with sense of smell)
Nurturing influences	• Prepare food in such a way that its natural taste can become apparent • "Tasteful" discernment of people and things • Aesthetically designed environment
Harmful influences	• Tendencies toward over-stimulation of taste buds (excessive ketchup, etc.—all tastes the same) • Tasteless comments • Tactlessness • Unaesthetic environment

SENSE OF SIGHT

Organ	• Eye
Conveys	• Experience of light and color
Nurturing influences	• Drawing attention to subtle nuances in nature by showing interest • tasteful color combinations in clothes and living space
Harmful influences	• Exposing to destructive or "silly" images • "Loud" colors • Excessive TV • Dark moods • Lack of interest • Colorless, dull environment

SENSE OF WARMTH

Organ	• Receptors for warmth and cold
Conveys	• Experience of warmth and cold
Nurturing influences	• Nurturing of warmth organism through adequate clothing • Providing a feeling of warmth in soul and spirit
Harmful influences	• Exaggerated "toughening-up" measures • Overheated rooms • Inefficient clothing • A cold, impersonal atmosphere • Exaggerated or hypocritical "warm-heartedness"

Senses that relate primarily to the thinking as mental capacity

SENSE OF HEARING

Organ	• Ears
Conveys	• Experience of sound • Access to inner soul realm
Nurturing influences	• Singing • Listening to and playing classical music, especially Bach, Handel, Haydn and Mozart • Adjust speed of reading and storytelling according to the child's ability to absorb • Allow time for inner pictures, tone memory and acoustic images to arise
Harmful influences	• Excessive acoustic intake, especially through media (too loud, too fast, lack of personal/human element) • Superficial or untruthful talk • Inhuman tone of voice

SENSE OF WORD

Organ	• Develops out of perception of movement and language
Conveys	• Experience of form and physiognomy (sense of form), grasping body language and the forming of word-sounds
Nurturing influences	• Warm and loving tone of voice • Awareness of body language and gesture • Ensuring that inner experiences match outer ones to avoid "untrue" impressions • Have a sense for individual expression
Harmful influences	• Conflict between what is said and what is done • Cold, neutral attitude, which leaves the child unclear if the parents are cheerful, sad, caring, or absent-minded • Any form of lying, where inner and outer experience do not match

SENSE OF THOUGHT

Organ	• Develops as a result of the complex processes of perceiving
Conveys	• Ability to grasp a line of thought immediately
Nurturing influences	• Cultivating surroundings where things are true and right

	• Coherence of things and events
	• Meaningful surroundings
Harmful influences	• Pointless actions
	• Erratic, uncoordinated thinking
	• Distortion of facts
	• Pointless associations

SENSE OF EGO

Organ	• Develops out of perceptions of touch and contact at the periphery of one's own body
Conveys	• Experience of essential being, immediate experience and recognition of the "I" of the other person
Nurturing influences	• Early experiences of sensing a loving and caring person to whom the child relates
	• Love between adults and toward the child
	• Culture of visiting friends and meeting people
	• Genuine perception of the other person (Martin Buber's "Thou"[9])
Harmful influences	• Disinterest, lack of attention, and other forms of lovelessness
	• Media consumption and exposure to virtual realities, which do not provide real experience of essential being
	• Materialistic view of the human being

If as a teacher I read these descriptions of how to nurture the senses, I have to ask myself the following questions as part of my lesson preparation: How will I meet the children tomorrow? What will my posture, my clothes, my facial expressions, my movements say to the child? Which sensory functions will be stimulated by the way I walk into the classroom, use gestures, speak, pause, ask questions, encourage activity, try to create habits for the whole class, decorate the classroom, so that the children can have a positive color experience, a sense that things are "just right," meaning: well-structured and ordered? How does it affect children to hear their names spoken in angry, reproachful, resigned, or aggressive tones?

Nothing helps discipline more than when the teacher is fully present, when she identifies physically with what she teaches, when she is "alive" and carries the pupils with her to a realm in which she herself has an existential interest. If adults are fully engaged and find their own subject exciting, then the children and adolescents will also be interested—they will find it difficult to switch off or disengage. Children know instinctively whether the adult is really fully aware of them, knows them, is genuinely interested in them. What is often seen as provocative behavior or rudeness in class is in reality a sympathy appeal from the students: an attempt to show that they are expecting more of their teacher. Is the teacher at all aware that a student has social difficulties, is being bullied, or is going through a difficult time at home? These kinds of problems often come out as aggression or rudeness towards the person from whom help is expected.

There is another question the adult can ask in view of the twelve sense activities: What about my own senses and the experiences I have in body, soul, and spirit that are dependent on them? Do I really experience myself in this human threefoldness, well incarnated in the body, sentient-perceptive in soul life, and mentally awake and sensitive to discern the different undertones and intermediate tones that accompany what is being said, and above all how it is being said? What can I do to keep developing my own senses? An important first step would consist in the realization that I have these sense-related qualities myself and that I can foster and develop them as part of my character. The twelve senses might well be the foundation for a healthy self-awareness, but that does not at all mean that this self-awareness is born out of the sense activity, rather that it is lifted into consciousness through the senses.

The fourteenth-century German mystic, Meister Eckhart, famously said: "If I were a king and did not know it, I would not be a king." Similarly, we could say: If I were a thoughtful, loving, good-natured creature of God, and I did not know it, what would I be? I would be that but without knowing it. That means it would have no significance for me. The sense activity shows that, especially for the young child, what comes first is the self-defining will, then, through the manner of activity, the sense organs develop further. It is through this development that the world is experienced by the self. The conflict between materialism and spirituality in the view of the world and humanity cannot be settled by outer evidence. There would be no sense in that. What would human freedom and dignity amount to if one could compel them by material means, if their existence could be determined and verified by a striking display of evidence? It lies in the nature of human freedom that it can only develop if I, as a human being, want it and if I develop thoughts and have experiences that are convincing inner proof of the eternity and indestructibility of a spiritual being, only then am I a king and know it.

That means for us, here, in this context: my spiritual being, my I, is indeed eternal, but it only knows about that which it has become conscious of during the life it has led on earth within an individual, sense-endowed body. Because this spiritual being, this "I am," is light, warm, capable of sympathy and antipathy, endowed with inner peace, freedom, harmony, and trust, it can—with the help of the physical body and the senses, through contact with the outer world, by meeting human beings—become conscious of itself and experience itself in the body in all its uniqueness and inner completeness. If we contemplate inner experience in this way we will not only become fully conscious of this self-experience, but we will be able to eternalize it by taking it into our thinking.

Everything we identify with in mental reflection constitutes the conscious part of our life and being. This experience, the apex of self-awareness that we have reached in and through our body, we can take with us when we die, as essential earth experience into the spiritual world. "Life in thinking, in the spirit" will continue after death, because thinking activity is spiritual activity and as such not tied to bodily life. By living in a sense-endowed body we gain the whole range of sense impressions and experiences. If this can be worked through in thinking and, especially, if growing self-awareness can be taken into this thinking, it will come to a so-called "second birth" through self-knowledge, which will allow the human being to fully become what his physical birth only provisionally makes him. Both in esoteric tradition and in the language of the New Testament, the second birth is described as "from the spirit."

Body life and thought life: The metamorphosis of the forces of growth and regeneration through thinking

Rudolf Steiner not only contributed to a qualitative as well as quantitative expansion of our view of the senses and their physiology, he also introduced a new basis for an understanding of human thinking. That spirituality, in the form of prayer, meditation, contemplation, devotion, and intercession, can positively influence, even heal, body and soul might be an accepted fact in modern medicine, but people still do not understand how this works in individual instances, especially in physiological terms. In short: the "what" is understood, but not the "how."

If we follow the development of the thinking capacity from childhood through adolescence to adulthood, and on into aging and death, we discover a different dynamic from the one we observed when we compared the generative and degenerative processes in the physical body. In the healthy person the development of thinking has a different gesture.

Rudolf Steiner calls the system of self-healing forces that are active in growth, development, and regeneration the etheric organism or life-generating organism. His findings were groundbreaking for the educational as well as medical field, because they showed that the activity of the life-generating forces and the thought-generating forces is identical. The knowledge that there is a complete congruence of thought and life leads to the conclusion that there is nothing in outer nature or in what we perceive with our senses that we could not take hold of with our thinking. This provides a clear answer to a question that remained unanswered during the conflict between nominalism and realism in the Middle Ages: Are thoughts real in themselves or are concepts merely names given to sense perceptions that are felt to be "reality"?

Only today, with the aid of modern science, can we find the inner evidence. Scientific fields like biochemistry, physiology, and micro- and macro-anatomy enable us to consciously access the functioning of life forces with their rhythms, regulatory circuits, interconnections, functional dynamics, and the interaction of all organs thanks to hormones, enzymes and other transmitter substances. With increasing astonishment, we realize that we are not only able to discover all kinds of minute details, but we are also able to grasp their lawfulness in our thinking. It goes even further: the more differentiated our thinking about them becomes, the more differentiated are the results of our research. Apart from this overall congruence of laws that can be grasped by thinking and the perceptible word, and the natural processes of which these laws exactly conform to, there exists another, even more impressive, congruence in the human organism itself.

Here we have, on the one hand, an external experience of our body and its biochemistry, physiology, and anatomy, when we look at it, accidentally cut our finger, have blood drawn, or have whole organs removed in operations. On the other hand, we try to follow, in our thinking, how the functions of our hands, our blood, our organs are reflected in our thinking. The sketch below illustrates how this affects our biography:

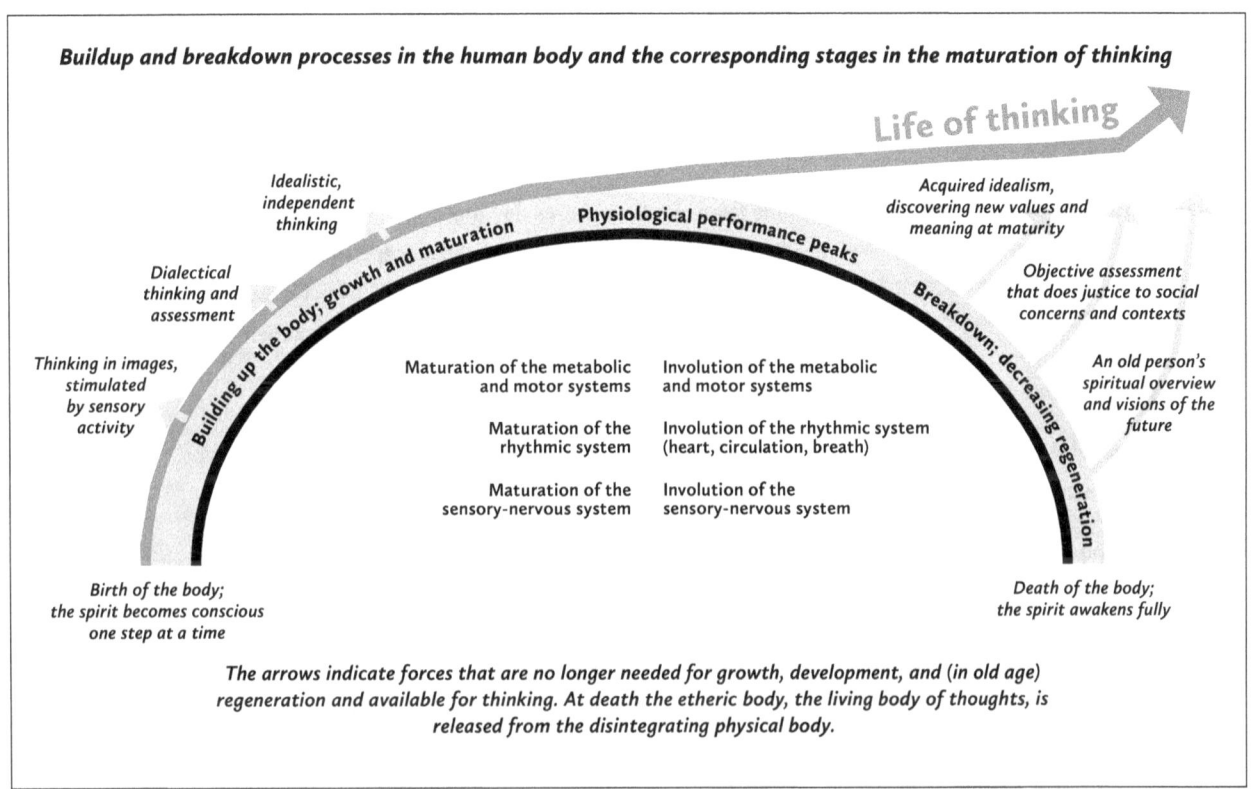

The generative and degenerative processes in the human organism and the corresponding maturation levels of the thought life.[10]

The following table shows examples of the congruence between the life activity in the physical body and that in the thinking life.

LIFE ACTIVITY	THOUGHT ACTIVITY
Digestion	Mental digestion
Analytic degenerative processes	Analytic thinking
Synthetic generative processes	Synthetic thinking
Eating	Taking in thoughts
Excretion	Thinking that orders and structures
Mobility	Mental flexibility
Bone formation	Generating structure and concept
Depositing, fixing, structuring	Forming fixed mental pictures flowing, dissolving, mediating processes forming flexible mental pictures, like the purely conceptual grasping of a thought without the presence of a particular mental picture; for example thinking the concept "lamp" without an actual lamp appearing as a mental picture
Breathing processes	Coming and going of ideas, letting ideas disappear
Thermoregulation, uniform body/warmth sensation	Being fired by a particular idea, having a "warm" feeling for a particular ideal, being filled with it
Separation processes	Clear conceptual, mentally pictured distinctions etc.

That which effects the bodily life processes regularly regulates the life organization of the organism: it remains in thinking as a function possibility for free decision. The link between educational influences and the state of health in later life goes even further. What happens if a child grows up with an irascible parent or teacher, if he often becomes suddenly rigid with fear when they have an outburst of anger? The child's circulation contracts and he turns pale. What will be the result if such angiospasms occur repeatedly as a consequence of circulatory disturbances and if they are not balanced sufficiently, because the child does not experience loving acceptance, if he cannot breathe out and is not allowed to make mistakes and to receive help? Such a one-sided education of the circulatory system will cause an underlying disposition towards arterial hypoperfusion. It is frequently the case that events which affect psychological functioning in the adult affect physical functioning in the child. Problems that adults have in the soul realm reappear in the child as a certain disposition towards medical problems. It is for example quite common that children who stutter have a parent who has the tendency towards stuttering: they have a fast and breathless way of speaking that never develops into an actual stutter. This also shows how a person's health is connected with questions of destiny and development and that self-education is the basis of all salutogenesis in education.

Laws of destiny in education and biographical development

This presentation aims to awaken an interest in these insights and encourage self-development. Some of the ideas described here might seem far-fetched, but it is inspiring to contemplate their potential, to consider orienting our educational methods toward them and observing the child to see if he finds his own destiny path. In his lectures on education, Rudolf Steiner gave numerous examples of such connections between educational influences and medical disposition in later life. The following health relationships are from publications of Klaus Rittersbacher, who has worked through the education lectures of Steiner in regard to this theme:[11]

EDUCATIONAL INFLUENCE	IMPLICATION IN LATER LIFE
Experiencing joy, love, happiness	Physical body stays supple and flexible for longer; the person finds it easy to relate to people and environment
Being astonished and full of admiration	Love toward the world
Finding life beautiful, being able to accept things out of love for an authority	Underlying feeling of contentment in life, ability to get something out of life
Education towards interest in the world	Growing interest in other people
Learning from life	Inner stability in life
Undisturbed imitation	Free and open exchange with the environment, open character
Independent search for truth	Courage and initiative
Taking in religious images, a religious mood	Tendency towards tolerance and philanthropy
Learning to pray during childhood	Ability to bless in later life
How one learns to play	How one stands in life and deals with what life brings
Getting to know and to love the plant world	Tendency towards living, flexible concepts
Getting to know and love the animal world	Strengthening of will
Being attracted to the mysteries of the world, contemplating questions	A healthy attitude to power and eroticism
A materialistic education	Decreasing interest in the world
Taking in mathematical laws without involving the feeling life	Tendency towards materialism
Education towards a critical and skeptical attitude to life (lack of idealism)	Disposition to feeling psychologically demoralized

Abstract grammar teaching	Disposition towards functional gastro-enteropathy
Absence of loved authority	Disposition towards life crises, not having the strength to help oneself
Excessive intellectual and mental demands during first school years	Tendency to sclerosis and premature degeneration of the nervous system
Learning to criticize and judge too early	Tendency to unkindness and harsh judgments
Inartistic, one-sidedly intellectual teaching	Disposition towards arrhythmia, especially an overemphasis on the in-breath, disturbed respiratory rhythm with corresponding tendency towards chest tightness and asthmatic complaints
Superficial, "quickly picked up" knowledge	Tendency to premature aging in the soul realm, as there are no deeper experiences left to work through

These and other indications are to be found in Steiner's pedagogical lecture presentations. He demonstrates how a teacher's interactions can influence the students in later life. This is independent of the individual destiny and home life of the child. There are many hours in the kindergarten and classroom where the teacher can strive to bring balance and personal development and uncover the child's gifts. This approach makes teaching today one of the most helpful and important interactions for the present and the future. The teacher will be the key for modern preventative medicine and education will, as Steiner said, become a gentle "healing."

CHAPTER 2

Pictures of the Development of Physiology

Michaela Glöckler

The following pictures are able to express more than words. They show the formative forces of the child's organism in their complexity, their totality, and their aesthetic. How can the environment and relationship-forming forces so influence a child that their consciousness development is in harmony with their physical maturation?

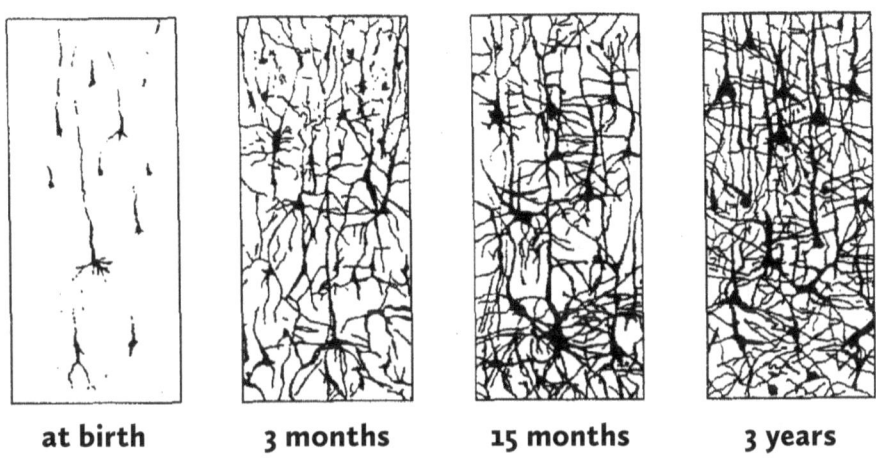

Figure 1: Microscopic sections of the human cerebrum showing synapses between brain cells.

These four images[1] of the development of neuronal networks show the drama, complexity, and simultaneity with which brain growth occurs in the first years of life, and how sensitive, pliant, and interlinked these developing structural processes are. In children's paintings and drawings—without any external direction—a parallel development is common to children throughout the world, a kind of universal marker of developmental stages. They draw their own growing awareness in the form of head, trunk, and limb development, and where no paper is available they draw these forms with their fingers in clay, sand or dust.[2]

Figure 2:
Circular ball, painted by a girl aged 1 year, 10 months.

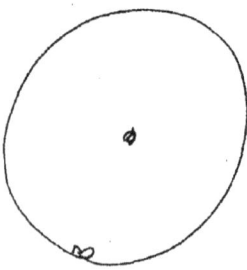

Figure 3:
Circle with focal point, painted by a girl aged 3 years, 3 months.

Figure 4:
"Head-footers," painted by a boy aged 3 years, 9 months.

Figure 5:
Two "ladder people" painted by a boy aged 4 years, 5 months.

Figure 6:
First representation of an action: mother with children and an infant going for a walk. Drawing by a girl aged 5 years, 2 months.

Figures 7, 8, 9: Children's drawings representing various actions and the surrounding environment.

Question: how different are the life and physical bodies of the three children who have drawn figure 7-9?[3] Figure 7 shows a strong limb quality but without hands and feet. Figure 8 shows an awakened face quality and far less self experience of the limbs. Figure 9 shows a distinct torso, with arms and hands, together with a shining sun on the left of the picture.

The same formative and self-healing forces with which the child builds up his body also quiver through his fingers and pass into external creative activity. Here we see a phenomenon that Rudolf Steiner highlights as typical of artistic skills in general, that the artist has an excess of life and formative forces that remain available to him beyond childhood and throughout his life, and give rise to his particular artistic gifts. Just as sculptural and pictorial forces are the upbuilding forces which anthroposophic study of the human being calls etheric forces, so in music the soul or astral forces come to expression, which are of a differentiating and proportioning—that is, mathematical-musical—nature.

The formative forces and the ego-organization integrate and ultimately shape the whole of the adult form, the "word" being the central context.

Figure 10: Developmental stages of the chimpanzee from birth to sexual maturity.[4]

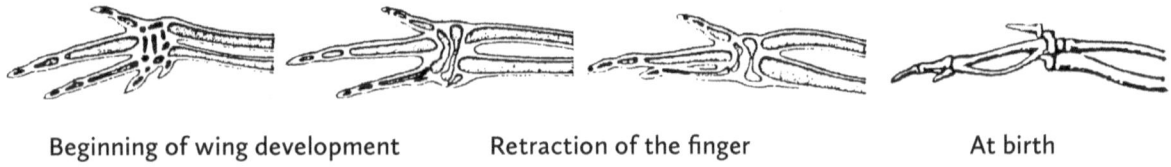

Beginning of wing development **Retraction of the finger** **At birth**

Figure 11: Developmental stages from the embryological phases of a bird's wing

These two picture sequences of the development of a chimpanzee and a bird's wing[5] show that more is involved in species evolution than a superficial Darwinian approach suggests. It is quite simply an observable phenomenon that a newborn mammal, particularly a young ape, more closely resembles the human being the more recently he has been born, and only gradually develops into the adult animal form. This applies to all vertebrates, including birds: their limbs pass through human-like hand

and foot forms, then develop into species-specific animal limb-types. The archetypal image of the human being holds sway in the background of all mammal and vertebrate evolution.

Instead of the human being descending from the ape, the animals descend from the human being. They have specialized prematurely. The human being, as youngest born of Creation, remained pliable and malleable for longer, integrating into his constitution a life-long capacity to learn and remain flexible. In this way specific human attributes have been able to continually evolve and develop to this day. The earlier that capacities are fixed and specialized, the less capable of change and development is the creature in question. These pictures endorse the concern of Waldorf education not to impose early training of intellectual or other faculties, but to support the slow development which distinguishes humans from animals. The more actively and consciously a child shares in the formation of his capacities, the more mastery he will later show in exercising them—in other words, the more autonomy he will have in their use.

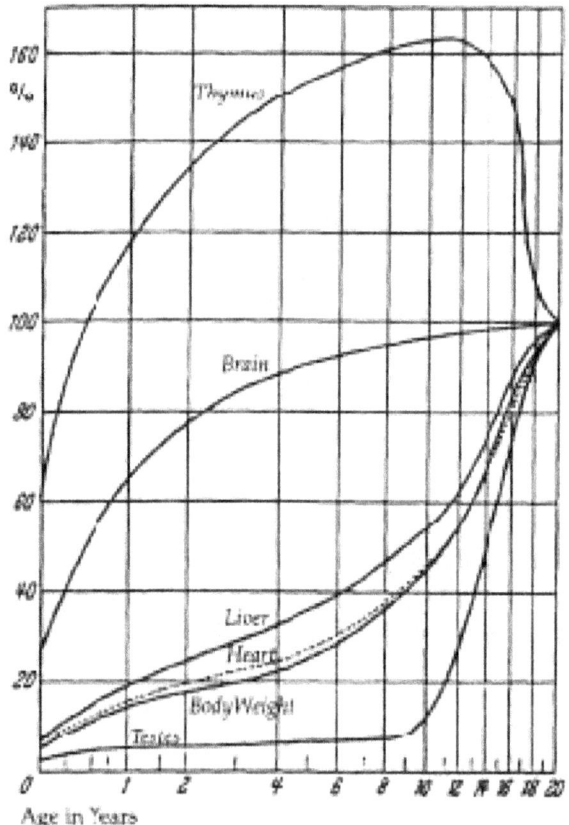

Figure 12: Converging of thymus, brain, and gonads (in the 20th year of human life).

This diagram[6] shows how the thymus (which stimulates the immune system), the brain, and the gonads (ovaries, testicles) converge at 100 percent development in the twentieth year of life. When pre-puberty starts at age 9, and gonad growth together with hormonal changes begin leading to a change in form, the cerebrum is 95 percent developed. One can almost tangibly grasp the fast-approaching end of the period when the growth spurt itself and formative influences from the child's environment have imparted the greatest gifts to him through both nature and education. From now on progress can only be achieved through increased exertion and conscious learning. Then the law of "Use it or lose it"[7] applies, which neurobiology has brought to light in the past twenty years. The body makes an enzyme that removes and thus forever erases extruding cerebral networks that have not been activated through learning processes. The only new developments now are those stimulated by active learning processes, though these become harder and less like child's play than formerly. We all know that the growth spurt at puberty is initially linked with enlargement of hands and feet, followed by lengthening of arms and legs, followed finally by lengthening of the trunk, then shoulder breadth and last of all trunk depth. Correspondingly unharmonious are beard and breast development—which do not appear in a uniform pattern (sculpturally) but differentiated (musically)—like a conductor who brings in individual players (body areas) at different times, and only unites them all in harmony at the end. Initially there is a little down on the upper lip, then on the chin, then on the side of the face—first there is one breast then a pause—some girls ask "how will it be with the other one?" Like a conductor, calling first on one player, then another, and then ultimately bringing all together. The diagram clearly shows that the head-focused growth of the first nine years diminishes in favor of a limb- and metabolism-focused growth spurt, which even causes some of the previous brain growth to recede again.

Thus it does not require too much imagination to understand why young people do not show the greatest motivation to learn intellectual subjects at the time of the main growth spurt (between age 12 and 15), but prefer to devote themselves to sports, music, and dance, as well as discussion and active pursuits. Their brain development at this time goes through a structural crisis—as with their experience of their own identity.

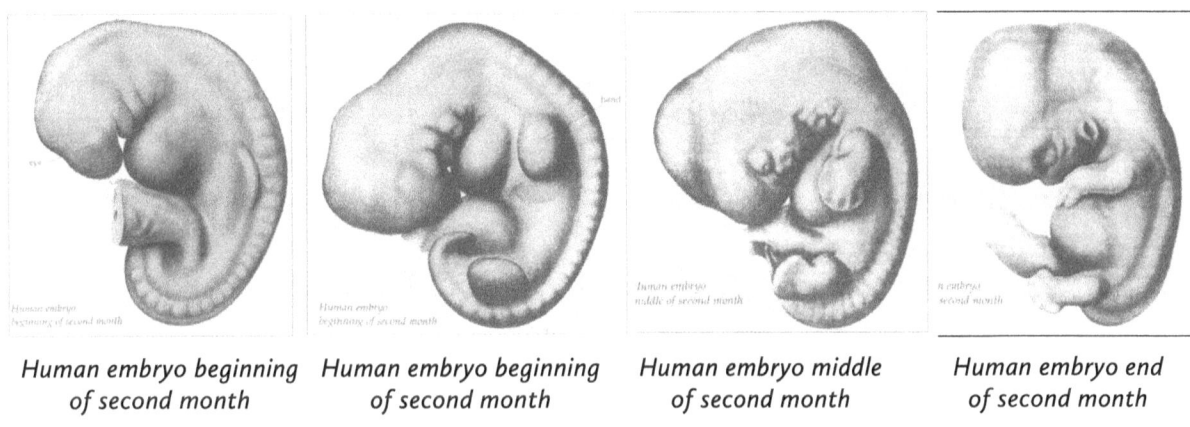

Human embryo beginning of second month   *Human embryo beginning of second month*   *Human embryo middle of second month*   *Human embryo end of second month*

Figures 13-16: Human development: beginning 13 & 14, middle 15, end of second month—16.

The stages of embryonic development in the second month[8] show how the interaction between sculptural/proliferative and musical/differentiating, proportioning, and holistic forces represents active influences which are penetrated by a third process, which harmonizes and integrates these two opposite systems of formative forces. The integration processes, to which the embryo and also later the developing child owe the harmonious interplay and holism of their form, are called the formative forces of the ego organization in anthroposophic study of the human being. It is to these three systems of forces—formative and upbuilding life forces, differentiating astral or soul forces, and integrating ego forces—that we owe not only our physical form but also the purely soul-spiritual potential for activity which becomes free as the body matures. The same forces after all promote physiological growth and underpin emotional and intellectual development and growth.[9]

In the adult human being the fourfold organism can be depicted as follows in relation to the unfolding of its physical and soul forces:

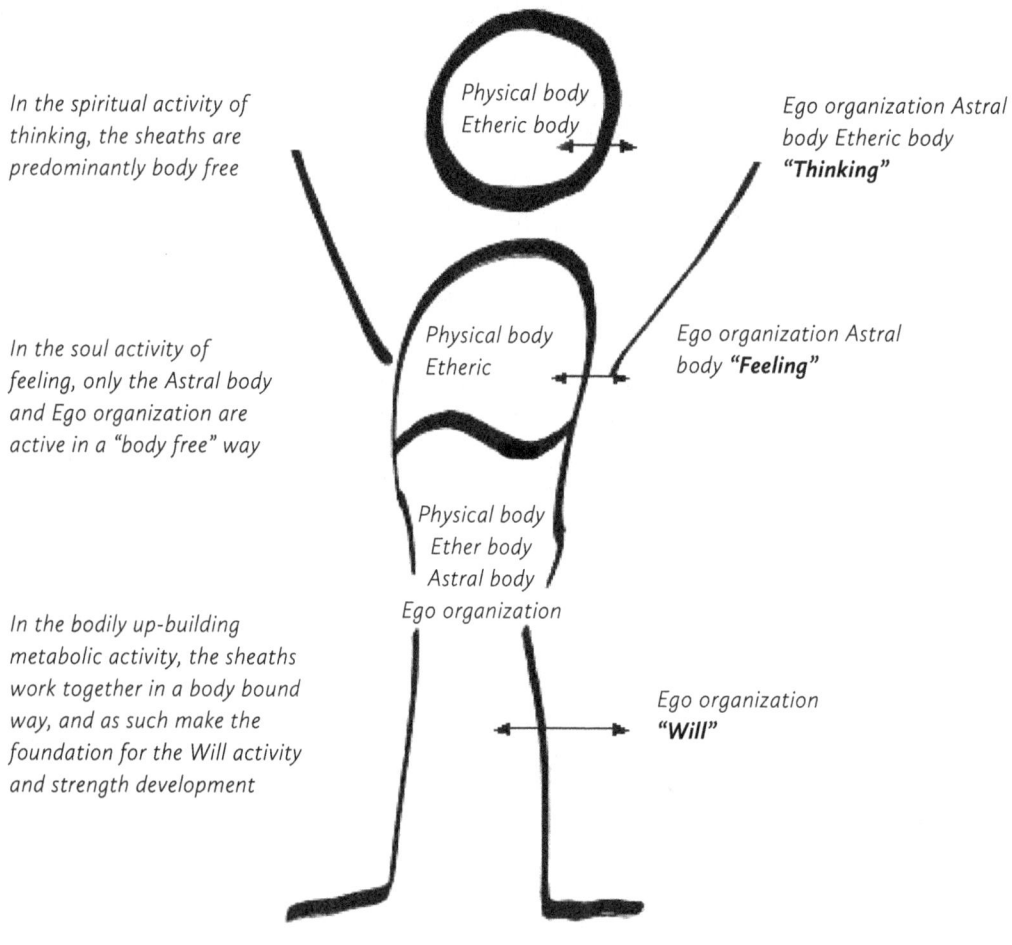

Figure 17

This illustration[10] shows that a healthy metabolism necessitates full incarnation in the physical body of the three bodily sheaths, which constitute the laws underpinning life forces, ensoulment, and penetration with spirit. Only by this means can the metabolic processes—which in a healthy person embody the specific type of one's own protein structure right into the subtlest differentiations of the physical body—imprint identity as intended by the ego organization. Here pure nature holds sway, one can say, almost entirely withdrawn from conscious human control. The limbs, in contrast, demonstrate a gradual emancipation and capacity for autonomous control of limbs by the ego organization. The latter is partly incarnated into the limbs, partly body-free: the freer and more self-determined the will, the more independent of the body is the activity of the ego organization in this sphere. It is different in the rhythmic system. Here, in the adult, the ego organization is completely body-free, while the astral body is partly incarnated—and more so on the inbreath. To this is due the special peculiarity of human feelings: on the one hand we are completely involved in what we feel—the ego organization is wholly *with* the other when experiencing genuine sympathy or active empathy; feelings go out to their object—but on the other hand feelings remain, at the same time, tied to personal experience.

Feelings are always relationships between—never wholly body-free nor completely tied to one's own experience of the physical body.

In the nerve-sense system the etheric body is also largely body-free, which is why we have to sleep. Animal experiments have shown that sleep deprivation harms the nervous system but not the other organs. During waking life, the nervous system not only suffers the physiological catabolism involved in every physical activity, which can be compensated for by the body's own regenerative and upbuilding forces, but an additional degeneration that can only be compensated for by sleep. The nervous system's formative life forces are largely body-free and available for reflective thinking activity, together with all other formative forces of the etheric, astral body, and ego organization which are liberated from involvement in growth.

In view of these insights, "thinking" is the interplay among the thought processes (the ether body), the emotional forces (the astral body), and the body-free will forces (ego organization). Thoughts can be experienced as having distinct qualities and, through the thinking process, influence conscious will engagement.

Feeling, in contrast, manifests as the deep wisdom of our identity-forming will and feeling forces. When we give ourselves wholly to feeling, it is always the human being himself, his "I," which feels and senses without being disturbed in this process by thinking. This world of feeling and emotion can develop in highly differentiated and subtly tuned ways, like a soul resonance, like a tensing and relaxing. Feeling is inner music, inner light, a spectrum of colors and shading.

Will, in its pure form, is the ego organization becoming free from the limbs. In directing the limbs, we experience our innate will most purely, however small the action.

The drawing below[11] shows the dramatic difference between day and night, between conscious and unconscious bodily experience. It is important to take account of the physiology of sleep in teaching, since it is by no means a matter of indifference what thought forms and content, soul experiences, and impulses for action we engage the child in during the day. In the night the astral body and "I" release themselves from the nerve-sense system and plunge back into the world of spirit from which they first incarnated. The etheric body, in contrast, immerses itself wholly in the physical body, in particular the nervous system, bearing the after-effects of conscious daytime experience into the whole organism. In other words, during the day the etheric body is not only the bearer of conscious experiences and of all thoughts that accompany thinking, feeling, and will. In sleep, the etheric carries the after-effects of this activity as formative impulses into the body, where—depending on their quality and life-nurturing or injurious tendencies—they exert either disruptive or beneficial influences on growth and development.

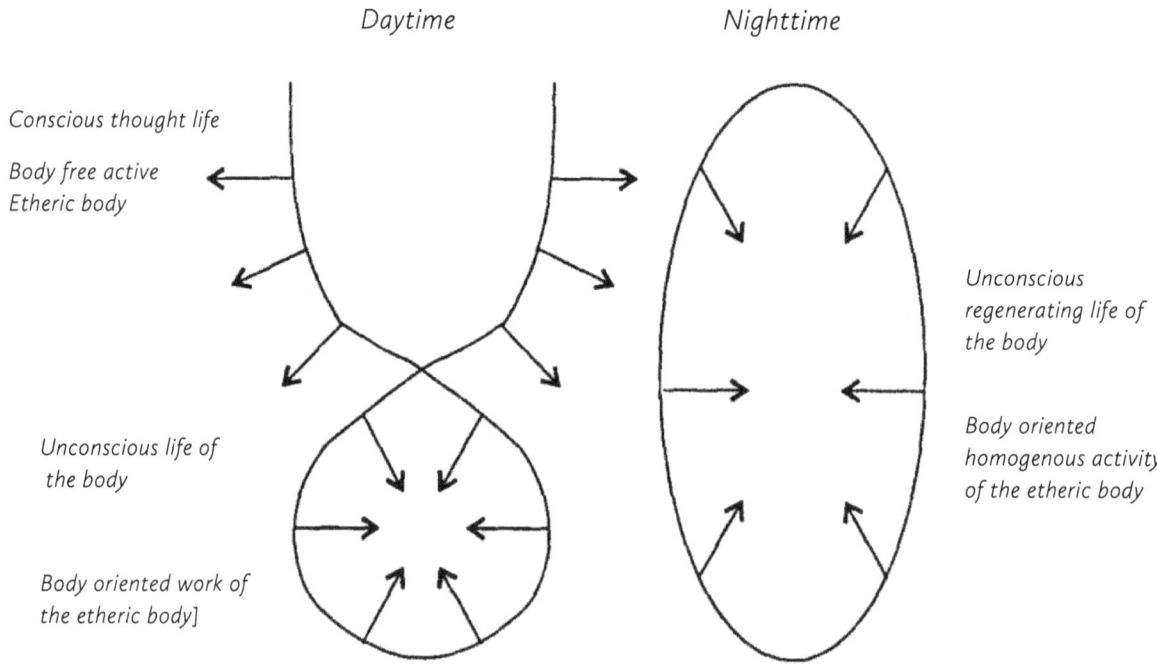

Figure 17

It is repeatedly asked: Where in Waldorf education is it necessary to speak of the four layers or "sheaths" of organization, meaning the physical body, ether body, astral body, and ego organization? The child-friendly ideas of this education could surely be applied without all this? Yes, this is possible, however in practice it is shown that exactly these complete ideas are needed, to be able to see the body and soul in a complex context, to find where to begin in working with the child. The dual aspects of natural and spiritual science can be used to understand the developing child and can support the child in a directed way. The four sheaths are no mere theoretical concept. This is a system of working principles and descriptors of phenomena that would otherwise remain unnoticed and unconsidered.

CHAPTER 3

Healthy Timetabling: Everything Has Its Time

Michaela Glöckler

Rudolf's Steiner's provocative questioning of timetables and curriculum design in his day is still as topical as ever: He states:

> If one wishes to educate children one also needs a certain amount of elbow-room. The normal, dreadful timetabling in schools rules this out: from 8 to 9 religious studies, from 9 to 10 gymnastics, from 10 to 11 history, from 11 to 12 math. Here all that follows cancels out what preceded it. There's nothing to be done, and as a teacher one despairs of achieving anything. That is why we have what one can call main lesson blocks in the Waldorf school. A child comes to school, and receives integrated teaching in the main lesson each day, during the main hours of the morning: from 8 to 10, or from 8 to 11, with appropriate short breaks. There is one teacher in the class, also in the higher grades. The subject does not change every hour, but a longer period—say 4 weeks—is devoted to each subject, for instance math. Each day from 8 to 10 the relevant aspect of the subject is dealt with, and each day succeeding work links back to what was done the day before. What comes later does not cancel out what came before, and this allows real focus. Once 4 weeks have passed and an area of math has been dealt with sufficiently, and concluded, a different lesson block begins, say history, and this in turn is pursued for as long as necessary, say 4 to 5 weeks; and so on.[1]

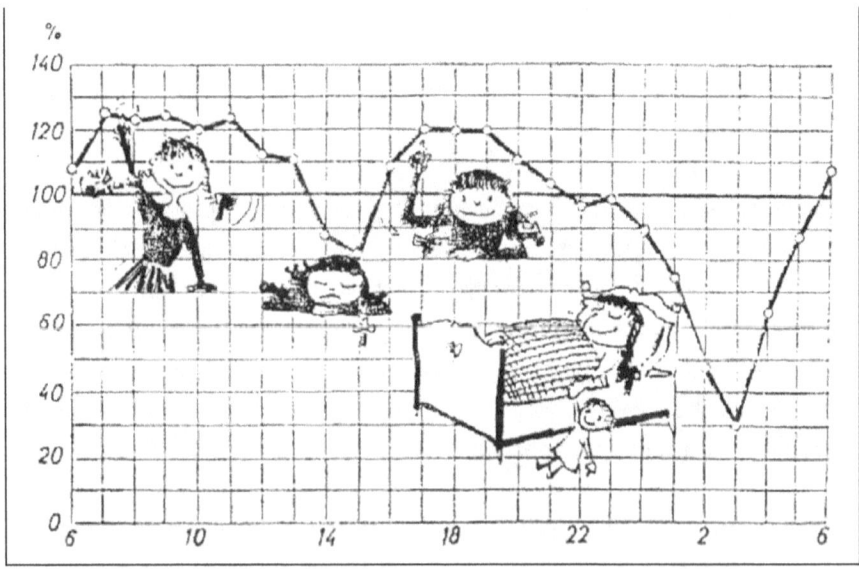

Figure 1: Daily course of physiological performance readiness according to examinations by Bjerner et al.[2]

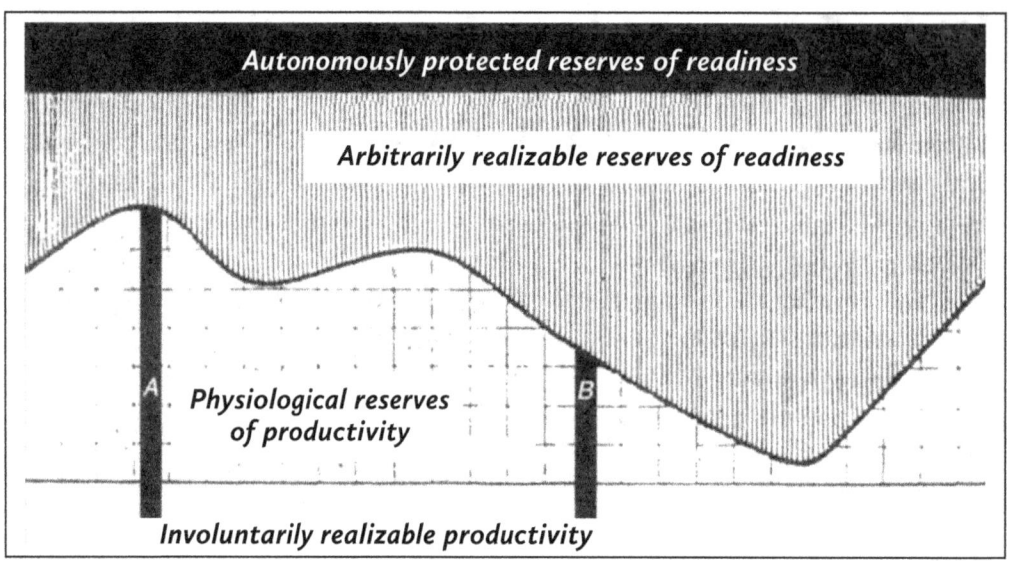

*Figure 2: The curve in the above chart which runs from left to right represents:
Limit of physiological readiness for productivity Table of performance areas related to time of day.³*

The peak performance rhythm familiar since the sixties is not only taken account of in Waldorf education but also enhanced by further physiological consequences arising from it. What does it mean that the child's circulation is centralized in the morning (the body core and head are better supplied with blood than the metabolic and limb system), and that this is reversed at the second performance peak in the afternoon and evening? At this second high point the periphery is better supplied with blood than the body core. For this reason, Steiner speaks of the need to focus morning lessons on subjects which primarily address the head, and require children to sit still, so that head activity can occur in an uninterrupted and concentrated way. Toward midday and afternoon, in contrast, lesson focus should be on subjects that address the will and the limbs.

These range from religion (in some countries)—where "good will" is involved—through artistic activities to eurythmy, sports, crafts, and practical life skills.

Unfortunately, for purely individual reasons, this ideal timetable cannot always be implemented and adhered to. But those who understand its importance will do everything to realize it practically as far as possible. The overview below of the major rhythms of interaction between nervous activity and adaptation to the environment show how sensible it is not just to consider Circadian rhythms but also weekly, monthly, and yearly rhythmic patterns when drawing up the timetable. In chronobiology and rhythm research studies of the weekly rhythm has shown itself to be particularly influential on the rhythm of regeneration and reactive recuperation.

It is all the more problematic when the modern 5-day week disrupts this health-giving endogenous rhythm. A 5-day plus a 2-day rhythm are quite different from a 7-day rhythm. Unfortunately, when schools throughout the world changed from a 6-day to a 5-day week, hardly any research was done into the potential effects on pupils and teachers. One of the few pilot studies, unfortunately not published, showed that the incidence of illness or missed days was significantly different after a weekend preceded either by a 5-day or 6-day week.[4] However, there was no interest in or commitment to such research, since parents, teachers and pupils were all in favor of the two-day weekend.

But such research is urgently needed! Where, however, there is sufficient understanding of the need to cultivate endogenous rhythms during childhood growth and development—to form the basis later for the physical resilience which is typical of a healthy rhythmic system—one can try the following compromise: giving as little homework as possible during the 5-day week, so that pupils still have sufficient leisure time; but then, on Saturday morning, organizing things in such a way that pupils get up at the same time as usual, gather in small groups at various parents' homes, and do their homework together. After which, unburdened and relieved, they can enter the seventh day to conclude the 7-day rhythm

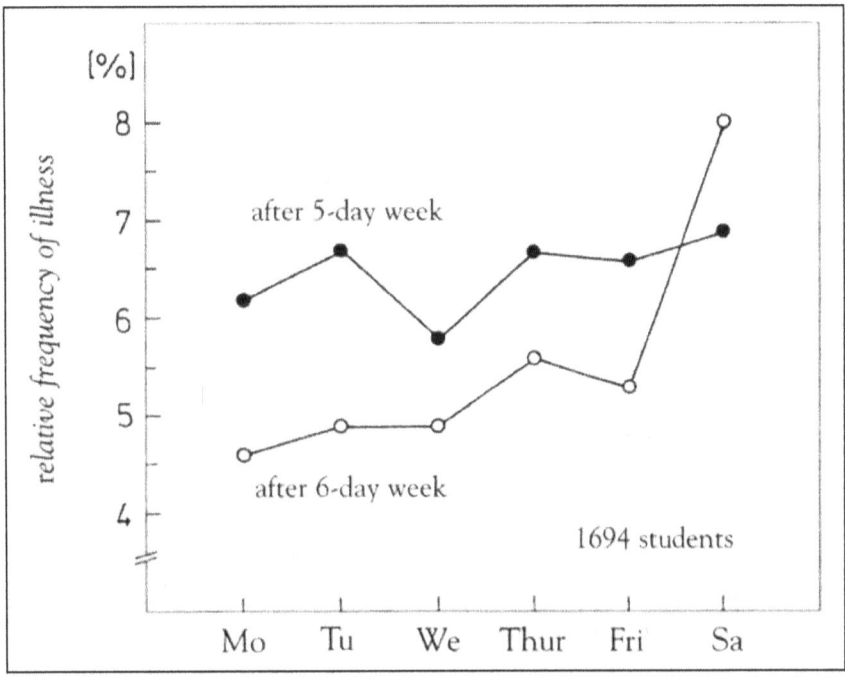

Figure 3: Incidence of missed days in a week following a weekend preceded by either a 5-day or 6-day week. A total of 1694 pupils took part (from unpublished data by Klemp).

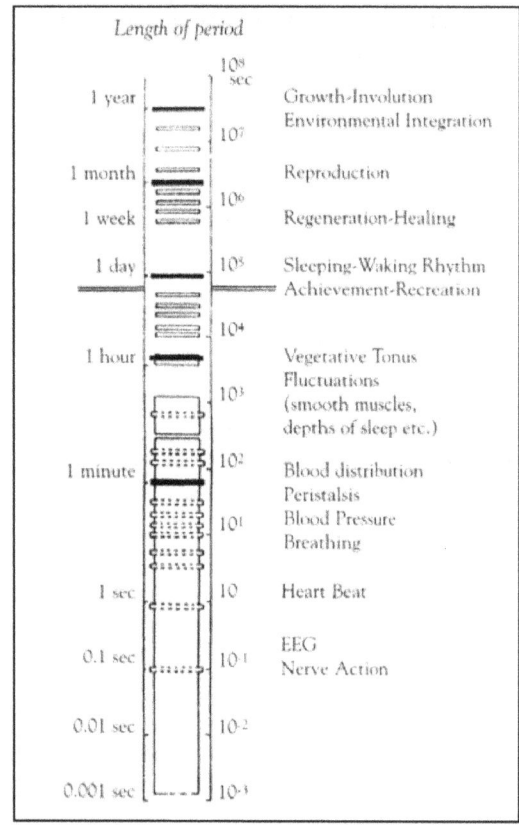

Figure 4

"Once is never" is a trusim of rhythm research. The One, or single occurrence, has no rhythmic and physiological effect. Rhythm only starts with two, with repetition, affecting living systems in a profound way. Single events are processed with the help of the rhythmic system. Recurring events, on the other hand, influence the rhythmic system itself and thus also its capacities for processing experience.

As far as the monthly rhythm is concerned, it is interesting how definitely Rudolf Steiner stresses the 4-week rhythm in the quote above, even speaking of 4-5 weeks. We know that the reproductive processes (menstruation in women, long-wave regeneration rhythm) follow a 4-week rhythm, but that in one to two weeks after the last week of the process, a "scarring over," must occur to ensure successful regeneration of the rhythm. Quite apart from this, the second month naturally reinforces the monthly rhythm established in the first. It is also interesting that Steiner does not just speak of two hours "with appropriate short breaks," but also of a period lasting from 8:00 to 11:00. It was his hope that the class teacher would be able to have sufficient time to really impart something to children, and to enter into intensive learning processes with them. How would it be if the main lesson ran from 8:00 to 11:00 and elements of specialist teaching were integrated into each current main lesson block? By this means a particular subject could be enriched from a variety of angles, and one or other specialist teacher could also be involved. Such a curriculum would, at least, be more consistent, interesting and alive than changing too rapidly from one subject to another during each school day. This would also ensure that the teacher really has a conscious overview of what his pupils absorb each day, that he could link up with the following day. On the other hand, it is also clear that such intense supervision of a class will demand an optimum pupil/teacher relationship. If things don't work here, every additional class will pose a problem. That is why Waldorf teacher training has great importance, and those who come to work in Waldorf schools without such preparation must be released regularly for further training and observing other teachers' lessons.

The annual rhythm is supported by whole-year learning targets, the celebration of seasonal festivals, and certain memorial and celebration days, as well as the special attention given to birthdays and death-days in the school and classroom.

CHAPTER 4

Salutogenic Approach to Education in Early Childhood

Peter Lang

Childhood at risk

In a speech delivered in December 1899, the Swedish educationalist and member of parliament, Ellen Key, voiced the demand and hope that the twentieth century should and would be a century of the child, in which the needs and interests of children would come to the fore and be put into practice. The twentieth century is now passed, a new century has begun. How much have we achieved?

On the positive side: in the industrialized countries, medical care has greatly improved. Almost all children attend school and have access to further education. Children have rights and are protected from arbitrary measures by the state. There is an international children's aid organization, UNESCO. Large sections of the population have developed an awareness that childhood is a commodity worth protecting.

Yet there are no grounds for complacency. According to the United Nations, more than 40,000 children all over the world suffer from hunger and disease each day.[1] Wars, epidemics and increasing poverty threaten millions of children in all parts of the world.

But even in the countries in which there is peace and affluence the developmental opportunities for children are not automatically good. Here, too, childhood is under attack—often hidden—in almost all areas of life and at all levels, social, political and private. It seems as if the needs of children are relegated to the background or are forgotten completely. Just like the elderly and people with disabilities, children are increasingly squeezed out of cityscapes, while cars, concrete, and neighbors sensitive to noise are often given precedence. Increasing unemployment and lack of integration of large sections of the population have a direct effect on children's life and developmental opportunities.

In the history of education, the path to a recognition and understanding of the particular laws and the special character of the early years of life was a long one. Not until the mid-nineteenth century did childhood become a social concept, at least in Central Europe.

But it seems that childhood as an independent concept is once again under attack, is at risk of disappearing again—but now under the guise of modernity. Children and adolescents are often treated as adults. The consumer and media age has long since discovered children as objects of interest, and they are pressured from all directions. Everywhere one finds childhood poverty.

The new task of the twenty-first century is to make this the century of the child—to protect, to pay attention, and to realize the developmental needs and life criteria for children.

The history and development of the Waldorf kindergarten and the International Association of Waldorf Kindergartens

Until now, we have essentially enrolled children in the same way that lower schools do. We start when the imitative age has finished. It would be nice if some things could be included in the first seven years.

(RUDOLF STEINER, JUNE 23, 1920)[2]

Rudolf Steiner thus indicated the necessity of practicing Waldorf education in the preschool years, and suggested the necessity of a child-centered preschool education.

Elisabeth von Grunelius started the first Waldorf kindergarten in 1926, the year after Steiner's death, as part of the Stuttgart Waldorf School. The establishment of a number of other kindergartens followed in other cities. This expansion ended with the Nazi ban on Waldorf schools and Waldorf kindergartens in 1933, followed by the Second World War.

After the war, a group of kindergarten teachers, teachers, and physicians formed around Waldorf educator Klara Hattermann in Hanover, Germany. Basing their work on Rudolf Steiner's study of the human being, they developed methodology and teaching skills for kindergartens and work with parents. From then on, the number of Waldorf kindergartens increased steadily.

In the late 1950s and early 1960s the attack on early childhood reached a further peak in many countries of the world. In 1956, the Soviet Union put a man-made satellite into earth orbit. This technical achievement triggered a shock wave in the West not only in the military and economic field, but also had a profound effect on the view of how children should be educated, particularly in early, preschool childhood.

The Western world now attempted, on the one hand, to reduce the technological lead of the Soviet Union by a huge military and economic effort, while shifting the focus of education of young children to a one-sided view that only promoted cognitive development. Making kindergarten more like school and lowering the school age became education policy objectives.

This attack on early childhood was countered by Klara Hattermann, Helmut von Kügelgen, and others in 1969 with the establishment of the International Association of Waldorf Kindergartens. In Germany, parents and educators responded to government education policies with the foundation of many Waldorf kindergartens and Waldorf schools.

The fall of the Iron Curtain, which had divided Europe since 1945, initiated a further wave of new kindergartens from 1990 onwards in almost all countries of the former eastern bloc. Today there are approximately 1,600 kindergartens in more than 50 countries throughout the world, including 550 in Germany alone.

The International Association of Waldorf Kindergartens has set itself the task of supporting the spread of Waldorf education worldwide and promoting professional dialog among Waldorf educators. They work closely together with the Waldorf school movement.

The 32 Organization for Economic Cooperation and Development (OECD) states regularly prepare a comparison of student performance in the countries participating in PISA (Program for International Student Assessment) studies. Germany has done comparatively poorly in these standardized studies. In recent years, this has led to renewed education policy debates and to consequences—such as lowering the school age, making the last year of kindergarten more like school, reducing the high school level by one year, and so forth—many of which totally ignore the fundamental needs of children.

By contrast, a study submitted to Darmstadt Technical University in October 2005 reaches the following conclusion:

> Children who, due to existing regulations, start formal schooling at the age of around seven instead of six, draw long-term advantages from this. The greater maturity of older first-grade pupils leads to them having much better reading comprehension by the end of the lower-school period, and they are more likely to be admitted to a Gymnasium [academic grammar school]. Given these findings, the benefits of a policy of continually lowering school entry age seems questionable.[3]

But these comparative studies have limitations. For example, countries with completely different educational methods achieve top places in the rankings. If we look at the structure of education in early childhood, children in one top country are enrolled earlier and are subject to cognitive education in kindergarten, whereas in another the children remain in kindergarten one year longer and are given the opportunity to develop their capacities in extended phases of play.

Furthermore, it is fundamentally questionable whether the performance of completely different education systems can be measured by OECD criteria. After all, human talents, propensities, and abilities such as imagination, pleasure in play, and social skills are not taken into account to the necessary extent, since they mostly play a key role with regard to success in later life, are not easily measured, and can certainly not be determined by a questionnaire. In general it is undoubtedly true that in education the point at issue is not so much the "what" but the "how": namely how childhood and adolescence are qualitatively lived.

Implementation of the findings in resilience research and salutogenesis

The reactor accident in Chernobyl in 1986 shattered people's long-term confidence in life and influenced their thinking about the risks of living in modern society.

In the same year, the book *Risikogesellschaft* ("Risk Society") by Ulrich Beck, which looks at the general risks to life and development in modern societies, was published in Germany.[4] In his book, Beck describes risks associated with civilization's environmentally destructive global advances, and draws attention to "the risks of modern lifestyles as a consequence of an enforced individualization process in modern societies, which forces individuals to take control of their own biography, compelling them to take and justify risky decisions on a permanent basis." On the benefit side, a high, hitherto unknown degree of self-determination opens up for people; on the risk side, people are experiencing fundamental changes brought about by global mass unemployment, poverty, and disease, with a direct effect particularly on children and adolescents.

This is where resilience research comes into play. In the social sciences, the term designates the general ability of people to cope successfully with stressful situations, not to allow themselves to be suppressed and not to founder on misfortune and failure.[5]

Against this background, two basic questions arise for modern resilience research in relation to the development and education of children:

1. What strengths and skills can best help children to develop positively—i.e. physically, mentally, spiritually, and socially in the healthiest possible way—despite the existing risk constellations?
2. How can we strengthen such powers of resistance through educational measures?

Furthermore, the following fundamental questions are also of interest: How does health arise? Why are most people healthy, despite all risks and dangers?

Starting from the observation that healthy people are not generally subject to scientific study, Abraham Maslow, one of the most influential psychologists of the twentieth century, investigated the nature of human health.[6] At the same time, Maslow treated severely traumatized people who had survived Nazi concentration camps between 1933 and 1945. It became apparent to him that many of his patients were not physically robust, but they had been guided during the the concentration camps by spiritual, artistic, religious, and social values that gave them the strength and the means to survive terrible events. In his quest to discover the nature of health, Maslow noticed that these healthy people were "very different, in some respects surprisingly different, to the average."[7]

According to Maslow, healthy people were distinguished by, among other things, the following characteristics:

- They possess a better perception of reality.
- They are able to accept themselves, others and nature.
- They possess naturalness, spontaneity, and simplicity.
- They are independent and active.
- They possess full esteem: basic aspects of life are valued with reverence, joy, wonder.
- They possess a sense of community.
- The structure of their character its democratic.
- They possess a strongly ethical outlook.
- Their humor is philosophical, not hostile.
- Without exception, healthy people are creative.

That this selection of positive human characteristics and behaviors raises questions about the types of educational objectives and methods for children is self-evident—and urgently needs implementation in practice.

Maslow's successor was the medical sociologist Aaron Antonovsky (1923-94), who is today considered the father of salutogenesis. Antonovky's fundamental critique of conventional medical thinking is that it is solely guided by how causes of disease (pathogenesis) can be avoided or combated, whereas there is hardly any interest in what causes health (salutogenesis).

In essence, Antonovsky's salutogenesis approach proposes three requirements for a healthy or health-promoting human lifestyle:[8]

1. Comprehensibility, or experiencing oneself and the world as making basic cognitive sense and being capable of study.
2. Manageability, or having confidence in one's own capacity to act and to master one's own life using one's own resources or with the help of others.
3. Meaningfulness, or being able to process one's experiences in life so that they make sense.

These three aspects of a health-promoting way of life together produce what Antonovsky describes as the sense of coherence: people experience themselves and the world around them as making coherent sense.

Understanding oneself and the world in which one lives, creating meaning, experiencing one's inner foothold—all of these things increase the chance of being physically, mentally, spiritually, and socially healthy, and not to be destroyed by life's challenges.

What salutogenesis characteristics, then, can be shown to exist in Waldorf education and the understanding of the human being which underlies it?

Using play to create a sense of coherence

Children come into the world as individuals who develop their gifts, affinities, interests and, indeed, disabilities and who want to pursue their own path. Education therefore starts with the observation of children: What are their intentions and how can we support them? How can a space be created in which they can imitate and repeat in play what they have experienced and seen?

The great Swiss educator Heinrich Pestalozzi said, early in the nineteenth century: "Education is example and love, nothing else!"[9]

The way in which a child plays reveals his stage of development and relationship to the environment. Through play, the child develops his capacity to relate to the world through activity, feelings, and thinking.

Even the very small child, lifting his head, using his arms to support himself, sitting up and engaging in continuous practice until he can stand up and take his first steps reveals human will, the zest for action. Such zest for action characterizes play in the very first years of life. The child directly puts into action what he perceives with his senses: playful activity arises which is still largely without purpose, often linked with the joy of repetition. If such zest for action and movement is given sufficient space and time, one component of the basis for an active and energetic adult, who wants to and can achieve things, is created.

At the second stage of play, approximately between the ages of 3 and 5, imagination is added to pure zest for action. The imaginative power of the child recreates the world, transforms it in the sense that what is perceived by the senses is inwardly developed, emotionally transformed and recreated in play; here the ground is prepared on which the active creativity of the future adult can take shape.

The third quality comes to expression approximately between the ages of 5 and 7. The power of ideas and reason increasingly permeates the child's play, his powers of memory grow strongly, and he matures into a social being. The children now organize their joint play, work out rules, plan and make agreements. They join together, sometimes to oppose adults, they gain an increasing command of language and discover their infinite expressive possibilities, their observation becomes more and more acute and detailed. This third quality of children's play prepares the later ability for clear conceptual penetration of the nature of the world.

None of these developmental stages in childhood play is dispensable or should be neglected or, indeed, limited; all of them are invaluable building blocks for the future adult's approach to life.

How children learn to understand the world

A Waldorf teacher visits a farm with her kindergarten. They begin by saying hello to the animals in the barn, experience the warm atmosphere, pet the cows and watch them eat and chew their cud. Then they go to the feed store, where sacks of grain are piled up, and all the children are allowed to put their hands into the grain. The children buy a small quantity of grain and take it back to the kindergarten. The next day, the grain is ground to flour using a hand grinder. The children keep relieving one another in this hard task. On the following day, the flour is made into dough and the children create rolls, dumplings, earthworm shapes, and many other things on the baking sheet. The baking sheets are put into the oven and the room is filled with delicious aromas. Now a verse is recited or a song is sung and everyone thanks the sun, the rain, mother earth, or Our Father in heaven who made everything grow. Everyone has a happy breakfast and thereafter the day takes its usual course.

In this small example, children learned to understand the world a little better through five levels of learning and life:

- Activity level: the children were active and intensively occupied, they worked.
- Social level: they undertook the work together and ate together.
- Cognitive level: nothing was explained but the children were allowed to experience and perceive the logic of the process and the meaningful sequence of the various actions.
- Feeling level: the visit to the barn, the smell of the rolls, the beautifully laid table.
- Ethical/moral level: the children expressed their gratitude, recited a verse, sang a song, and experienced reverence towards creation through ordinary actions.

Such learning and life experiences should take place repeatedly at the five levels set out above in order to allow small children to understand the world in gradual stages in a healthy way before starting school. None of these aspects should be missing, and none should dominate or replace the others.

The teacher and the children could of course visit the field in which the grain is grown in the spring and they could watch it being harvested and the grain being threshed in the autumn—the process of learning to understand the world is unlimited and extensive.

There are no computers or any other communication technologies in the preschool curriculum. Working with ready-made products instead of self-made products takes away developmental possibilities and encourages us to use and apply instead of being creative.

That is why, later on, Waldorf high school students not only learn how to operate a computer but they also build simple hardware and software in order to understand how it works.

Children are active beings, so Waldorf education for preschool children is activity-based rather than explanation-based. Life in a Waldorf kindergarten consists of a wealth of activities.

When children enter the communal room in the morning, the teacher may be sewing, repairing a toy, or fixing breakfast with a group of children. Other children are at play, allowing themselves to be inspired by the existing materials, which are characterized by their simplicity, beauty, and authenticity. Dolls, boards, cloths, pine cones, ropes, stones, and so forth await the children. Some children are quite independent in organizing themselves in mixed-age groups whereas others need an adult's guidance.

The is structured with play in the communal room and outside in the garden; the seasons are reflected in the daily activities; the nature of different animals and plants can be experienced; poems, songs, and different forms of movement turn the day into an experience for the children.

Meaningful stories with clear plots, told repeatedly, create a homely atmosphere in the souls of the children. Children who experience a story, a festival, certain aspects of the course of the day on a recurring basis thereby acquire inner assurance and a feeling of familiarity—and children in familiar surroundings need have no fear.

When small children have plenty of opportunity to do things themselves, when the day, the week, the year are clearly structured, self-confidence in the child's growing forces increases. The child acquires the certainty: I can do that and I know what I'm doing. In this way healthy self-confidence and self-assurance are nurtured.

But for such a development process to take place, the child needs to get his bearings from an adult. Education means giving guidance and being a role model. Children learn from their own impulses and in doing so imitate the adult. Small children possess the deep conviction that what adults do and how they do it is correct and good. Children enter the world without preconceptions, inquisitive and open, but without an adult role model, they are lost.

> We must interpret physical environment in the broadest possible sense. It not only includes what exists physically around the child but also the events which take place in the child's environment which can be perceived by the child with his senses and which act from the physical environment on his spiritual forces. This includes all moral or immoral, failed or foolish actions.[10]

Children observe exactly how adults do things. Are their actions meaningful or unkind, superficial or undertaken with commitment? Do actions and words coincide or not? In the way that a person lives, speaks, and acts, children can also recognize that person's soul and spiritual outlook.

Hence in educational processes recognition and support of the individual gifts and abilities of each child must always be accompanied by the communication of basic ethical, moral, and religious values that support the individual person and the culture—and this must be done not with words, but by making the inner attitude of the adult apparent to the child. These educational processes can only be developed in a positive sense if the educating adult continuously endeavors to achieve such inner meaning and attitude to life.

Children do not look for the perfect educator—such a thing does not exist—but they seek people who strive for inner truthfulness and clarity. In this way they prepare themselves to find meaning in their own life.

These examples clearly illustrate how salutogenesis research—comprehensibility, manageability, and meaningfulness—are integral to Waldorf education. Waldorf education is supported by this health studies research field.

Play time is learning time

It is often thought that children in kindergarten merely play, and real learning only starts in school. We must meet this erroneous view head on and try to correct it. The child in kindergarten learns with the greatest intensity, but he does so in a different way from the child in school.

Many education policymakers perpetuate this erroneous view and try to impose the learning content and learning methods of school on the kindergarten.

Such a view, which we encounter in all parts of the world and which threatens childhood, must be opposed. In this context neurobiological research provides important supporting evidence.

If we ask what children want to and should learn before they are ready for school, then we should be concerned with the basic abilities, so called basic skills, on which later school learning can build.

Physical and movement skills

In recent years, scientists, physicians, teachers, and educators have noticed increasing numbers of children with bad posture, who are overweight, or who suffer from balance disorders. The children suffer from lack of movement, their gross and fine motor skills are insufficiently developed. But the mental and spiritual wellbeing of human beings corresponds to their physical mobility; anyone who cannot maintain physical balance is more likely to have difficulties in maintaining balance in her soul.

The ability to move with agility and purpose also influences the acquisition of language. Understanding something and being able to move toward it affects perception, broadens the horizon of experience of the child, and activates the language development process.

Particular attention is therefore paid in Waldorf kindergartens to children moving in many different ways. Regular walks, play, and gardening are as much a part of the day as circle games, finger games, handwork, painting, crafts, and kneading.

In summary, children who move actively and in many different ways prepare themselves for the skilled use of language and thinking.

Sensory and perception skills

Children require an alert awareness of what is happening around and to them. This develops with the trust in one's own perception. That is why children in the preschool years require reliable, unadulterated sensory impressions. In the Waldorf kindergarten, children experience the real world in a way that has been qualitatively formed by the adult. They perceive relationships with the senses and learn to understand them. Coupled with their joy of discovery, they gradually experience basic laws of nature.

Care of the twelve human senses, such as the sense of touch, sense of life, sense of own movement, sense of balance, sense of smell, sense of hearing, and sense of sight, is crucial educational work. Healthy foods, produced in close proximity to nature, and the authenticity of the materials used, which are not designed to deceive the senses, support this development, as do harmoniously designed rooms and a pleasant coordination of colors and materials in the child's environment.

The media skills required at a later time also require the corresponding educational basis.

Children should enter a direct reciprocal relationship with the world in childhood in order to be able properly to understand it. Only by touching water do I learn what it means that water is wet. At the same time I hear it gurgling or dripping, see waves, perhaps smell the sea or the grass at the edge of a lake and thus gain an overall impression which turns—together with many other such experiences—into a complex and differentiated representation of water.... The experienced reciprocal relationship with actual reality is thus the prerequisite for being able to begin to cope with the virtual reality of computers. Computers therefore have absolutely no business in children's rooms, kindergartens and in pre-school.[11]

In summary, virtual worlds are expanding, they deceive us with the illusion of qualities which do not, in reality, exist in such a form. In order not to be deceived by such illusions, children must be able to rely on their senses.

Language skills

Thinking and speaking are closely connected. Only through language can we give expression to our thoughts, give everything in the world a name, and enter into conversation with others. Children only learn to speak if they grow up in a speaking environment. In this context the linguistic relationship between child and adult, based on warmth of soul, provides the foundation for a good and differentiated way of speaking. In many countries, the number of preschool children with speech disorders or delayed development of speech has been on rise for the last 20 years. A 2002 study by the Clinic for Communication Disorders at the University of Mainz in Germany showed that 20 percent of three- to four-year-old kindergarten children are delayed in their speech development, half of them so seriously that they required urgent treatment. An additional alarming factor in these children is that there are no medical reasons for such a delayed development. Professor Heinemann, head of the research project, explains this by a lack of conversation in families, too little reading aloud or telling stories. The concept of the "silent family" is gaining currency among specialists.

When children learn to relate things from their own perspective, they form the world in accordance with their impressions. But this can also cause problems through the dominance at an early age of modern screen media. Neurobiologists such as Manfred Spitzer and Gerald Hüther[12] describe the danger of "mental impairment" when the child's brain is flooded with external images at a time when he should be learning to develop his own versions of stories and produce images out of himself.

As early as 1907, Rudolf Steiner repeatedly drew attention to the direct connection between the quality of perceptions and brain development in children: "If before the age of seven a child only perceives foolish actions in its environment, the brain takes on a form which later makes it suitable only for foolish things."[13]

The point at which children begin to speak varies from child to child. But all children require good linguistic role models in order to grow into speech. Songs, stories, fairytales, poems, finger games, and rhymes play a major part in the Waldorf kindergarten. The teacher's speech should be loving, clear, without ambiguity, and full of images, and should be age-appropriate. So-called baby-talk will as little be found here as cerebral, abstract explanations.

In summary, an early, active, and careful concern for language, the opportunity to say everything, not to be corrected, and adults who are willing to listen—all these things provide the basis for subsequent joy in reading, the ability to read and a good understanding of reading subject matter among adolescents and adults.

Imaginative and creative skills

Being imaginative and creative is a growing challenge in our increasingly standardized, prefabricated, and predetermined world.

Children come with their creative and imaginative forces. They want to develop them in kindergarten, but they require the proper opportunities. Thus the following conversation took place among some four- and five-year-olds in kindergarten: "I'll be mother and you go to work because you earn the money. You are the baby and you can be the dog. I'll make lunch. We're having pizza today. I can build a pizza flattening machine…"

The child's imagination grasps the elements of the world of perception and experience, reforms that world, enters new roles, invents wonderful machines.

That is what the German psychologist William Stern refers to the "child's creativity,"[14] which is based on the one hand on perceptions and real experiences and on the other hand is a "force in its own right" that enables children to create the world in a way which does not exist in the here and now. Human social and cultural development cannot be imagined without creativity and imagination.

Thus development and nurturing of the forces of childhood imagination assumes tangible form in the Waldorf kindergarten. There are no single-function, industrially produced toys but all materials from the environment can be used creatively in play, all the furnishings are included in role play; stories which have been told stimulate the children to use and transform what they have heard into creative, playing activity. Puppet shows performed by the teacher stimulate the imagination of the children and animate them to become creative with the puppets themselves.

The child's imagination grasps everything it is offered and since children do not yet differentiate between good and bad, it is our job to do so for them.

In summary, everything imaginative and artistic expands the human soul and consciousness. Imaginative and creative skills applied in early childhood help develop inventiveness, soul and spiritual agility, and imagination in life and work.

Social skills

Children are social beings from birth and want to settle into human relationships as they learn. These learning processes originate in families and continue in kindergarten. Here kindergarten must, more than ever, provide the basis for social fields of experience, since family structures have changed a great deal and some nuclear families provide insufficient spheres for practice.

In social interactions it is always a matter of placing the interests, wishes, needs of the individual in relationship to the social community—communities in which there should be room for the concerns of the individual and in which agreements can be relied upon, where rules apply and in which trust lives. Children in particular require communities in which they can learn as many as possible of these rules of social coexistence and in which they can be guided by them.

The Waldorf kindergarten is such a space. Here children learn, embedded in a supportive daily and weekly rhythm, that there are rules, just as there are tasks for the individual children in the group (tidying up, laying the table, watering the flowers, and so forth). In these activities they can always be guided by imitating adults. They learn to take responsibility. But they also experience the parents who take an active part in the communal life of the kindergarten, for example in redecorating the rooms, gardening, and the like.

When toys are repaired, laundry is washed, festivals are jointly celebrated, children experience that a community requires many active people.

For us adults, Rudolf Steiner's motto of the social ethic of modern communities might be of help: "The healing social life is only found when in the mirror of each human soul the whole community finds its reflection and when in the community the virtue of each one is living."[15]

In summary, without social skills, the life of the individual in a community is full of conflict and often destructive. If rules for living are learned at an early age, communities can arise in which everyone together and each person individually can contribute with their interests and abilities.

Motivational and concentration skills

For years, educators and pediatricians have had special concern about children who are hyperactive, have attention deficit syndrome, who have difficulty concentrating, or who are nervous and suffer from sleeping disorders. These children are disadvantaged in their creative pleasure, and their capacity to undertake specific tasks suffers.

Increasing numbers of kindergarten- and school-age children are already being medicated daily to help them calm down. But it is symptoms that are treated, not causes; and the consequences may only appear decades later.

Kindergarten work in general cannot start giving medical treatment to children with disorders, but there are certainly preventive actions that can be taken, particularly as many of these childhood disorders are the result of modern life, in which lack of time, a hectic pace, stress, pressure to perform, noise, and media consumption disable our children.

Waldorf kindergarten teachers work hard to ensure a happy, stress-free atmosphere in which children can feel well. Such an environment creates health.

Today, more than ever, children need opportunities to experience things in context and be allowed to realize them in their own activities. Small children have many interests, they are inquisitive and their attention can quickly and happily be diverted; this to a certain extent lies in the nature of small children. But it is just as important that the general hectic pace of things, the superficiality and boredom do not spread to the kindergarten.

Regular repetition and rhythmical elements in the course of the day and extending throughout the course of the year with its many highlights and festivals help to strengthen children's concentration.

Children want to be active themselves and thus the important thing is to meet this basic need wherever possible and sensible. Here it should be observed that it is not a surfeit of things to do which motivates activity but precisely the opposite: "less is more." Thus there is absolute abstinence in Waldorf kindergartens from electronic media, not because of an anti-technology attitude but because children must be protected from the pathological influences which can affect the very processes which form the brain.

In summary, it is important to be aware of the health-giving and stabilizing factors in education for young children. Children who build up inner security and stability within themselves can become strong, committed adolescents and adults.

Learning ethical and moral values

Children, like adults, need orientation of soul and spirit, values and tasks with which they can inwardly associate themselves in determining their lives. Children need rules, rituals, clarity and truthfulness. This does not mean attempting to preach morals. Anyone who preaches morals to children may, at most, teach them to preach, but is not teaching them about morals.

As far as this area is concerned, the relationship between having a role model and imitating it applies in a special way.

> Children are not influenced by moralizing phrases, by reasoned instruction, but by how adults in their surroundings visibly behave.... Healthy vision is developed if we provide the proper color and light relationships in the child's environment, and the physical basis for a healthy moral sense is formed in the brain and the blood circulation if the child sees morality in his environment.[16]

Thus children want to experience adults who lovingly care for nature; they want to perceive gratitude, for example in saying grace; they want to encounter parents and educators who look after elderly or sick people or people in need and who endeavor to create a social life that is compassionate, free of hate, jealousy, and malevolence. Children need parents and educators who are committed—in the kindergarten, in an association they work for, or in politics.

Perspective: Children who experience adults who keep striving for clarity and truthfulness, who work on an ethical and moral outlook on life—such children have a good chance as adolescents and adults of becoming collaborators in a world in which human beings can live with dignity.

In 1998, a Waldorf education center was opened in a South African township. Nelson Mandela, still president at the time, gave the opening address and we will end this chapter with the spirit of his words to encourage us all in our common task not to relax in our commitment to safeguard children's right to their childhood: A society nowhere reveals itself more clearly than in the way it treats its children. Our success must be measured against the happiness and welfare of our children which in any society are both its most vulnerable citizens and its greatest wealth.[17]

CHAPTER 5

Questions from Waldorf Educators

Michaela Glöckler

In preparing the Kolisko conferences many discussions took place in faculty groups, at teachers' conferences, among Waldorf school doctors. A series of questions arose from this, and the desire was expressed to find some answers to them in this book and conference companion. I hope that the following attempts to answer these questions are stimulating and useful.

Question: How do I master the material for the next class, for the coming school year? When do I start and how do I find the reading matter I need?

School years are not just calendar periods. Daily, weekly, monthly and yearly rhythms are, rather, *the central physiological development rhythms* of the human constitution. It is therefore best if the curriculum theme for a whole year is studied and prepared together by a class's teachers at the end of the school year or before the new year begins—i.e. at the beginning or end of the summer holidays. The class teacher can tell specialist teachers which main lesson themes will be taught during this school year. He can discuss with these colleagues questions which he himself has about these main lesson blocks. The specialist teachers for their part will explore how they can approach their specialist material so as to accentuate its inner connection with the year's main themes. It has proven very helpful if an experienced class teacher—perhaps one who has already retired—can be invited to such an *annual class meeting,* and bring his own experiences to bear. Literature for the various main lesson themes should be drawn from the questions and issues that are of most interest and that give the impression that working with pupils on these particular questions will be particularly rewarding. It has also proven very useful to ask colleagues who have themselves recently dealt with this subject matter, or to consult the research department at the Association of Waldorf schools (Bund der Freien Waldorfschulen) in Stuttgart, Germany. In many areas, older literature is often more accessible and suitable for teaching. We can then add to it through internet searches or discussion with colleagues about more recent findings. At all events it is also important to include current research findings or perspectives drawn from a contemporary social context.

The most economical use of time is to undertake the main literature research consecutively, primarily during the peace of the summer holidays, rather than in the daily rush between main lessons. In his lectures on the curriculum (GA 295),[1] Rudolf Steiner uses the example of the nutrition and health main lesson to show, in particularly clear fashion, that a main lesson does not involve specialist areas that are sharply defined and distinguished from each other; rather, it aims to make intelligent links between various specialist areas in order to illumine a central idea in a wide-ranging context of ideas and viewpoints. The aim is then to work at this for a period of four weeks. In the health and nutrition main lesson the overarching idea is that of healing and regulation based on a grasp of complex wholes: the aim is to address both questions relating to the health of the human organism and also those of global and territorial health, as these arise in issues of transport and distribution in the fields of agriculture and global economy. Human health cannot be seen in isolation from the health of the earth and the health or sickness of the economy and distribution processes. This development of the idea of a main lesson requires collaboration, and at the same time brings an inspiring direction to social interaction between colleagues. This annual class meeting always also requires the input of particular high school teachers, whose specialist knowledge can give help in certain main lessons. Planning can go as far as to include inviting the history or social sciences teacher, for example, to give a special main lesson class on the theme of the global economy, or to answer difficult specialist questions. If pupils experience the community of teachers as one that is also learning and developing, then they will experience themselves, in their own class context, as a reflection of this, and it will motivate their own learning.

Once the school year exists in rough outline, details can be planned and noted in the calendar, including dates reserved for marking main lesson books, class studies, or preparing new teaching material.

Question: How about inner preparation?

This can be divided into two areas: in relation to the pupils and to oneself as teacher. In relation to pupils the most important thing is to conjure as vividly before one's soul as possible each child's bodily and soul constitution. Memories of one's own childhood, observation of pupils of this age, discussion with experienced colleagues and/or child and adolescent psychiatrists can lay the right underlying soul mood to deepen one's interest in detailed study of Rudolf Steiner's advice and curriculum suggestions, given for various ages. These are now available in a very well-structured form in curricula and texts published by the Association of Waldorf schools (Bund der Freien Waldorf Schulen) in Stuttgart, Germany, and by the Steiner Schools Fellowship in the UK and the Association of Waldorf Schools in North America. It is therefore easy to find the relevant references, and it is best to study them in a group of two or three colleagues. Sometimes it is also possible to study such issues relating to the nature of the human being and child development in a group of interested parents and teachers.

The better we engage with a young person's developmental conditions, the more sensitive we become for the way his being expresses itself, and the less likely we are to take provocation and misdemeanors personally. Instead we view them as pedagogical challenges to give pupils what they really need in their current developmental stage.

For the teacher, the most important inner preparation in relation to teaching material is his *own life questions* that unite him with the subject in question. It is one's own personal perspective that provides a source of creative teaching. If this is lacking, one seeks formulas and advice—but these can only temporarily compensate for a lack of real interest and personal perspective. Pupils are most interested in what truly interests the teacher, and soon lose interest if they notice the teacher's indifference to the subject.

It is of decisive importance to understand why, for instance, Norse mythology, alliteration, and fractions accompany pre-puberty in fourth grade. Inner preparation means seeking an inner connection with the spirit of each particular subject—e.g. in a chemistry experiment, a historical event, a poem, or whatever the subject may be.

Question: How do I manage to love my students, particularly the difficult ones?

Every person that we do not understand is difficult. Why is this so? Because the less a person feels understood—whether child or adult—the less happy he feels in his own skin. And anyone who feels uncomfortable is likely to be easily provoked. In other words, he is more likely to react negatively to us, and to do so more quickly, than he would do in a situation where he feels accepted, supported, and understood. It is similar with forgiveness. I can really only forgive what I have properly understood. Only then does the knot of misunderstanding resolve itself. If children feel one is inwardly struggling to understand them and serve them well, this has a calming effect, and positively stimulates their learning behavior. But if they get the sense that one expects something of them that they either feel is beyond them or does not align with their own feelings and ideas, they begin—more or less successfully—to challenge this and to build up defenses.

What can be done to help in practical terms? It helps to imagine the "difficult" child very vividly in the evenings. One should form an image, look upon the child or pupil without antipathy, *purely as he is.* Doing so, and allowing all the expressions which a child manifests to surface in one's soul, without judging, and without involving one's own antipathy and sympathy, allows true spiritual empathy to arise. Then we can succeed in identifying with a child, inwardly experiencing the way he is, and understanding how things currently seem to be, and within this human being, and also what the next helpful steps might be, in terms of teaching, support measures, conversation, etc.

Question: What do I want, and what am I able to achieve in the course of a school year?

At the end of each school year comes the "Waldorf testimonial," or report for each pupil, where he and his parents can read an evaluation of his progress and challenges. Instead of graded achievements, *development processes are described.* This can be done all the better and more objectively the clearer the teacher has considered—either before the beginning of the school year, or at the end of the previous year—what each pupil can achieve in the coming year. Just as no medical treatment is given without diagnosis and therapeutic aim, there should really be no school year without envisaging certain learning objectives in different subjects, formulated on the basis of a pupil's development so far and the demands of the coming school year. If a teacher is confident that a particular pupil can learn something in the coming year, and is committed to doing everything possible to help him achieve this goal, this is a hugely motivating force that not only unites teacher and pupil in their daily work, but also helps overcome difficult periods. If the teacher notices that his formulated goal was wrong, he must consciously change the goal. This also applies if he notices that the pupil succeeds in doing something more quickly or easily than expected. Rudolf Steiner's meditations for teachers are an indispensable aid in cultivating this personal connection. They facilitate a dialog from heart to heart, one which does not rise to the surface in daily life but which takes place as it were in the silent reaches of the night.

Question: Is there any means to help develop composure?

The most important aid for practicing composure is to ask oneself: What can I be happy about and grateful for? The happier a person is the more composure he can find. That is why trust and confidence in destiny are the best help here.[2]

It is precisely because there are so many reasons for dissatisfaction—both in one's personal life and in society at large—that the irritation threshold is often so low that we allow our unhappiness free rein, sometimes getting far more worked up about small things than the cause itself would justify. We react in an inappropriately emotional or severe way, and our pupils or colleagues feel hurt.

A second aid is the evening review, at the end of which one calls to mind moments of impatience, aggression, and dissatisfaction, and what triggered them. The more clearly one recognizes when and under what circumstances one loses self-control, the better one can avoid such moments on the one hand, or, on the other, undertake to react in a more self-aware way when a similar situation occurs. It will then quickly become apparent when we react aggressively, we are allowing ourselves and our own conduct to be determined and manipulated by the other—whether child or adult. That is why it is crucial to learn, through schooling and working on inner calm and composure, to *act out of oneself,* rather than just *react* to the other.

The most frequent cause of loss of composure is increased irritability caused by fatigue, hunger, personal problems, or our own temperamental constitution (choleric-melancholics have the hardest time here).

Question: How do I develop a nurturing relationship with my colleagues?

A nurturing relationship with colleagues can be cultivated in the same way as described above for children. The better I understand why a particular colleague thinks and feels the way he does, the more constructively I can relate to him. The only question then is what to do if the other person strikes me as very unsympathetic for certain reasons (self-centered, dishonest, cliquish, loquacious, disinclined to take Waldorf education seriously etc.) Two things can help here: first, we can observe which colleagues or other people have a different impression of the colleague we are judging in this way—i.e. try to discover when the latter can show a better side of himself, and note and study this. The other aid is to repeatedly approach him afresh and without prejudice, addressing things that belong to normal, everyday life, in which the negative underlying feelings and judgments play no part. It has a particularly positive effect if, for instance, one asks a "difficult" colleague for help—by coming on an excursion, attending a parents' evening, or the like—and at the same time tries to bring one's relationship to this colleague into a more objective realm. Sometimes apparent episodes of dishonesty and prevailing problems are resolved when it becomes evident that these involved misunderstandings or a lack of ability on the part of the colleague. One may notice that lack of knowledge or understanding, or a sense of being overlooked, were at work here, rather than actual intention or even bad will. Such processes make a deep impression on pupils. They usually have a better sense of the nature of relationships between faculty members than many staff themselves. In his lecture entitled "How Can the Destitution of the Soul in Modern Times Be Overcome?"[3] Rudolf Steiner advises that *we should take each person as he is, and try to make the very best out of what he is.* In stark contrast to this advice, we usually lay emphasis on being accepted *ourselves* as we are, while happily stressing the need to correct *the other.*

Question: What enables us to form the chalice which Rudolf Steiner speaks of in lecture 1 of The Foundations of Human Experience (Study of Man)?[4]

Human thoughts, feelings, and will intentions are not just the expression of personal ideas, wishes, or actions. Over and above this they exert an effect on the interpersonal sphere, sundering, uniting, motivating, or paralyzing. The effects of moods and atmospheres between people can be highly diverse in institutions and also in a faculty of teachers. Thus there is such a thing as the "overarching spirit" of a family, a factory, a school. Every person can easily observe in himself what thoughts, feelings, or impulses for action he is capable of, depending on whether he lives in a constructive or destructive environment. Consciously working on making the psychosocial environment of the school as constructive and spiritually sustaining as possible was one of Steiner's concerns when assembling the faculty of the first Waldorf school. It is important to engender and maintain awareness within the faculty that the possibility of forming such a chalice does indeed exist, and that it truly must become a reality. What is involved in the act of founding a school? Such a foundation only makes sense if it is an enduring basis for what follows. This original faculty structure founded by Rudolf Steiner continues to have an effect whenever it is newly formed in a community of collaborating colleagues. And like every spiritual impulse, such an act of founding must be nurtured. This can be done, for instance, by referring each new colleague who becomes a permanent faculty member—and thus also belongs to the internal, or school management group—to this original act of founding of the Waldorf school and the transcripts recorded by Herbert Hahn, Caroline Heidebrandt, and Walter Johannes Stein. He will be given the teacher's meditations, the book in which are compiled all meditative verses relating to the teaching profession, which is available for everyone who wishes to engage with it. It has also proven useful to read one of these transcripts together at the first faculty meeting of the new school year, and also when a colleague is newly accepted into the faculty group.

It is usually up to the chair of the meeting to refer to this founding act in his own words, to present its importance for faculty work from his own experience, and then to read out the initial text. It is good for a faculty to establish its own rituals and sustaining habits. (On this point see also Christoph Wiechert's comments in Chapter 10, "Meditation and Community Building.") In order to understand the endeavor to create a chalice, capable of bringing spiritual substance and help from the spiritual world into daily school work, it can be helpful to recall Rudolf Steiner's remarks about the activity of the hierarchies of angels, archangels, and archai[5] (time spirits), in the human soul. It is the angels who can be active in human thinking, with their winged lightness and transparency, when spiritual content holds sway in our thinking, when light and warmth, the fire of idealism, directs our thoughts. Correspondingly the archangels have their sphere of activity in human feeling, which unites human beings and groups of people. Experience tells us that negative emotions always arise by themselves and have something of a demonic quality; they can often only be overcome and processed through arduous work. It is not archangel beings who reign here but demons or "fallen angels."

Positive feelings in contrast do not generally arise by themselves, but always require a certain openness and positivity towards life and other people. As far as impulses of action and will are concerned, the sphere of deed is the time spirits' realm of activity. Through action they continually form present and future. The question is only which spirit inspires human actions, which "trends" or culture-creating ideas have a motivating effect. And here the critical question of human freedom and susceptibility to manipulation always arises; or, in the language of religion or spirituality: to which spirit do I entrust the guidance of my soul, which spirit do I wish to serve? Waldorf education and the anthroposophic underpinning takes a clear stance here: *what is involved is the spiritual guidance of human beings and humanity, which feels itself devoted to the evolutionary principles of truthfulness (for thinking and observation), love (for feeling life), and freedom (for the life of will and action)*. This does not signify adherence to a religious denomination or a particular spiritual stream. Instead it addresses a general science of the human spirit and soul which must be available to every single human being no matter what the cultural milieu and scientific, artistic, or religious education he receives as he grows up. *The human spirit itself is the essential thing, as is unprejudiced thinking, feeling, and will, and the free decision about which thoughts, feelings, and will impulses one wishes to give space to in one's own soul, and also ultimately be governed by*. It can therefore move us deeply to recall that at the foundation stone ceremony for the new Waldorf school in Stuttgart on December 16, 1921, Rudolf Steiner wrote this foundation stone verse:

> May there reign what spirit strength in love
> May there reign what spirit light in goodness
> In heart's certainty
> In soul's steadfastness
> Can bring
> To the young human being
> For the body's strength for work
> For the soul's inwardness
> For the spirit's brightness.
> To this goal we dedicate this place:
> May young sense and purpose find in it
> Strength-endowed, light-devoted Human care.

> May those who here lower the stone
> As emblem, remember in their hearts the spirit
> Which is to reign here, so that this stone
> Fixes the foundation; over which should live, hold sway, be active
> Liberating wisdom
> Strengthening spiritual might
> Manifest spiritual life.
> Let them acknowledge this:
> In Christ's name
> In pure intent
> With good will.[6]

There follow the 42 personal signatures of the teachers and those responsible for the new school building. When the name of Christ appears at the end of this foundation stone verse it is quite evident that this name is not used in terms of the Christian religion or in a denominational way. Rather it stands for the universally human that must come to expression in the school in individual and social development, and permeate all teaching, if mutual understanding is to exist and if the *totality of humanity* into which the pupils are to grow is to make sense. This universal human quality, expressed in the striving for truth, love, and freedom, is the developmental substance that the angel hierarchies also nurture and further in humanity's evolution. But since they respect human freedom, they can only intervene by sending good ideas which inspire feeling life and motivate actions if the individual desires this, and opens himself to these powers and forces of good by working on his own soul. Rudolf Steiner wanted to awaken consciousness for this, and give the necessary help for forming the "chalice" through the striving for good thoughts, feelings and actions.

Question: How do I maintain my enthusiasm for teaching?

Enthusiasm for teaching can continually be renewed by three things: interest in pupils' individual destinies and their social milieu, interest in the subjects taught, which one represents as teacher, and interest in the destiny of the age into which children and adolescents grow. It is this interest which unites parents, teachers, and pupils, and helps promote an atmosphere of warmth and affection that can help prevent burnout in the daily routine. It certainly gives pause for thought to read in German newspapers that the teaching profession is currently the one with the highest drop-out rate.

Question: How do I develop a spiritual relationship with my children?

The spiritual relationship with other people and in particular with the child can be forged in the most selfless way by thinking of his angel, this is, of his destiny's guidance. Our task is to unite with this guidance and to live with the attitude: *"Not my will but your will be done."* Any teacher and educator who lives with the question of both approaching the child and setting limits, so that the latter learns to develop his *own, self-directed* activity as far as possible and unfolds his capacities, is living in a nurturing, spiritual relationship with the child.

Question: Can self-administration improve teaching, and how much self-administration can teaching cope with?

Self-administration at the Waldorf school is a must. Why? Only self-determining people who take responsibility for their own actions can educate children and adolescents to freedom. The free life of the spirit as we may call it stands or falls with individual responsibility and thus also self-administration. Self-administration can also directly improve teaching: important administrative decisions, right into the area of salary arrangements, can affect teachers' daily lives. The more that teachers have a hand in such decisions and help determine their own circumstances and destiny, the freer, more conscious, and above all self-determined they will be within the school organism, giving pupils an example of how to control one's own life. However, self-administration also requires special training, which must be overseen by a faculty of teachers. Administration must be learned, and this is where things often get stuck. For instance, I find it hard to understand that people might prefer to spend money on a director's position, similar to that of a manager, instead of further training faculty members in administrative questions and distributing tasks in a sensible way. Naturally much can also be delegated, but in administrative matters teachers themselves should always take final responsibility.

Question: Can meditation improve my work? If so, how should I begin?

What is meditation? How can it improve my work? It can do so simply because meditation describes a soul stance which includes inner peace and healthy feelings such as reverence, gratitude, truthfulness, inner independence, and courage. A particularly helpful commentary on meditation by Rudolf Steiner can be found in his book *At the Gates of the Spiritual World.*[7] In Chapter 1, Steiner speaks of the trust one can have in thinking, and explains the nature of meditation. If we succeed in establishing a certain degree of soul composure, thinking is simultaneously experienced more intensely and we can notice, if we are honest, that each of us trusts in our own thinking. Even someone who is full of doubt knows that it is *his own thinking* that grants him his capacity for doubt; and that ultimately he can only overcome doubt with the help of *his own thinking.* So a first meditative activity can begin by becoming aware of the trust we have in our own thinking. This is a safe starting point for calmly calling to mind words, thoughts, and meditative content, and initiating the inner, soul-spiritual dialog that we call meditation. When people—particularly teachers—ask how they should begin, one can suggest working in two directions. Firstly, as Rudolf Steiner writes in the Afterword to his book on meditation *Knowledge of the Higher Worlds*[8] one can regard this book as a conversation between the author and the reader. This means nothing less than that one can read this book with one's own life questions in mind, and, for instance, also with the question "How shall I begin?" One can be struck by the subtle way in which, as one reads, certain thoughts or feelings arise in the soul, which one can understand as a direct answer to one's own life questions.

Even if we take these thoughts and feelings as just possible suggestions, they are still there and—if one wishes—can be the very help that is needed. The second way of approaching meditation is to study meditatively acquired knowledge of the human being,[9] to meditate on it, and to bring it alive in oneself through artistic processes. This is the *teacher's meditative work.* To understand the human being ever more profoundly enlivens pedagogical intuitions, and deepens one's love both for the growing child and for questions about how his development can be nurtured.

Question: How do I mobilize the forces to stay healthy? How do I access the salutogenic forces?

We have addressed this question to some extent in this book. In addition, we can say that each person ultimately acquires the greatest strength from what he can inwardly and outwardly unite with, and with which he can stay connected. Nothing weakens a person more than living at odds with himself or other people or biographical situations. That is why, in difficult life situations, it is better to act, and thus remain connected to others, than to withdraw, with the attendant danger of "letting oneself go" or growing bitter. But if one has to withdraw, for reasons connected with time or strength, one should ensure that this does not happen out of negation or frustration, but to achieve a positive goal—for instance to rest, recover one's health, or pamper oneself so that one can then return to school again and set to work with new strength.

Ultimately life itself is the best model in relation to this core question: an organism is healthier the more that all its functions and activities are coordinated with, and linked to each other. The same applies to soul and spiritual health, and thus to all our reserves of strength. (Cf. here also the seven conditions for the path of schooling.)

Question: How much sleep do I need to stay healthy?

The amount of sleep a person needs depends on his physical constitution, diet, and physical environment. As a rule the body shows it is in need of sleep through tiredness. However, the problem is that one cannot always give in to this need, often going to sleep later, and thus sleeping less, than one would like. But the astonishing thing is that in such situations we experience a variable range between "cheerful but rather tired, yet still healthy" and "irritable about not having considered one's own needs enough and not having slept enough"; or "frustrated with one's own life situation, and with colleagues and pupils whose demands and related telephone calls or other conversations have deprived us of sleep." Whether and when these frustrations and associated bitterness express themselves in psychosomatic complaints or serious illnesses is an open question. What is certain is that we all can notice, to some extent, whether we are in the healthy realm, or in one that is making us sick: this is the fundamental sense of whether we still enjoy life and do our work gladly. Where this positive sense of things is impaired we shouldn't let things go any further downhill before we seek respite—also by consulting a doctor—so as to restore in ourselves a sense of purpose in life and work.

The quality of our sleep depends on our waking life. Someone who is wakeful and has presence of mind during the day sleeps more deeply and healthily, and often needs less sleep. Someone who enters the night having made peace with the day, keeping in dialog with himself through practice of the daily review and preview, and also calls to mind the night's sacred and healing effect, can draw on inexhaustible reserves of strength.

Question: Remedial help or waiting—we need guidelines! How long can one wait, and when has one missed the vital moment?

In relation to a pupil, the teacher should not make such a decision alone. It is good to discuss this with other colleagues who teach the child, as well as the school doctor or the child's pediatrician, and with his parents and the child himself. Of course, as class teacher, one should take the final decision, but only after having consulted widely if one is unsure. Ultimately these are questions of destiny and conscience. We know of Waldorf pupils who only really connected with their studies in high school, but then had glowing professional careers. They looked back with gratitude to their lower school days when they were left in peace and not woken too early. They were thus able to dream, gradually come to themselves, store up strength for a strenuous life later on, and lay down reserves. Likewise there are pupils who for years suffered from the fact that they didn't make proper headway, that they didn't receive the right help. They were prevented from feeling at ease and integrated in the class, and from developing a healthy sense of themselves. The work of the school doctor is guided by the principle of taking one's lead from the child himself in such a decision: he can convey whether he is happy in his current school situation or not.

Even if he is unable to verbalize whether he is on the right path, as teacher one can perceive this if one earnestly asks this question and observes the child carefully to find out.

Question: Individual support work—what age can this start?

Remedial or support measures can be undertaken at any age. This already starts in the way an infant is handled. For instance, if I observe that the infant is turning his head to the side where there is something interesting to watch, and this is leading to a twisted position, I have to take remedial action. If the infant is to avoid harm, head- and feet-ends must be swapped now and then, or the crib turned round. What is important is that remedial measures take their lead from the age of the child and his capacities. Rather than ambitious parental wishes, the child's own developmental needs should be the deciding factor. This also includes support work for highly gifted children. A pupil who is highly gifted in math should naturally be released sometimes from classes and allowed to attend higher courses at university, as long as one also, at the same time, helps him to integrate his gifts socially, and use them to help others. Strengths are frequently connected with weaknesses, and vice versa. However, it is also important not only to consider individual support but to support groups of children with similar problems together. Ultimately the best support is that given by the *class teacher himself*. It is ideal if every class teacher can be covered for at least two lessons per week so he can attend to the individual needs of the children in his own class.

Question: What techniques exist to teach calculations?

There are children who have next to no rhythmic memory, and cannot remember any times tables. They only learn to calculate when they are given a written sheet of tables which is anyway the accepted way at the end of a learning process.

It is important to practice three things: movement without speech, speech without movement, and movement with speech. Depending on how a child spends his preschool period, one can have children who move very awkwardly but speak a great deal, or very active children who do not speak well, and also those who can do both perfectly well. In the class group we should work in the way the children need. One can also divide them so that a certain group in the class only does the movements, while another group speaks, and a third group does both. This can alternate or be done altogether. The starting point is always observation of the children themselves, and offering them activities which help them develop. Calculation is a self-movement-style learning in the realm of counting. The times table is based on rhythms, counting has names and qualities, and has visually graspable forms.

In grades 5 and 6 in Germany, the focus is on the higher times table and algebra, which are developed from the first rules of mathematics as applied in grades 1 through 3. In grade 4 come fractions. Mental arithmetic is naturally very important, which must be practiced together with basic arithmetic in the first three school years. With this foundation the children have an inner "counting room" and are flexible with calculations.

Question: What about premature development?

Little attention has been given to premature developmental steps before puberty. Does this mean one should place curriculum content earlier than we normally do? Or is it actually good for children if one presents curriculum content to them in line with the right stage and order? A few detailed questions about this:

Deciding things for oneself at too early an age:

Parents increasingly assume that children younger than 9 should be asked to make many of their own decisions (about clothes, afterschool activities, etc.). Some children become "partners" of single parents, or the parents use Gordon's "family meeting"[11] for children younger than 9. Children are increasingly becoming small adults.

Premature independence:

- Time orientation. 7-year-olds already spend the whole day away from home because their parents work. They have to know: I'm going to this place at lunch time, that place in the afternoon, then I'll be picked up by Mummy at 5. It is not unusual for children in first grade to have a wrist watch.

- Spatial orientation. Children at rural schools may have to manage an hour-long bus trip to school on their own, including changing buses. For some children this begins in grade 1. At grade 2 this affects the majority of children.
- Over-planning of leisure time, too little free play.

Question: I have cancelled homework in the first three grades and begged parents to give their children time to do what they like. Is that good?

Once again, the first thing to do is observe the children. Physical acceleration is usually connected with marked emotional immaturity or infantilism. Sometimes there are family-related or environmentally-determined leaps in knowledge and skill that cause the child to be bored in class. One has to decide in each case whether to consider supporting the child in class and encouraging him to support weaker members of the group, or to send him up to the next grade for certain classes. Mostly the problem can be solved by using the age-appropriate teaching material but enhancing it with questions and also additional tasks which are suited to each pupil's interests and situation. Of course such teaching demands more preparation by the teacher, but also offers good opportunities for making the lessons more lively and interesting.

On the theme of making decisions for oneself at too early an age, or when one should teach children to tell time, something very interesting arises here. There is a difference between showing a child the position of hands on the clock so that he knows when he should get home if no one else can tell him this reliably, or whether the whole process that led to the development of the clock is described at school: how the clock imitates the movement of the sun, and a sundial works. It is a long path from the sundial to the wrist watch. Waldorf education consistently avoids explanations in the lower school. Its method and pedagogical approach are based on characterizing living processes, historic developments, natural phenomena, etc., in a way that enables children to develop a feeling relationship to the subject and form their own ideas. Those who present explanations and definitions usually expect pupils to remember them as precisely as possible, and be able to repeat them. But if processes are characterized, the paths leading to a particular result can take very different forms. This gives rise to interesting questions for lesson discussions, and things come alive.

Here are two examples: a first-grade pupil had already been taught to read and write by her older siblings before introduction of the letters, one after the other, in her Waldorf class. Her parents were very concerned that the child might be bored and considered having her moved up to the next grade. Since the teacher was experienced, they soon realized their mistake and changed their minds. Each day their daughter came home from school and enthusiastically told them about the latest letter story. She enjoyed hearing where the letters came from, and what they do. It didn't matter at all that she already knew them. On the contrary, the child was very pleased to hear such interesting new things about them. Another child did not want to stay in bed despite being ill, simply because "I will miss a letter, Mummy!" Beginners and more advanced pupils are both properly served if they can develop interest in the subjects taught. How to prepare teaching that makes the subject matter continually new often requires a discussion between colleagues, research, and mobilization of one's own questions.

To stop giving homework if children have too little time for movement and free play is a good idea. One should also consider the goal of giving homework. It certainly shouldn't serve to catch up with or practice things one didn't manage to do in class. Children should feel that "I learn at school," and that homework—if given—involves interesting reflections which make me think of school when I'm at home, and necessitates asking my mother or father something, or making my own observation in the garden or on the street. Homework should not "cost time," but awaken interest, and help one to reflect on and process what has been learned. From fourth or fifth grade this changes: homework then becomes a way of undertaking additional practice, learning something by heart, or the like.

Question: It is my experience that premature independence can lead to anxiety.
Likewise, ambition and an increased sense of shame when failure occurs at school. Children often seem inhibited by this, and blocks to learning develop. How can we counter this?

This touches on a theme that currently also figures under names such as "new children," "indigo children," "star children," and similar. It is evident that children today enter kindergarten and school with a very sensitive self-awareness that wakens much earlier, and also a fragile sense of self-worth. This confronts teachers with challenges. Irrespective of whether this is accompanied by symptoms such as attention deficit, motor restlessness, hyperactivity, aggression, the basic problem is prematurely awakened self-awareness and thus also much more sensitive vulnerability and liability to become frustrated. Many things work into this change: the influence of the adult world with its tendency to sensory overload, rigid time scheduling, and frantic schedules, passing each other by without connecting, taking little account of children or burdening them with responsibility too soon because circumstances at home necessitate it. In addition, all children bring their own destiny with them and the new element that they are trying to bring to the world, together with their particular gifts. Much storms toward them, causing anxiety that cannot be properly processed.

This and much else shows, ultimately, that doctors and teachers must realize the extent to which the school today needs to be more than just a place of learning, but also, primarily, a space for life and development. What use is intellectual progress if human relationships and self-discovery are left floundering, or are not nurtured sufficiently? The more fragile a child's sense of self-worth, the easier it is for blocks to learning to develop, and the more necessary it is for pupils to feel accepted and understood by their teacher. Trusting human relationships is often more important here than the teaching material. But where both come together—a good relationship and subject matter presented in a way that reaches and speaks to the child—then Waldorf education has achieved its goal. Anxiety vanishes where trust and love are established; blocks to learning resolve themselves when learning is offered in small enough steps for the child to have courage to embark on the process.

Question: What should one do when a seventh- or eighth-grader no longer sings?
Should one take advantage of the time in grades five and six to embark on the songs for grades seven and eight in advance?

The music curriculum is exposed to attacks in a way similar to the eurythmy curriculum. Finding methodologies which allow us to present age-appropriate, artistic, developmental experiences to children requires a great deal of pedagogical know-how on the one hand, and on the other often the help of the faculty. If the class teacher sings regularly with her pupils, and does not stop doing so before grades seven or eight, the music lessons will work out. But if the class teacher does not manage this, the music teacher can help her by periodically attending the start of lessons in the morning. Sometimes the presence of a class teacher or specialist teacher is needed for some time to create the basic discipline for tackling an artistic process at all. What is involved here are subtle perception, process structuring, quality of hearing and creative forming. These "soft skills" often find little space in today's culture. In other words, pupils only find these qualities at school, and are often not at all open to them initially. It is all the more rewarding if they can open up in this way, and if children can develop enthusiasm in such areas.

Staging a dramatic performance can help here, in which there is much song and music, and the music teacher collaborates. Sometimes it also helps if, in a limited way, melodies and songs which children and adolescents hear at home are integrated into music lessons, thus building a bridge between daily home-life and school—where capacities are developed in a way that requires practice and learning. When pupils sense that teachers are working together, are helping each other and consider it important that these particular experiences arise in classes, one is already half way there.

Question: What would you say to professed Waldorf teachers using make-up, lighting, and scenery for lower-school plays—and not just in grade seven or eight for the final class play?
Here external apparatus is used to cover up a lack of skill in performing a role expressively. And what do you say of cases where it becomes the norm to introduce—often loudly amplified—electronic music at school festivals, or even coffee mornings or school bazaars? Is this kind of concession to the spirit of our age reconcilable with the Waldorf curriculum?

Waldorf education can only take root where people understand it and also really implement it. That is the problem. Whether one engages a band at school festivals—there are still some that play without amplifiers, or are willing to turn down the volume—is after all just a question of making a decision, and money. That is, if people want to do this it happens, and if not, then it doesn't. The same applies where alcohol and nicotine are involved. Here too the teachers' example has a decisive effect, as does the question of whether they wish to realize true Waldorf education or prefer just to cobble together an alternative school. It is hard to say anything helpful in response to this sort of question. Children and adolescents always join in if adults are truly convinced of something and enjoy doing it. Pupils also understand that things can be different at home and at school, and that they can also learn styles of music at school that may not be their natural inclination at present. It is always problematic if teachers entrench themselves behind Waldorf phrases and espouse prohibitions and views that they cannot really defend. The students do not particularly want to push their own will, rather they want to know honestly what the facts are.

Question: In commentary on the health and nutrition main lesson in seventh grade we are told that this block should take place before "health egotism" has awoken. *By seventh grade it's really too late for that. Should we bring this main lesson forward to sixth grade?*

Waldorf education aims to do everything at its proper time, at the right moment. It is therefore absolutely appropriate to observe individual class groups carefully to see whether a particular main lesson such as health and nutrition might well come at the end of sixth grade, or at the beginning of seventh. In some circumstances it makes sense to focus more strongly on what was already referred to as enhancement of the subject matter by including factors relating to commerce and economy, and to highlight issues of healthy agriculture and social health in general. By doing so children are diverted to some extent from self-preoccupation, and can examine health and nutrition issues in a more objective way.

Question: There is a rumor going around our Waldorf school that Waldorf pupils frequently get pregnant at a young age, before they have completed a training. *Are we doing too little about sex education, are we focusing on it too little?*

Whether too little attention is given to this theme must certainly be examined in each individual case. It has proven useful to invite the school doctor to a parents' evening at least once in fourth, fifth, or sixth grade, to discuss all issues relating to this. The parent evenings in fourth grade are of particular importance, where help is given on the degree to which sex education should be approached at home. It is frequently apparent that this area is full of taboos and silence. Of course, the school doctor does not have to get involved, but this can be helpful for clarifying the theme and drawing on practical experience. Under no circumstances should parents get a sense that this theme is taboo in Waldorf schools. We also very much welcome the fact that a volume relating to this field has been published by the German association of Waldorf schools (Bund der Waldorfschulen).[12] It is important that sex education be included as part of the annual class meetings we have mentioned. The Waldorf curriculum is structured in a way which, if properly understood, can make a contribution to ongoing sex education: this starts in first grade, where a king and queen wish to have a baby, through to the human and animal main lesson in twelfth grade, when pregnancy, birth, and care in the first years of life are dealt with. Biological questions, interpersonal issues, social issues, or also events which children often pick up on far too early through the media, must all be tackled in class of course, must be properly illumined, ordered and shown in a light that as far as possible reflects human dignity. However, it is also important to seek personal discussions with individual pupils whom one senses are at risk in some way, or showing a particular interest in this area. There really are some things which are not suitable for general lessons in the whole class group, and would merely use up valuable time. Another question to the issue of high rates of student pregnancy: The social environment may mean there are fewer abortions, rather it may be encouraged to see a pregnancy to full term. Without this fuller information I have no indication that public school students have lower pregnancy rates than Waldorf students.

Question: Foreign language teachers tackle grammatical themes before the class teacher has dealt with them. *Of course one can attribute this to lack of discussion between colleagues. But this is also a fundamental problem—foreign language teachers are often also class teachers, and ought really to know this!*

These questions cannot be answered in the abstract—they are a good example of the need often mentioned here for discussion in annual class meetings. The better a foreign language is coordinated with mother-tongue instruction, the more constructive will be the synergy between them. Then you can easily delegate something to foreign language teaching which you pick up again in a main lesson, and vice versa. Teaching foreign languages without books and written text work is a purely methodological problem. We can refer here to the excellent foreign language training course for teachers in Mannheim, Germany, and in other countries, or the annual specialist conferences organized by the Association of Waldorf Schools (Bund). New foreign-language teachers should be required to attend such training.

Question: What about Steiner's curriculum suggestions?
He places many things much earlier than we do, or demands greater achievement. For example, his recommendation for second-grade grammar: "Teach the child concepts of what a noun is, and a verb. Discussions of sentence structure." This normally happens in third grade, and we are also warned that all children must be at the "Rubicon stage" so that they are able to distinguish between a word and the concept it represents.

Teaching the child concepts does not mean defining concepts and grasping an idea as pure concept independently of a word. Rather, teaching concepts means the characterization or description, already mentioned, of processes and realities. Experiencing a process that has come to rest, which embodies a noun; and standing within the whole as a process, in time, in action, as applies to verbs, is what counts here. We should cultivate enjoyment of the intelligence in words, in what is going on there, what it can mean, distinguishing how differently sentences can be built up, how differently one can stress them. Apart from this the division of word and concept only takes place when pupils enter the stage, around fifth grade, of delighting in words with multiple meanings. They find it exciting that "shift" means both to move something and an article of clothing. This is the first time that they experience a word's autonomy and independence from an idea or meaning, and it gives them pleasure to sense that they bear ideas in themselves that are independent of words; that, indeed, they can seek words for certain ideas and that sometimes one word can convey multiple ideas. Handling language in a conscious way, as learned gradually through grammar, strengthens self-awareness and self-experience in terms of thought and spirit, and is thus an important prerequisite for the subsequent search for one's own identity. It is therefore particularly harmful if grammar is boring or arduous, and if pupils do not notice that relating to language is actually relating to oneself and one's own spiritual and creative potential. Pedagogical meetings and conferences should discuss the phenomena of language in relation to the various teaching areas. A poem such as this one by Rilke can also touch us profoundly:

> The poor words languishing in the everyday,
> Those inconspicuous words I love.
> From my festivities I give them colors:
> They smile, grow slowly happy, move… [13]

Question: Maths in seventh and eighth grade.

In math Rudolf Steiner gives the material for seventh grade which nowadays is usually done in eighth grade, and for eighth grade the material usually taught in ninth grade.

This is a sign to show how important it is for each teacher to take time to study the overall teaching plans, which can be inherited from the teacher above, and to relate these to the original indications from Steiner and the concrete developments of his school situation. Words such as "generally" or "typically" are not appropriate. Much more must the typical be reviewed in light of the current situation: "Why do I teach this now? What is my relationship to this material? What interests me today on this? Why do I say that my students must work on this now? What do I want to bring about with this?"

Question: Why is reading and writing a problem in Waldorf schools?

This comes about due to the lack of working through of the method. Both for learning to read and to write there are two ways: one sees through the eyes and for others through the ears. This is important because there are typically people who tend more toward eye or ear, as well as those who learn best when both ways support each other. The eye path passes from story to an image that is painted, and ends in the letter or number. These can also be beautifully formed with the fingers, using modeling wax or clay; or they can also be drawn with the feet, that is by holding a crayon between the toes and drawing on large sheets of wrapping paper. The ear path is based on the story that leads to the letter's or number's sound. The relevant form is then moved or drawn with the hand in the air, with large and small movements. Words are sought in which these sounds appear, and the number sequences are rhythmically repeated. In this second path, too, via the ear to sound and movement, the process ultimately ends in a form drawn on paper, or with chalk on the board. When both methods are practiced in the classroom, then all children can learn—slowly but surely. Those who can understand quickly, or can read can only profit as they have the motor movements in addition and also to have the social observation to the degree that they may also learn to assist another.

Question: I have heard that the times table should first be written in the third grade.

There is no doubt a serious misunderstanding here. Naturally the numbers are already written down in first grade, at the same time as the multiplication tables; also the sequential numbers where the rhythms (1, 2, 3, 4, 5, 6) can be made clear with arcs under the numbers.

In fifth and sixth grade we come to the extended multiplication tables and algebra, which are based on the four math processes taught in the first three school years. In fourth grade come fractions already. Mental arithmetic is also very important, and this must be practiced in the first three school years in particular, in combination with the four processes. This opens the interior number space and children become flexible in handling numbers.

Question: Nature study. *There are various suggestions by Steiner—for instance in lecture 7 of Practical Advice to Teachers, he speaks of the nine-year-old child. Should one therefore bring nature study forward to third grade?*

It is in fact the case that the curriculum contains more, and more condensed material, than is usually practiced. For this reason too it is very important that people work together in the class faculty group to prepare the content of a school year! Steiner's curriculum lectures are essential reading and ought to be studied thoroughly by young faculties in particular, as part of their pedagogical meetings. Instead of asking whether one should bring nature study forward to third grade, we can ask: which aspects of nature study would be especially good for third grade, and which for fourth grade? Steiner's various comments about this actually provide a very clear answer.

Question: Rhythm and speech, i.e. long and short qualities in speech, is increasingly being lost. *This is a cultural problem—deficient heart forces. Will and thinking—or one can say beat and accentuation—remain. As a result, class teachers practice class recitation almost entirely without rhythmic quality, just with beat and emphasis. This is particularly bad with the hexameter in fifth grade. Even colleagues who actually know what is involved are unable to do it properly. However, a very large number do not know, and directions for speaking the hexameter are not taken seriously enough due to lack of skill. I believe this is a grave problem, since language is one of our prime tasks, sustaining communication and mediating human culture. Language is also our chief medium as teachers. Everything comes toward children through language in the elementary school and largely also in middle school. What can be done?*

Basic staffing of a Waldorf school faculty should include not only subject teachers but also a school doctor, a teacher trained in curative and remedial work, a therapeutic eurythmist, and a speech formation practitioner. At the original Stuttgart Waldorf School these tasks were filled by Eugen Kolisko (school doctor), Elisabeth Baumann (therapeutic eurythmy), Karl Schubert (curative education) and Marie Steiner (speech formation). We strongly recommend including a speech professional in the faculty, who works with both teachers and pupils, helping produce plays and also keeping an eye on questions relating to discussion skills and communication. Sometimes it is also necessary to offer the speech practitioner the opportunity to train further in valuable mediating and discussion techniques.

Question: Why are Waldorf schools not safe from bullying?
Does this have something to do with our system of social education, i.e. with "rubbing off each other's rough edges" by grouping of pupils according to temperament? Does it have anything to do with big class sizes? We do not suppress pupils after all. So is our system perhaps enticing something out of pupils? This isn't a new theme in Waldorf schools, even if the concept is a relatively new one. As long ago as the mid-sixties I myself experienced bullying at first hand at a Christian Community camp. I was 10 or 11 at the time, and in public school. I have been experiencing things in my own classes, and also among children I know in other schools that are very similar to what I witnessed in the sixties. Little has changed. This makes me suspect that this is a problem in all Waldorf schools before conscience awakens (i.e. before age 14). In my current class I had a real bullying problem at the end of first grade. Has anyone really worked on the concept of bullying in anthroposophic terms? I also ask myself whether bullying could be a violent processing and rejection of sheaths experienced as "alien" in the form of inherited characteristics and residual family qualities, or even karmic limitations. Does this perhaps have something to do with an incipient perception of the "double"?

The word "mob" is derived from the Latin *mobile vulgus*, a crowd of people, usually not organized, who egg each other on to commit acts against individuals, groups, or institutions. Mobs are characterized by aggression and low self-control. The same applies to bullying. Here we usually meet ostracism or cliquish behavior. Two against three, three against six, four against two, etc. It doesn't matter what the bullied individual or group does—the aggressors will always find a reason for cynical remarks, verbal insults or even physical aggression. Study material on bullying from an anthroposophic perspective has been published in the USA.[14]

There is a great deal of literature on the theme of the shadow or double, and not just from an anthroposophic viewpoint: unconscious projections of expectations, wishes, sympathies and antipathies have been prevailing themes in psychology, psychotherapy, psychoanalysis, and also the social sciences, since the end of the nineteenth century. This also includes examination, still ongoing, of the demagogic propaganda that surfaced in Nazi Germany. All such phenomena lead us to consider evil in human nature. When asked about the purpose of evil, Rudolf Steiner replied that evil was not in the world for its own sake but in order to lead human beings to the path of initiation, that is, to awaken them for what is good and true. It is indispensable not only for doctors and psychologists to engage with this question of evil and its effects, but also teachers. Children and adolescents experience—and not just through the media—so much destructiveness and aggression that they are all highly sensitive to whether and in what way this arises in the subjects they are taught. Thus fairy tales in kindergarten and first grade can already help focus on this theme of the battle between good and evil in human nature in a healthy way, using appropriate images. One reason that Waldorf education prefers the Brothers Grimm fairy tales is that they are derived from Rosicrucianism and have a developmental orientation.

The focus is always on the human being's developing ego, and the confrontation with its soul forces, with the elemental world, nature, other human beings and spirits. For this reason things also always end well: development continues, and a solution is found for every problem. Everything has its proper time and its just compensation in due course. Healthy self-awareness cannot develop without such a developmentally orientated, constructive view of the world. Your question—"We do not 'suppress' pupils after all. So is 'our system' perhaps enticing something out of pupils?"—needs to be put with more precision. Of course we do not wish to suppress anything in children, for that is an educational method (like fear, compulsion, drilling, conditioning) that quells much of a child's spontaneous capacity for response, allowing it to accumulate in the unconscious and thus creating a potential for aggression that can express itself in bullying. The other extreme would be *laissez faire*, undisciplined teaching in which little is learned and the children just have fun.

Waldorf education tries to replace compulsion and power with voluntary involvement, something that is only possible if a child either develops interest out of himself, or else does something out of love for his teacher. Acting out of love always takes place with the full soul-spiritual involvement of the child, which is why it does not involve any splitting or suppressing of aspects of the personality. That is why Waldorf education stands or falls on the relationship between teacher and child. This relationship is the sole means which the teacher can use to deal constructively with bullying. If pupils see and experience that their beloved teacher absolutely cannot bear this kind of thing, and does everything possible to exert a clarifying and ordering effect on such phenomena, this will give them a clear model and also the necessary basic orientation for their own conduct. Since children, due to the incomplete foundation of their personality development, are not yet capable of conscious self-control and emotional balance, the teacher has to add what is lacking through his own presence and conduct. In the second and fourth lectures of the *Curative Education Course*,[15] Rudolf Steiner speaks of the pedagogical law, which states that there is an influence between people such that one effects the other on various levels depending on the individual's impact or strengthening influence on the other. When a person experiences his own ego in a situation this can take place because of his thinking, feeling, and willing abilities—his soul forces. The way in which this happens inwardly either enhances or impairs our sense of life or vital functions. Ultimately the body's state of health is dependent on the quality of life function. That is, up to a certain point, each day has its own health, depending on how we deal with and process our daily experiences. This lawfulness underpinning self-education also applies to the interpersonal realm and can work in a nurturing or obstructive way in the teacher-pupil relationship. How the ego of the teacher meets the child affects the latter's soul and the way his soul capacities respond to a task or word spoken to him. On this depends, in turn, how the child feels, and whether he is spurred on or demotivated. Children also react in a correspondingly sensitive, and physiological, physical way to psychosocial stress, for instance becoming ill through fear of a math test, or developing a headache in response to an inability to work. Being clear as teacher about the extent to which one's own soul-spiritual and physical state affects the child either positively or negatively, is the sustaining foundation of Waldorf education. Ultimately, unlike the adult, the child cannot yet act out of himself in situations of daily life but usually reacts. In other words, it depends largely on the teacher himself what reactions he draws forth from pupils, and how, consequently, he stimulates their soul and physical development.

A further question relating to bullying is: When is there time and desire for it. Usually it occurs when people are bored, or for some reason have a low inhibition threshold, or also because they are in some way unhappy with themselves and their situation. It is rarely pure destructiveness. One of the main issues of prevention, therefore, is how pupils' interactions can be kept as lively and interesting as possible, so that there is as little space as possible for inertia.

What form of punishment is appropriate for misconduct? It is disastrous if mistakes or misconduct by pupils meets with a punishment-happy teacher, or with unimaginative punitive actions that have no real link with the misbehavior, mistake, or misdemeanor. Making mistakes relates to development and being human in the same way as the sun to plant growth. One always learns most when one can work through a mistake in a meaningful way. The formation of conscience also occurs in the child through actual, self-discovered experiences. This is why mistakes—however big or small—should always be regarded as a valuable treasure for individual growth. Pedagogically valuable punishments are those that give a pupil the experience of how a mistake or a problem can be made good again, or solved.

Depending on a child's age it is also important to let children discover for themselves what they need to do to make up for their misconduct, and what deficient skill they can learn or practice. This requires a stance on the part of the teacher or educator that we also adopt in regard to our own mistakes: we assume that the other would have preferred to have behaved properly, rather than imputing to him intent, negligence, or bad will. Even if this does appear to be the case, we still have to assume that the person concerned was unable to act differently, and therefore is in need of help. One can find a model for this in the legend of young Parsifal, who kills a swan, not knowing that animals deserve compassion. One aspect of this is being pleased to have hit a moving target in flight, being proud at one's sure aim; but alongside this are many other aspects, which can show the selfsame deed in a very different and negative light, and brand it as misconduct.

For instance, if something is broken or destroyed, we should examine the result of the destruction calmly together and discuss how the damage can be made good. If the damage is linked with expense, we need to think where we can procure the money, and what the pupil in question can contribute as compensation. If we are dealing with a chronically tardy pupil, we must discuss together how this can be overcome. Perhaps we can give another pupil the task of reminding him for a certain period; or of organizing someone to accompany the latecomer on his way to school. Discipline is not punishment, it is help in learning something one is as yet unable to do. The punitive teacher in the classroom, who lays bare pupils' errors, can strike children like a döppelganger, and many pupils feel bullied by teachers, and express this as such when they are older. How can the teacher bring something to the situation in an objective way, especially in a way that does not show favoritism? We need to develop an atmosphere based on nurturing individual relationships with pupils in a class, which gives children a sense that they are part of a community of collaborating and mutually supporting people. One can develop a kind of common sense in which can live pleasure at successful actions or achievements but also genuine sympathy if something does not work out. It is not only individual pupils who are responsible for this, but also the whole context in which they are embedded.

A profound meditation on bullying is contained in these words of Paul the Apostle (1 Corinthians 13:4-8):

> Love is great-hearted, love is kind.
>
> Love does not envy,
>
> love does not vaunt itself, is not proud,
>
> does not hurt others' dignity, does not seek its own ends,
>
> does not allow itself to grow bitter, does not impute evil to others, does not rejoice in injustice, rejoices only in truth.
>
> It encompasses everything, is all-trusting,
>
> all-hoping, all-enduring.
>
> Love can never fail.

Eight identifying qualities of love are here contrasted with eight characteristics that can be overcome through love, since the latter have no part in the nature of love—despite the fact that love can comprehend and thus avoid or overcome these negative propensities. Viewed individually, we can also clearly see that these named characteristics of love are precisely what can compensate for the potential, eightfold lack of love or humanity:

- Envy through great-heartedness.

- Self-aggrandizement through kindness.

- Pride through pleasure in truth.

- Hurting others' dignity through loving encompassing and comprehending of a situation.

- Selfishness through trust, the fear that something will be taken from us, indeed also that one will not find oneself. Fear is usually the basis of selfishness. This existential anxiety can only be healed by trust in the spirit, given to us through love.

- Bitterness at others can be healed by hope—hope in the capacity to develop of those involved, and evolution's future goals.

- If injustice occurs, or mistakes have been made, this can best be endured if it is initially accepted and tolerated as the reality that has happened. This most quickly releases the forces to work on possible strategies for preventing a recurrence, or forgiveness based on understanding why the other acted in this way.

- Pleasure at others' discomfort and enjoyment of injustice, of sensation and catastrophe—or, put simply, fascination with evil—can only be avoided by calling to mind a stance of love as basic gesture toward life. This does not distance or aggrandize itself, and cannot fall or fail. Instead it integrates things that have fallen asunder or split off, and can understand and order, and thus place things and possibilities into the right context where they show themselves as purposeful and not harmful.

CHAPTER 6

The Nature of the Human Being

Astrid Schmitt-Stegmann

As Waldorf teachers, we must have a comprehensive understanding of the child and of child development, because the whole marvelous movement of the Waldorf curriculum, and the artistic way that the teachers bring it, is keyed to the changing inner condition of the child. Steiner stresses that the subtle organizations of the human being and how they interact should be second nature to the Waldorf teacher. However, even when we make the conscientious effort to attend to this foundation of our work, we may soon notice that we have to return to it intensively again and again so that our understanding remains living, flexible, and artistic. Therefore, it is good to approach the nature of the human being and child development from as many different sides as possible, so that our knowledge does not become merely informational, fixed and stale.

This understanding is the door for the teacher to know what to teach when, and how to approach the children. By addresses the inner age-appropriate needs of the child, healing elements stream to the child with the curriculum. In our present time, Waldorf teachers need to be conscious healers. The more teachers will contemplate and meditate on the changing nature of the human being, the more secure, imaginative, and inspired they will be, and the more Waldorf education will be a source of renewal for both students and teachers.

Every movement, every gesture, every look of the child must become for teachers an outer revelation of the inner constitution. When this becomes a reality, then we have teachers of initiative, inwardly free and able to stand fully behind the curriculum, for the teacher has both knowledge and inner experience of why, for instance, fairy tales are appropriate for grade one, and why Norse mythology is appropriate for grade four. The teacher then asks what the inner constitutional moment is that Norse mythology addresses, and recognize this moment in the child of that grade.

We are familiar with the fourfold organization that Rudolf Steiner speaks about. This creates four fields of experience for us. We have the visible physical body, the life body (etheric organization), the soul (astral organization), and the spirit ("I"). We also realize that merely knowing the names is not enough. Naming must be given substance by our capacity to see and experience how each of these subtle bodies expresses itself in the child, and how we as teachers can either nourish and strengthen these organizations, or influence them in a negative way. Each of the subtle bodies has an effect on the physical body, and they also affect each other. According to Rudolf Steiner,

> A concrete knowledge of the human being is of the utmost importance in human life. A really concrete knowledge of the human being, with the power of seeing right into the human himself, is the only possible basis for a true art of education.

Steiner then goes on:

> We can only see the whole human being if we have the wisdom and knowledge to recognize the soul in its true nature as clearly as we recognize the physical body; and further, if we are able to recognize the spirit...as an independent being.[1]

Insight into the working of these subtle bodies over years of teaching is not only a necessity but a joy for any serious Waldorf educator. For in our present time and even more so in the future, children will bring greater gifts but also greater challenges. Restlessness, uncontrolled movement, inability to listen and focus, constant talking, or difficulty getting engaged in what is asked of them—these traits are only the tip of the iceberg.

The gift of the physical body

How we work with the child during the first seven years of life is extremely important, because the physical body is the foundation on which the subtle human organizations build. The physical body is also the basis upon which the human "I" achieves self-awareness. If the body is not developed in a proper way, what is the impact on the much needed healthy self-consciousness and self-assurance of the child? The physical brain makes it possible for the etheric forces to create mental images. The physical body supplies the astral body with a basis for feeling by way of the rhythmic system. Our awareness of the physical body enables the "I," our eternal essence, to experience itself as the central core of the human being. Our thoughts, feelings, and actions need the physical body in order to have conscious experiences in earthly life. In addition, we need our senses so that the "I" can take in the world and organize our perceptions. Our experiences here in the earthly environment depend on our healthy physical body. Therefore, the care of the physical body is of utmost importance, especially in the first seven years of life, when it is still being cast into the necessary and healthy forms.

Steiner elaborates the physiological point of view:

> Every part of the body involved in the activity of the metabolic system is directly connected with human will. The circulatory or rhythmic system forms the physiological basis for the human feeling, and the nerves-sense system is immediately connected with thinking and the life of conscious ideation.[2]

In the middle grades, especially from ages nine to twelve, rhythm, repetition, breathing, and artistic activity are essential because the middle or chest area of the child is being elaborated. We see how physical growth moves from the head (ages 1-7) to the rhythmic system (especially ages 9-12) and down into the metabolic and limb system (at age 14-15). We see how this system now becomes the focus, how the limbs grow and become strong.

As Waldorf teachers, we need to be aware that before the change of teeth, a stream of forces works from the head downward. These are the forming forces that shape the organs and organ processes and the whole body. After the change of teeth, the focus shifts more to the etheric organization, and the stream of life forces. Breathing and circulation are connected with the middle system, with life. A mood of stress or fear in the classroom works against developing healthy breathing and circulation rhythms. Healthy adults have a four-to-one rhythm of pulse to breath that establishes itself around age 12 to 14. Stress or fear in the classroom affects the rhythmic system and may incline the child towards asthma. A warm, harmonious atmosphere is a necessity for learning; as teachers we can stimulate or hinder the development of these physiological processes.

Life, vitality, and form

When we speak about life, vitality, and formative forces, we speak of our etheric forces or etheric organization. This subtle body works closely together with the physical body,

in fact it never leaves it during life on earth. The etheric organization shapes and forms the physical body. We experience it and its forces in the growing, healing, and regenerating capacities, and also in our level of energy and vitality. In short, its forces keep our physical body alive, energetic, and functioning. Looking at the body from the physical perspective, we are aware that when the etheric life forces withdraw at death, very quickly disintegration sets in. Our etheric body needs to remain closely bound up with our physical body to keep it alive.

In addition, we need to consider that the etheric organization is the bearer of our more permanent tendencies in life. It is the bearer of our character, talents, and temperament, also of our habits and inclinations, of our compassion and our memory. The care and strengthening of the child's etheric forces should be a high priority for the teacher, especially during the time when it is most accessible, from age six to seven onwards.

How can we work in a healing and strengthening way on the etheric life organization? We can begin by caring for the mood and social climate in the classroom, by establishing a good rhythm in our lessons with thorough repetition. Developing good habits will go a long way (for example, finishing the work at hand before starting a new project). The arts of form drawing, modeling, and eurythmy strengthen the life and forming forces. The story material in every grade, including pedagogical and nature stories, and also seating by temperament, support the developing etheric body. Furthermore, it is important to establish moods of reverence, gratitude, and awe in the classroom.

It also helps for the teacher to be aware of her own effect on the children. She should ask herself questions like: How is my speech? Is it monotonous, too fast, does it lack flow, does it sound too heady, intellectual? How is the pitch of my voice? Is it too high? All these factors affect the children's life forces.

We also need to study the life forces from another perspective. Steiner's insight that life and form forces metamorphose into thought forces during the first seven years of life highlights the reciprocal relationship between life and health forces (in the body) and our thinking activity (which is body-free).

The forces we use to think are in fact refined form and growth forces. Knowing this, we can reflect on the connection between the quality of our thinking and our physical health. It can become clear to us that illness, or even fatigue, stress, over-stimulation, will affect the quality of our thinking—or even our ability to think. On the other hand, scattered, illogical, erroneous thinking, cold-hearted, over-intellectualized thinking, will affect our physical health.

Keeping this reciprocal relationship in mind is tremendously helpful for the teacher. It explains why, when the teacher's lessons are well organized, when one thought logically follows the next, this clarity is felt by the children and has a positive effect on their health.

> In our thinking, then, we meet a body-free invisible activity. We experience it, because it is we who are doing the thinking. Thinking lets us withdraw from the world, it gives us distance from objects and people, so that we can observe and distinguish them. Thinking also gives us distance from ourselves, and hopefully gives us some self-awareness and self-knowledge. This certainly is helpful in faculty meetings! When emotions rise, thinking brings in reason and cools the situation.
>
> It is helpful to live again and again with the concept: life is incarnated thinking and thinking is excarnated life. It is helpful to recognize this double nature of life: incarnated life works in time and space, excarnated life works in our thinking and connects us with eternity.

A healthy breathing between world and self is necessary. And if the ego is actively engaged during the day, taking things in with interest, then the life of the etheric forces is strengthened and enhanced. The etheric forces can then bring regenerative powers into the physical organism. When there is little self-engagement, little active, attentive participation, or perhaps emotionally aggressive, destructive behavior, or a bombardment of sense impressions, the after-effect will be negative and destructive to the vitality of the organism. Please think about the media use in this connection.

Rhythms and relationships

When we look at our soul, our inner space, then we speak of our astral organization or our astral forces. The astral organization has as its physical basis the rhythmic system. Its gesture is in-breathing and out-breathing. Physically breathing connects us with our environment. That is key for the astral body: to be connected. We can say that no astral body is healthy unless it feels itself to be connected with the world and with other human beings. The astral organization is the body of relationships.

Having a strong sense of connectedness, having good relationships, gives a child health and security. Resiliency research points to a third important factor beyond heredity and environment that is crucial for physical health: human relationships. Therefore, a harmonious, joyful relationship between teacher and students is crucial. A child's interest and motivation to learn depend on this loving and genuine relationship. Children also need to feel included in all that happens in the classroom. When a child feels isolated, sidelined, not appreciated or accepted, illness can result.

Our emotional and feeling life, our astral forces, have quite a different quality from our thought life. We can align our thoughts clearly and logically. We can think in pictures that have continuity. Our feelings, however, can be unsteady. They come and go, and may change from one moment to the next. Yet mature and purified feelings can be sensitive organs of perception. We can use them to assess and judge situations. With them we can "read" what is needed. But we do not like to have mixed feelings; they make us uneasy and hesitant.

Rudolf Steiner tells us, "Whereas our etheric forces are our sculptural-pictorial forces, the astral forces are the musical-poetic forces."[3]

Our astral body (or soul) is a body of music. It produces melodies that change their arrangements and moods constantly as we take in and respond to other human beings, to nature, and to our environment. Rudolf Steiner often draws the teacher's attention to this musicality:

> The astral body itself, in its true inner being and function…can only be comprehended by understanding music—not just externally, but inwardly…. The only thing that is earthly about the astral body is time, the musical measure. Rhythm and melody work directly out of the cosmos, and the astral body consists of rhythm and melody.[4]

In the classroom, music itself plays a major role in harmonizing the incoming astral forces. At the time of adolescence, quality music has the power to bring a palpable harmony into the classroom. This harmony is felt in the soul as relief, a freeing, an expansion—all feelings that are helpful when young people are struggling with inner disharmony, emotional ups and downs, and awkwardness in the body (affecting boys particularly). The teacher can do much in the years starting with grades four or five to harmonize the incoming astral, emotional forces by engaging the students in playing the recorder or other instruments. This is the time when main lesson movement should change from outer physical to inner soul movement, and inner soul movement is music. That is the shift that Steiner makes teachers aware of in the middle grades. We move from doing (willing) to feeling (the rhythmic system).

Feelings and emotions have a powerful role in stimulating learning. Waldorf education guides all learning to engage the feeling and will life in the lower grades, which then gradually awaken the thought life. When thinking is awakened through feeling, it develops with compassion, and by way of willing, thinking also will remain practical and connected to reality.

The agent of transformation

Every human being has a fourth member: the ego, the "I," the Self. The "I" is a uniquely human dimension. It finds expression in our very own path through life, our biography. We sense the holy mystery of the human being when Steiner says that "the name 'I' can never reach my ear as a description of myself…. With the 'I,' the 'God' who in lower creatures reveals himself only externally in the phenomena of the surrounding world, begins to speak internally."[5]

The "I" is the transforming agent. It connects with and enters into all other subtle organizations of the human being and develops them.

How do I experience the "I"? When I concentrate on what I do and am fully present in it, then I am; I create out of my center. When I concentrate like that, then there is no room for stress or hectic energy. I become stressed when I lose myself. As long as I realize myself as "I" and am active in the present, concentrated, giving myself direction, then I remain calm, inwardly centered, and at the same time active. Then I am connected to myself. Stress and fear are always indications of the absence of the "I." One way we can strengthen the presence of the "I" as teachers and adults is by working with exercises that school attention, such as the six essential exercises given by Steiner. Attention is an "I" activity.

Also, what we do shows who we are. Initiative and interest are "I" capacities, as well. The "I" is always in the here and now, in the present. The "I" is fresh, open, taking in, responding. Everything that enters into our consciousness enters through the "I." We can, of course, be on overload because of too much input. Then the "I" is circumvented. This is the case when technologically-produced images encroach on the individual soul in rapid-fire fashion. They allow no time for the "I" to connect and thus weaken its activity. Images then enter below the threshold of consciousness. Then images are not digested, not thought through, not questioned, even as they take up residence in us.

The "I" engages in two polar activities: one is that of complete identification, as we often experience when we engage in artistic exercises; the other is that of separation. We can distance ourselves, withdraw from activities, we can ponder, we can contemplate. Even though we have these two activities of the "I," the "I" itself is the *indivisible* Self that is our undivided and eternal core. The "I" is an active form-giving force in us. We may experience it as the "manager" of our whole being. It is the thinker and the planner. When the "I" lives in the body, it is anchored through cognition in the nerve-sense system, through feeling in the rhythmic system, and through willing in the metabolic and limb system.

When we speak of the ego, we can feel this as self-consciousness, more under the influence of the physical body, while we often speak of the "I" to designate our higher self, which shines into us and is our connection with the spiritual world. According to Steiner, the "I" is a gift from high spiritual beings, the Spirits of Form.

In the course of child development, the "I" penetrates the part of the human being that becomes free, or "has been born," as Steiner often puts it. Therefore, to develop the "I" presence takes time. Ideally the "I" is fully developed by age 21. That is when responsibility for one's own life is really taken up. Between the ages of seven and fourteen, the teacher needs to be the "authority" in the classroom. In other words, the teacher needs to be the "I-presence" in the classroom. That means being conscious of all students at all times. The teacher needs to be the planner and activator, giving form and guidance to the students. Teachers who have this strong "I-presence" usually have fewer challenges in classroom management, because the students are clear that someone is truly present. This presence of the "I" has to be cultivated by teachers.

I want to conclude with a chart that makes it clear what the activity of the "I" is at what age.

0-7	"I" works in the physical organization	Schooling it, forming it, by way of the child's imitative capacities.	
		It develops the will.	
7-14	"I" enters the etheric organization	Partially freed from the physical body.	
		It develops thinking and memory.	
14-21	"I" works in the astral organization	Partially freed from the life body (physical and etheric) beginning at age 12-14.	
		It develops the feeling life.	
21-28	"I" in the "I-carrier"	"I-carrier" (all subtle bodies) has established itself and the "I" can enter into it.	

CHAPTER 7

The Curriculum Physiology: Age-Specific Subjects and Therapeutic Pedagogy

Christof Wiechert

> *It is therefore necessary that in teaching we we are dealing with subject matter that speaks to the etheric and physical bodies, or which speaks more to ego and astral organization.*
>
> – RUDOLF STEINER[1]

It is a common experience that teaching can have a healthy effect on the teacher. She learns to overcome herself, to persist, and keeps trying to be kind, loving and lively towards the children. For hours at a time we can quite rightly forget our daily worries! Indeed, one tries to be as one always wished to be. After six hours, when the teaching day has ended, one could easily carry on for another hour or so. The body may be tired, but the soul is not.

This may be a little exaggerated, but don't we all strive to work like this? And do we consider how such conduct affects our pupils? A dynamic flow streams back and forth between teacher and pupils. In everything she says, in every moment of self-conquest, the teacher acts as an example to her pupils. Alongside everything contained in the curriculum, the basis for pupils' healthy schooling lies in the soul disposition of the teacher.

And here the phrase about self-education applies: It is not perfect capacities that count, but the striving and efforts one makes. This is actually the prime source of health for the children and the class. Our attention is drawn to this when Rudolf Steiner describes the effect of the teacher's temperament on pupils.[2]

Once we have grasped this then we can turn to the question of how the lesson or subject matter affects pupils. What happens in the child when we do math? What happens in the child when we write, sing, or paint? Quite apart from learning, all these activities have an effect on the pupils' whole disposition. We can have some inkling of this through a more or less developed educational instinct. If we have done math fairly intensively together in the morning, we won't conclude with singing, for that would stimulate children still further—for we have found by experience that math has a very stimulating effect. Instead we may do form drawing or tell a story. On the other hand, if we have been trying to write beautifully for quite a while, we are likely to think of singing at the end, for we notice that everything has calmed down through writing, and the children may even have grown a little sleepy. We will sense such simple balances in ourselves.

But we have to try to answer the question of what in the child is affected by different subjects.

Everything we do is absorbed by the nerve-sense system. The children look, listen, and are wakeful and engaged. But they also experience something from what they absorb, which works on into the rhythmic system. In an exciting experiment in physics they hold their breath; when the whole class paints, their breathing is different from when we do mental arithmetic together. And when the children listen to a story, their breathing is different than when they speak a poem together. In other words, the lesson's breathing process is reflected in the breathing of the class.

In this sphere of the fluctuating motion of immediate experience working in but also expressing itself through breathing processes, lies a second source of health for pupils, for a class group.

Reaching this point in pondering the interconnections, we are left with the question of how subject matter and my teaching affect the children's motivating force and desire for activity. An important pointer here is that the three soul forces strongly interpenetrate in the child (certainly up to the age of 14). No thought is experienced without a connected feeling, no activity takes place without feeling-imbued thinking. For the teacher this means she is on the right tracks if (certainly in lower school) she addresses the forces of the center. But this requires that the teacher herself resides in her center.

Let us return to the will forces. If thinking and feeling are awakened through our activity, the path to doing becomes almost inevitable for the child. But once again the example set by the teacher is of particular importance here. Does he always do what she asks? Children have a fine sense for anything promised. If homework is not marked this represents a hole in a class's will body; or if, months after the end of a main lesson, main lesson books have still not been marked and returned; or if something is threatened that is not subsequently carried out. The opposite is healing: if the teacher says "We will play ball games tomorrow in the gymnastics hall," or "I'll be collecting your workbooks in a week, make sure they are ready by then," and everything happens as promised, this is healing for both the children and the teacher.

In relation to this theme there is an insightful story about Friedrich Rittelmeyer as a young man:[3]

> When I look back at the events of my youth which continued to affect and influence me, I encounter an experience that happened a year later, when I was eleven. One day our "Professor" declared: "You mustn't copy from others, but nor must you let others copy from you—that is just as bad. The handler of stolen goods is as bad as the thief." I was still used to taking teachers' words seriously. In particular the words of this teacher, who was the only one for whom I held a spark of reverence. It was not due to trying to get on, or sycophancy, but an innate conscientiousness, and even a certain striving for freedom. I often experienced in my fellow pupils how "dishonorable" it was to be caught and then make long-winded excuses to the teacher. But there wasn't the least understanding for such feelings amongst my fellow pupils. When I no longer wanted to let others copy from my books, I was made a complete outcast. None of my fellow pupils spoke to me, and I was excluded

from everything—for many weeks. A sole pupil, who wanted to keep in with my parents and continue to enjoy the delicacies of their table, once spoke a few quiet words to me in a barn. I found that particularly ignominious. It was even more embarrassing when my father, who had learned about this, wanted to intervene, and as confirmation teacher tried to insist that this banishment should be lifted. Finally this, my first attempt at moral heroism, collapsed pitifully. I said that I myself would not copy anyone else, but would let anyone else copy from me if they wanted to. Now everything returned to its former state, apart from the fact that I remained tainted forever with having broken pupil confederacy. The teacher never found out what had resulted from his words for the only pupil who had taken him seriously. He didn't protect him—neither wanted to nor was able to—but simply left him in the lurch, indeed, made a martyr of him. He was the one who had really been vanquished. But with him, for me, all teachers and their authority were overthrown. Twelve years later, when I myself was to take on a position as teacher at high school, this memory resurfaced and formed into two principles which accompanied my teaching: never demand something whose effect you cannot foretell or control! Always keep the pupils' world of feeling very vividly in mind!

For daily educational practice we can draw here on Rudolf Steiner's suggestion for waking the will, which has great educational scope for the child. The path to the will in the child, as we know, does not pass through reason and understanding. Today it is the problem of education that the will is constrained and compelled through instruction and learning which addresses the head. The tasks here are quite different. We have already seen how thinking, feeling, and will are interconnected:[4] The approach to will education therefore lies in feeling. Daily repetition as an integral part of school life works on the child's whole disposition of soul (each day the same greeting, a lovely song sung together at the beginning of the day, the morning verse—all these are "recognition moments" from which the soul can kindle enthusiasm). If we bring wakefulness into this repetition we raise it from something that runs by itself, and then a small effort of will is required for it. We practice and promote the will:

> The more things remain as unconscious habit, the better it is for the development of feeling. The more the child becomes aware of the need to do deeds out of devotion to repetition, because they should and must be done, the more you elevate these to true will impulses. Thus, unconscious repetition cultivates feeling; fully conscious repetition cultivates the will impulse because through it the power of decision increases.[5]

Having now to some extent characterized the effect of learning on thinking, feeling, and will, let us turn to the question of how the subject being taught itself affects the child.

Here a mighty panorama opens up, which can give us insight into how each subject originated. We here approach the polarity of eye and ear, time and space, picture and sound. But at the same time we will encounter in teaching material the synthesis of each of these pairs. We can develop a primary experience of this when we ask ourselves what our teaching actually proceeds from. When do we mainly address the eye, when the ear?

When are we in pictorial image, and when in dynamic flow and movement?

When we learn the letters with children, when we write, draw, paint, or model, when we teach plant studies, we are working primarily with pictorial images and the eyes. We are involved with what is visible. In math or singing, in contrast, when we speak a poem together, do a concentration exercise, or listen to a story, then we are primarily active in the nonpictorial realm. Here we encounter a polarity that informs the whole of human life. All earthly existence unfolds in this realm, and the soul, indeed, draws nourishment from it to a large degree. We can also call it the polarity between the pictorial and the musical.

Now we become aware that the pictorial primarily holds sway at the beginning of life. The formative, structuring, imaging force actually leads us into life, so that we gradually take shape in space. This is a process that begins in the invisible, in the pre-birth state, and gradually reveals itself ever more powerfully in the realm of visibility. It is therefore understandable that this beginning is nourished by pre-birth forces: we step from invisibility, from unborn-hood, into visibility, but for a long time continue to be sustained by forces from the pre-birth sphere. Growth creates spatial form and image, giving rise to the lovely term "body of formative forces" for the etheric body. These forces, which come from our sphere of origin, come to a certain conclusion as they complete their work on our physical body. Nowadays we call this moment of completion the age of school readiness. The forces which previously worked on our form and shape now acquire a new field of activity: they become the forces of reason, the power of imagination, the power of memory. This now begins to work into the child's life as a force he can use.

But how is it with the stream of musical forces? They do not come from the pre-birth sphere but work into life out of the after-death realm. These are the will forces which slowly, as in a long, sustained crescendo, begin to connect with the child. They first work in the unconscious on developing physical functions, and once they have come to a certain conclusion, the child's soul awakens to autonomy. This moment more or less coincides with what in anthroposophic terminology is accurately called "earth readiness"—in German, Erdenreife, or the arrival of puberty. Whereas children's schooling primarily starts through pictorial forces, over the years these are joined by the musical forces. What does this mean? It means that everything which has too strong an emotional tinge cannot yet meet with a response from the child. If, for instance, we tell a fairy tale, then we can experience how the dramatic element only affects the child as stark fact, not as dramatic fiction. Soul drama really comes into its own only in eighth grade; and tragedy can only be properly experienced and affect the soul in a good way in the high school years.

Now there are, additionally, three activities in which these two polar forces work together. These are activities named in the curriculum. However we should remember that they are not new just in the Waldorf school, but new for the whole of civilization. They are: storytelling as an active constituent of lessons, watercolor painting, and eurythmy. In storytelling we use the word, which is a musical element, but by doing so we awaken (inner) pictures in the child. When we do watercolor painting with the children, and remain (initially) in the formless element, we are working pictorially but creating moods through the colors, which delicately affect the soul. The truth of this fact can be experienced by anyone who has witnessed the mood in a class when children are painting. They grow quiet, as though through the activity itself. (How different this is from straightforward drawing, which exists only in image, when there is always a need to chatter.) In this context eurythmy as visible word and visible music has a quite astonishing effect: space and time reach out to each other; the audible becomes visible and the visible can be heard.

If we turn our attention away from these three areas for a moment, it can be said that other subject lessons all exist somewhere on the scale between these polarities. But let us go further and ask about other subjects. How does this relate to learning to read, to geography, to history, to plant and animal studies, to handwork, to craft lessons? We can ask how all these activities affect us. But to provide an answer we have to distinguish two things. In trying to show how a subject affects a child we examine the subject's effect. Besides this, though, there is also the perspective of the diverse ways in which a relationship to the child comes to expression through the way the particular subject is presented.

Let us look at the first approach, recalling the quote at the start of this chapter, and trying to answer the question it contains.

Everything that requires imaginative activity, but also comes to expression pictorially, primarily works on the physical body, and on the etheric body (body of formative forces).

This applies to:

- Drawing in paint
- Painting illustration
- Geometry (initially freely drawn)
- Writing, and learning to write
- Form drawing
- Plant studies

What does this signify for their effect? Let us recall a primary fact of life: sleeping and waking. When we fall asleep something divides in us. Body and life functions remain in the bed but day-consciousness and self-awareness are absent. Put in terms of *Study of Man*, the spirit-soul or soul-spirit is in the world of spirit, while the physical body remains on earth. In other words, physical and etheric bodies remain here while astral body and "I" are in the world of spirit.[6] However, we know from experience that sleep is not a static condition. Much occurs in our nightly sleep. The first experience we have is of reinvigoration, of regeneration of life forces. One can sense that this regeneration does not affect physical and etheric forces alone, but also soul forces. Here we are primarily experiencing the effect of the etheric body, whose activity works more strongly at night. This activity incorporates daytime experiences of learning. Steiner now cites a peculiarity of the etheric body, saying that the latter continues to learn during the night, carrying on what it experienced during the day and bringing it to greater completion. This truth is also accessible to normal experience in the simple fact that something can occur to us in the morning which was still an unresolved question for us the evening before. The etheric body therefore continues to learn.

The first step for a teacher in the modern world who seeks to be aware of this fact is to try to carry this knowledge within her. The period dividing one day from the next is not an empty hole but a continued weaving and working. The next day I do not begin again afresh, but build further.

Our attention is also drawn to two further important facts. What has been learned does not go on into the world of spirit. And what has been experienced is not sustained by conscious awareness. We can put it still more strongly and say: consciousness actually disturbs this learning process continuing on through days and nights.

A second step in a modern teacher's awareness is the following: we need to develop trust in this activity at work in the child. This is in stark contrast to current opinions in education which rely very heavily on consciousness, perception, knowledge, and early self-reliance. If the teacher is carried along by this view, she shuts children off from the formative force of the etheric. Until age twelve, children are primarily dependent on the process described above. If the teacher tries to work in accordance with it, her lessons will have a health-giving effect. If, instead, we prematurely involve the child's awareness, we will increasingly have to deal with stones impeding the path of child development. (The question of the increase in so-called "difficult" children has nothing to do with this, in my opinion.) To sum up, we can call this task learning to sleep and wake in the right way.[7] What does this mean for our practice of teaching? It means working to develop activity and repeated activities, so that learning comes more to resemble a life process than a learning process. It is self-evident that a teacher should draw on the whole picture, on pictorial image and pictorial comparison. But we must always experience this requirement alongside another: to allow ourselves to be inspired by life, by authentic reality.

Let us summarize what has been said in a picture. The child has built up his body. The ship is ready. The craftsmen who have built the ship are now retrained to serve as the ship's crew: they become sailors. The bosun and crew have been allocated their tasks, but the helmsman and captain are not yet on board.

Now let us look at other teaching subjects. What is the situation as regards:

- Animal studies (Man and Animal)
- History
- The human being

We can feel that these subjects have a more direct link with us than the previous ones. In the case of animal studies there is always the question of how the subject relates to us. What do I experience in the description of a lion or a mole? A subject like history also refers only to humanity, presenting us with inner questions. Was this or that historical figure a good person or a villain? It is clear that history in the lower grades is not striving for objectivity but for living images of the past. One can sense that children's relationship to the subject matter is more emotional than activity-focused. The subject asks the child to relate to it. This is also very clearly the case in studying the human being.

Steiner said of these subjects that they work on the astral body and the ego organization. What does this mean? Let us imagine a lower school pupil. His soul resonates with the soul impulses that approach him in life and thus also in school. Only gradually does he find the means to pass from a general mood into work and learning. He has to awaken himself first, so as to independently grasp hold of the subject. As we can observe from teaching, the greatest possible differences exist between pupils in this respect. But we can conclude that the soul (astral body) and ego organization do not yet have the maturity within the child which leads to self-reliance. That is, firstly, the reason why the teaching of these subjects is linked to a particular age; and secondly, a fact exists which Steiner describes in simple words: "The human being takes this [the subject matter in the lessons named] with him into sleep, out of the physical and etheric bodies and into the world of spirit."[8] In other words, it is not "learned further" during sleep! It is actually the case that the effect on the soul-spiritual organization gives rise to the tendency to forget the lesson during sleep: it becomes less perfect and paler.[9] What we can already sense as a vague inkling in our teaching appears as a stark contrast in the effect of different subjects on children. It now becomes comprehensible that in these subjects (which leave the body during sleep) we should also try to make a connection and relationship with the etheric body. This can happen if the teacher uses pictorial language to give graphic and vivid lessons. In relating a historical event, describing a plant, or attending to the skeleton, we give a description that is as living and vivid as possible.

The next step is to add something to what has been described which characterizes it, as an addendum, no longer pictorially. We no longer inhabit the subject but are saying something about it. The first mode of working focuses on the etheric body, while the second addresses the soul. Then we let the subject rest. Steiner says of this procedure that in the following night, the material thus treated lodges in the etheric body "like a photograph." We can draw on this fact the next morning, by speaking with the children in age-appropriate ways about what we taught the day before, and evaluating it. Then one can sense that a connection is created between the physical-etheric and the soul-spiritual.

A new teacher may initially feel that this way of working has a somewhat artificial quality, which seems to run counter to spontaneity. But one should simply try it out. One will find that it works, that teaching goes more smoothly. And if one practices this repeatedly one will notice that it becomes a kind of instinct for doing the right thing in teaching. (This mode of working is also known as the so-called "three-step" process.[10])

As far as the effect on the child is concerned, geography, math, and geometry occupy a special position. First geography, whose effect is described as follows:

> And if we observe this spatially, then in a certain sense teaching geography to the child always represents, for our astral body, a "standing up on our own legs." The astral body actually does become stronger and denser below. We engage with what is spatial and so make the human being's soul and spirit denser toward the ground.[11]

Steiner also explains how this subject matter awakens a moral impulse in children, so that the child develops a more loving attitude towards his fellow human beings if he experiences insightful geography lessons. This applies from age 12 onward.[12]

We experience that this subject, when properly taught, has an effect on consolidating the soul and spirit in a downward direction. Geography is therefore suitable for strengthening the human being's earthly soul capacities by cultivating interest in the spatial world, and this has a moral effect. The importance of this subject is characterized in unmistakable terms by Steiner when he says: "And the downgrading of geography's importance means nothing other than an aversion to love of our fellow human beings, something that has increasingly diminished in our times."[13] If we look at all this together, then we can sense in the background, gently resonating, the intimate but at the same time significant change that occurs in the child around age ten, when he learns to distinguish himself from the external world. This subject is as it were the birth attendant in this delicate process.

When teaching history we can sense how we are active in another part of the soul. One could say at a higher level; and also distinguishing, structuring, and modeling through the fact that children are strongly urged to form feeling judgments: one figure was a hero, the other rather the reverse; one thing was wisely done, the other was a bold trick; and so forth. Let us put this in a different way: geography tends to address the feeling will, while history lessons speak more to feeling thinking.

Math and geometry

In most subjects, we pay careful attention to the right moment for beginning with the subject in question (learning to read, history, geology, multi-part singing, physics, chemistry, etc.). But we do math continually from first grade to twelfth.

Does this fact tell us something? It tells us that math is a very general human activity that starts as soon as the human being can think and enter into a relationship with the world. And the world itself is ordered according to measure and number. Perceiving distinctions and structures is the basis in the child for starting math, which then progresses to the high art which soon no longer needs the world of objects any more.

If we consider this then the following statement by Steiner about math can have a simply joyful effect on us.

First he describes how the lesson subjects have their various spheres of activity in the human being, that is, have a more nurturing effect either on the etheric and physical, or on the soul and astral, together with what happens to these experiences during the night.

Then he comes to math and geometry: "Math and geometry speaks to both—that is the remarkable thing." Math and geometry thus work on both the etheric-physical and the soul-spirit. "And thus, in relation to teaching and education, math and geometry are, one can say, like a chameleon. They adapt their own intrinsic nature to the totality of the human being."[14]

This sentence conceals several mysteries. In the case of the lesson subjects discussed above there were always potentially one-sided effects which we must take account of in teaching a child. Here we find the reverse: the subject adapts to the child, and indeed to the whole child. This answers the question why one can always do math with children (of course in age-appropriate ways). It also tells us that forces lie in math that have a healthy effect on the child, since it addresses the whole human being. In other words, this activity is intrinsically healthy. But the fact that one can do math in a way which reverses this—that is, has an unhealthy effect—is something most people are aware of from their own experience.

As already described, in the lower school soul activities (such as the capacity to form judgments), and in high school ego activity (such as forming and pursuing intentions, doing what one believes to be right) are only active to a limited extent since they have not yet emancipated themselves as autonomous tools. Indeed, the whole curriculum aims to bring about this emancipation. You cannot play a violin that is still being made. If you try to do it nevertheless, stringing it and starting to bow, you can be sure that the sound produced will not be very good.

Steiner does not embark on such long detours when he wishes to describe this, but simply says that in contrast to the etheric body's capacity for learning and dynamic movement, the astral and ego organizations seem dull or stupid; and, if drawn on, stupefying. But the etheric body continues to do math during the night, perfecting the capacities that have been practiced during the day, engendering joy in feeling and fire in the will. In other words: if I do math in such a way that only feeling understands what I do, and furthermore this activity is continually repeated, I not only learn math but also strengthen the body of formative forces and the soul body, by leaving the latter in peace. Here lies a fundamental principle of Waldorf education, one that is worth dwelling on. When we find that politics today is really wholly dictated by economic factors and money, when we look at a simple pocket calculator and see that the key with the "+" symbol is four times bigger than the keys for dividing, subtracting, or multiplying, when we experience how world events are very largely evaluated in financial terms, then we can develop a sense of how profoundly math is hemmed in by the forces of egotism. If we do math based on this approach, then its healthy effect on the whole human being is rendered null and void. If we try to understand this, it becomes clear that math does indeed work both on the physical-etheric and on the soul-spirit. It is generally known that Steiner recommended approaching math not from addition but from division, because the aim is to start from a unified whole. How can we understand this? Firstly, addition is an image of acquisitive egotism. This in itself would be enough of a reason for not starting math teaching with it—in other words a moral motive that affects the soul and spirit. A further motive however, rooted in the nature of the human being, is that addition is not an activity that corresponds to the organizing etheric body. This activity is as it were alien to the etheric body, whereas it recognizes itself in all activities in which a dividing and self-organizing unity plays a role. Once this activity has consolidated itself through teaching, then additive counting can no longer do any harm: "…for this is an activity which only has significance here in physical space, whereas dividing a unity has an inner significance which makes it resonate on in the etheric body, even if the human being is no longer engaged in it."[15]

In conclusion let me say the following. The principle that applies to all teaching—that it must be engaging, awaken interest and draw on life—applies even more to geometry and math for the very reason that these are so strongly involved in the interacting life of the human being's upper and lower poles. When this happens we open up a source for bodily and soul health.

The issues are different when we turn to subjects such as handwork, crafts, gymnastics, gardening, and so forth. In these subjects the chief focus of experience is, naturally, physical activity, finger dexterity and effort. What does this signify for the child?

Where previously the polarity of pre-birth and after-death, or idea and will, or picture and sound have helped us form perspectives, now another polarity appears. The physical body's polarity is spirit and the spiritual. And we can have a quite unsophisticated experience of how these relate to each other. We all know what it is like to have studied hard before an exam. You may have studied and crammed for days at a time. After several days of this you notice that you are more physically tired than after physical exertion. If you have ever worked through the night too, this experience is even stronger: the intellect has been called on, but the body has to pay the price.

The opposite is also familiar: physical work regenerates the spirit, refreshes it again. This mutual interaction of body and mind is a fact of life. Those who have learned to make proper use of this pendulum swing gain great benefit from it. How does this enter into education?

The teacher should be aware of one thing: the will expressed in movement is a mystery! At a time when science has unlocked almost all the mysteries of inheritance, the following daily experience has still not been solved and remains a mystery: how does it happen that, when I decide to take a step or lift a cup, it actually happens? How can we explain this mystery of movement? How does it happen that an intention is actually carried out? Science does not ask this question, because—according to Steiner—it mistakenly assumes that the nerves receive and pass on commands. In contrast, Steiner asserts that the nerves can only perceive movements, not initiate them. The transition from idea to action is, in Steiner's view, a spiritual process, which in essence has no physical correlate, thus representing a leap. (For instance, if we examine finger dexterity used in writing and playing the piano, or the physical abilities used in sport, and reflect that all such movements are willed by an ego, we can see this manifest secret of the will and movement taking place before our eyes.) Only slowly is scientific debate beginning to edge towards the direction contained in Rudolf Steiner's comments. Now we can understand what Steiner meant when he said: "When you activate your limbs in work, whether useful or un-useful work, you are continually paddling around in the spirit, are continually involved with the spirit."[16] We will not go wrong if we see the spirit here as a supersensible activity rather than a state of consciousness. However, this is a type of spirituality of unusual quality. Just as we bear the soul and spirit within us, and are partly aware of it, and can work on it, so there is also a soul-spiritual element outside us in the world. We therefore encounter a quite new polarity—that of inner and outer, point and periphery. We thus grow into the following idea:

> Whenever we work physically our inner soul and spirit is involved, at most, through the fact that our thoughts dictate the direction we should walk in, and exert an orientating effect. But the soul and spirit in the external world participates fully. We continually work out into the spirit of the world. We continually connect ourselves with the spirit of the world by working physically. Physical work is spiritual, spiritual work is physical, both upon and within the human being.... The spirit encompasses us when we work physically. Matter is active within us when we work spiritually.[17]

Here we have two pointers: so-called physical work is spiritual by nature, and so-called spiritual work (learning in the narrower sense) affects the physical human body.

We must not omit a mention of eurythmy at this point, that extraordinary spiritual creation of Rudolf Steiner's. Others are better placed to speak about its essential qualities, but in the context of this essay, Steiner himself described how eurythmy works between spirit and body. Following on from what was characterized above, a description is then given of how all organs involved in eurythmy activity are as though penetrated with spirit. Through these purposeful movements the spiritual is released from the organs and streams upwards. This works like "a redemption of the spirit.... The spiritual element with which the limbs are replete detaches itself. That is the actual process." Then he describes how the "liberated" spirit waits to be used, to be consolidated in the human being. Then comes the mighty thought that this is brought about by the subsequent moments of rest: a real microcosmic process of the macrocosmic law of movement, which is spirit; and of rest, which becomes matter.[18]

Instead of this fact totally revolutionizing education in the western world, things have just continued along pre-ordained tracks, with these two realms growing ever more distant from each other. One can see this in the way sport has become more one-sided, an end in itself (Steiner: "Sport is practical Darwinism"). One can also see this in learning processes in schools which—despite the best efforts—are handled like sport. Learning performance becomes an end in itself, without the learner developing a relationship to the content of what is learned.

On this topic, Friedrich Rittelmeyer's account of his adolescence is very pertinent:

> I have to say of the "humanities Gymnasium" [selective high school specializing in humanities subjects] that, aside from very fleeting impressions, none of our teachers ever

came close to succeeding in involving our hearts and feelings in the "teaching material." Everything was compulsory labor from start to finish. Scarcely any of my fellow pupils ever came remotely close to thinking, for a moment, that one could be interested in what one had to learn. Anything of interest was consigned to out-of-school activities, once the bell had, at last, rung at the end of the day. It was not until I reached university that I realized, with real fury, what crimes had been committed upon our young souls. If young hearts have been denied the living cordial of enthusiasm, this cannot be made good again in the whole course of their further life.[19]

We can set a new kind of education against this, which has the task of integrating these realms. How? In education we can fill physical work or activity with sense and purpose; and spiritual or intellectual work with interest. This is nothing other than the harmonizing of light and warmth. Once we understand this we can grasp Steiner's demand that teaching should work on in the soul so that not only what has been learned remains, but that the very act of learning also becomes a soul constituent:

> What is undertaken in learning to read condenses into the ability of being able to read. What is undertaken in learning math condenses into the ability to do math. But consider how this relates to things that are based more on feeling and memory: today's children actually learn a very great deal only in order to forget it again, only in order for it not to figure in their lives. This is something which will really mark out an education of the future, that all the things to which the child is introduced will remain in him throughout life.[20]

Here Goethe's (often misunderstood) phrase from *Faust*, Part II, really comes into its own: "Consider the 'what'; but still more, consider the 'how'." Here are two instances of this:

At school we had a most revered German teacher. Everything he did with us had an aura of originality and significance, whether it was grammar or literature. His name was Matthieu Laffrée. One day he told us that we were going to read together the little book *The Life of a Good for Nothing* by Joseph Eichendorff. We found this text not only dumb but also thought it a shame to waste our time with it. In eleventh grade we had more important things to do. He sensed our reluctance, smiled at our arrogance and said that we ought, nevertheless, to read a few passages from it. Then we read this stupid story about the baron who pulled himself and his horse out of a swamp by his own hair. Did we really have to read this nonsense as an example of German Romanticism? Over twenty years later the picture came back to me, in a flash of illumination: as metaphor for someone who is always capable of giving himself a leg-up, of transforming himself. This resulted not only in an "Aha" experience, a step in self-knowledge, but a warm feeling of gratitude rose up in me for the fact that what I had learned worked on in my soul. It was as if my teacher gave me a friendly wave from beyond the threshold.

Our chemistry and biology teacher was an outstanding phenomenologist, one of the first to introduce Goetheanism into science, based on a path of consistent practice. The legacy of his works still breathes with a germinating power. His name was Frits Julius. However, we were also his pupils, and did not experience his genius so directly, although in his chemistry lessons, when he stood behind the experiment table, we felt we were witnessing a priest at nature's altar. I was interested, but not necessarily a good pupil. In my report for eleventh grade he acknowledged my efforts and assessed the abilities I had developed, concluding with the phrase: "How far have you come in love of perception and observation?"

At the time I read this I believed that my abilities were fine in that area. It was only much, much later that I realized this very realm was actually a weakness in my character. Since then this phrase has accompanied me throughout my life as a quiet but powerful admonition.

Let us return to the child study, in particular to the third step: How do we help the child in question? This is a path that does not necessarily have to involve a child study. We saw that it can be necessary to adopt specific therapeutic measures. But now we also see how we can affect the child in a health-giving way quite specifically through the curriculum itself. If we recall the different ways in which all lesson subjects so far discussed affect the child, then we can also find in the curriculum itself things that can help the individual child. Education can heal.

The last perspective is of special importance today. I refer to the polarity between the ego drawn too deeply or too little into the body. Let me first highlight a possible misunderstanding. This polarity does not refer to the way incarnation occurs. Incarnation takes place at birth. That is not the issue. The issue is how the ego (and here I do not mean the ego organization, but the human being's core and essence) relates to the body. The dynamic here is that of the ego sucked in too deeply by the body contrasted with a too loose connection. How can we perceive this?

Whereas, in the polarity between cosmic and earthly we are in the realm of soul, here we are in the realm of spirit, of the "I." The ego drawn too deeply into the body is apparent in thinking in a pronounced tendency toward matter: thinking wishes to live solely in facts, in mundane realities. Everything clear and logical is preferable to the artistic and pictorial. Expressing oneself artistically is problematic, as is, likewise, sustaining a mood in ideas. It is not simple to listen to a story. When the soul approaches adulthood it faces the question of whether I work to live or live to work. The ego is the prisoner of the body, and physical functions, and demands overlay the silent questions of the "I." Instead of a means, enjoyment becomes an end in itself (*Knowledge of Higher Worlds*). Steiner makes a striking comment that these facts explain criminal tendencies.[21]

If the ego is too loosely connected with the body this gives rise to arbitrariness, lack of involvement, idealism which does not succeed in realizing ideals, let alone meeting reality. We see before us the utopian, full of the best intentions, but these are forgotten as soon as spoken. The idea finds no path to deed. Wonderful discussions are held but they stay in never-never land. As the soul approaches adulthood the question arises: What am I to do with my life, what am I here for? Here too we can experience how strikingly topical these characterizations are for our times. Everything that civilization produces in both directions is detailed here in sharp focus. At the same time so is the almost inestimable importance of education.

One should remember that these descriptions sound absolute. If we moderate them to the tendencies that are present in each person (also in us educators), then we will find the path to self-conquest in ourselves. I believe it is an essential step of self-knowledge if we can observe that our own constitution tends in one direction or the other. If we become aware of this in ourselves, we take a step toward pedagogy. What I perceive in myself is of use in helping children when I teach.

It is always astonishing how delicate the pedagogical suggestions are that aim to remedy a one-sided constitutional tendency. If the tendency is towards a too deep immersion of the ego, Steiner recommends structuring teaching in such a way that a strong personal pictorial relationship to the subject matter arises. The soul is stimulated and communicates itself to the ego.

If the connection of the ego to the body is too tenuous, Steiner suggests keeping the teaching material at a certain distance, and remaining more in the thought realm. Something that one could otherwise communicate with a strong emotional content can instead be retained in the mathematical or thought sphere. We see that a direct appeal is made to the higher soul faculties. Geographic presentations, historical stories, mathematical-geographical understanding, in these ways can this be worked with.

All recommendations from Steiner ask that the teacher be challenged to present his work artistically. How does art affect us? We go to the museum. Apart from the fact that we get tired feet after an hour or two, what happens to us? One can experience the need to send a certain force into the eyes in order to "open" our experience of the picture or sculpture, so that it says something to the soul. For some this is a self-evident process, while others have to make more of an effort. Then we leave the museum, and it is as though we still have the pictures around our head. One feels like a bee that has visited a flower: a sense of being enriched in the area of the head. Gradually these experiences settle. One can feel it as a new structural anchorage, as inner solidity, or like a cleansing of vision. The soul sucks in these pictorial experiences, though more in the realm of the nerve-sense system.

We go to a concert and sit down, and in doing so completely forget the body. We become wholly ear. One can almost experience how one forgets to breathe, and enters wholly into the stream of sounds, how the soul resonates with them. Then the concert is over. One leaves and is out on the street again, as though wrapped in a cloud of sound. One feels fully refreshed, not physically but in the soul.

These are delicate experiences, but no less valuable for us to try to grasp and experience. For instance if, with this kind of sensitivity, we attend a monthly celebration at school, where both modes of observing come together, this can become not only a rich experience but also an educational experience of the effect of art in education. To enter into such experiences is important today. How often we teachers doubt the need for artistic approaches because we are unaware of their effect. Isn't it rather easy for the artistic to be seen as an end, not a means, in the Waldorf environment?

If we set ourselves the task of learning to understand how the artistic works in children and pupils through the polarities which have been described, we will have taken a step closer to the relevance of the art of education today. If we make efforts to do this then the justified questions about the proper degree of artistic work in lessons can be answered. The questioning thought of what is purposeful here, and what not, has a cleansing power for the "how" of teaching.

CHAPTER 8

Projective Geometry: A Holistic Understanding of Space

Georg Glöckler

With special thanks to Beth Weisburn for her editorial contribution to the English version

Developmental epochs of geometry

> *In all cultures mathematics and geometry were regarded as a preparatory school for initiation or spiritual knowledge.*
>
> – LOUIS LOCHER-ERNST[1]

Math and geometry are based on directed thinking activity. This can be directed to sense-perceptible objects but can also largely become independent of these. Thus, numbers and angles are not derived from external sense perception, although they can naturally be related to it. True mathematical activity lies in the realm of *sense-free thinking*. A thinking which can rely on itself is not only independent of external supports, but also renders the person who thinks inwardly independent. On this is based the educational task of math. The Waldorf school math curriculum is developed on this foundation.

Geometry is a particularly pictorial area of math, and makes immediately apparent thought forms that are of the greatest significance for detailed understanding of time-space processes in the fields of embryology, medicine, pharmacy, botany, architecture and general morphology. To integrate these insights into various subjects taught at school is one of the greatest challenges facing an education that tries to include and embody the spiritual dimension in a scientific way.

Geometry—like all of mathematics—is one of the most important integrative studies in Waldorf education, and can be realized there in a particularly striking way. Those interested in the foundations of the math curriculum, and especially in possible evidence supporting it, are referred to the introductory or more advanced literature on the subject.

Geometry's development through the course of human history is largely divided into four eras:

1. Geometry as preparatory schooling for spiritual knowledge, and also as wisdom inspiring architecture, in the mystery centers of ancient times (Babylon, Egypt, South America/Tiahuanaco/Bolivia).

2. Publishing of geometry by Euclid (365-300 BC), who compiled the knowledge of his time and also traditional mystery knowledge, and made its elements generally available. In medieval

monastery schools, Euclid's writings were the most widely read, second only to the Bible. This was why the mathematician Georg Unger stated that Euclidian geometry served to sustain human powers of reason for 2000 years, right up to our own times.

3. The Renaissance period, with the discovery of perspective in painting, gave rise to a new experience and understanding of space. This also made it possible to grasp the periphery of space using the so-called projective or distance elements (vanishing point, horizon).

4. Based on findings derived from perspective, projective geometry was able to develop from the seventeenth to the nineteenth century. Inherent in this is the basic knowledge that space has a dual structure, i.e. that for every spatial form there is a complementary form belonging to it. Drawing on this, Rudolf Steiner introduced the concept of *space and counterspace.* Through projective geometry views of perspective are also definitively expanded. The distance elements of vanishing point and horizon—as used in perspective—are now joined by the projective plane. Thus, in the field of projective geometry, the three basic geometric elements of point, line, and plane also arise as the function of distance elements.

Pyramids as Witness to the Mystery Wisdom of Ancient Times[2]

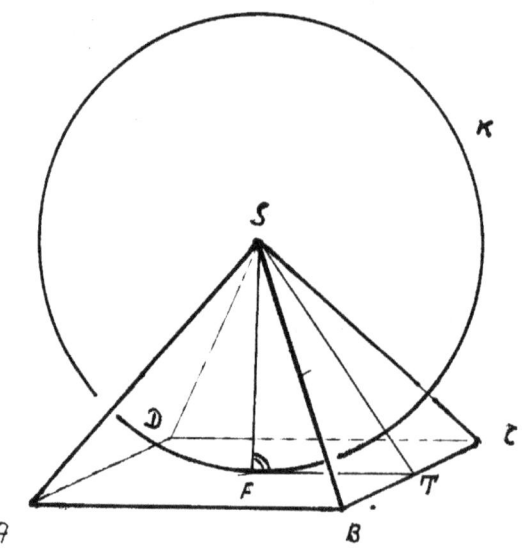

Diagram 1

At the Great Pyramid of the Pharaoh Cheops in Egypt, close to Giza, various measurements have been taken. These found, among other things, the following in relation to the ideal right-angled triangle SFT (see diagram 1):

$$\frac{FT}{ST} \approx \frac{55}{89} = 0.61787... \left(\approx 0.618033988... = \frac{1}{2}(\sqrt{5} - 1) = g \right)$$

This numerical value closely corresponds fairly precisely to the value g, the golden section (the concept of "golden section" is explained in section 2, below). This is remarkable in itself. The following analysis may be still more remarkable. The ideal circle K drawn with the height of the pyramid as radius can be seen as a symbol of the sun's trajectory. If one makes the circumference of this circle equal to the perimeter of the square base of the pyramid, then the above numerical relationship is obtained exactly. This process would correspond to the squaring of the circle. The calculations needed are as follows:

Calculation:

Analysis: With $FS = r$ and $BC = CD = s$

   let $2\pi \cdot r = 4 \cdot s$ (Circumference of circle = measurement of the perimeter of the base).

   Now $(ST)^2 = (\frac{s}{2})^2 + r^2$ (Pythagoras' theorem in the right-angled triangle SFT).

Furthermore $FT = \frac{s}{2} = \frac{\pi \cdot r}{4}$.

This gives, after a short calculation:

$$\frac{FT}{ST} = \frac{\pi}{\sqrt{\pi^2 + 16}} = 0.61766...$$

This path is expressed as follows with the ratio series of best possible approximations for g and small numerals (see section 2 below):

$$\frac{1}{1}, \frac{1}{2}, \frac{2}{3}, \frac{3}{5}, \frac{5}{8}, \frac{8}{13}, \frac{13}{21}, \frac{21}{34} ...$$

One can formulate this result as follows: if the Egyptians knew the constant π, then based on it they could symbolically express the number g by manifesting it in the ideal triangle. If, on the other hand, they knew the number g of the golden section, then the constant π would come to symbolic representation in the circumference of the ideal circle. Corresponding to these principles, for the circle constant π a short calculation would then give rise to the value

$$\pi = \sqrt{4g} \approx 3.1446...$$

It is clear that in building the Cheops pyramid use was made of the geometric knowledge that the value *g* of the golden section and the constant π stand in a mathematical relationship to one another.

The Pentagram, the Golden Section Ratio, and Four Fundamental Insights

Why are we talking of Euclidean geometry here? This encourages the soul to establish its dwelling in the finite, spatial conditions of earth. It describes the latter's measurability, consistency and structural character. In every way, it supports a sense of being here and now in daily life, in so-called objective reality. In the context of these

Euclidean laws, the geometry of the pentagram occupies a special position. The geometric laws that manifest here lead beyond a purely geometric grasp of space into the dimension of time processes. This results from the fact that the forms of thinking to be developed through the pentagram point far beyond grasping the pentagram as a purely spatial form. The forms of thought that can be developed through the pentagram lead to four fundamental insights.

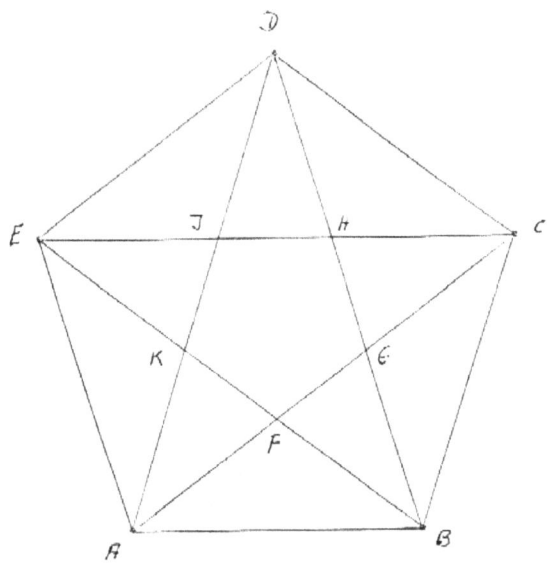

Diagram 2: Pentagram

Given elementary knowledge of geometry, once can see from the drawing that, *DG* = *AG* = *AB* and the two triangles *ABD* and *BGA* are similar triangles, i.e. for instance the corresponding angles are the same. This means that:

$$\frac{BG}{AB} = \frac{AB}{BD}$$

and because *DG* = *AB* it is also true that

$$\frac{BG}{DG} = \frac{DG}{DB}$$

The line *BD* is thus divided by *G* in such a way that the shorter distance *BG* relates to the greater distance *GD* in the same way as the longer distance *GD* to the whole line *BD*. This division is called the *Golden Section* (section aurea). It appears frequently in nature and art, but also in the human form, and is therefore also called the "divine proportion."

If now *BD* = 1 and *DG* = *g*, then:

$$\frac{1-g}{g} = \frac{g}{1} \lor g^2 + g = 1$$

and

$$g = \tfrac{1}{2}(\sqrt{5} - 1) \approx 0.6180339...$$

The value *g* is thus a quadratic irrational number.

All quadratic irrational numbers can be constructed using compass and ruler. For *g* the following construction arises:

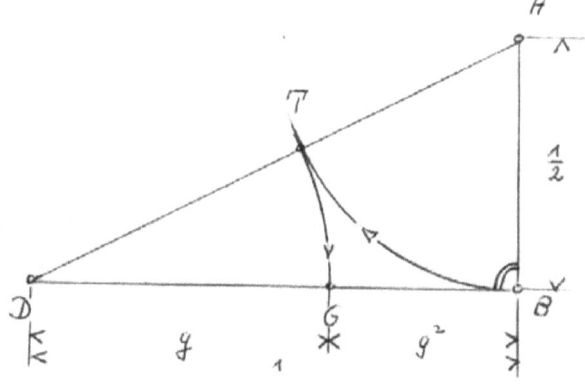

Diagram 3

From the construction:

$$(DH)^2 = 1^2 + (\tfrac{1}{2})^2 = \tfrac{5}{4} \qquad \text{(Pythagoras's theorem)}$$

$$DH = \tfrac{1}{2}\sqrt{5}$$

$$DT = DG = \tfrac{1}{2}\sqrt{5} - \tfrac{1}{2} = \tfrac{1}{2}(\sqrt{5} - 1) = g$$

where $DG = 1 - g = g^2 \approx 0.38196601...$

Alongside purely quantitative ratios, a series of qualitative properties are also connected with the value g of the golden section, whose character goes far beyond the purely mathematical context. To properly describe these properties, we must first clarify an important concept, that of the series of values that converge to g.

From $g^2 + g = 1$ follows initially

$$g = \frac{1}{1+g}$$

Continuing this, we get:

$$g = \frac{1}{1+\frac{1}{1+g}} = \frac{1}{1+\frac{1}{1+\frac{1}{1+g}}} = ...$$

The value g can thus be represented as a so-called continuous fraction.

For this continuous fraction, we now have to find approximate values in the form of fraction numbers (approximation fractions). These arise as follows:

$$N_1 = \tfrac{1}{1}, N_2 = \tfrac{1}{1+1} = \tfrac{1}{2}, N_3 = \tfrac{1}{1+\tfrac{1}{1+1}} = \tfrac{2}{3}, N_4 = \tfrac{3}{5}, N_5 = \tfrac{5}{8}, N_6 = \tfrac{8}{13}, etc.$$

$N_6 = \tfrac{8}{13}$ is already a useable approximation value for g, being in fact:

$$\tfrac{8}{13} = 0.615394 \text{ repeating}$$

Here we can also recognize the law of formation of these approximation fractions. In these approximation fractions numbers appear in their enumerator and denominator, which belong to a famous number sequence, the Fibonacci sequence discovered by Fibonacci (Leonardo of Pisa, ca. 1170–ca. 1240).

$$f_1 = 1$$
$$f_2 = 1$$
$$f_3 = 1 + 1 = 2$$
$$f_4 = 1 + 2 = 3$$
$$f_5 = 2 + 3 = 5$$
$$f_6 = 3 + 5 = 8$$
$$f_7 = 5 + 8 = 13$$

Generally formulated: $f_n = f_{n-1} + f_{n-2}$

In a Fibonacci sequence a value always appears as sum of the two preceding values. For the above sequence of approximation values for g, we get the sequence of ratios from two respective consecutive Fibonacci numbers. Consequently, the Fibonacci numbers themselves are inherently linked by the value g.

Four fundamental insights relating to the value g

1. There are processes which depend on and are sensitive to their starting conditions. This is taught by chaos theory. However, in general starting conditions participate in the end result in a co-determining way.

   Above and beyond this, however, there are processes which are *stronger than the starting conditions,* i.e. the process *itself* overcomes its starting conditions.

   We already know that an ever closer approximation to g can be gained through the sequence of approximation values N_1, N_2, N_3. But if, instead of the starting values f_1 and $f_2 = 1$, we were to set arbitrary starting values such as $a_1 = 1, a_2 = 3$, with $a_n = a_{n-1} + a_{n-2}$ (where $n = 3, 4, 5, \ldots$), and apply the same arithmetic process to this, the result of the approximations would also tend toward g.

   Example:

   $a_1 = 1 \; a_2 = 3 \; a_3 = 4 \; a_4 = 7 \; a_5 = 11 \; a_6 = 18$

   $N_1 = \frac{1}{3} \; N_2 = \frac{3}{4} \; N_3 = \frac{4}{7} \; N_4 = \frac{7}{11} \; N_5 = \frac{11}{18}$

   $N_6 = \frac{18}{29} \; N_7 = \frac{29}{47} \; N_8 = \frac{47}{76} \; N_9 = \frac{76}{123} \; N_{10} = \frac{123}{199}$

   $N_{10} = \frac{123}{199} \approx 0.6181\ldots$

The mathematical proof can, for instance, be formulated as follows:

$$n = \lim_{n \to \infty} \frac{a_n}{a_{n+1}} = \lim_{n \to \infty} \frac{a_n}{a_n + a_{n-1}} = \lim_{n \to \infty} \frac{1}{1 + \frac{a_{n-1}}{a_n}} = \frac{1}{1+g}, QED.$$

This principle can for instance be observed in homeopathy.

Potentization in homeopathy is based on two founding principles:

- Repetition of the dilution process resulting in a numerically recordable sequence, e.g. as potency multiples of ten: 1x, 2x, 3x, in which one part of mother tincture (starting substance) is wholly intermixed with 9 parts of a receptive medium.

- Absorption of the starting substance via the shaking process in the water medium, or the intermixing process in the lactose medium. This absorption into the medium can be seen as dilution on the one hand, but on the other hand a transformation of substance occurs since, through ever-increasing dispersion, the substance releases its essential spirit into the medium. The process of absorption and imprinting into the medium becomes more important than the starting substance. Thus, a thought form is achieved which facilitates recording and observation of the transition from static, spatial conditions to *active realities* in the realm of time processes.

A process analogous to potentization is the arithmetically infinite one which has led to the value g independently of both starting numbers. The starting number corresponds to the starting substance, and the value g to the process of complete "death" or spiritualization.

2. Typical of an organism is the fact that the whole always works in its parts. Some outstanding examples of this are starfish or the plant Bryophyllum, which are directly able to reproduce themselves as a whole from one of their parts (for instance in isolation). In this connection, one should also examine what is presented in section 4. It is this precise qualitative state of affairs that we find in observing the value g. This is:

$$g = \frac{1}{1+\frac{1}{1+g}} = \frac{1}{1+\frac{1}{1+\frac{1}{1+g}}} = \ldots$$

In the living world, the law applies that the whole is more than the sum of its separate parts. Through the mutual interactions by means of which everything is connected with everything else, every living process withdraws from linear-causal description. Apparently simple life rhythms and effects live within complex interactions. In the same way, endless relations and associations live within the value g.

3. There are processes which run more slowly than others. The process of human development, especially the aspects concerned with the form of homo sapiens, is the slowest of all mammals. The human figure is wholly proportioned in accordance with the golden number. Within evolution the human being appears as last of the species. He stands at the end of the evolution of species, integrating them and their processes and capacities in a new plainness, beauty and simplicity.

Now one can show that any irrational number can best be approached through the approximation fractions of its continuous fraction expansion. In specific terms this means that for 8/13 as the approximation fraction of *g* there is no fraction with smaller numbers in the numerator and denominator that would be a better approximation to *g*. If one now compares the various sequences of approximation fractions of irrational numbers, the appropriate sequence for *g* is the one whose numbers in the numerator and denominator *grow most slowly*.

Three examples of sequences of the best possible approximations for the values *g,h* and *k*:

$g = \frac{1}{2}(\sqrt{5} - 1) : 1, \frac{1}{2}, \frac{2}{3}, \frac{3}{5}, \frac{5}{8}, \frac{8}{13}, ...$ slowest 'growth' of numerical values

$h = \sqrt{2} - 1 : \frac{1}{2}, \frac{2}{5}, \frac{5}{12}, \frac{12}{29}, \frac{29}{70}, \frac{70}{169}, ...$ quicker 'growth'

$k = \sqrt[3]{5} : \frac{1}{1}, \frac{2}{3}, \frac{5}{7}, \frac{22}{31}, \frac{71}{100}, \frac{235}{331}, ...$ still quicker 'growth'

It is apparent that *among all irrational numbers, g is the one to which a successive approach through the best possible approximations is the slowest of all.* Thus, it becomes directly mathematically comprehensible why the golden section with its value *g* holds sway over all the proportions of the human body. The slowness of his development gives the human being the potential to involve his emotions, to be present, to develop integrity and identity. It also becomes apparent here why *patience* is the core virtue of all educational and developmental work.

4. For all Fibonacci numbers, and also for *g*, the remarkable fact arises *that they reconstitute out of themselves*. Here are three examples:

    a) Reconstitution through squares of the Fibonacci numbers

    General law:

    $$\sum_1^n (-1)^{n+1} f_{2n-1} = (-1)^{n+1} f_n^2$$

So, for example:

$1 = 1 \quad 1 - 2 = -(1^2) \quad 1 - 2 + 5 = 2^2 \quad 1 - 2 + 5 - 13 = -(3^2) \quad 1 - 2 + 5 - 13 + 3 = 5^2$
$= f_1 - f_3 + f_5 - f_7 + f_9$

b) Reconstitution of a Fibonacci number from the latter's total spectrum:

General law: $f_{n+v-2} = f_v \cdot f_n - f_{v-2} \cdot f_{n-2}$

Thus, for instance:

$34 = 5 \cdot 8 - 2 \cdot 3 = f_5 \cdot f_6 - f_3 \cdot f_4 \quad 8 \cdot 13 - 1 \cdot 5 \quad 2 \cdot 21 - 1 \cdot 8 \quad 1 \cdot 34 - 0 \cdot 21$

c) Reconstitution of g from the total spectrum of the Fibonacci numbers:

General law:

$$(-1)^{n+1} \cdot g = (f_n + f_{n-1} \cdot g) \cdot (f_n \cdot g - f_{n-1})$$

Thus, for instance:

$$g = (1-0) \cdot (g-0) - g = (1+g) \cdot (g-1)g = (2+g) \cdot (2g-1) - g = (3+2g) \cdot (3g-2)g$$
$$= (5-3g) \cdot (5g-3)$$

These examples demonstrate mathematical thought forms which are inherent in living processes: if one wishes to characterize life as such, the first capacity to highlight is that of renewing or reconstituting oneself out of one's own forces. The loveliest example of this can be found in the plant kingdom itself. In the 19th century Schimper and Braun investigated the arrangement of leaves around the stem (phyllotaxis). Leaves grow in a spiral around the stem, with a constant angle between two consecutive leaves. Related to a full circle, the following arises for the most frequent leaf positions, expressed in fractions:

$$\frac{1}{2}, \frac{1}{3}, \frac{2}{5}, \frac{3}{8}, \frac{5}{13}, \frac{8}{21}, \frac{13}{34}, \frac{21}{55}, \frac{34}{89} \ldots$$

These are the fractions we get when, in the Fibonacci sequence, we repeatedly skip one step: e.g. the leaf position 2/5 in the rose corresponds to 5 leaves in 2 turns around the stem. These surprising facts were no doubt in Johannes Kepler's mind when he formulated the following principles:

> In my view, the capacity to propagate is formed in similarity to this sequence developing out of itself. That is why in plants we see the characteristic of this capacity in the pentagram. At this point I pass over all further proofs which one can here provide after long cogitation.[3]

> The most common leaf positions, in the above sequence of fractions, point to a second remarkable fact: this sequence does not converge toward g but toward the first potency of g, that is g^2. If we recall Goethe's view of the archetypal plant, whose further development corresponds to diverse plant types, the above ratio sequence gives us the applicable arithmetical correlation. This shows that the plant world is revealed to us in its formative processes, that it bears within itself an inherent potentization law.

These four fundamental insights relating to the value g point us directly to the realm of living things. This is characterized by processes of integration, mutual interaction, potentization, simplification, reproducibility. Thought forms based on math and geometry of the golden section can help make the intelligence of living systems transparent, and enable us to study life's spatial and temporal laws.

Perspective and the new consciousness of space

Initially it was artists who experienced modern spatial consciousness and represented it, particularly in the field of painting. They evidently experience themselves as standing autonomously in the space surrounding them. Pictures painted using color perspective (see the famous *Madonna of the Rocks* by Leonardo da Vinci) or later linear perspective representations (see the *School of Athens* by Rafael) demonstrate this new spatial experience. Later on, the principles and laws underlying it are also described and grasped in thinking by mathematicians and geometers. The following sketches show three variations on ways in which parallel lines, such as of a road, meet at a vanishing point, thus making it possible to pursue foreshortening perspective into unlimited dimensions, and to describe this in terms of geometric laws.

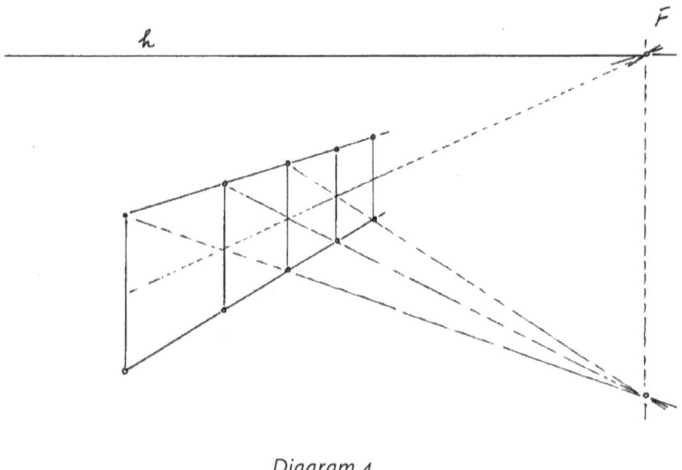

Diagram 4

Diagram 4 shows how the 'parallel lines' intersect at the vanishing point F on the horizon h. This vanishing point for the first time introduces to perceiving awareness, and describes in terms of geometry, the infinitely distant point of the horizon, for instance of a road which runs toward the horizon.

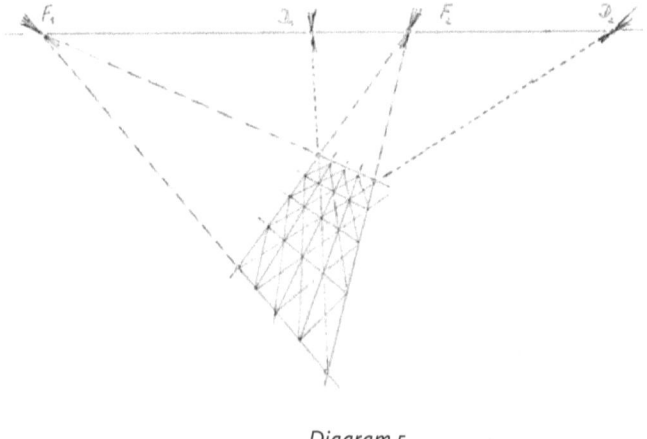

Diagram 5

Diagram 5 shows the same for perspective distortion of a regularly structured rectangle.

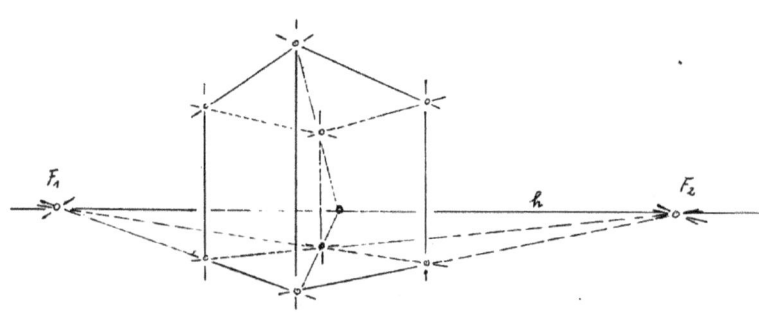

Diagram 6

Diagram 6 represents the corner perspective of a cuboid. This is not yet the general case, as diagram 7 shows.

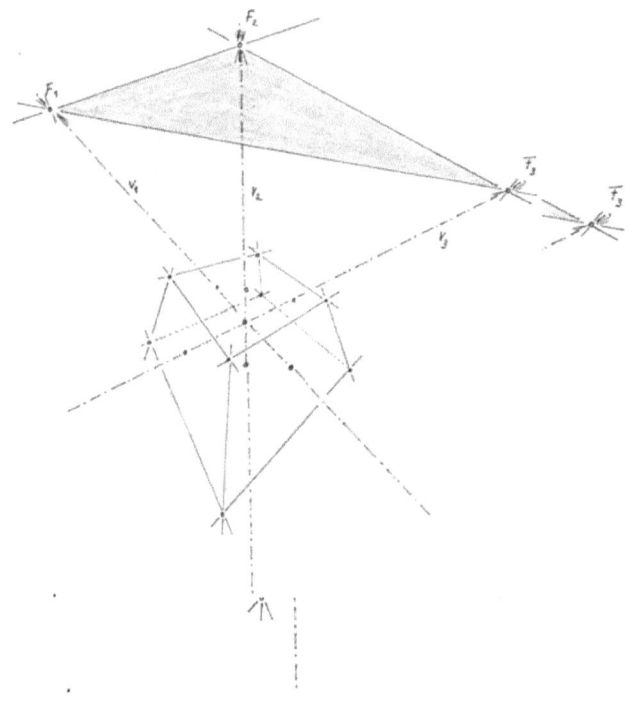

Diagram 7

Whereas in diagrams 4, 5, and 6 only one or two vanishing points are needed to describe spatial relationships, in diagram 7 we have three vanishing points. In diagram 6, in the special position of the cuboid represented there, one can make do with two vanishing points, since the third cannot be represented due to the particular circumstances: the vertical parallels here remain parallel for immediate perception, and therefore cannot meet in a common vanishing point. In diagram 7 this is fundamentally different: the cuboid shown here is drawn in a general perspective with no parallel lines remaining as such to immediate perception, but all moving toward or relating to their respective vanishing point. The drawing represents a cuboid (which could also be a cube) with twelve edges, of which each set of four are parallel and have a common vanishing point. These three vanishing points in turn determine a plane, called the projective plane, which corresponds to the horizon in diagrams 4 to 6. In place of the horizon, therefore, we now have a plane which, in accordance with the laws of perspective, brings infinite distance into tangible geometric visibility.

Which new form of perception was therefore made conscious by the painters of the Renaissance and the mathematical and geometric calculations that followed them? We see here that the well-known basic elements of geometry—point, line and plane—now appear in the function of distance elements, and do so in the form of a vanishing point, a distant line (as horizon), and a projective plane. By including the projective plane a form such as, in this case, the cuboid, can be imagined as being determined by the distance elements. Thus, the point-orientated internal view can be extended by the perspective from the periphery. A crystal—e.g. the cuboid of a salt crystal—appears on the one hand to be internally structured by its crystal framework, but on the other it can also be described as structured by its distance elements. This gave rise for the first time to geometric concepts which describe the circumference, that is the periphery of space, as precisely as Euclidean geometry described finitely conceived spatial forms and shapes.

Perspective thus shows itself to be a concept of space which mediates between conceptions of finite and peripheral space. Whereas Euclidean space conceives the forms and shapes of this world in their finite limitation, thus providing the bases for a world view enclosed and complete in itself, space conceived of in perspective terms goes to the very edge of infinity, though *without stepping over this threshold.* In other words: the realm of the infinite is here brought back into visible perception in the form of projective plane, horizon line, and vanishing point, thus for the first time making fully conscious in thought our relationship with the so-called infinite. In the field of perspective representation, the distance elements are grasped as functional constructions, and can thus be used in drawing. Points, lines, and planes can be used in drawing in their role as distance elements.

Discovery and study of projective geometry: Breakthrough to a spatial consciousness independent of sensory perception.

Terms such as projective geometry or synthetic geometry describe laws which go beyond those of Euclidean geometry and perspective. These fields uncover new laws in the form of the law of polarity and the description of dual, or geometric, multi-perspective relationships. It was found that every basic geometric element (point, line and plane) has a complementary correspondence: the point with the plane, the plane with the point, and the line with another line. The line thus has a polar correspondence to itself. Likewise forms such as a point-field on a plane and a plane bundle are polar to each other. (The seventeenth-century mathematicians Paucelet, Reye, and von Staudt, to some extent independently of each other, discovered and investigated these laws.)

The study of projective geometry thus leads to overcoming one-sided, point-focused awareness in favor of a dynamic view of space that includes the context, the periphery. Thus, one can for instance view a line or plane as a totality of all these structuring points. As a result, such forms then appear as though composed of or structured from an infinite number of tiny constituents or points. Reversing this, lines and points can be seen as the totality of all these structuring planes, etc.

The seven basic forms of projective space are:

$$P(\varepsilon) \leftrightarrow \varepsilon(P)$$

plane bundle   point-field in a plane

$$P(g) \leftrightarrow \varepsilon(g)$$

ray bundle   plane field of lines

$$g(\varepsilon) \leftrightarrow g(P)$$

plane cluster   straight row of points

$$P(g)\varepsilon = \varepsilon(g)P$$

ray cluster

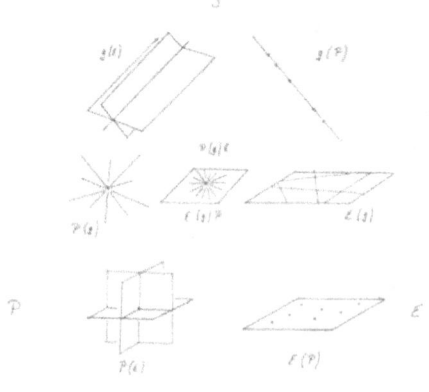

Diagram 8a

A single point can thus be formed by planes and lines, and in turn a line can be formed from planes and points. The three basic components of geometry become in projective geometry forms of manifestation equal in value. Alongside the point-focused consciousness of people schooled in Euclidean geometry, comes an awareness of lines and planes capable of understanding the spatial-temporal structure of processes, forms, and objects in a quite new way. Space ceases to be nothing more than a vessel in which objects exist and move. Instead it becomes a dynamic quality accessible to thinking. In other words, space ceases to be a sense-based perception and becomes a perspective of thinking. In practical terms this means that every form can be described as consisting of points, lines or planes. However, Louis Locher[4] is right when he says that it is easy for modern people to grasp with their everyday consciousness that a line can be the totality of the points composing it, but that it is more difficult to view a line as the totality of its planes. Here therefore are a few examples to practice this:

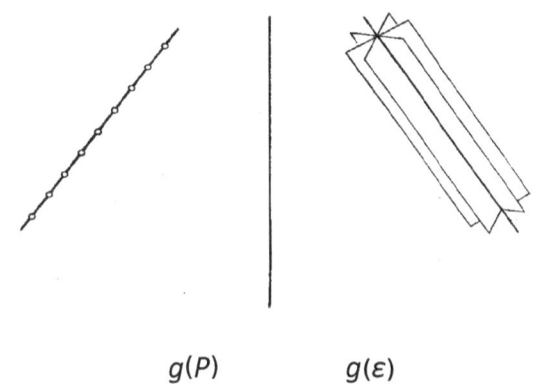

g(P) g(ε)

Diagram 8b: Line as a bearer of points and line as a bearer of planes.

We spontaneously experience points as parts of a whole, and the line as the bearer of this whole. Correspondingly it is also possible to conceive of the point as the whole and the planes and lines of a point, in contrast, as its parts.

P(g) P(ε)

Diagram 8c: Point as bearer of lines and point as bearer of planes.

Normal, self-focused consciousness, which proceeds from itself as the center of an occurrence, and observes the world from that standpoint, can be perceived as one-sided by such a threefold mode of observation. It can be extended by means of line or plane consciousness. The question is only *where awareness draws its respective basis of experience from in relation to consciousness of points, lines, and planes.* Here Louis Locher made some noteworthy comments:

> In recent decades people have arrived at the view that the task of all mathematics is to provide structural schema which are thought out by the human mind for functional reasons in approximation to the phenomenological world. This represents an advance on the view formerly put forward by Kant, that space is a fixed form of perception which one simply has to accept as a given. It will signify further progress to recognize how thinking adds very specific structural schema to this. To acquire this insight, we need to observe human development. In the first years of life we work our way into the vertical—without conceptual thought. In the interplay between the right and left sides of our organism we experience breadth, and in seeing with both eyes—also in grasping by the arms—the dimension of depth is realized. As substrate of these inner experiences—not as abstraction from the world of phenomena—we are able, once the formative forces have been partially freed from their work of shaping the physical body, to form abstract space in our thinking. Thus, the dimensions of normal space appear as subsequent abstract reflections of former, organic activities.
>
> When we succeed, perhaps without a direct awareness of this, in creating mirror images of activities that lie still further back—such as in the years before birth where the individuality, descending to earth, wraps itself in the formative forces from the cosmic periphery—another concept of space can arise, that of counterspace.[5]

However, we need to hold on to the fact that this law of polarity of point and plane, with the lines mediating between the two, *is not derived from empirical investigation,* but is a *phenomenon*, that is, it is axiomatic in character. The following drawings make this phenomenological lawfulness tangible. Diagram 10 depicts the polar form of a cube, giving rise to an octahedron. It is easy to construct an octahedron inside a previously drawn cube by following the law of polarity and, wherever we find a plane in the cube, placing there instead the mid-point of the square adjoining the respective cube surface. Likewise, following the law of polarity, instead of the eight cube corners (in each of which three edges meet), a plane bordered by three lines must appear. These eight planes of the octahedron thus formed arise through connecting the square centers of the six cube surfaces. It is evident that these two polar-related bodies are two of the five Platonic solids. These five Platonic solids are distinguished from all other geometric bodies through the fact that their corner points and surfaces are regularly structured. Just as cube and octahedron are polar to each other, this is also true of the pentagonal dodecahedron (consisting of twelve regular pentagons) and the icosahedron (consisting of twenty regular triangles). The fifth Platonic solid, the tetrahedron, is polar with itself.

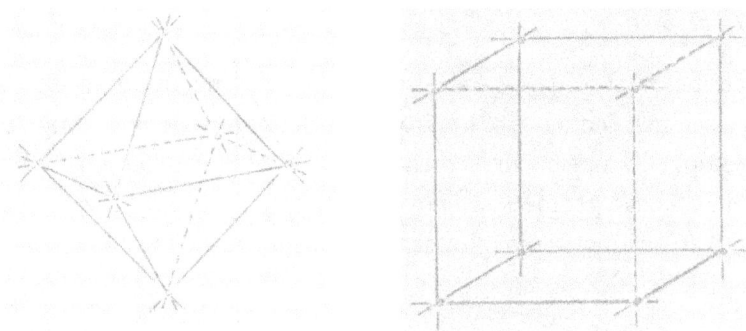

Diagram 9: Hexahedron and octahedron are polar to each other as wholly regular solids

The solids represented below, the cuboctahedron and rhomboid dodecahedron do not belong to the Platonic solids but are nevertheless polar to each other.

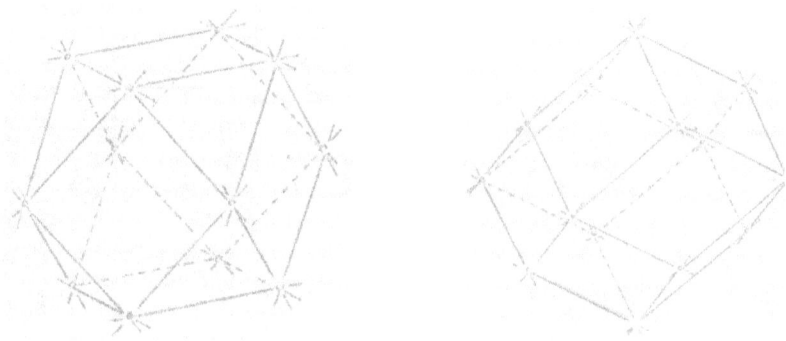

Diagram 10: Cuboctahedron and rhomboid dodecahedron are polar to each other as semi-regular (i.e. non-Platonic) solids

On handling distance elements

The diagram sequences below show two geometric processes of metamorphosis which carry a regular point through infinity. The first sequence starts from an ellipse whose point B migrates upward through infinity and returns from below in diagram 11c. An ellipse becomes a hyperbola. Interesting here is the fact that in Euclidean geometry infinity already plays into the drawing of a hyperbola, but that this did not lead to an abstract grasp of distance elements (see diagrams 11a, b, c).

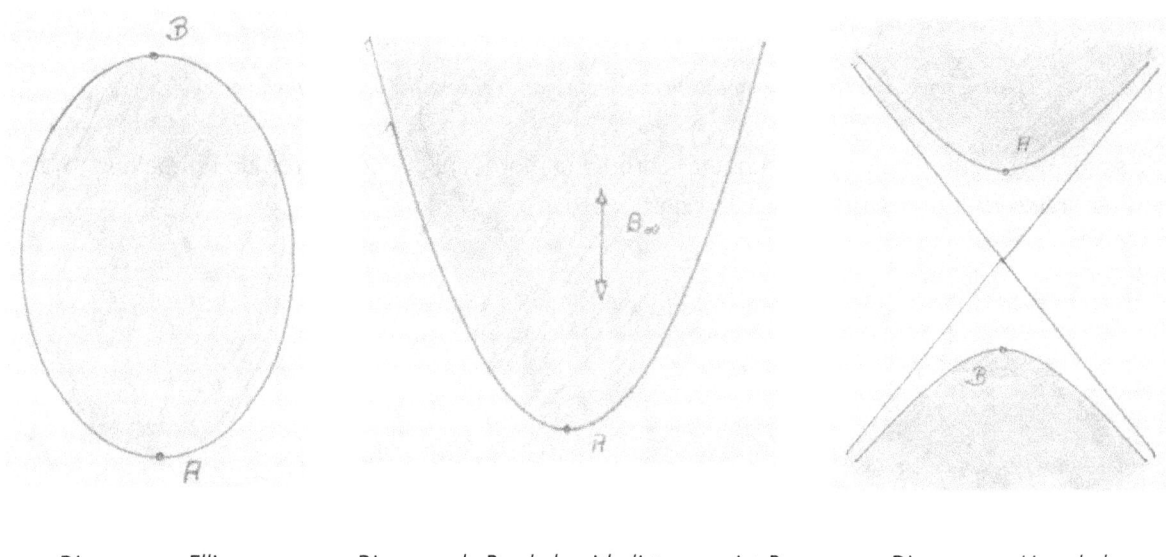

Diagram 11a: Ellipse *Diagram 11b: Parabola with distance point B* *Diagram 11c: Hyperbola*

The second sequence starts with a triangle, whose point C leads upward through infinity, and returns again from below in the last diagram. The fourth triangle is called the Möbius triangle after the mathematician August Ferdinand Möbius (see diagrams 12a, b, c, d).

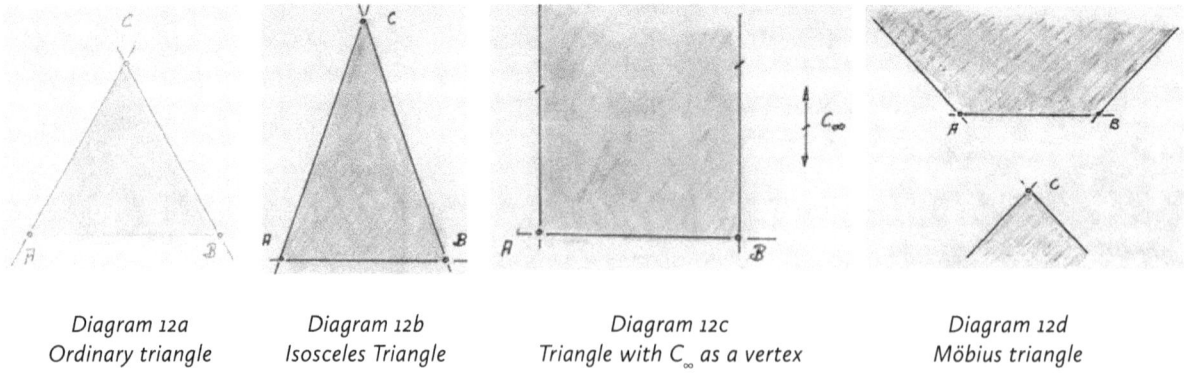

Diagram 12a
Ordinary triangle

Diagram 12b
Isosceles Triangle

Diagram 12c
Triangle with C_∞ as a vertex

Diagram 12d
Möbius triangle

Expanding the concepts of inner and outer

When one draws a circle, it is initially clear that everything inside the circumference is within, and everything outside the circumference is seen as external to it. A view based on projective geometry, however, shows us that only points can come to rest within the circle's interior. (In this description, only points and lines enter into consideration as characteristic elements.) In contrast, the entire line can lie outside the circle (see diagrams 13a, b).

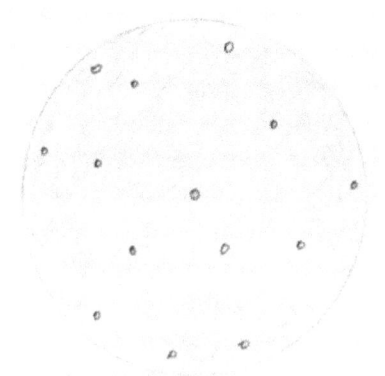

Diagram 13a
Interior (point, focused consciousnes)

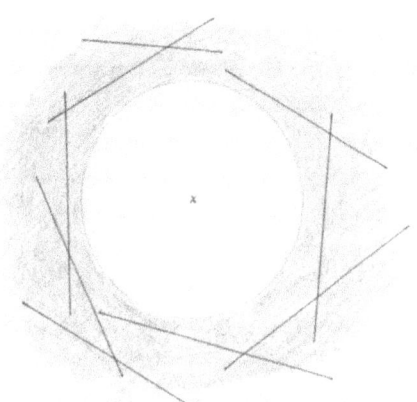

Diagram 13b
Shaded area: interior (line consciousnes)

Diagram 14a makes clear that through any arbitrary point S *within* the plane of the circle two lines can be drawn, each of which intersects the circle at two points. In the adjoining, polar drawing the line s appears as polar to the point S. The two intersecting lines p and q in diagram 14a correspond in the polar representation to points P and Q. The point of intersection S within the circle, in contrast, becomes the line s, which therefore likewise lies in the *interior*, since each of its points sends two tangents to the circle (see diagrams 14a and 14b). Thus, we can geometrically characterize the interior position of a point S in the case of a line s.

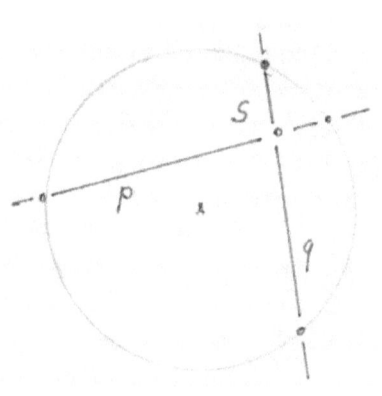

Diagram 14a

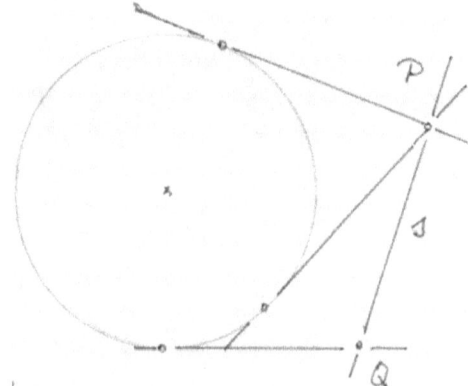

Diagram 14b

In the last diagram, 15a shows a point S_1 outside the circle, which lies outside it because lines can pass through it which intersect the circle at two points, and also lines which do not intersect it at all.

The polar diagram, in contrast, shows that the line s_1 does not lie within but outside the circle, because it contains points, for instance P_1, which can send two tangents to the circle, and points such as Q_1 which send no tangents to the circle (see diagrams 15a and 15b). Thus, we can also geometrically characterize the exterior position of points and lines in relation to a circle.

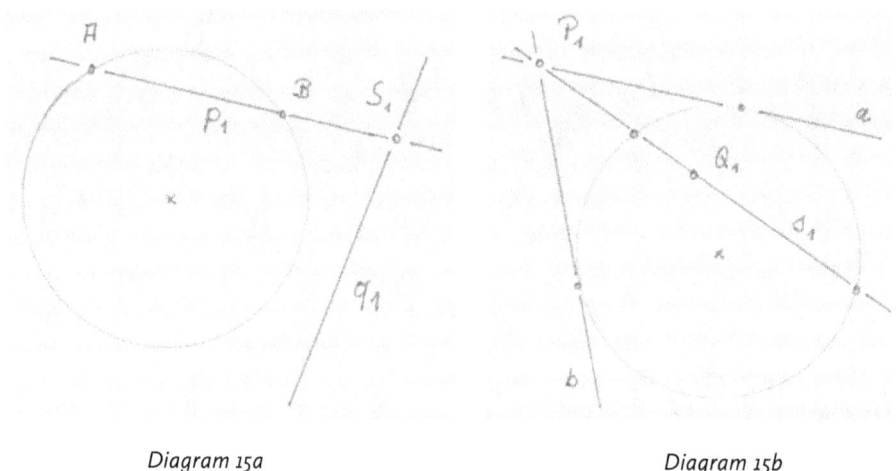

Diagram 15a   Diagram 15b

The two polar diagram sequences of points and lines in the plane make evident that in the field of projective geometry the question of within and without has to be put differently from Euclidean geometry. Projective geometry shows that the two characterizations well-known from Euclidean geometry of what a circle is (the circle as geometric location of all points that are equidistant from a central point, and the circle as body enclosing all tangents) give rise in projective geometry to the creation of new concepts relating to interior and exterior (see diagrams 16a and 16b).

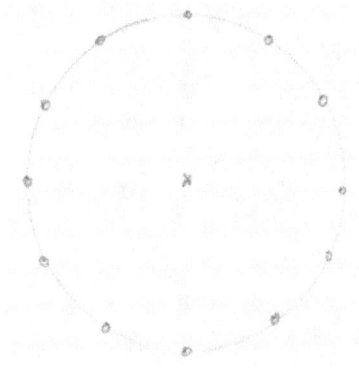 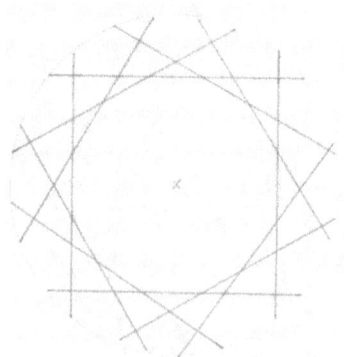

Diagram 16a   Diagram 16b

In projective geometric representation the apparent interior is shown through points which lie inside the circle. In contrast to this the apparent exterior is marked in the polar diagram by lines. Here, the inmost line in the function of distance lines corresponds and is polar to the center of the circle as inmost *point* (compare once more with diagrams 13a and 13b). From this it is evident that, in correspondence with mathematical and geometric laws, whether something is situated inside or outside depends on one's point of reference. In his interesting book *Mistel and Krebs* (*Cancer and Mistletoe*), cancer researcher and doctor Dietrich Boie based his scientific understanding of cancer on this insight.[6] There, referring to Steiner's lecture at the philosophical congress in Bologna, he writes:

> …In normal life the human being feels as though his conscious life issues from a unity, differentiated according to the concepts that derive from the perceptions of individual senses. Our normal view of ourselves consists in reflection on ourselves as bearer of sense impressions, and the cognitive processing of these sense impressions. In normal self-observation, our attention is derived from what we perceive in our surroundings and reflected onto the perceiving self. Here the content of consciousness increasingly contracts to the center point of the "ego." In the epistemological views of the nineteenth century the ego is conceived as residing within our physical organization, and the impressions are received from "outside." For normal, empirical consciousness the ego is enclosed in the bodily organization.
>
> Rudolf Steiner's epistemological investigations show that the view of the ego as enclosed within our physical body is incorrect for the cognitive ego. During its cognitive and perceiving activity, the ego is actually outside the body in a full inward immersion and experience of the lawfulness of the world. The physical body is connected to this ego like a mirror which reflects the mental/spiritual life of the ego beyond the mirror by means of the body's organic activity. The ego lives in the content of knowledge, i.e. it experiences its links with the objective world within this objective world itself, with which it is identical in the cognitive process. It receives its experiences through the fact that it receives them from the bodily organization as mirror images of conceptual life. The experiences of the ego within the objective world include thought contents as well as the contents of sense perception. Both are reflected back by the physical body and thus brought to consciousness in the cognitive process of the ego dwelling outside the body.
>
> This relationship between the perceiving and thinking ego and the physical body was farther clarified by Rudolf Steiner in a later lecture on cancer, in which he also referred back to the fundamental importance of the Bologna lecture for understanding cancer's origin. The ego, he says, is not directly perceived. It is connected with every sense perception, with everything that occurs outside the body. It is only active within us to the extent that it directs, from without, forces into the head's physical organization that are derived from perception. In the head, the etheric and astral bodies and ego are active outside the physical body, in other words they are body-free.

The relationship of the supersensible sheaths is quite different within the metabolism and the limbs: here the etheric and astral bodies are bound within the body, and only the ego is active in a body-free state. The ego is directly active in the movements of our arms and leg, "taking the legs with it" when they move.

The core of the problem consists in the fact that the reality of the ego active outside the body in the perception and thinking can only be experienced in a fully conscious way if we undergo a spiritual schooling as described by Rudolf Steiner in his Bologna lecture. This path of schooling leads to the insight that the theory of knowledge which the ego conceives as residing within our physical organization is based not only on illusion, but also mistakes a process of cognition that occurs outside the body as one within the body, in which metabolic processes normally occur rather than sense perception and thinking. In other words, the process of cognition is mistakenly transposed from outside the body onto the metabolic processes.

Cancer arises precisely because the astral body in the metabolic-limb system behaves in a way that is normal only for the astral body in the head. The metabolic-limb system's astral body takes on a head-type configuration, i.e. it withdraws from its activity within the body and becomes body-free. The consequence of this is that the physical body develops a tendency to assume the nature of sense organs within the metabolic system. Carcinoma formation derives from this tendency to try to form sense organs "in the wrong place."

This actually means that the epistemology of the nineteenth century represents, in the philosophical domain, what Rudolf Steiner describes as a cancer-inducing constitution. From this perspective, one can say that the cultural life derived from the nineteenth-century theory of knowledge predisposes us to cancer if its philosophical approach is implemented in daily life.

The normal, empirical consciousness, which only considers the sense-perceptible world to be real and has become blind to the world of spirit, was personified by Nordic initiates in the figure of the blind Hodur. In this context, it seems illuminating that Rudolf Steiner described the Hodur-type consciousness as parasitic: the body-free principle of the perceiving ego which is justified and necessary in the head realm and the domain of nerves and senses is shifted to the metabolic and limb system within the physical body, and there becomes a parasitic principle.

When Rudolf Steiner in one of his last lectures on the carcinoma problem refers to over-developed ego development as cause of the tendency to form misplaced sense organs, he characterizes something that is essential for understanding cancer as an ego-related illness: the conscious ego experiences itself too strongly within the physical body and too little in the true nature of its being, which can only be grasped in purely spiritual, body-free consciousness. Blindness toward the objective, spiritual outer world allows only a constricted ego consciousness that normal self-observation represents. The ego identifies itself, both inwardly and outwardly, only with the material phenomena: "The human being becomes too earthly" (July 24, 1924). Basically, therefore, an over-developed ego within the material world is an ego weakness in relation to spiritual mastery of the sensory content of perception. Thus, the cancer patient is in fact in a "Baldur" situation: the past's spiritual legacy is no longer sufficient to master the "Hodur principle." The problem of ego development shows clearly why cancer is an illness of our time.[7]

This view of cancer, developed from spiritual science, underpinned Dietrich Boie's oncology practice but also his work as school doctor at Marburg Waldorf School in the 60s and 70s of the last century. He was profoundly convinced that education—specifically in the domains of math and geometry—is preventative medicine.

Another approach to developing a link with reality based on new concepts of inner and outer is implicit in the field of physics, in the question of whether we are inside or outside the sun. In purely empirical terms the truth was summed up in a Moscow publication by the well-known Soviet science writer Felix Sigel, in 1972:

> The corpuscular and electron streams emitted from the sun at very great speed form the solar corona. The sun's light rays are reflected by means of these electrons, thus giving rise to the silvery, mother-of-pearl illumination surrounding the sun, which we can observe from earth. The solar corona's fan of rays is formed by both the corpuscular streams and a large number of released electrons.
>
> Apart from these corpuscular streams relatively slow particles are continually and evenly emitted from the sun in all directions of interplanetary space. These have a speed of 300 to 500 km/h and from what modern astrophysicists call the solar wind. This solar wind is a peculiar phenomenon, which one can best compare with a rain falling from below upwards. But Reality remains reality: the sun emits particles continually and evenly in all directions. The sun eruptions, as far as we know, represent only an unusual and extreme intensification of these continual emissions.
>
> Following these observations let us try to answer the question about the extent of the sun, or, to put it more precisely, the extent of the solar atmosphere. The sun certainly does not end where the human eye perceives the edge of the corona during a total eclipse....
>
> Based on corona ray density investigations once can calculate how density diminishes as function of distance from the sun. In terms of these laws and by assuming, in addition, that the solar corona extends to the earth's path of orbit, one can work out the density which the corona must have in proximity to the earth. Furthermore, by using astronomical measuring instruments, one can determine the density of electrons in the earth's proximity.

These calculations initially gave rise to a wholly unexpected accord. The measured density of electrons was exactly the same as it ought to be if the sun's corona extended to our earth. Could this be accidental? Of course not! These calculations, often repeated, led to the paradoxical conclusion that we live within the sun. Even if in extremely dilute form, the sun's corona extends to the surface of the earth and even further. If we take this thought further it becomes apparent that, in a certain sense, we do not just live on the earth, but are also inhabitants of solar space. This indicates that solar activity must be evident in processes occurring on earth, and even within ourselves.[8]

Concepts of large and small

The following drawings again show polar representations in the plane. Diagram 17a shows a parallelogram with the parallel pairs of lines p and q on the one hand, and on the other r and t. The shaded parallelogram constructed within the larger parallelogram with the center S appears visibly smaller in area.

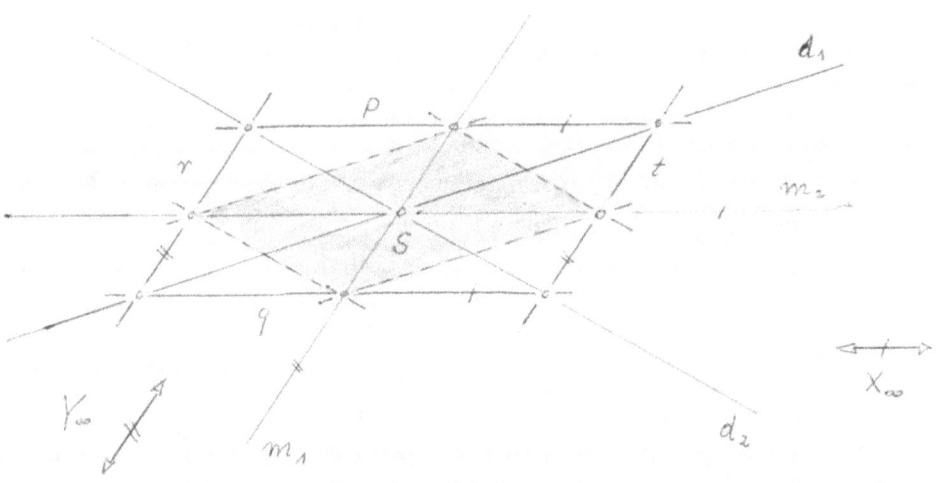

Diagram 17a

The polar representation (diagram 17b) to this shows, in the place of the four pairs of parallel lines, the four pairs of centered points: P and Q on the one hand, and R and T on the other. In this case, "centered" means that the connecting lines Q and P, or R and T, meet at a point Ω, corresponding to the projective line Y_∞ in diagram 17a. A major difference between the two polar drawings consists in the remarkable fact that the projective line of the plane is intrinsically pre-determined, while the choice of the corresponding point Ω can be arbitrary. (The connoisseur will recognize here the aspect of a polar affinity observation in the plane.) The four points cited above mark a centigram, which has a polar correspondence in the plane to the parallelogram in the first drawing. The second centigram *circumscribing* the first parallelogram (PTQR) corresponds to the shaded *smaller* parallelogram in diagram 17a. To the inscribed, shaded, smaller parallelogram in this first drawing corresponds, in the second drawing the second centigram circumscribing the first centigram (RTQR) whose area of enclosure (shaded) corresponds to the centrigram inscribed in the first drawing. This area of enclosure, although apparently more expansive if seen from the center, is smaller than the first area of enclosure.

In the realm of living things this relativity of large and small is something we can encounter in tangible ways: a plant seed, such as an acorn, is great in growth potential. A hundred-year-old oak tree, on the other hand, has acquired physical size but is diminished in growth potential.

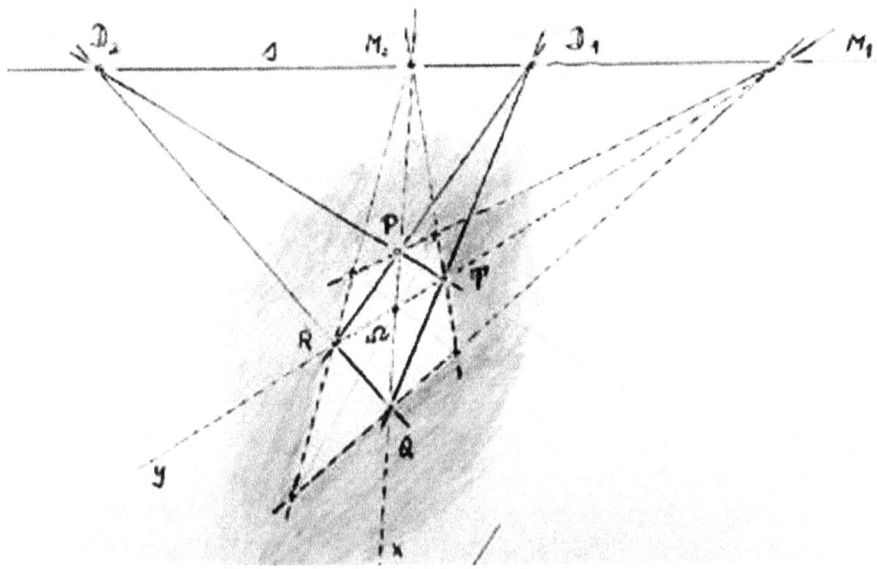

Diagram 17b Ω is the ∩ of RT ∧ PQ

Different ways of seeing the same

We now turn to the Desargues Configuration in the plane, named after French mathematician Gérard Desargues (1591-1661).

Where three lines passing through a point S contain, respectively, two assigned points A → A', B → B', C → C', then the connecting lines of corresponding points (such as AB and A'B' etc.) intersect at a line s. Now the Desargues Configuration is distinguished by the fact that it is polar to itself in the plane. This derives from its property of having ten points and ten lines, with the peculiarity that three lines pass through each of its points and, complementary to this, three points of the configuration lie on each line. All points and lines thus respectively fill the same function. This is the reason why, for instance, in place of S any other point of the configuration such as S_1 can be chosen, for which the corresponding line s_1 must be sought. In this way the Desargues Configuration can be viewed in ten different ways. It thus offers a significant basis for thinking and describing the same in different terms.

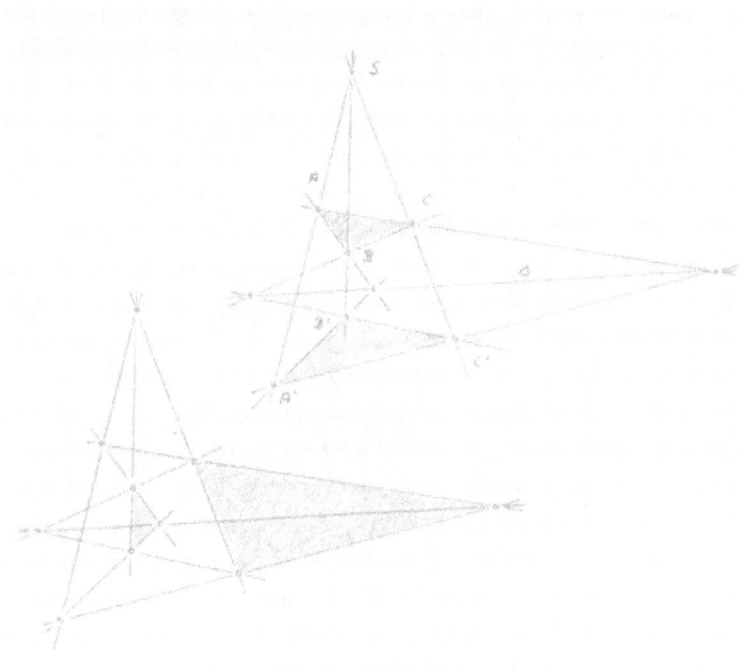

Diagram 18

In the field of medicine, it is evident how necessary complementary, extending perspectives are. Naturally one can regard the human being as an object and analyze his body in terms of molecular substance. To every question one asks one receives the answer that corresponds to it. Thus, in line with Paracelsus,[9] one can for instance describe the five causes of illness. Standing before a patient who died of cholera, one can say:

- that he died from infection
- that his self-healing forces were weak and failed to compensate
- that he impaired his self-healing forces through an anxious and depressive mood of soul
- that he was too weak in his ego to cope with his life circumstances and confidence
- that the moment of his death, pre-ordained in his destiny, was God's will

It is clear from this how fruitful it is to observe life in a more differentiated way. What is right? What is true?

Being "right" is a relative business. It accords with life to know from what perspective we ourselves or others are "right." Knowing this brings us closer to reality—which nurtures understanding and promotes peace.

Division of the plane by three lines and three points

Three lines divide the plane into four core areas which adjoin each other (diagram 19a). Three points divide the plane into four areas each of which enclose a core area (diagram 19b). Inside the core areas lie points, and polar to them lie internal lines alongside enclosing areas.

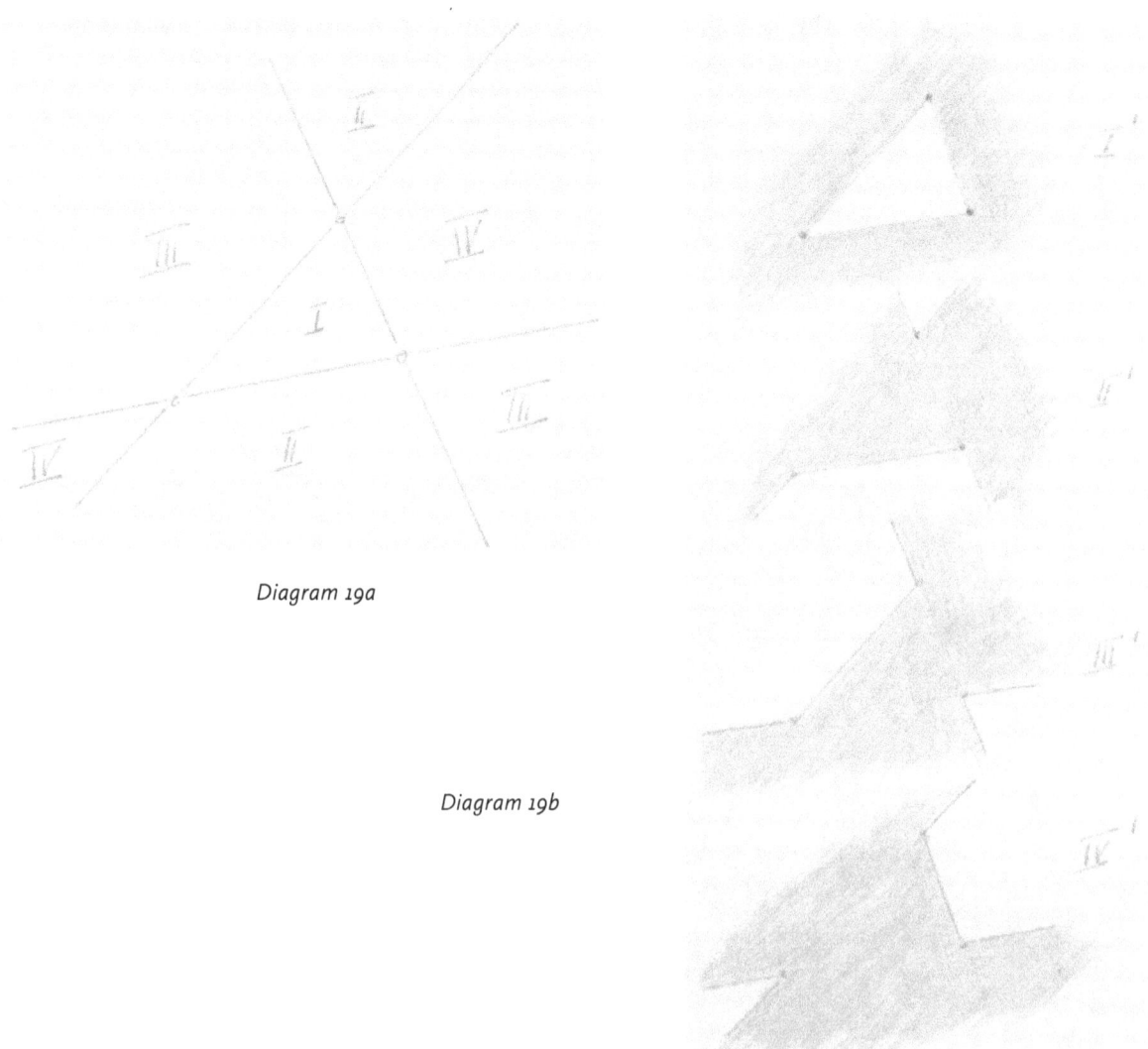

Diagram 19a

Diagram 19b

Where do we find this polarity in daily life? Whenever we calmly observe a surrounding landscape: fields, meadows, water-meadows and forest: differentiated surfaces, plains, often modified by hills, mountains and valleys. If, in contrast, we look up to the starry heavens at night, we see an arched dome, the far plane divided by points of light from the stars. Heaven and earth are as polar to each other as are point and plane, mediated by the line.

The special quality of holistic observation

To observe a form holistically we need to consider not only the form itself but also the division of its surroundings by this form. Diagram 20a shows how the indented oval, with its two crossing tangents, structures and divides the plane. The division gives rise to distinct and separate areas. Here a so-called two-point area, for instance, means that two tangents to the oval can be drawn from each point of this area. Diagram 20b shows the aspect polar to this. Here the O' core area corresponds to the O' area of enclosure.

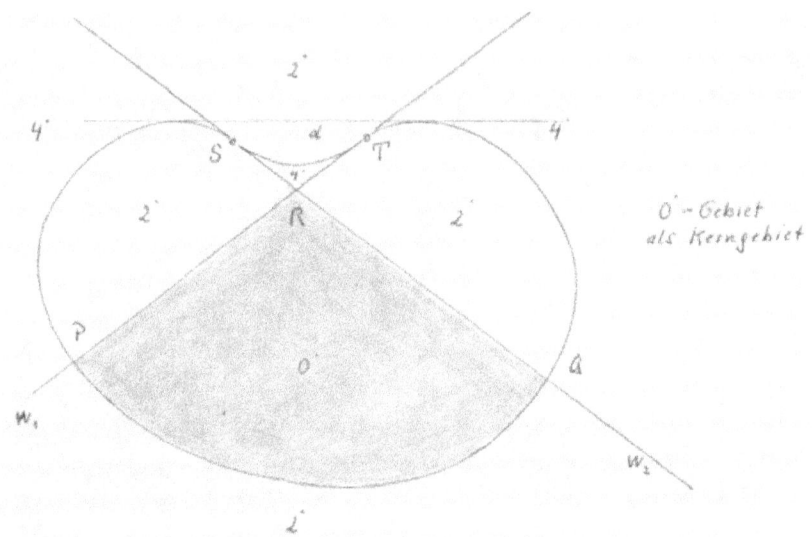

Diagram 20a O' area as score area

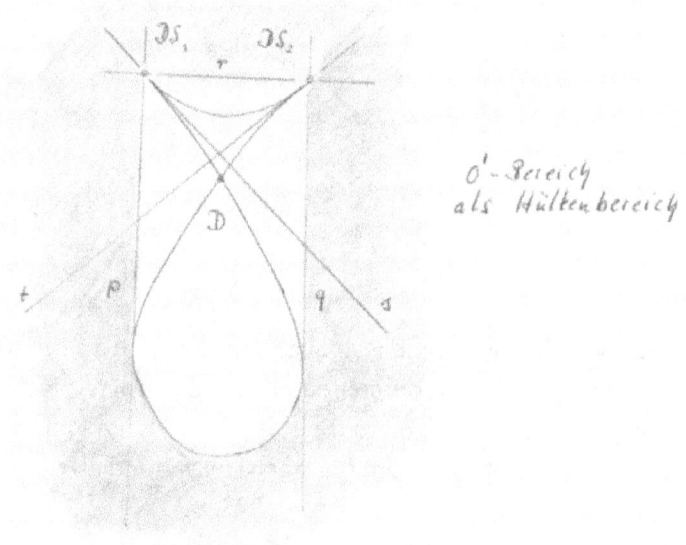

Diagram 20b O' area as enclosure area

It is evident that such a view opens completely new outlooks on embryonic development. One can see almost tangibly what must occur and differentiate before an invagination can take place as formative embryonic gesture.

Examples of polar forms

The following diagrams of closed curves in the plane show how diverse are the complementary forms that can be grasped using the polarity laws of projective geometry. All these forms must be imagined in the plane. Three-dimensional spatial forms are generally more complex. The forms depicted here possess peculiarities (singularities) which can likewise be assigned to the laws of polarity.

Singularities of two-dimensional curves in polar opposition

These compatible polar singularities are shown in diagrams 21-23, paired with their opposites. There are five fundamental form elements whose understanding is important when one wants to characterize a form, or more precisely a curve, in the plane.

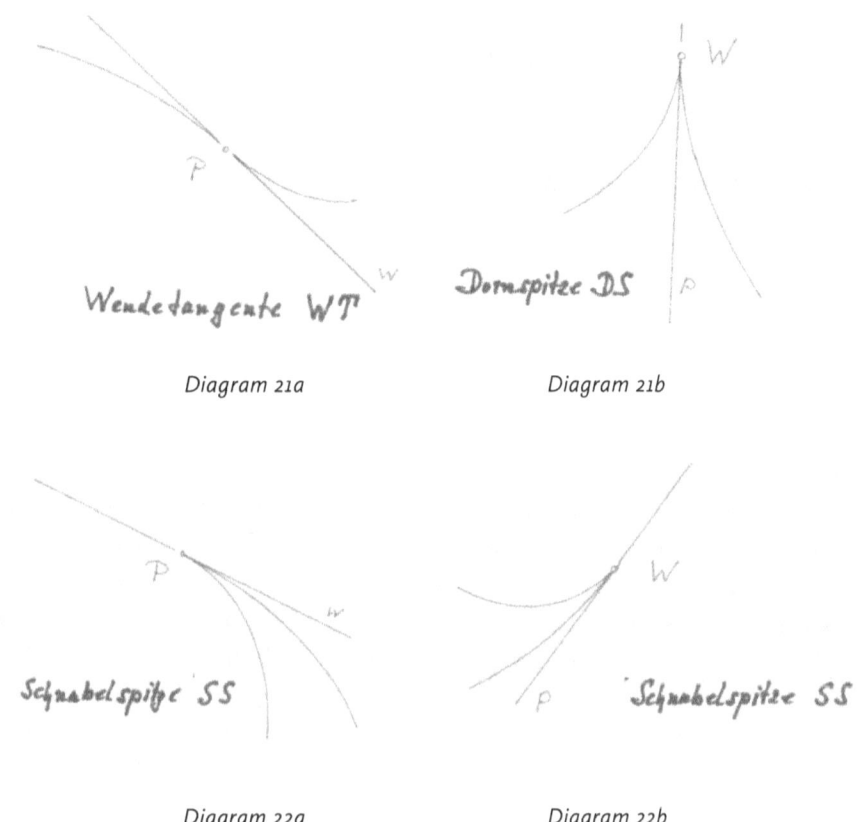

Diagram 21a　　　　　Diagram 21b

Diagram 22a　　　　　Diagram 22b

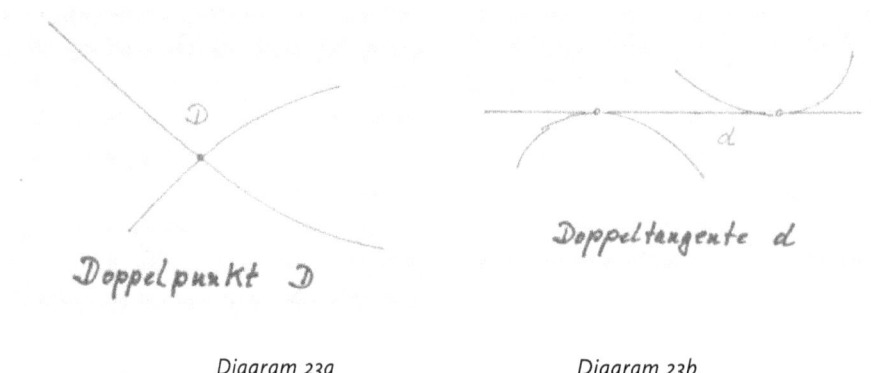

Diagram 23a   Diagram 23b

Six manifestations of one and the same type of curve in the plane

The curves in diagram 24a possess two singularities: a crossing tangent W and a double point D. In diagram 24a one can discern this directly. The curves can simply be traced in their entirety. However, some practice is needed to perceive the other 5 curves as belonging to the same type. This is due to the fact that certain elements of the curve (usually certain singularities) appear in the function of projective elements. Such observations are of a kind that lead us to the first threshold of imaginative capacity. If one compares these observations with those made in relation to the Desargues Configuration, it is noticeable that *one and the same* configuration can be viewed in different ways, and that in the case of the *six different curves* what is important is to discern the same within the altered forms. This only succeeds by using the capacity referred to above.

Curve shapes polar to each other

The forms that are shown in diagrams 24-27 are examples of the existence of these characteristically occurring singularities.

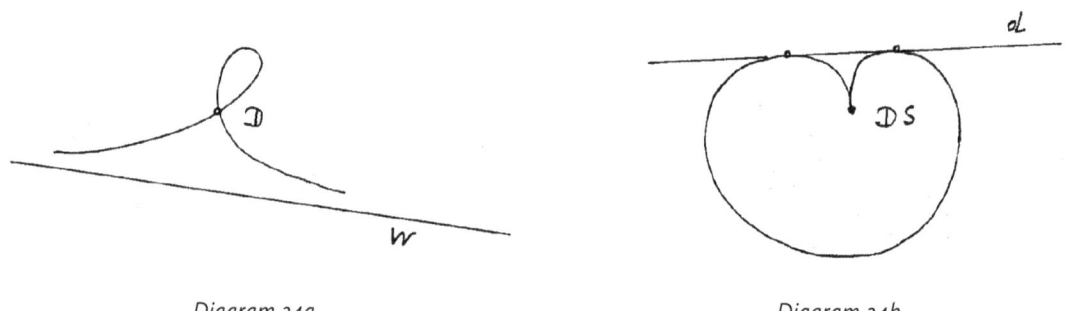

Diagram 24a   Diagram 24b

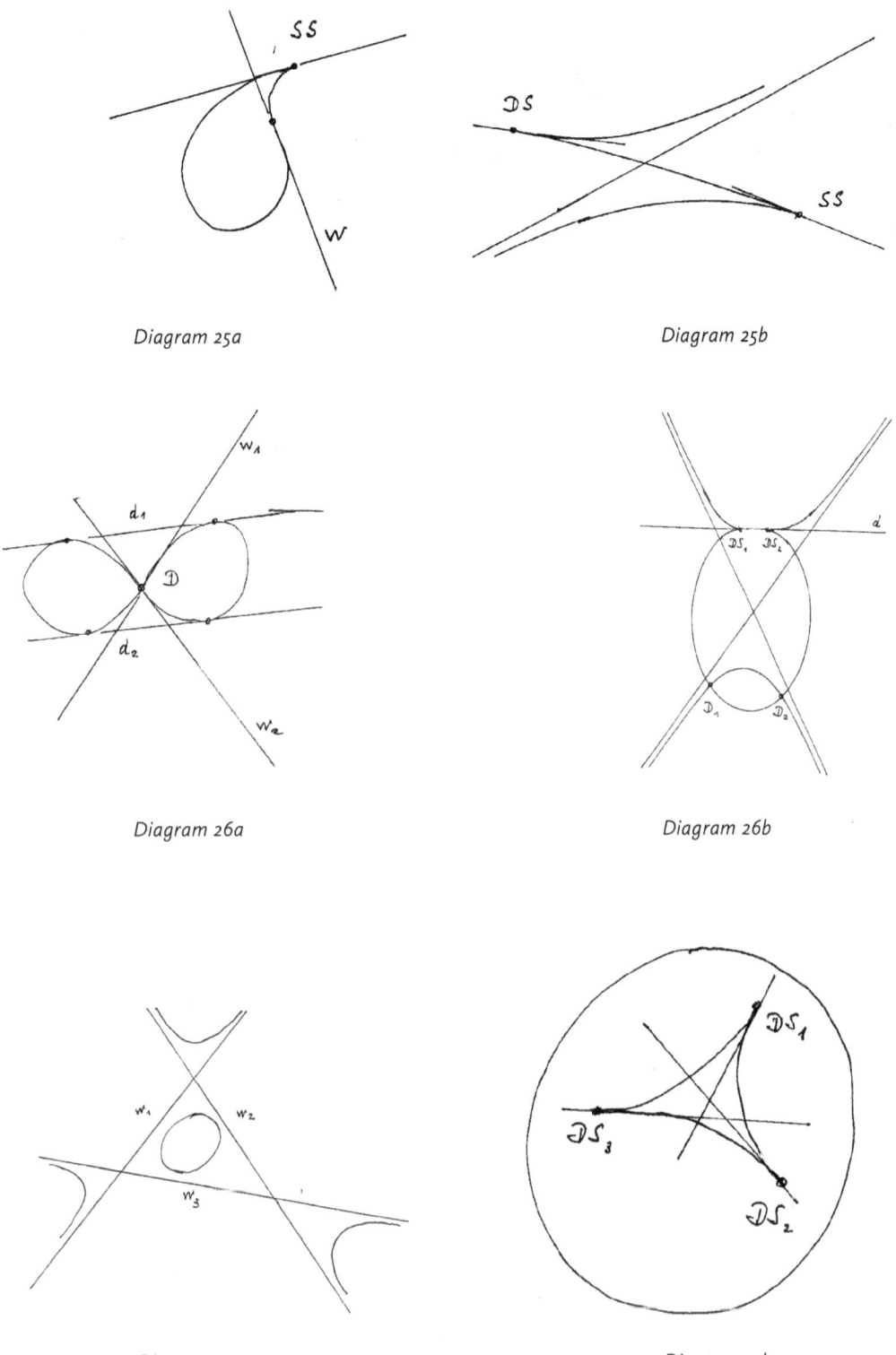

Diagram 25a

Diagram 25b

Diagram 26a

Diagram 26b

Diagram 27a

Diagram 27b

The polar curves (diagrams 27a and 27b) have the peculiarity, in contrast to the curves depicted in diagrams 24-26 that they are clearly not unicursal—that is, simply continuous. Instead they clearly diverge despite representing *a single* curve. To the three-pointed form element in an oval of diagram 27b corresponds the complementary form which extends beyond the projective straight line in three ways, and possesses three crossing tangents and an "inner" oval.

Such a mode of observation shows that something that appears seemingly divided spatially nevertheless belongs together. Thus, projective geometry facilitates the development of thought forms that can be directly applied in embryology and physiology to functional structuring principles and patterns. Here we are in an area, after all, where a hormone can have various areas of activity, or where, in one and the same cell, quite different processes of synthesis and breakdown occur simultaneously, and can correspond with relevant organ activities. But it goes further than this. As long ago as 1952 Hermann Poppelbaum linked this fact to observations which still today act as inspiration for biology and medicine:

> In contrast to normal, to some extent inert, indifferently extending space, the space of etheric (formative) forces is differentiated and configured. As a result, substances which "come to lie within it" have a quite diverse significance depending on where they are situated. The identity of the particle, a self-evident property in commonly-held concepts of matter, is thus in flux. A substance is what is only in connection with the place it currently occupies....Let us examine a liver cell for instance: It forms glycogen from sugar and vice versa, produces urea and uric acid from amino acids and ammonia, breaks down hemoglobin, produces bile acids, is capable of fixing the toxins it receives or rendering them harmless etc. In a cell whose size can be estimated at a hundred times smaller than the head of a pin, at least ten and probably many more chemical processes unfold alongside each other. The fact that the cell can continue to perform all these functions is due to the fact that it is not sustained from within the cell interior but from the periphery. R. Steiner tells us that the whole cosmos is active within a single cell.
>
> The compression of many conflicting processes into a tiny space is only comprehensible if one takes account of the fact that the cell content is situated in the "counterspace" which in its own way is as infinite as the surrounding trivial space.
>
> The investigations mentioned...by Adams and Locher into the space of formative forces also enable us to conceive of the link between organs in one and the same organism in a multiple and differentiated way. Organs belonging more closely to one another do not have to be physical neighbors but are as it were alongside each other in "counterspace" as "etheric neighbors"—such as kidneys and organs of vision, large intestine and forebrain. Many facts are known in pathology which point to common affliction of distant organs by the same illness, while the anatomical space between remains unaffected.[10]

Another view of the same

First let us ask: What is a curve-type? We speak of curves of the same type if they have the same singularities, in the same respective number. The curves represented in diagrams 28a-f each possess singularities: a crossing tangent *w* and a double point *D*. In diagram 28a one can discern this directly. The curves in diagrams 28b-f can however also be traced in their entirety. However, some practice is needed to perceive them as belonging to the same type. This is due to the fact that certain elements of the curve (at least certain singularities) appear in the function of projective elements. The directional arrows inscribed on the curves give one of two possibilities of tracing each one. They thus provide the so-called traversing direction and require of the observer a capacity to perceive a curve—passing through infinity—as connected. Such observations are of a kind that lead us to the first threshold of imaginative capacity. If one compares these observations with those made in relation to the Desargues Configuration, above, it is noticeable that one and the same configuration can be viewed in different ways, and that in the case of the 6 different curves what is important is to discern the same within the altered forms. This only succeeds by using the capacity referred to above, which can be systematically developed on the geometric path described. It is evident that this simultaneously schools our observation to recognize types in the plant and animal kingdom, and to work through them methodically. The laws of math and geometry, after all, underlie all of evolution. It is ancient Mystery knowledge that "the Gods do geometry." The human being can recognize this divine wisdom within and learn to use it. It was for this reason that Rudolf Steiner once wrote down for Count Polzer-Hoditz the remarkable phrase: "If a young person studies math, a divine child will be born in him." This divine child, this pure capacity of imagination is what we need to develop. The imaginative capacity integral to pure mathematical thinking should not be dissipated or lost by applying math and geometry only, without perceiving its pure source. To perceive oneself in the creative reproduction and acquisition of these pure thought forms gives rise to a core dimension of spiritual self-experience.

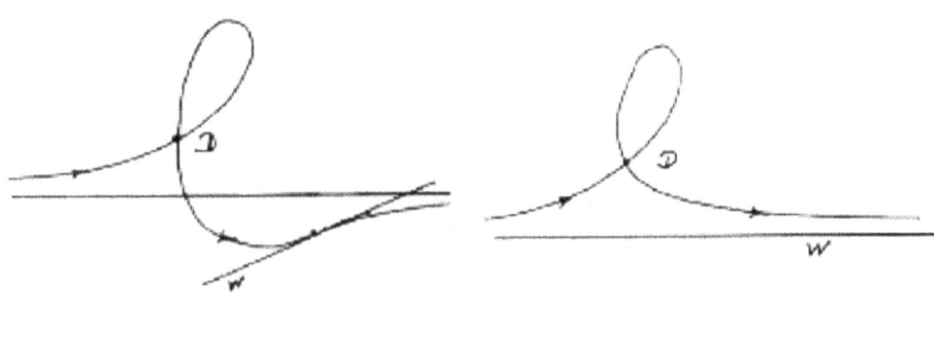

Diagram 28a   *Diagram 28b*

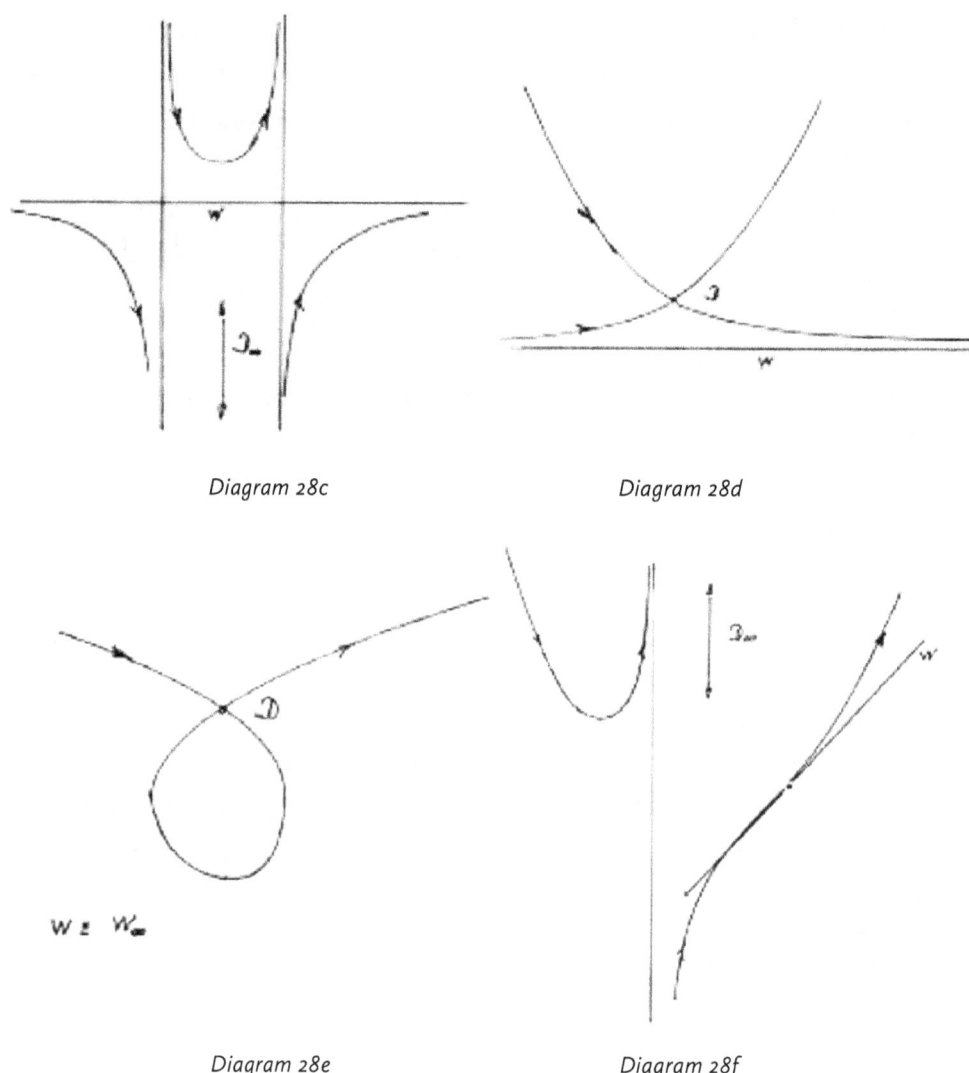

Diagram 28c

Diagram 28d

Diagram 28e

Diagram 28f

Concluding remarks

Abstract observations are useful where singularities or specifics of a larger context need to be grasped in detail: a specific singularity of a curve, the single leaf of an oak, the liver as human organ, etc. But one always needs to remember that such details are only isolated parts of a superordinate whole. Space as an idea is such a superordinate whole. This fact is one we can only gradually approach, through practice. A primary example of this is the following:

Let a finite horizontal distance be limited by the two points A and B. A straight line g through the two points passes, however, beyond them to both right and left, and extends infinitely far. Here a point that moves toward the left distances itself continuously from one moving toward the right. The infinitely distant point F_∞ lying toward the right is the same as that lying toward the left. The double arrow gives symbolic expression to this fact.

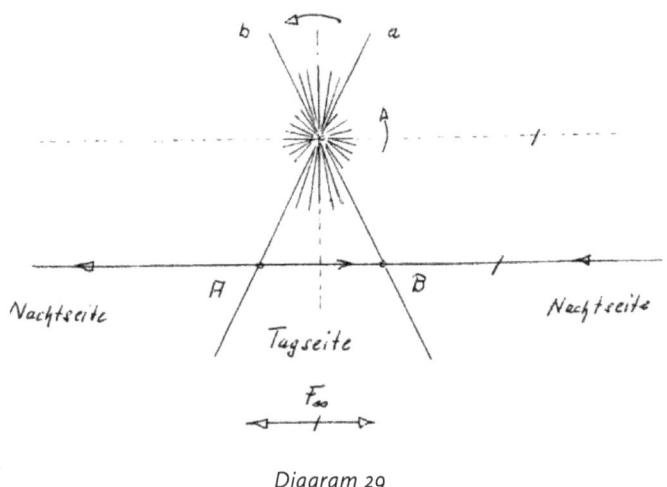

Diagram 29

Projective geometry shows us that these two initially opposite movement directions can be seen as moving toward each other, both meeting at the projective point F_∞ on the straight line *g*. Grasped qualitatively we can say that the finite distance from *A* to *B*, is traversed as the day aspect, while the "infinite distance" from *A* to *B*, in contrast, is the night aspect. Now we can grasp the straight line as a whole.

The significance of such an elemental expansion of consciousness for a human being can be seen from the example described by the young Rudolf Steiner in his *Autobiography*:

> A decisive experience was vouchsafed me at the time, specifically from a mathematical perspective. I had the greatest inner difficulties with the concept of space. As a void expanding in all directions in space, the basis for all prevailing scientific theories of the time, it could not be grasped in a comprehensive way. Through the newer (synthetic) geometry which I came to know in lectures and private studies, it dawned on my soul that a line extended to the right into infinity will return to its point of departure from the left. The infinitely distant point lying to the right is the same as the point of infinity lying to the left.
>
> It appeared to me that, with such concepts of modern geometry, one might form a concept of space as other than a void. The straight line returning to itself is like a circular trajectory struck me as a revelation. I left the lecture where this first occurred to me as though a burden had fallen from my shoulders. I felt liberated, and once more geometry gave me, as in the days of my boyhood, a sense of joy.[11]

CHAPTER 9

Professional Ethics and a Spiritual Approach in the Teaching Profession

Michaela Glöckler

> ***Seven Social Sins:***
> *Politics without Principles*
> *Pleasure without Conscience*
> *Wealth without Work*
> *Knowledge without Character*
> *Commerce without Morality*
> *Science without Humanity*
> *Worship without Sacrifice*
>
> – MAHATMA GANDHI[1]

Ethics questions what "the good" is. What is the meaning of this for the teaching profession? Where does the good come from?

In an unparalleled way the twentieth century revealed sources of evil. World wars were instigated by power struggles and financial interests, radical fundamentalism of both left and right, collective socialism and totalitarian regimes. Military and political dictatorships, genocide and engulfing hatred have plagued the destinies of countless millions of people.

What good and evil have in common is that they affect us from without but can also surface more or less consciously from within and come to expression outwardly. Thus we can be appalled at examples of corruption and deception that are reported every day in the media, but at the same time we fail to notice tendencies towards the very same kinds of behavior in ourselves. A convenient lie or a good deed done to obtain something in return may seem to us both natural and harmless.

We need a new kind of ethics, one that begins where the battle for humanity and humane values is being fought today: in each one of us. The time has passed when decisions were taken by great leaders on behalf of the immature masses. In modern democracies, everything depends on the many individuals who ultimately decide who comes to power and which products are consumed. Taking this seriously is the beginning of a new ethics.

Just as individual actions by terrorists, and their use of violence, can destabilize any society and cause chaos, so fundamentalist outlooks and slogans, herd opinions and extremism can be neutralized and opposed in every single individual. This capacity is one that pupils can experience in their teacher.

They sit or stand opposite him with the unspoken question: Who are you? How do you face life and deal with it? What do you have to learn? Who is your teacher? Are you a full human being already? Can you help me to become one?

Examining Rudolf Steiner's remarks about the human capacity for self-development, one can feel optimistic when one reads: "The capacities which give us insights into higher worlds slumber within each one of us."[2]

Each and every person can learn to become more human if she grows aware of, and awakens to, divine, spiritual realms of existence. Development means that a later stage proceeds from an earlier one, that we transform ourselves, growing on beyond what we are at present. The very special secondary aspect of the path of self-development that Steiner outlines is that he describes life itself as a path of initiation. He clearly demonstrates that the acquisition of knowledge, impulses for higher development or meditative practice, will only bring blessing if one does not regard the fruits of such work as an end in themselves, but integrates them into daily life. Viewed in this way, self-development means enhancing one's experience of life, and discovering life in all its aspects, with its highs and lows. How, ultimately, can we learn to develop qualities of character such as reverence, inner peace, courage and confidence, hope, loyalty, love, truthfulness—through to an autonomy that also affirms the autonomy of others—if these qualities are not learned in such a way that they also enter our daily lives, clearly demonstrating that life itself is the best educator of these very characteristics.

This affirms also that there can be no "un-spiritual" teaching. As a teacher one is challenged to bring teaching material in a way that serves the physical, soul, and spiritual development of the child. In order to do this, one must enter a path of self-development. For this reason, Rudolf Steiner gave the seven character-building pathways. Those who work with these will soon notice what is gained through inner stance and life orientation. Steiner called these the "seven conditions" for the inner path, and remarked about them:

> It must be stressed that none of these conditions must be fully achieved but that what is required is the striving to achieve them. No one can wholly fulfill these conditions, but everyone can start on the path toward doing so. What counts is the will, the intention to pursue this path.[3]

Seven Conditions for a Fundamentally Ethical Stance

The first condition is: to direct one's attention to promoting physical and spiritual health. How healthy a human being is naturally does not initially depend on him. But every person can try to nurture this in himself.[4]

It would be possible to interpret this as proposing that we egotistically promote our own health. But in the following passages Steiner describes how we can learn to find the right relationship to enjoyment—and also to duty. Body and soul are involved in our daily work, and it often happens that we have to ignore our health to perform our duty. We may miss a meal, or work through the night to meet and obligation. In other words, work often requires us to overlook our health. What can have an injurious effect should then be balanced by the right relationship to enjoyment. We can learn to enjoy intensely, but in such a way that this enjoyment gives us the strength to perform our work better and with more satisfaction. We need to learn never to seek enjoyment as an end in itself—which then robs us of strength—but to learn to enjoy in a way that gives rise to new strength and motivation for life and self-development. For people unable to enjoy themselves it is particularly important to realize that enjoyment is a fundamental precondition for maintaining health of soul and body. The problem is just to be able to remain aware and to stop again at the right moment, in line with the adage: "Stop eating while it still tastes good." If we carry on enjoying ourselves beyond the height of enjoyment, or by using health-impairing drugs or stimulants, we will have to recover from such consumption afterwards.

The second condition is to feel oneself as part of all life. Fulfilling this condition involves a great deal, but each person can only fulfill it in his own way. If I am a teacher and my pupil does not meet my expectations, I should not, initially, direct my feeling toward the pupil but toward myself. I should feel myself one with the pupil in my care to the extent that I ask: "Is the insufficiency in my pupil not the consequence of my own deed?" Instead of directing my feelings against him I will then, instead, reflect on how I myself should behave so that my pupil can better fulfill my hopes in future. Cultivating this kind of stance leads to a gradual change in the way people think. This applies both to the smallest and greatest things. By adopting such a stance for instance I will view a criminal differently. I will withhold judgment and say to myself: "I am just a person like he is. It may be that the only thing protecting me from his fate was the education which circumstances granted me." This also kindles in me the thought that this human brother of mine would have turned out differently if the teachers who expended their efforts on me had devoted such attention to him. I will realize that I was granted something which he was denied, that I owe what is good in me to the very circumstances that he was deprived of. And from there it is only a short distance to realizing I am a part of all humanity and thus co-responsible for everything that happens.[5]

Those who practice this condition will notice—with some dismay—the degree to which they exercise power through their behavior. If someone verbally attacks me, and I react on the same level, the situation can easily escalate, or lead to a lasting atmosphere of conflict. But I can refuse to allow an insult to provoke a similar reaction in me, and instead ask how I can defuse the situation. How must I behave so that this person, too, can show his better side? Or: What must have happened within him, what did he experience at home, for instance, which sent his tolerance level plummeting so low that he came out with this whole litany of accusations? Even if we cannot answer such questions, the very fact that we genuinely ask them, instead of condemning the other, represents an important step. It can often happen that, after a while, the other will then change his behavior.

This is directly linked with the third condition for esoteric schooling: The awareness

> ...that his thoughts and feelings have as much significance for the world as his actions. It must be acknowledged that it is just as injurious to hate a fellow human being as to strike him. Then I also realize that, when I seek to perfect myself, I am not just doing something for myself but also for the world. The world draws as much benefit from my pure feelings and thoughts as from my right action.[6]

How effective good thoughts and feelings are in relation to others is something we all know if we have people around us whom we think of with love, esteem, and respect. Children who meet loving respect grow in such an atmosphere as though in a moral haven. This enables them to cope with ordinary, everyday annoyances and frightening experiences with an assurance that would be impossible otherwise.

The fourth condition is to acquire

> ...the view that the real nature of the human being does not lie in externalities but in inner life. Someone who regards himself merely as a product of the outer, physical world cannot get anywhere with esoteric schooling. Feeling oneself as a soul-spiritual being is a basis for such schooling. Someone who penetrates to such feelings is then able to distinguish between inner obligation and outer success. He learns to see that the one cannot directly be measured against the other. The esoteric pupil must find the happy medium between what outer conditions demand and what he acknowledges as the right course of action and conduct for himself. He should not impose on his environment something which it will not meet with understanding; but he should also be quite free of the urge only to do what will bring him external acknowledgement. Acknowledgment of his truths is something he must seek solely in the inner voice of his authentic, knowledge-seeking soul. But he should learn from his environment as much as he can about what is beneficial and useful to it. By doing so he will develop in himself what is called in esoteric knowledge the "spiritual balance." On one side of the balancing scales lies an "open heart" for the needs of the external world, and on the other, "inner certainty and unshakable endurance."[7]

The fifth condition is

> ...steadfastness in following a decision one has taken. Nothing must induce the esoteric pupil to deviate from a decision he has once taken, except the insight that he is mistaken. Every decision is a power, and if this power does not lead directly to success in the domain it initially addresses, it will still take effect in its own way. Success is only decisive where one does something out of craving or desire. But all actions instigated by cravings or desire are without value to the higher world. There love of an action is of sole importance. In this love should be expressed everything that motivates an esoteric pupil to an action. Then he will never tire of repeatedly carrying out a decision, no matter how often it may fail.[8]

To work from an inner position of love for the work or for people, and not to work just for money, recognition, or success, is today like a thought from another planet. It is only through such an approach that the inner character can develop a work-related morality with a quality of steadfastness. If work is done for the latter reasons above for money alone and so on, then the ego becomes dependent, and can easily be undermined by being more easily manipulated and vulnerable.

Resolutions bring the strength of implementation. Steadfastness requires resolution and love of the matter to be dealt with in order to accomplish what is required. On the other hand, it also requires strength, the strength of selfless love, to deal with mistakes or disappointments. These qualities also support the steadfastness in life and prevent potential breakdowns, when negative reactions or disappointments come from one's decisions, which comes to everyone at some stage.

When students meet teachers who radiate this quality of steadiness, then the students have a feeling of a second home. They gain the positive experience of "learning to live" and feel that their own expressions of insecurity, idealism, and disappointment are understood and taken on board.

A sixth condition is to develop a feeling of

> …gratitude toward everything that comes to meet us. One has to realize that one's own existence is a gift of the whole universe. How much is necessary before each of us can be granted a life to live out our existence! How much we owe to nature and other human beings! Those who aspire to esoteric schooling must incline to such thoughts. Someone who cannot devote himself to them will be unable to develop in himself the universal love which is necessary to come to higher knowledge. Something I do not love cannot reveal itself to me. And every such revelation must fill me with gratitude, for I become richer in consequence.[9]

It is precisely in the school that it is important to be aware and awake to the fact that destiny, which gives so many small and large gifts in life, gives the possibility to take on the positive aspects of life development. Students experience the teacher as an artist of life when the teacher has really worked on this sixth condition. Gratitude is the soul breathing between human beings. People feel themselves to be free and light in an atmosphere of gratitude. The mood of gratitude brings together openness and trust. Rudolf Steiner also describes gratitude as the bridge to the dead. It is the gratitude on earth, which is bound to space and time, which can be taken up in life after death. In gratitude, every experience—be it difficult, beautiful, or colored by a painful longing—comes to rest in the constancy of our own being.

Rudolf Steiner concludes:

> All these conditions must be united and reconciled in a seventh: tirelessly to view life in the way these conditions require. By doing so the pupil will develop the capacity to make his life a unified whole. The various different expressions of his life will harmonize with and not contradict one another. He will thus prepare the composure which he needs to develop as he takes the first steps in esoteric schooling.[10]

The results of working with the seven conditions can be seen in:

- Healthy life structures
- Ability to integrate
- Sense of reality
- Inner self-reliance and independence
- Patience
- Trust in destiny ("all is love")
- Inner peace

Using the basis of such inner work, the teacher can stand as a model for the path of human development.

Examining the path of self-development shows clearly that although we human beings are imperfect and lacking in knowledge, we are above all capable of development. We can learn ever-increasing humanity if we are prepared to think and feel it, to practice it and repeatedly will it anew. This cannot be forced, it also cannot come from outside, from Nature. This is a product of soul and spiritual work, and comes from within, from the heart.

CHAPTER 10

Meditation and Community Building

Christof Wiechert

There are three areas for development of an inner meditation life: for the personal inner path, for the esoteric enrichment of the professional daily life and for the connection to modern life—to humanity of today. If a person cannot come to terms with these three areas in his life, then he will sooner or later become ill, or become to a degree paralyzed in his life.

So it is no wonder that Rudolf Steiner not only spoke about teaching methods and pedagogy, but also about the spiritual underpinnings of the school. He encouraged the grounding of a community of teachers to support the students and the school. In order to call on the necessary conditions of the collaborative work, he gave a leading thought, a leading imagination. He gave this to the teachers as described in the diary of Caroline von Heydebrand:

> On September 9 at 9am Rudolf Steiner assembled the first Waldorf teachers. He asked them always to remember to work as he had shown them, namely in full consciousness of the reality of the spiritual world. He said: In the evenings before your meditation ask the angels, archangels and archai that they may help you in your work on the following day. In the mornings, after the meditation, you may feel yourself united with the beings of the Third Hierarchy. Then Dr. Steiner walked around the table, shaking hands with each teacher and looking deeply and with moving, utmost earnestness into the eyes of each.[1]

Walter Johannes Stein wrote the following short note into his diary:

> 9am Dr. Steiner asks us, clasping the hand of each teacher in turn, to promise to work together in the way he has shown us: in the evening, before the meditation, ask the angeloi, archangeloi and archai to help in our work on the next day. In the morning, after the meditation, know ourselves united with them.[2]

This took place before the first school day, after a lecture from Steiner on the *Study of Man* (now published as *Foundations of Human Experience*)[3] which looked at the didactic methods and the curriculum in relation to the work of the school.

The event described in these short notes is known as "the vow." Just imagine the deep earnestness that came out of this. This event shows clearly that we are not just dealing with an act of remembrance, as for example once a year at the meeting before school restarts, but with a daily striving for unity with the third hierarchy. It also shows that Rudolf Steiner took it for granted that teachers had a meditative life. The expression "before and after the meditation" clearly indicates this, even more so as at this point in the history of the Waldorf school the so-called teachers' meditations had not yet been given.

Lecture 1 of *The Foundations of Human Experience* now contains a short paragraph, which was not originally recorded by the stenographer and which describes how the beings of the third hierarchy work on the teacher who is striving to approach them.

> Behind each one of us stands his Angel, gently laying his hands on the head of each. This Angel gives you the strength which you need.
>
> Above your heads there sweep the circling Archangels. They carry from one to the other what each has to give to the other. They unite your souls. Thereby you are given the courage of which you stand in need. (Out of this courage the Archangels form a chalice.)
>
> The light of wisdom is given to us by the exalted beings of the Archai, who are not limited to the circling movements, but who, coming forth from primal beginnings (Urbeginnen), manifest themselves and disappear into primal distances (Urfernen). They reveal themselves only in form of a drop (of light) in this place.
>
> (Into the chalice of courage there falls a drop of light, enlightening our times [Zeitenlicht], bestowed by the ruling Spirit of our Age.)[4]

We have a meditation picture in front of us. What does this mean? It wants to stimulate in us the experience that we do not stand alone in our work to support the developing child. When one really works to take this picture into one's own inner world, then strength from the spiritual worlds, whence the children come, will help us. Strength, courage, and light (of wisdom) will strengthen our soul forces.

Let us now consider the following questions: What do strength, courage, and light (of wisdom) signify in our profession? Where are they needed? How can we experience that we need these precise qualities as teachers?

Looking at "strength" leads us straight into the situation of the school movement as we experience it today. The question of life forces in general and the life forces for the teacher in particular lives strongly in our time. Deficiencies arise where teachers have not enough strength to cope with their life and work. It is characteristic for the anthroposophic approach that it does not seek in the physical realm forces that strengthen the physical, but in the realm where the forces live, in the etheric. We can renew our life forces by turning to the etheric. And the path that leads us there is the path of meditation. A peculiar phenomenon of the anthroposophic approach is that we need to invest strength first (in the meditation) in order to receive strength. And here lies the first obstacle on the way to a meditative life that can give us strength, conviction and direction and that could be the starting point for self-development.

The decision to embark on a meditative path is easily taken. We can decide, for example, to read the teachers' meditation once a day (late evening is usually the best time), in a quiet moment that we have to ourselves, to concentrate on it, to speak it as clearly as possible, softly, letting it work on us. We will then experience how internal disturbances assail us, how thoughts and associations start interfering with our mental pictures. We try again, this time by concentrating even harder on the words of the meditation. Depending on our disposition we might well find that we are still not very good at it, but at least we have tried. This in itself will have an effect.

The second major hurdle presents itself as soon as we have made a start. This is faithfulness to ourselves. Out of our own free will we made a start. Nobody can force us, no faculty can dictate it; we could just leave it; it is up to us if we are willing to take this step; nothing will change externally. This freedom, the absence of any obligation, puts our loyalty to our own decision to the test. In this situation we are confronted with the will forces that are available to us. If we are not used to directing our will to an area which is free of causal obligations we will need to make a special effort to adhere to our original decision. In short, there is quite some danger that we might stop before this hurdle and realize to our shame that we have given up meditating without even noticing it. It will help in the beginning if we limit the time set aside for the meditation. Once we have managed a shorter time we can extend it.

We should aim to make a habit of meditative practice—a habit that is indispensable because we have come to love it like an encounter with a friend. If that is achieved the meditation will sooner or later show its effects. According to Rudolf Steiner the effect occurs generally quite soon, but we tend not to notice it. It is like fishing. We have to drag our net through the sea of our experiences now and again in order to see what is in it.

We will attempt to mention some of the effects here, so that we can have an idea of what we have caught in the net of our experience. The first effect is quite mundane. We feel a certain contentment about having set a task for ourselves and having persevered with it. Then we will notice that we are in a better state during our waking life, that we are more "with it." This can go as far as finding ourselves in the right place at the right time to do something, that one we had not thought about before. It is as if we had been led to the place where we were needed. Some things just "fall into place." It is important that we become conscious of these little daily miracles. We will notice that no day will pass without a smaller or greater "miracle." It is like a gentle hint that the practicing person is dwelling with the forces of the spiritual world.[5] (In his lecture "How Do I Find the Christ," Rudolf Steiner presents this exercise in a different context.) We might also find that the feelings which arise out of our daily perceptions are considerably enhanced. Everything that affects us in our thinking, feeling or will might become more intense[6]—a reason to strengthen those even more, as indicated in *A Way of Self-Knowledge*, the sequel to *Knowledge of the Higher Worlds*. We should also be aware that our dream life might undergo a change. We can differentiate more easily if a dream is the after-effect of yesterday's dinner or if something more significant tries to reveal itself.[7]

What strikes us as rather mysterious is that a gift of "courage necessary for our work" is imparted to the faculty of teachers. When and where do we as teachers need courage? At the end of *The Foundations of Human Experience*, Rudolf Steiner speaks of having "courage for the truth," after having encouraged his readers to imbue themselves with the "power of imagination." Could he be speaking about the truths that underlie all visible reality? The truths of the source?

What follows can evoke another question: on the path towards enlivened imagination and creativity we pass through several phases. Our aim is to teach our pupils certain things. The question is how.

Once we have dedicated ourselves to this question an abyss opens in front of us. We don't know how we got there; we can't see our way. We start doubting ourselves. Now the question of courage arises. Should I try to cross this abyss (with uncertain outcome), or do I choose the safe way? We can compare this to the performing artist's courage, which helps him to overcome his stage fright. The greater the art, the greater the stage fright, which may bring a performer close to despair. The teacher-artist also undergoes this kind of process, even if on a smaller scale.

The lectures collected in *Practical Advice to Teachers* deal in detail with the question of courage. There are, of course, other situations where courage is important for the teacher: in Waldorf schools it is, after all, often the case that what is considered the right thing to do is also an unusual thing to do. It is a well-known fact that one has to swim against the current to get to the source. We need the courage of our insight and knowledge.

It is important to keep in mind that, in this case, we are not concerned with an individual path (it is different with the question of strength); we are concerned with a path that passes through the souls of the faculty of teachers. How should we picture this? In the circle of the faculty the "vessel of courage" is formed. It is made up of the qualities that the individual teachers bring to the school through their work. Being aware of this generates courage. It becomes apparent when we feel ourselves as a member of the circle, not as an individual person who happens to be part of the faculty. We feel connected with each other and know that through this connection we are carrying a common responsibility.

This experience makes us realize that the faculty of teachers is more than the totality of its individual members. The faculty is necessary for the work of those higher beings who will, in turn, impart the "drop of light," the decision imbued with wisdom, to the work of the faculty. Many people have experienced this. A difficult decision needs to be taken and the faculty struggles and struggles. Suddenly the solution stands clearly before us. Where does it come from? Did somebody bring it up? Looking back, we realize that it was not one individual person who spoke the enlightening word first, but the solution appeared out of the faculty's collaborative work.

Let us turn again to the triad of forces and look at strength.

In physics, we would call it energy, a word which is, however, also used in connection with human beings: I am full of energy; somebody works energetically. But we also hear the opposite: my batteries are drained; I need to recharge my batteries. The concept of strength, of energy seems to be connected with the physical realm (just as healing is often seen as repair work).

In everyday language, these expressions usually refer to what one experiences as energy or the lack of it. What is meant here by strength? By energy? From research on the physical resilience of human beings we have long known that the actual point of complete physical exhaustion—certainly for us in the Western world—lies considerably further away than we think.[8] What lies much closer is our *feeling* of being exhausted. This means that the question of forces or of strength belongs to the soul realm. In order to understand strength the way Rudolf Steiner explains it we have to look for the place where the body is given strength out of the soul-spiritual realm. This is essential and it is, for education as well as for our own self-knowledge, the key to understanding lecture 3 of *The Foundations of Human Experience*.

> When viewed broadly, what is the significance of the Law of Conservation of Energy for our civilization? It is the main hurdle to understanding the human being at all. When we believe that forces are never created, we can no longer achieve an understanding of true human nature. We can find the true essence of humanity in the very fact that through human beings new forces are continually created. In the world in which we live, human beings are the only beings in whom new forces and, as we will hear later, even new matter, are formed. However, because the current world view is incapable of accepting thoughts through which we can fully recognize the human being, people come along with this Law of Conservation of Energy. In a certain sense this law disturbs nothing if we look only at the other kingdoms of nature—the mineral, plant and animal kingdoms—but it immediately destroys all real understanding when we attempt to get close to human nature.[9]

An increase in force or strength is not a material but a soul-spiritual process. Rudolf Steiner once put it this way: "Somebody who is enthused cannot be tired." We know this from our own experience. If we are really enthusiastic about something we will have strength.

On our search for the source of strength we have to look at what it is that inspires enthusiasm. We are looking for renewable enthusiasm, not for one-off experiences. But where do we find this sustained enthusiasm?

In lecture 2 of *The Foundations of Human Experience*, Rudolf Steiner explains the foundation of our thinking and will: our thinking is of a pictorial nature and therefore not existential; it is appearance, not reality. Our will, in contrast, is willingness to act, is real, it exists. (It is on this that Rudolf Steiner bases his criticism of the Cogito of Descartes). The appearance he calls sub-real, the will potential which is seed, which is still forming, he calls super-real. One can say that these are two different worlds. By connecting these two poles we find what is new. In other words: Can mental pictures and thoughts be enlivened from within so that something living arises out of them? Can we enliven a thought to such an extent that its shadow existence fades away and something real emerges? Again, life itself provides the answer. "Love" is just a word for some people, for others it conveys a whole world of reality, and the same applies to words like "child" or "peace." These terms can be filled with meaning, when they refer to (a part of) our existence. It is more difficult with words like "soul" or "spirit." This is where anthroposophy comes in, because it gives us living seeds in the realm of thinking, which, if used in the right way, will result not in mere appearance but in an actual force. We are not talking just about meditating here, but about studying. By studying we mean a process of internalization and strengthening of thought. This means that we don't absorb content on which we can reflect without involving ourselves. It is this process of internalization that makes us autonomous human beings. And this process is today, a hundred years after the advent of anthroposophy, of great significance: will we succeed in becoming autonomous human beings with the help of anthroposophy? If we do, anthroposophy will become a new moral force in us. Then we will invalidate Mayer's Law of Conservation of Energy[10]: we will have entered new territory.

For most people brought up in the late twentieth century, this is not a self-evident path. It is therefore very important that the school's faculty members help each other to find it. The study of anthroposophy is, after all, a path of becoming conscious of what one really thinks and could do. It is now our task to find the right form for this. Experiencing this through talking together about how to interpret part of a lecture, or discussing with others the fact that we still find a train of thought difficult, or that we have just found a way to grasp a particular idea, seems more appropriate for our faculty meetings today than listening to the revealed wisdom of one colleague who "knows it all." We are touching here on the social possibilities within the faculty that can either hinder or support our work.[11]

Rudolf Steiner, in any case, emphatically expressed his opinion that in the faculty meeting "there is study, steady continual study."[12] He explicitly describes this path for the circle of teachers (Rudolf Steiner rarely gives such direct guidelines because of the importance he attaches to the individual's own search). We are referring here to a paragraph in lecture 3 of *Meditatively Acquired Knowledge of Man* which can be applied to all his observations about knowledge of the human being:

> He has to absorb the knowledge of the human being, to understand knowledge of the human being through meditation, to remember this knowledge of the human being: then remembering will come to life. It is not an ordinary remembering, but a remembering which initiates new, inner impulses out of itself. The remembering comes flowing out of the fountain of spiritual life, and into our outer work is transferred what follows as the third step: after meditative understanding follows creating, creative remembering, which is at the same time an absorbing from the spiritual world.[13]

The task is to inform and help oneself through this outline of the working process. We need courage in relation to somebody or something else. I enter into a relationship with the world or with another person or with a cause, and for this I need a certain degree of courage. Courage, therefore, has not just to do with me individually but with my environment also. This environment—and this can be understood at a physical as well as at a soul level—can give me courage, a gesture that comes toward me from without. The opposite of courage is fear. Fear can be inside me, but it can also be evoked in me through my environment. Fear is a poor counselor, says the proverb. What has this got to do with the work of the teacher?

If we see the work of the teacher in the wider sense, as it is described in the opening words of *The Foundations of Human Experience*, and if we compare these with the words at the end of the same lecture course, we arrive at an interesting image. This image might help us to come to an understanding of the word "courage" in the educational context.

The opening sentence of lecture 1 of *The Foundations of Human Experience* is extraordinary because it leads us from the soul level of the teacher's activity (intellect, feeling) straight to the moral and spiritual level: "We can accomplish our work only if we do not see it as simply a matter of intellect or feeling, but, in the highest sense, as a moral spiritual task."[14] The moral-spiritual element can only exist if the soul strives toward it, if it takes responsibility for its deeds and actions. We all know the difference between pondering something in our thoughts, with feeling, between having an opinion, for example, or arguing a point, even teaching something, and taking responsibility for our actions. If we take responsibility we involve ourselves, we can't let go of it in the evening, when we have made a connection. We need courage for life itself and courage for the responsibility, especially as teachers, because the children also occupy our mind in the evening.

At the very end of *The Foundations of Human Experience* this motif appears again in a different form, when the threefold categorical imperative of the art of education is pronounced: imbue yourself with the power of imagination, have courage for the truth, sharpen your feeling for responsibility of soul.

The marriage of courage and imaginative power in this context seems unusual. At the end of the book we find the following paragraph:

> During the second half of the nineteenth century, people understood this spirit [of education] in a masked form. Then, people were cowardly about the life of the soul and complained about whatever entered the human soul through the direct path of imagination, because they believed that if they accepted imagination, they would fall directly into the arms of untruthfulness. People did not have the courage for independence, for freedom in their thinking and, at the same time, for a marriage to truth instead of lies. People feared freedom in thinking because they believed they would immediately take lies into the soul. To what I just said—that is, filling their lessons with imagination—teachers must add courage for the truth. Without this courage for truth, teachers will achieve nothing with the will in teaching, especially with the older children. We must join what develops as courage for truth with a strong sense of responsibility toward truth.[15]

How deeply are the nineteenth-century thinking habits still ingrained in our educational work? Everybody is still afraid of using their power of imagination. It is like walking on ice if one relies on these forces during lessons. People prefer to hold fast to a well-prepared lesson plan. Books, methods, printed lesson aids—they are all valuable, but they cannot replace a teacher who draws on his free imaginative creativity. Another problem of our time is the constant use of photocopies. We can say without exaggerating that educational work today is more often determined by the photocopier or the copies than by the subject and the state of the class.

This also brings us to the question of courage.

Can I put together creatively what I am going to teach so that it is *my* achievement, *my* way to the students, and can I be unique and original without violating the truth? When Rudolf Steiner looked back after the first years of Waldorf education he saw many things that were worthy of praise, many things that had considerably improved in the educational work. Nevertheless, he asked for one thing: Could the teachers stand in front of the class, speaking freely, without having recourse to notes or a book in their hand?[16] One could argue, of course, that times have changed and these things are not important any more. But one could also ask oneself if Rudolf Steiner was not alluding in his humble request to the archetype of the free human being. This free human being should be visible to the students, every day, apparent also in details such as the one just described.

We have looked at the question of courage in the teacher's inner relationship with his pupils at a sense-perceptible level. There is something else that needs courage.

All educational methods worldwide are based on the principle that one can only educate others if one educates oneself, even if people have not been consciously aware of this principle for a long time.

Anthroposophy can also be described as a path of self-education. Because we are constantly widening our horizon through anthroposophy, we tend to forget that anthroposophy is a path to self-knowledge. The work of the teacher, if rightly understood, is a help in this respect. If we are not aware of ourselves, we cannot see where we have to change in order to improve our teaching or our relationship with pupils. In other words, teaching can accelerate the process of gaining self-knowledge. If we do not heed the question of self-knowledge then we cease to inquire how *we affect things,* instead asking what our colleagues or students should do differently. Not looking at ourselves will sooner or later lead into crises.

The step in the direction of self-knowledge, toward asking myself how I can change to become a better teacher, needs courage. This is the inner aspect of courage: working on myself.

CHAPTER 11

Two Meditations for Teachers

Christof Wiechert

During our daily work an avalanche of impressions comes towards us; impressions to which we react in our thinking, feeling, and will. Depending on circumstances we find that a day was successful if we have managed to achieve a balance between these impressions and our reactions. Were we in control, or did we end up in a state of breathlessness?

We may feel that we need an inner counterpoint, an inner perception that helps us keep this balance. Each of us will try to find this balance in the way that best suits us. Rudolf Steiner created three ways to help Waldorf teachers find the inner space that is particularly necessary for the work of educators.

The first, as discussed in Chapter 10, is the teacher's imagination.[1] It is based on the already mentioned aspects for community building in the form of an inner reverence towards the angel realm of the third hierarchy (angels, archangels, and archai). The others are the two teacher's meditations.

The first of these meditations was given to the teachers by Rudolf Steiner on September 30, 1919, shortly after the first Waldorf school had opened its doors. They received the second meditation after a short lecture course given in autumn 1923, now published under the title *Deeper Insights into Education*.[2]

The same applies to these meditations as to any other—to only work with these meditations if it comes from a heartfelt wish to do so. Therefore, the meditations are taken care of by someone in the faculty, who can pass them on to those who wish to work with them. A colleague who changes to a different job can, out of respect for the meaning of the meditations and from their own free will, hand the meditations back to this teacher in charge. The meditations were given especially to nourish educational work and they need to be held consciously in this context. They belong to the spiritual substance of the Waldorf school, and as with every spiritual substance, should be looked after in the realm they belong in order to distribute the blessing of the verses.

This applies even more today as, given the expiration of the copyright of Steiner's works, the meditations have been published openly.[3] During the preparation of the Kolisko 2006 conferences, we made the decision, after much thought and discussion, to include the Imagination and meditations in this book. This was a result of having been asked about this inner path of the teacher many times over the last years. At the same time we hope to contribute to a new consciousness of the preconditions of care needed for these mediations by having done so.

The Imagination and meditations have an inherent soul-spiritual intimacy to which the individual human being can find access. They need to be protected by outer sheaths, even though we live in a time that is generally without protective sheaths. It is up to the individual to find out for him- or herself how this can be achieved. We can, however, talk about the meditative contents in the intimate and protected environment of the faculty meeting. We can ask how one works with these verses, and discuss their meaning and usage, and the individual is left in freedom as to how he or she approaches the content. The meditations can be entrusted to people who are familiar with the path of anthroposophy. The decision about who is to receive them should not lie solely with one person. It seems right that those colleagues receive them who are willing to take on responsibility within the school. It is a question of tact, to feel the right time to let new colleagues know about the meditations, doing this in such a way that leaves them free to take them up or not. On the other hand, it is important that all colleagues see the importance and relevance of this inner path for the professional work.

One can inform new colleagues about the meditations and let them know that when they feel ready, they can have more information about them. The protection, which we have spoken of above, does not need to prevent there being an openness about these things. Both teacher meditations are word meditations. When the words of the meditations can live in the soul life and be articulated, something seed-like which lies within the words, can be embraced through thought and inner activity.

One could say that by using one, the other, or both meditations, one is in conversation with the soul. How this can be achieved is up to each person: it is a gift, for the deep self to find. Rudolf Steiner gave different indications in relation to the being of the Meditations: transform knowledge through devotion or contemplative reflection or let it live in thinking or let the word content resound through the soul, let it live in the soul or listen inwardly to the words, to hear inwardly what certain thoughts, words and sense perceptions want to say. The meditative exactness calls on a soul attitude, which allows the veneration towards the reality of the Spirit and devotion to the smallest details and greater aspects. The first meditation is more directed in relation to the world of the human being, and encourages the search for the illumination of teaching. The second has a focus, in contrast, to the higher and lower worlds, the spiritual and earthly worlds, and seeks to bring the experience of the relationship of the higher self of the teacher to that of the being of the students entrusted to him, to a higher consciousness.

First Teacher's Meditation

In the semblance of sense being
There lives the spirit's will,
Giving itself as wisdom's light
And concealing inner strength.

In the "I" of one's own being
There shines forth human will,
As thinking's revelation,
Supporting itself on its own strength;

And its own strength united
With world wisdom's light
Powerfully in the Self:

Forms me, as I turn toward
The heights divine and seek
Powers of enlightenment.

Second Teacher's Meditation

Spiritual looking,
Turn inwards, perceiving;
Touch the soul's tender being;
In the spirit's intuitive looking,
In the soul's heart-felt apprehending
Consciousness Being weaves itself;
Consciousness, which from the upper
And the lower of man's being,
Binds the brightness of worlds
To the darkness of earth.

Spiritual looking,
Hearts' apprehending,
Perceive and grasp
In man's inner being,
Weaving brightness of worlds
Within the sway of earth's darkness:
My own
Human formative force
Engendering
Strength creating
Will-bearing Self.

The outer world surrounds us, we are standing in it, it makes its demands on us, in short, we devote ourselves wholly to it. The inner world has to be established first through meditation and in complete independence from the outer world. We can put it even more strongly: it should not be mixed up with the ordinary physical world, if it is ever to reveal its own power. What does this mean in practice?

It means that for our meditative life, we have to create a free space into which our ordinary life cannot intrude: a moment of peace, of solitude, established by me, during which I can turn my thoughts to my chosen object, without disturbance from outside. This object could, for example, be the content of the first meditation. Many find that the end of the day, when all tasks of the day have been dealt with, is a suitable moment. Others prefer the beginning of the day, before they start their daily work. Others, again, find it best to use both times. Whichever time one chooses, creating this free space is essential.

Once one has created it one notices that it is necessary to defend it: there will always be reasons to give it up because there are more urgent things to do.

How can this moment of inner peace be achieved? It is best if one tries to create it oneself. It is important that everything that moves in our soul from our day's work can fade away. We can achieve this by looking at a picture or by concentrating on a particular thought, which has an inner meaning for us. We can also try to become inwardly completely calm. Into this calmness, into this peacefulness, one can then speak for oneself the words of the teachers' meditation and leave them to resound within.

If one has decided to establish this moment of inner peace in the evening, following it with a review of the past day is recommended. Steiner points out on many occasions how important this daily review is: in reverse order, starting from the end of the day, one lets the images of the day pass before one's inner eye. Only the images. Not the thoughts and emotions that went with them. One should observe oneself while one goes back through the day. If one has developed a certain aptitude with this one can move to another level and let a particular part of the day, moment for moment, pass before one's soul in reverse order. The more detailed the better.

If one chooses the beginning of the day for these exercises it has a special effect on the soul in anticipation of the coming day. What are my tasks, what will be expected of me and my work? It is like a survey of the future, a preparation that comes out of the ego, short but intense. The review breaks through the earthly continuation of time; the preview goes along with it.

We need to emphasize that these exercises have to become habit. In the same way as it is usually not easy for an adult to change established habits it will not be easy to establish a completely new habit, free from all daily obligations, out of sheer effort of will. For this reason, one should not set one's expectations too high to begin with. It is important to keep a balance between one's ambitions and what one can realistically achieve.

One thing is certain, however: the more accomplished we become at having an active inner life, the more strength we develop for meeting the daily challenges of the world.

CHAPTER 12

The Seven Virtues of the Art of Teaching

Christof Wiechert

When Rudolf Steiner established his educational approach with the lectures collected in *The Foundations of Human Experience* (*Study of Man*), *Practical Advice to Teachers*, and *Discussions with Teachers*, he gave the first Waldorf teachers seven virtues to accompany them on their professional path. In this chapter I will examine Rudolf Steiner's seven virtues from a skills perspective.

Three are:

> Need for imagination, sense of truth, feeling of responsibility; these are the three forces which represent the nerve fibers of education. And any person who intends to make education his own should preface it with the motto: imbue yourself with imagination, have courage for the truth, and sharpen your feeling for responsibility of soul…
>
> Allow me to close these observations today by referring once more to what I wanted to commend to you, which is that you should adhere to four things:…[1]

And four are as follows:

> This is the first: the teacher should be a person who exercises initiative both in great and small matters….
>
> This is the second: the teacher should be a person who is interested in all worldly and human existence….
>
> And the third is: the teacher should be a person who never compromises inwardly with untruth…. And then [a fourth is] something which is easier said than done, but which is also a golden rule for the teaching profession: the teacher must not wither and go stale. A mood of soul which is fresh and unspoilt![2]

The first noticeable feature here is the fact that there is a structure. We might almost experience it in a runic way; first mention is made of three abilities and then later, at the final conclusion, of four. What do the "three" and "four" signify in this context? In observing the human being, when do we focus on the three and when on the four? The three always rule when we are dealing with capacities of the soul. If the soul comes to expression in conjunction with our physical body, we are dealing with the four.

If we consider "imbue yourself with imagination," "have courage for the truth," and "sharpen your feeling for responsibility of soul," we experience that thinking, feeling, and the will are only indirectly addressed. That begins to change as soon as we think of three qualities—as expressed in Goethe's fairy tale—which represent an important factor in the nurture of human development: wisdom, beauty and strength. Beauty, wisdom, and strength are mentioned in *Foundations of Human Experience* in that order.

If we look at the verbs used above, we can experience two things: the will element is emphasized when we imbue something, when we display courage and hone responsibility. We are not told "develop yourself," but to have these abilities is clearly a prerequisite; then they only need to be activated. When we engage these three abilities, our soul develops wisdom, beauty, and strength. Then we experience development. And that is what is actually perceived by the child in the teacher: the developing human being. Children will happily accept that.

There is another way in which we can penetrate the mystery of the three: by asking ourselves whether it is really these three characteristics that determine whether a teacher becomes truly skilled. We can also ask how Christ's saying "I am the Way, the Truth and the Life" can be applied to teaching.

Every teacher knows the search for the right, effective, and inspiring way in education. It is a question of methodology, of being inventive in response to the situation. Everyone knows that in education, the "how" is of immense importance, and I can only find the way if the subject I am teaching is of profound interest to me. The teacher will only find the way if he loves his material, if he can sanctify it and raise it from the mundane. That is what constantly renews teaching, even if the material remains the same. This is the sphere in which the forces in both teacher and child are revitalized.

How does the teacher relate to truth? How do we act in response to our true selves? Do we have the courage to face up to our own truth? What am I capable of, what am I not? Where and when am I someone different to the real me when I am with students or fellow teachers? When in my contact with my students am I truly driven to understand and help them? Or is my wish to help others restricted by my own ideas of right and wrong? This sphere represents the true application of what I have learned in my effort to understand the foundations of human experience. If we cultivate such an aspiration, something in us combats the naked spirit of our personality.

How should we understand life in this context? Is teaching a nine-to-five job, or am I involved to a far greater extent than I thought? When people say that teaching cannot simply be approached in an intellectually complacent way, but must be understood in a spiritual and moral context, this means no more and no less than taking and carrying responsibility for everything which this profession involves. And is that not our attitude to life? Teaching is a responsibility that corresponds to our responsibility toward life (that is, toward our fellow human beings).

We begin to fathom that these three competencies have their source in a mighty origin. If wisdom, beauty and strength are concepts originating in a mystery tradition in which these powers were developed purely for the soul, we can experience their ordinary reflection in science, art, and religion.[3]

With art and science, the relationship is easy to comprehend. The question is whether "sharpen your feeling for responsibility of soul" bears the religious element within it. What is a feeling of responsibility in the soul? Surely the fact that I can never be indifferent toward my fellow human beings—in this context the pupils. Is it not a religious attitude to know our fellow human beings and to take responsibility in the soul sphere?

Every student can thus have the (unconscious) confidence that there will be a true interest shown in him.

We will now turn to the fourth virtue. In a lecture Steiner reflected on a passage in his book *Theosophy*:[4]

> When I wrote my book Theosophy, I could not simply note the sequence physical body, etheric body, astral body, ego—as we can summarize it if the subject has already been dealt with and inwardly comprehended. I had to proceed in triads. Physical body, etheric body, sentient body: first triad. Then the interlinked triad: sentient soul, intellectual soul, consciousness soul. Then the associated triad: spirit self, life spirit, spirit man. Three times three, interlinked, producing seven. But this seven is an interlinked three times three. And the four, which is actually really only a secondary number, does not emerge until we look at the current stage of human development.

This is depicted as follows in *Theosophy*:[5]

1	Physical body	1			
2	Etheric body	2			
3	Sentient body	3	Sentient soul	4
		4	Intellectual soul	5
7	Spirit self	5	Consciousness soul	6
8	Life spirit	6			
9	Spirit man	7			

This diagram not only gives us an insight into the incredibly alive process of thinking in Rudolf Steiner's work but also shows clearly how the three is active in the creative principle, the principle of what is still developing: a cosmic process. The four, by contrast, is something that is complete in its development. When everything already exists, has been created, understood—then the four appears, which is actually a secondary number, that is 2 times 2.

This also applies to the four temperaments. They are produced from the fourfold constitution and enable a development of the ego forces. We must work on our temperament with our "I" to avoid it becoming an obstacle. The temperament must be "elevated" so that it can be used appropriately as the self determines, transformed to become something we can utilize. The following sequence gives us some idea of the transition:

Choleric	: tyrant	→	initiative
Sanguine	: scattered	→	interest
Phlegmatic	: inertia	→	loyalty (no compromise)
Melancholic	: going stale	→	staying fresh

In this way we can transform what is rooted in our body. Then we can engage the four qualities.

Is there another way of looking at the figure seven? Is there a different relationship? Are we simply dealing with three plus four, or is there an internal connection? Let us look at the three and the four as if they really were seven. Then we get the following (the seven qualities are only listed as keywords for the sake of clarity):

1. Imaginative ability
2. Sense of truth
3. Responsibility
4. Initiative
5. Interest
6. No compromise
7. Staying fresh

If we now compare these qualities with one another, the following emerges:

1 ↔ 7 : Without imagination we go stale

2 ↔ 6 : The sense of truth gives us strength not to make compromises

3 ↔ 5 : Feeling of responsibility wakens interest, interest wakens responsibility

4 : In the middle, the power of the ego, initiative: the origin of everything that makes us a developing human being

The proactive human being can take initiative either on his own behalf or for a cause. The more he succeeds in becoming active for a cause the more beneficial the social effect of his action will be. His initiative becomes a force which does not serve the individual person but has a community-enhancing effect. We approach the way of working of the spirit of our age: "When human beings seek freedom without egotism, when freedom for them turns into pure love for the action to be performed, then they have the opportunity to draw near to Michael."[6]

Now most people will reject the suggestion that they act out of egotism. In our consciousness we "of course" act altruistically as the need arises; for on earth we live between appearance and reality. Step by step we must free ourselves from appearances, because our consciousness is at first based on the realm of illusion. It takes a long time and needs a lot of life experience until our consciousness can meet reality and others can live in a period after consciousness.

CHAPTER 13

What Helps in Daily Practice?

Christof Wiechert

For diverse reasons the teaching profession is not an easy one nowadays. Some of the reasons for this are socially determined (pressure of time, complex life circumstances, the organizational complexity of schools, high demands, high expectations, social dynamics, financial pressure…) and some lie in teachers' personal lives.

In relation to the latter it is a fact that not every teacher can look back on happy schooldays. *The following exercise shows how significant this fact is.*

Without pondering on it for too long, try recalling your own school days. Whatever you may remember, one thing is certain: the memories will be easily accessible, there's no need to think too long and hard to recall them. They are close to the surface of awareness. It therefore seems likely that such memories, even if from a long time back, somehow color our daily life. Is the basic tone more sunny or cloudy? It's worth discovering this for oneself. The memories, even if they have slumbered for years, are there, and it is important to clarify for oneself what sort of tinge came to color the soul as a result. Memories are deeply connected with our ego, but where they enter the soul they, to some degree, affect our quality of life.

(Charles Dickens recorded this fact in inimitable fashion in the last of his four Christmas stories. While the first became world famous, the other three remained almost unknown. The last of these, *The Haunted Man*, describes how someone is deprived of the sad memories of his youth by a seductive spirit, acting with supposed good intentions. Through the loss of these treasures of memory, however, he falls prey to appalling changes in his character. Fortunately, though, it is a Christmas story, and at the critical moment everything comes right again through the love of a young woman. The message is summed up in the phrase "God, keep my memory green!")[1]

Relationship to the Class

How do I relate to a class, how do I conduct myself? Am I only happy and in harmony with myself when the pupils do exactly as I say? Can I cope when they do exactly the opposite of what I want? Can I retain my equanimity if children are badly behaved or inattentive? Can I maintain the same state of soul when all around me things are happening that are not what I wished and hoped for? How often do I overreact? Am I aware of doing this, or is my state such that I hardly even notice this?

Someone who is only happy when pupils are "good" is always tense. How long will this last? Those who have adopted this frame of mind are in danger of trying to use their will to dominate pupils. There will be an undertow of tension in the class, even if everything is outwardly lovely. We often notice that classes managed in this way exhale when specialty teachers step in, which also gives rise to problems. The first thing a new teacher needs to acquire is a sunny disposition which he can maintain whatever the situation in the class. Getting children to be good cannot be our main goal!

Here's an example: a teacher in a fifth-grade class places a great deal of importance on teaching the children some aspects of grammar, but her pupils simply don't get it. They are full of good will but unfortunately don't understand. The teacher is almost in despair. She decides on the spur of the moment to change the subject, and allow the children to cheerfully forget about it. We'll try again next main lesson, she thinks. Such a decision may not be rational, but it is courageous. She saves the mood, and who knows what the next main lesson will bring? We know that there is no point in moral indignation directed at pupils if they do not understand something.

Another example: in seventh grade, once more grammar, relating to compound sentences. A group of girls has "decided" not to understand ("Why do we have to learn this?"). If one isn't careful this becomes a power struggle or a judgment that they are just being obstinate. But in agreement with the parents one could, instead, say something like: "Let's sit down together after school, have a cup of tea, and see if we can't sort this out. And behold, in a relaxed mood things fall into place and it seems easy to make the subject comprehensible. The only problem is that after a few such sessions, they won't want to give up this special privilege.

It is natural that being unable to do something or other leads to nervousness in the teacher. We should be aware of this danger in advance, and not let such a mood engulf us. Nevertheless, this latent pressure arising from children not being able to do what I want is a real threat to the mood of teaching. One should take preventive measures!

These may seem small matters, but such small details of teaching have an effect on the health of both class and teacher.

Manner of Discipline

Another thing that contributes to a healthy atmosphere in the class is the way in which the teacher handles discipline. This is an important indicator of the teacher's position in the class. It is well known that bad behavior by the children will easily cause us displeasure. That's the first trap one can fall into as teacher. Acts worthy of reprimand should not affect what the teacher feels. She should remain free of them. This is easy to say but harder to do. Then one should also hold fast to the principle given by Rudolf Steiner to judge the deed but not the doer (they are children after all).

The next thing is to try to think up something original as instructive discipline. It is an enormous contribution to the life of the class if one can avoid fixed punishments such as copying a text, staying behind after school or sending children out of the classroom. This is an area in which one can directly monitor one's own powers of invention and imagination.

Here is an example:

A fifth grade was invaded by a chewing-gum craze. The teacher wondered what to do about it. He entered into the phenomenon and found the following. Those who chew gum stimulate all the secretions in the mouth which are necessary for breaking down food. Saliva starts flowing. Not just in the mouth but also in the stomach, secretions start which prepare for the food that is coming. But in this case nothing comes. So now the teacher told his pupils the following:

> Dear children, listen to me for a moment. Imagine you are at home, waiting for a friend to come. You're going to play together and eat something too. Your mother is making a special meal for you both, lovingly cooking a wonderful meal. But your friend doesn't turn up, without even telling you beforehand. How do you feel? A bit empty, perhaps a little disillusioned? That's what your stomach feels like when you chew gum.

Whether or not this solves the problem is not important. This deed has exposed the actual moral situation. In this case, in fact, the chewing gum habit remained. Then the teacher looked closely at a pack of gum and saw in the list of ingredients a raft of chemicals, and that gave him another idea. He told the children that if he caught anyone chewing gum during lessons they would have to learn the list of ingredients on the pack by the following morning. Then he read out all the ingredients, and this did actually help.

Another example. A tenth-grade boy was being quite impossible in a eurythmy lesson. The teacher's patience snapped and she asked him: "Do you know how hard it is to teach eurythmy? Next time you will take over half the lesson. You will teach eurythmy, for exactly 25 minutes!" It turned into a wonderful, unforgettable eurythmy lesson. From then on the student was fully involved.

A misdeed discovered can also lead to progress for a pupil and the class, to a breakthrough—although only if the teacher keeps her head. For instance, word reached the teacher that a pupil had been stealing from a local shop. The teacher took the offending pupil aside and asked him about it. After hesitating he admitted it. The teacher then went to the shop and talked to the owner, and they agreed that the boy would help in the shop for a few afternoons. He overcame his shame and did this, and a very warm relationship developed between the student and the shop owner ("I was young myself once"). One will often find that a conversation with the parents is necessary in such cases to put the situation in perspective and not subject the child to excessively heavy pressure.

Temperament and Life Quality

Understanding temperament is the same for the quality of life in a class as air is for breathing. We can understand one another or come up against an invisible wall that blocks the way. Understanding begins when we know our own temperament. We have all listened to discussions about a class in educational faculty meetings. The teacher is keen to stress to the faculty that he has a choleric class.

Those listening, though, can have the quiet suspicion that he is talking about himself....

One should know one's own temperament and try to balance any one-sidedness. How do I find out my temperament? There are many ways. I can picture my own physical form, for instance, and ask what it tells me. Am I tall and slim, or more compact? How do I relate to gravity—is this straightforward, or do I need to keep overcoming myself? I can also ask what I am *not*. Is my handwriting loose-knit or compact? Is it large or small, angular or rounded? These simple indicators can tell me a lot. A more subtle path is to visualize how colleagues or parents react to me. Do the same communication difficulties continually surface?

With adults we need to remember that the basic temperament can manifest differently in thinking, feeling, and will. Someone can be choleric in his willing, sanguine in his thinking, and melancholic in his feeling life. A tall, slender colleague may be completely sanguine in nature, but nevertheless a choleric thinker. A monochromatic temperament is unusual in adults, although a dominant temperament is very much the norm. Knowing our own temperament helps us address the children in the temperaments that correspond to them.

A related question is: How inwardly flexible am I? Inner flexibility is a great virtue in working with the community of pupils (unless it leads to arbitrariness and superficiality). How can one manage this? The following self-questions can help: How stuck am I in my habits? Do I suffer emotionally or physically if something disturbs my habit life? Or do I have the habit of having no habits?

We all know that a teacher who blows with every wind will have as much difficulty with the children as one who sticks inflexibly to his own habits and ideas. Let us examine the life of habits from the perspective of the *Study of Man*. Habits "live" in the etheric body. This body of forces has in thinking an aspect accessible to the ego and consciousness. It also has an aspect that is not accessible to the ego and consciousness, the life functions autonomously managed by the etheric body. Between these, in a transitional sphere, dwell the habits. They are accessible to awareness, but not without effort. Strong participation by the ego is needed to access habits. Changing a habit is therefore something that does not come easily, and for some temperaments this is almost impossible. To be able to penetrate this realm with the ego is a very helpful capacity for teachers. We work on our inner flexibility when we try to change a habit. The smaller and simpler the habits, the greater is the effect. As a consequence one experiences reinvigoration and increase in strength. The ego reaches a part of the body which it previously only seldom entered.[2]

CHAPTER 14

How Long to Work with a Class as a Class Teacher?

Christof Wiechert

From the beginning, Waldorf education was based on the principle that the class teacher should move up with the class from grade one through grade eight. Initially this was so self-evident that it is not simple to find a clear statement about this in Steiner's writings on education. I will quote two brief remarks that can stand for others. The first is remarkable because of its open-ended formulation:

> Nothing is more useful and fruitful in teaching than giving something to children pictorially between the ages of 7 and 8; and then later, perhaps at age 13 or 14, returning to it in some form. That is why we try in the Waldorf School to keep children with the same teacher for as long as possible. When they come to school at age seven the children are entrusted to a teacher who, as far as possible, accompanies them through the years.[1]

At the end of lecture 11 of *Study of Man*, Steiner speaks of how the teacher can balance out one-sided tendencies in a class community over the years:

> You see, that's also why it is so important to keep the same pupils through all the [elementary and middle] school years, and that is why it is so crazy to hand pupils on to a new teacher each year.[2]

Today this approach is no longer so self-evident, and people ask whether such a demand can still apply. (I am leaving aside superficial objections, such as "What happens if a teacher doesn't like a child in the class?") The following considerations may be helpful in assessing how long a class teacher should stay with a class:

It is clear that this wish of Steiner's has many levels. The most important is that the teacher also develops by moving up with the children through the years. This ensures that teaching is continually new for the teacher, both as regards subject matter and the changing situation. The teacher grows too. He changes his skills not only through the changing curriculum, but also becomes a different person, for the first grade requires a quite different stance from the fourth, sixth, or eighth grade.

For the children, this unconscious experience of the teacher's capacity to change is enormously significant. One need only think of how the tone of address has to change as the children grow older. Just think of how one meets a sixth grade, compared to how one met them two years previously. It is this capacity to change which we must examine. If things no longer work in seventh and eighth grade, this has more to do with the teacher's capacity to change than his competence. For competence is generally held to mean "specialist teaching skills." The necessary specialist knowledge grows through the years, but the class teacher remains a generalist.

The concept of middle school really has to do with the teacher's capacity to transform. It is at the middle school age that we should avoid teaching according to specialization. At this age the educational direction changes to pave the way towards puberty. Steiner's statements about this age are quite unmistakable:

> And just as soul teething shows itself in the first school years in the capacity for learning to read and write, so all imaginative activity, imbued with inner warmth, announces everything which the soul develops at the end of the elementary school years from age twelve, thirteen, fourteen and fifteen onward... The power of imagination is something we must appeal to particularly in the last years of elementary school. **Whereas much more can be expected of the child when it enters elementary school at age seven, in terms of developing the intellect through reading and writing, we cannot afford to fail imbuing with imagination the incipient power of judgment that slowly matures from age twelve.** [Emphasis added.]
>
> The teacher must keep the teaching material alive within himself, must permeate it with imagination. One cannot do this except by penetrating it with feeling will.... What must be enhanced in the last years of elementary school, and is of very special importance, is the social interaction, the whole harmonious community between the teacher and the pupils.[3]

It seems to me that this is the only passage in which Steiner links the demand to keep imagination alive—which he calls the pedagogical imperative—with a remark that those who are not minded to develop this should seek another profession. He thus stresses the vital importance particularly of middle school education.

It may be that this remark corresponds to the fact that the activity of imagination needs to be properly understood and newly grasped. But in this activity of imagination we also have a quality that is very close to the capacity for self-transformation. If we now examine this polarity between the early grades and middle school, then we sees the range of work which the class teacher has to undertake. Those who wish to do justice to this, need to be able to change.

Now a remarkable fact exists. In economic life, in industry and professional life in general, people speak a great deal about flexibility. Alongside social abilities, flexibility is nowadays counted amongst the most important skills. One needs to be able to cope with change, reorganization, new tasks. There is no longer such a thing as a job for life, and so the capacity to adapt and change is needed.

At the same time however, we know how difficult this is. Anyone who isn't distinctly sanguine finds it hard to change and be flexible. Why is this? Rudolf Steiner characterized the etheric body as the habit body. Without a certain fixed basis of habits we would scarcely be able to cope with life. Every person needs habitual ways of acting, and as he matures acquires habits of feeling, of thought, and of speech. But the question is how fixed these are. Can we discern them when we examine ourselves? Can we scrutinize our habits without prejudice? Can we, when we do this, change a habit?

Here we enter an important realm of self-education, which for the teacher above all can be decisive for success or tragedy in her interaction with the developing children in her class. Someone can be a good teacher, but if she does not change her habits in the natural course of the children's change and development, then suddenly things don't work anymore. The symbiosis that previously functioned with the class breaks down, the teacher doesn't understand what is wrong, doubts herself, is in danger of emotional hardening and external projection of blame—for one wishes to understand what is wrong but cannot find the reason in oneself.

A teacher can expose her lack of capacity for change in how she addresses the class. Someone who greets the children in the mornings in fourth grade in the same way she did in grades one and two, fixes habits in herself and the class community which are binding rather than freeing. Specialist teachers are the first to feel this. They meet a difficult reception in the class, for these habits are like a defense that is hard to overcome.

This is indeed a complex reality, for naturally a class teacher must develop good habits in a class community. But not habits that create dependency. How can one distinguish between these? The difference lies in whether the teacher's habits are freely willed by her, or whether they arise unconsciously. The difference is scarcely perceptible to external view, but all the greater is the difference of effect.

The habit body, the etheric body, has a certain degree of flexibility depending on temperament, constitution, and education. This mobility shows itself in the soul forces, in thinking, feeling and willing, and their expressions. We won't go far wrong in assuming that today's circumstances inhibit the etheric body's mobility. One can check this in oneself, for instance by seeing to what extent one depends on a lesson running exactly as one pictured it. If a disruption occurs, how disconcerted am I?

This is the central question when it comes to how long a teacher should stay with a class. If a teacher is not capable of changing with her pupils, a hole develops in their relationship, of which all involved are aware. One fills the hole with increased competence. One moves closer to the style of high-school teaching, at the very age at which pupils need a holistic education. This is a change of direction with severe consequences.

How can we educate our own flexibility? Art is an important teacher here. All artistic work, including in the classroom, has an enhancing and strengthening effect on the etheric body. Another aid comes from a certain way of relating to thinking, in study of spiritual-scientific ideas. These promote flexibility of thought, and we have already referred to the relevant passages. Nevertheless this remains a difficult area.

Recall that Steiner said, "as far as possible." Let us for a moment imagine an ideal case if it doesn't prove possible. A teacher notices in the course of sixth grade that teaching requires increasing efforts and no longer goes smoothly. This may be a temporary problem, but as time goes on it doesn't get better.

The teacher views this calmly, and after mature reflection, perhaps after discussing it with a trusted colleague, makes the decision that she should share her doubts with the faculty. She also has a good relationship with the parents in the class, and she may have asked one or two trusted parents for advice. Then she presents the problem to the faculty and states that she wishes to give up the class at the end of sixth grade.

Her colleagues may be astonished, but she knows that this is the right decision, and preparations can be made for a change of teacher.

Someone who acts in this way is acting out of inner strength and can have well-founded hopes that following this decision the right new teacher will be found to take the class. When this decision is taken in good time, we have a fully justified process in which there are no losers.

A proper assessment of one's own situation, and a mature decision taken by oneself, give strength.

Those who cannot continue need not do so. On the contrary, such a decision spares pupils, parents, and the school a lot of suffering.

In conclusion I would just like to say the following. One should not draw the retrospective conclusion from this that such a procedure should be fixed in some way. It would be a failure to acknowledge the true nature of education if, due to bad experiences, a school decided to limit the class-teacher period to six years.

CHAPTER 15

Perspectives on Pedagogic-Medical Diagnostics and Therapies

THE TASK OF THE SCHOOL DOCTOR

Michaela Glöckler

In his January 1920 lecture entitled "Hygiene: A Social Problem"[1] Rudolf Steiner characterized the new discipline of "school doctor/specialist in preventive medicine" as follows:

As far as healthcare is concerned, one social sphere will have to be subject quite particularly and intensively to acquired knowledge of the human being: this is the area of education and teaching. Without a really comprehensive knowledge of the human being one simply cannot evaluate what it means for children to sit in school bowed over their desks, so that their breathing is continually disturbed; or what it means when one fails to ask children to speak loudly and clearly, forming clear vowels and consonants. The whole of their later life depends substantially on whether children breathe in the right way at school, and whether they are encouraged to speak in a fully voiced and clearly articulated way.

> In such things—and these are just examples, for in other areas similar things could be applied—we can discover how general healthcare can be specifically related to schooling. And it is precisely in this that the whole social significance of healthcare can be found, but at the same time it is also clear that life urges us not to specialize further, but instead to integrate specialization in an overall view. We do not just need the insight that allows the teacher to know how to educate a child according to certain educational norms, but teachers need to be able to form a judgment about what it means to get a child to speak a particular phrase in a clearly articulated way; or the effect, in contrast, of allowing the child to snatch a breath after just half a phrase, and not ensuring that he uses up all the breath as he speaks the phrase. Certainly, there are also many reference points and rules in relation to such things. But we can properly recognize and apply these things only if they enter our hearts, and this will happen only when we gain insight into their whole significance for human life and social health. Only then will this acquire the quality of a social impulse...
>
> In other words, we do not need a school doctor to work alongside teachers who teach only according to some abstract educational discipline—someone who turns up every fortnight or so and is unable to really engage with things. No, we need instead a living connection between medical science and the art of education. We need an art of education in every one of whose measures the children are educated and taught in a way that promotes health. This is what makes healthcare a social issue, for the social question is to a large

extent a question of education, and the question of education is to a large extent a medical question—but a question only for a kind of medicine that has been made fruitful by spiritual science, a healthcare imbued by the science of the spirit.[2]

In practical terms this means that the school doctor has the following tasks, depending on if he has a full-time position with the school, or other clinical obligations.

School Doctor Examinations, Class and Year-Group Examinations

On behalf of or in collaboration with public medical departments, the school doctor undertakes school medical examinations as required by law; and, by agreement with teachers and parents, other interim medical examinations of year groups. This is to ensure that the school doctor knows the state of health of pupils at his school, and the results are available to teachers and parents for questions of health-promoting educational measures—where necessary enhanced by effective constitutional remedies.

Some question whether the school doctor should, as faculty member, gain such intimate and detailed insight into the children's health. Is it not up to the parents to ensure that their children receive any needed medical care or therapy? The answer is, simply, that the school doctor is of course subject to the duty of confidentiality, and in child studies in the faculty group or teachers' meeting can only divulge what has been agreed with the parents or where applicable with the pupil. Likewise, it is clear that the school doctor cannot replace the pediatrician or family practitioner. However, the school doctor and family physician can offer each other valuable insights. It is self-evident that parents should have the last word if there is any doubt about which doctor to involve in consultations on their child's health or need for support. In my own practice as school doctor, however, I found that the family physician would call me up if parents arrived for a consultation with questions she was unable to answer through lack of knowledge of Waldorf education.

For instance, a teacher once told the mother of a ten-year-old girl that her daughter's "ego forces were too weak." The mother asked her pediatrician to explain how one could discern strength or weakness of ego forces. For me this highlighted the problem of Waldorf jargon, which needs to be translated into language that "outsiders" can understand. The school doctor can help here by choosing a form of speech that takes account of specialist terms but is at the same time as comprehensible as possible. The vital thing is always to clarify the evidence for such phenomena. In relation to the example mentioned here, observation of the so-called ego forces relates, primarily, to attentiveness, capacity for concentration, memory, presence of mind, reliability, and perseverance. The best solution is always to describe as vividly and clearly as possible what one observes in a child's behavior, rather than resorting to abstract, generalized concepts or psychological terms.

The school doctor is also confronted by questions such as whether there are classical problems in children resulting from in vitro fertilization (IVF). Do such children show typical characteristics, do they lack anything in particular? Here it is helpful to recall how artificial fertilization is accomplished, and that it is only successful in 10-15 percent of cases. These statistical facts alone already show that a clear, pre-birth decision by the human soul is involved in either accepting or rejecting this opportunity of incarnation, and that in the majority of cases it is rejected. In fact, the children who attend consultations because of developmental problems are not, by and large, those from artificially induced conception. Whatever a child's psychosocial or constitutional family background, help can always be given to see the individual child and, as far as possible, to avoid stereotyping a child or declaring him to be abnormal. It is a vital task to show that every child has the right to be as he is, and that one can pursue with him an individual path of development through which he can be allowed to develop his own norm.

In comparing children of the same age one always finds the most varied combinations of capacities and their lack. It is frequently possible for a great gift to exist side by side with a problem or lack of skill.[3]

Specifics of School Doctor Diagnosis and Therapy

An international working group of Waldorf school doctors, founded in 1978, is developing the professional profile of the school doctor and school-related diagnosis and therapy.[4] This work has given rise to a quarterly periodical entitled *Die medizinisch-pädagogische Konferenz* (*Discussions on Medicine in Education*).[5] Unfortunately this is published only in German. This journal hosts a lively exchange on support and remedial measures and the experiences of school doctors. At the same time, it also serves as in-service training support since, apart from regular further training events organized by this international school doctors' working group, specific training to become a Waldorf school doctor does not yet exist. The Medical Section at the Goetheanum in Dornach, Switzerland, publishes information about these trainings.

The school doctor diagnostic procedures outlined below show the trends of this work, and detail the areas of interest to teachers and parents, and therefore also of importance for the Kolisko conferences.

1. For the school doctor, medical diagnosis is based first and foremost on mainstream medical knowledge.

2. Building on this, there follows a study of the child's temperament and constitution, based on anthroposophic understanding of the human being.

3. This leads to a pedagogical and medical diagnosis of the bodily sheaths, which we explain in greater detail below. Rudolf Steiner's comments on ADHS, ADD, and developmental disorders do not include diagnoses such as minimal brain dysfunction, aggressive behavioral disorder, hyperkinesis, or milieu-reactive change. As contemporaries who live with this terminology we first have to feel our way into the manner and mode of approaching a child that Steiner models. In the meeting of February 6, 1923,[6] and in the lectures collected in *Education for Adolescents*,[7] he describes six possible one-sided tendencies

arising in incarnation: children who are large- or small-headed, more earthly or more cosmic, and either richer or poorer in imaginative capacity. These tendencies, together with his references to the four temperaments, provide fundamental diagnostic criteria. Every child learns to unfold his personality in as full a way as possible through this innate constitutional potential for expression, and to become "himself" to an ever-increasing extent. The shared task of education and medicine in childhood and adolescence is to help the child to thoroughly individualize his physical and soul constitution. Based on the three polar expressive possibilities sketched by Steiner *(large-headed / small-headed, earthly / cosmic and rich / poor in imaginative capacity)* we need to discover where a child is placed developmentally in relation to these criteria. This involves functional descriptions of the state of incarnation or the degree of individualization of a child's personality and of his bodily sheaths. We must try to grasp this and where necessary support the developmental process through homeopathic and/or anthroposophic constitutional remedies.

Incarnation into the Physical Organization

Large- and small-headed children: In physical terms each person communicates with his surroundings in three ways: through the senses, through the breath, and through nutrition. In the realm of the senses we are wholly open: we hear, taste, smell, touch, and see the world. In the nerve-sense realm we have the capacity to absorb the world and receive its impressions as it is. The wealth of our conscious life of soul is largely formed from these impressions and the thoughts and feelings associated with them.

Our relationship to the world via the metabolic system—mouth, intestines and anus—is something altogether different. Here we absorb all the various foodstuffs and radically alter, destroy and digest them. The very opposite happens here to nerve-sense processes. If we enjoy good digestion, nothing remains as it was. As soon as food touches our teeth we start making an impression on the world, instead of vice versa. The intrinsic, autonomous nature of our food dies away and provides the basis for the substance of our own bodies. A process of dying and birth occurs here. Just as we "become world" as we perceive, so the world "becomes human" through the work of the metabolic organs.

Our third relationship to the world is through breathing. Here we are concerned neither with fluids and solids as in nutrition, nor with light, air, sound, or warmth as in sense impressions, but with an opening to air.

From the air we breathe we take around 4 percent oxygen, then breathe out what forms in us, which we no longer need: carbon dioxide. Thus most of the air we inhale leaves our body again without having been exchanged. This is also apparent from the fact that the exhaled air contains enough oxygen (around 17 percent) to revive another human being who has stopped breathing. Here the relationship between human being and world is mediated—but with a clear direction and devotion toward the world.

The human center also breathes between the weight of the body and the force which raises and propels it upwards—its lightness or levity. Correspondingly the nervous system is more exposed to this upward motion and—being surrounded on all sides by cerebrospinal fluid—is partially relieved of gravity. The area of the stomach below the diaphragm, in contrast, is subject to weight. In a thin person, for instance, the stomach hangs down properly, whereas in a more corpulent person the cushion of fat makes it seem to be pushed upward.

We can experience the soul faculties belonging to the threefold organism in a similar way. We feel our conscious experiences and thoughts as light-filled and light, non-material, not heavy. Even when we have weighty thoughts these are still light in this respect. At our center, in the lung function of the thorax, there is a continual vacuum that increases when we inhale and continues as we exhale so that the lungs remain inflated and do not collapse. Thus we experience our feeling life as light and dynamic on the one hand, but, on the other, a good deal more tied to the body than thinking. The will, in contrast, is experienced as wholly tied to the body and its weight. It expresses itself physically in active conquest of gravity.

Now it is important to look carefully at every child to see how these three systems relate to one another in him, and to ask: How, in each case, can I help to strengthen the center, which is the physiological and psychological foundation for harmony between the needs and concerns of the self and the world?

If a child's head is more pronounced than his torso and limbs, we can see that the nerve-sense system is not harmoniously integrated into the rest of the body.[8] In relation to this constitution type, Steiner remarks that the child's astral body and ego are disinclined to approach the nerve-sense system, which is why such children have a tendency to drift off, removing themselves from earthly conditions instead of participating attentively and actively in earthly processes through their sense organs. Just as the brain is largely removed from the force of gravity by the cerebrospinal fluid, and is enclosed and protected by the skull, so these children run the risk of giving themselves up too much to the nerve-sense system's autonomous dynamic. The large-headedness linked to this is not just a matter of external dimensions (which can be discerned more or less from the head's circumference), but rather, above all, a question of the functional predominance of thinking—as opposed to alert interaction with one's surroundings through sense perceptions—due to lack of integration of nerve-sense processes with the rest of the organism.

In this regard let us imagine a large-headed child. He moves dreamily or thoughtfully through the classroom, often just standing and looking around lost in thought. One doesn't get the sense that he is observing anything very carefully, but rather that he has an overall picture of what is going on. When we arrive at school in the morning we may find this child already seated at his desk, or looking out of the window, and in winter he likes sitting close to the radiator. He finds it rather hard to concentrate and to make precise distinctions, and his attention easily wanders when listening and trying to understand things. He doesn't find it easy to grasp the things he encounters in clear thoughts, and to access them. But instead he carries around a wealth of images and dreams, has a rich soul life, and is gifted with a certain cheerfulness. His temperament is largely sanguine-phlegmatic.

The question is how to balance this tendency. What sort of feelings need to be awakened to stimulate the child to distinguish things, to grasp them and bring them down to earth? To put it metaphorically, the child needs to learn to feel the difference between heat and cold, in particular to oppose dissipating warmth with inner boundaries, and to awaken through the sensory experience of cold. We can also directly experience the fact that a cool head benefits clear reflection. Thus Steiner recommends engendering feelings of cold in these so-called large-headed children, particularly in the head region. In some children it is enough to wash the head in cool water in the morning, while others need this doing down to the waist. What effect does this have? By awakening these sensory feelings, by distinguishing between hot and cold, the child's life of thought gains access to the sensory organ functions. Imbalance between the systems arises, after all, from the fact that the child's ego and astral body are hesitant about connecting fully with the physical instrument of the nervous system. If strong stimulus is used, however, which awakens distinguishing perception, and shakes the child awake from hazy dream, the astral body and ego are stimulated to connect more strongly with nerve-sense activity. By lovingly washing down a child in the morning in cool water, one is helping him to enter the world of the senses, the world of distinction, coldness, hardness, clarity.

Steiner also recommends supporting this process of awakening for the sensory world via the metabolism by giving enough salt in food, with the aid of potentized lead or lead compounds.[9]

The small-headed child does not tend toward an experience of uplift, of being drawn up and out. In him the dynamic of metabolism is not sufficiently mastered. His astral body and ego do not intervene properly in metabolism, and connect insufficiently with the process of annihilating and resurrecting substance. What occurs if this connection fails to take place adequately, and the metabolism is not sufficiently penetrated by the child's individuality? Then we have someone who is always in some degree of tension, who must assert himself against the autonomous dynamic and power of substances and matter that he absorbs in food. These children are somewhat driven by the food they eat and by processes of digestion. They like eating and do so hungrily, hastily, and unevenly, depending on what is there before them. Their digestion is often irregular. Sometimes they have massive, not wholly digested stools; or then sometimes pass no stool for two days, after which things run smoothly again. On enquiring more carefully one discovers that the rest of their behavior also has a somewhat driven, desiring quality:

> If a child has too little capacity for synthesis of ideas, for constructive conceptualization, if he cannot pictorialize things enough, he will be a kind of little wild man when it comes to art, and this is a symptom for a disorder of the metabolic-limb system...[10]

Here the astral body is reluctant to intervene in the metabolic-limb organism, and needs support to do so. How does one help such a child to cope with the autonomous tendencies of the metabolism?

By what means can the integrating work of the child's astral body and ego be supported from the metabolic pole into the whole organism? Here warmth is indicated—a warm stomach compress after lunch or in the evening before going to sleep. In the language of modern medicine one would say: warmth relaxes the vegetative nervous system, stimulates and harmonizes the digestive nerves, has a stimulating, uncramping, digestion-promoting effect.

Steiner gives us an imaginative picture to bring this home: "The divine, spiritual powers allow the world to grow warm in summer and cold in winter: these are spiritual activities which the divine-spiritual powers achieve through material means."[11] These children too can be helped nutritionally, by stimulating the metabolism through easily digestible foods with a sufficient, integral sugar content. This can be enhanced medicinally with homeopathic doses of silver (Argentum).

In educational terms treatment of the large- and small-headed children is as follows: winter and summer correspond to cold and warmth, to antipathy and sympathy in feeling. Antipathy involves detaching oneself, separating from things around one, sealing oneself off; and sympathy involves opening oneself. Between these is a pause or neutral place as in breathing. Opening—closing—rest, always a threefold dynamic; and in the rest moment lies the turning point where inhalation changes to exhalation. Correspondingly, feeling also has its mid-point in inner calm. Now Rudolf Steiner suggests that in every lesson the children should be brought to the edge of laughter, and then again to seriousness and sympathy, almost to the point of crying. In this way, in lively involvement in the teaching content, children can experience and develop this center between extremes. They enter into anger, annoyance, indignation—and then connect themselves again in sympathetic experience wholly with what is said. Steiner describes it as an educational and therapeutic necessity for the teacher to teach by heart, fully identified with the teaching content and knowing it fully. If the teacher has no clear picture of the content, she is not immersed enough in what she wishes to say to be able to create the mood the child needs to unite himself with it in full interest and involvement. What the teacher says should not just be read from a book or drawn only from her thinking. It must also be present in her life of feeling and will if it is to bring the child into movement and be of interest and importance for him. The being of the child must meet the essence of the content that speaks through the teacher. It is astonishing how this high expectation works back on the person teaching. This kind of identification with the content of teaching also has a strengthening and stabilizing effect on the teacher. Steiner formulated the therapeutic dynamic that is revealed here, which lies in identification with the teaching content, as follows:

> One should really try not to bring one's private personal self into the classroom, but instead have a picture of what one becomes through the material dealt with in any particular lesson…The teacher should feel that, if she herself is indisposed, she can overcome this indisposition through teaching, at least to some extent. Then she will affect the children in the most favorable way imaginable. She should teach out of a sense that teaching is something healing for herself. While teaching she can change from a morose to a cheerful person.[12]

Earthly and Cosmic Children: In the diagnostics practiced by modern mainstream medicine we repeatedly find descriptions of end states. Because of this there is a frequent need to clear a good deal of space before one can open one's eyes for a diagnosis in the real meaning of the word: "Dia" means "through," and "gnosis" means "perception" or "insight"—in other words, passing through another being, thoroughly perceiving it as it expresses and manifests itself.

What is the human being? When someone has died or has not yet been born, we imagine him in a purely spiritual state, dwelling in the spheres, cosmic, somehow very far away. When he is there on earth and begins to cry, eat, and fill his diapers, we experience him as being very earthly, physical, often also as a burden. Not all children of course enter into circumstances where they adapt to daily life without any problem; one often has to adjust oneself to earthly conditions. But what is the actual being? The core human being is linked both to the earth and to the whole cosmos. That is why the human being can manifest his connection to the heavenly, spiritual world as an innate characteristic. The same person however also manifests a connection to the earthly through what he has received from the earth, the metabolism, the limbs, the capacity to be active. Based on previous lives, each person brings along wholly individual affinities with the heaven and earth, which live in the differentiated form and configuration of the etheric body. Rudolf Steiner draws the attention of teachers and school doctors to the fact that the spherical dome of the human head is a reflection of the heavens.

It is here that thinking can rise to the spirit. Now there are children whose heads are strikingly well-formed and sculpted, and stand in a certain polarity to the formation of the limbs. In his lectures *Education for Adolescents*,[13] Steiner speaks of the thoroughly formed and modeled shape of the head that predominates in these children. In contrast, the limbs are less well formed. Some children's faces strike us as "typical." One finds it hard to experience the facial expression, the sculptural formation of the head as something finished and fully shaped, as imbued with individual personality. When we see hands with soft, round fingers, so-called chubby hands that grasp weakly, and ask whether the child is as yet wholly present, or whether he is yet to arrive fully. Suddenly, in fifth grade one may get a proper handshake from such a child for the first time, and one realizes: Now you're there!

Other children seem always to have dirty hands no matter how often they wash them. Their hands and feet simply get into everything: the earth in all its aspects, but also colorful, noisy media that stimulates the senses so much—everything is fascinating. These children are tied in to this world by their hands and feet, and have a gift for engagement with earthly things.

Steiner's descriptions of children are not defect analyses that highlight what is lacking or wrong. Rather, they reveal innate gifts, characteristics, and affinities. We have earth-gifted children who engage with their surroundings and with things, but who are less thoughtful or reflective, and therefore cannot yet make any real use of their gift, and therefore need our help. And we have heaven-gifted children who somehow bear richness within themselves which they cannot properly express or make fruitful for the earth because they are not yet earth-gifted enough.

Here Steiner recommends treatment that is primarily pedagogical, since the one-sided tendencies in this case are in the etheric and functional realm, and can be balanced through strengthening feeling life.

Why? Because the feeling for an idea (cosmic child) or for an action (earthly child) are what make this child conscious of them. And only by this means—through conscious feeling and emotion—does the child learn to handle his one-sided and as yet unconscious gift. Whatever their temperament—whether sanguine, choleric, melancholic, or phlegmatic—earth-gifted children have a mild melancholic undertone to their nature, a certain tendency to ill humor. Of course this can lead to a variety of so-called behavioral problems. If someone is already in ill humor and then something unpleasant happens, he will lose his equilibrium sooner than someone who is in a good mood to begin with. The melancholic undertone is there because the earth gift also involves an earth burden. Inherited aspects that infuse us from the earth predominate in these children when they incarnate. Since the heavenly aspect is not strong enough it is unable to compensate sufficiently for the earthly, and so these children tend to be overwhelmed and determined by what comes toward them from inheritance. The recommendation for therapy here is to start with the children where they are. This is a kind of fundamental principle which we, as teachers and doctors, must continually recall, particularly in child psychiatry, psychology and in remedial teaching: Engage with each child where he is at present, using the relevant measures. If there is a melancholic undertone to his character, engage it through a minor-key melody, leading over to major. In other words, one only changes the mood after finding the tone that accords with the child. As a rule, earthly children have a pronounced gift for movement, and one can start with them there. Music and singing is inner movement.

Physical movement is outer movement. Thus in therapy for earthly children music and eurythmy play a key role. This is a challenge to teachers, for these children are precisely the ones who hurl themselves to the ground in eurythmy and refuse to join in. And yet eurythmy is the most therapeutic thing for them.

If one has some "wild" children in the class, it may be good to start with an activity in which they are allowed to move almost unrestricted. One engages the children where they are: some enjoy being allowed to run properly wild, especially when this follows a lesson when they had to sit still. One then leads this free movement into movement practice, for instance by getting such earthly children to watch the rest of the class, assigning them the task of observing where a movement or form succeeds and is beautiful. Then these children are allowed to show the others the same thing. In other words, one draws awareness to the beauty of a movement. What is the effect of this? A feeling for one's own gift awakens. The children learn to develop a feeling for what they have received as innate talent—that is, the capacity to move and enter into connection with everything earthly. The frequent repetition of such experiences enables the child to recognize her own talent ever more clearly, and thus learn to use and manage it.

In this way feelings are awakened for music, for movement, for beauty; for light and dark, contraction and expansion. This wealth of awakened feeling helps wake up the sleeping head. Whenever we have a feeling, when we want to learn something, ideas come to us more easily than when the feeling realm is grey and unaddressed. The feelings are what can awaken sleeping thoughts, so that the heavens can begin to say something to the child.

For the cosmic child, who brings with him the possibility of moving in ideas, Rudolf Steiner draws our attention to more reflective lesson content: history, geography, nature study, literature, poetry. Here too the teacher is urged to start with the child where he is. But now what is needed is to present the content so that it evokes strong feelings in the child. I was once told of a parents' evening where a mother related how her son, in fifth grade, came home every day and excitedly told her the latest news from Rome. But one day he came in without a word, passed the open kitchen door, threw his things in the corner and just called out despairingly as he passed: "Mum, Caesar is dead!" After this he ran to his room and didn't appear for a while. Here is an instance where the teacher evoked strong, dynamic feelings that reverberated even at home. That is ideal for cosmic children. Here it is less important to know the precise year Caesar lived, and whether all the imaginative details the teacher relates are completely correct. What clothes Caesar wore, how he smiled, the way he walked, will no doubt be described differently in every school. That is not so important. What is important is that the being of Caesar lives in the teacher and speaks to the child through the teacher; that Caesar enters his feeling and a personal relationship to him develops. The thing is to create the feeling basis and motivation for subsequent acquisition of knowledge.

The earthly and cosmic child both need an artistic treatment of lesson content. In art we are always involved with feeling and living experience, and with never-ending practice. These children need the teacher to be an artist who dramatically represents what he relates, and who can also, for instance, use moving words and personal involvement to describe granite and what this undergoes in the course of evolution in the Nordic mountains and fjords; what bears down on it, what it upholds—so that involvement, a feeling relationship, a relationship to reality and interest in the world arise.

Such teaching brings the cosmic children down to earth, enabling them to imbue with feeling what they experience as thought in the teacher's description. This awakens interest in the world, in the surrounding environment, and through this awakened feeling the child's being finds a connection to the metabolic-limb pole, to his earthly tools.

The reverse is also true: the "headless," movement-talented, earth-gifted child comes to himself by experiencing the strength and beauty of a form, and being able to master a movement, thus slowly finding a connection to what he brought with him from pre-birth realms as thinking and spiritual capacities. Rudolf Steiner's core phrase for treating earthly and cosmic children is: developing "feeling for the world."[14] The world does not just consist of light, color, and story, but also of musical dynamic and earthly tone. The task is to enter into all this with feeling. A teacher may say: "I can't do something specific and special for every single child in the class—that's impossible." But if, as teachers, we take this core phrase as guide—developing feeling for the world—and work at our gestures, our mode of expression, our speech melody, because we realize that for earthly children every nuance signifies a feeling, then we educate the center in us that mediates between earth and heaven, thinking and deed: our life of feeling.

People often ask whether small-headedness is identical with the earthly child aspect, and similarly, large-headedness with the cosmic child. Observation shows that this is not the case. Both large-headed and small-headed children can show either an earthly or cosmic orientation. Large- and small-headedness is an expression of the interplay of the nerve-sense system and the metabolism. Accordingly, treatment aims to support physical functions, such as nutrition and sensory perception. This is not the case with the earthly or cosmic child. Here the etheric level is addressed, and everything depends on whether the child can individualize head or limbs in an appropriate way. Only the ego-penetrated etheric organism has the capacity to wholly adapt to what comes from inheritance, and to transform it appropriately. Where this doesn't succeed sufficiently, one of the polar realms predominates. Here therapy aims primarily to address the life of feeling, since feelings can mediate between the etheric and astral bodies. The vivacity of the etheric organism receives its impulse through feelings. To have a "living experience" means immersing one's attention (ego activity) in the etheric body through the mediation of the feeling life.

The Child Rich or Poor in Imagination: In *Education for Adolescents*,[15] Rudolf Steiner next describes children who are either rich or poor in imagination. What does this mean? One way is to consider whether children have weak powers of concentration or have fixed ideas. Children who are poor in imagination find it hard to bring their ideas to conscious awareness, while children rich in imagination have trouble disregarding anything that has entered their consciousness. In the broadest sense, the term "rich in imagination" denotes conscious thought content, and also memory. Memories and thoughts do indeed arise from the etheric organism, but they are rendered conscious by the astral body and consciously controlled by the ego. This control and directing of thoughts by the ego only succeeds, however, if the physical-etheric constitution is well and thoroughly formed, and the metamorphosis of growth forces into thought forces has occurred in the proper way. If this metamorphosis occurs too weakly or irregularly, the astral body has either one-sided conscious thought content, or too little. So-called mental illnesses arise, according to Steiner, when an immature metamorphosis of growth forces occurs, or does not take place at the right time.[16]

A child rich in imagination who cannot get rid of his thoughts is not actually mentally ill, but is in a situation where somewhat more of growth forces are released than the ego can really deal with. His thoughts retain their autonomous, body-forming dynamic, and are not sufficiently susceptible to the ego's control. One can observe this in such children: for instance, a teacher's expressing what is important to her can profoundly affect a richly imaginative child. He then ponders on this until the very end of the lesson, and is no longer open to anything else that is taught or discussed. A tendency to illness already lies in this phenomenon, for illness is ultimately always linked to the fact that the ego can no longer integrate the many capacities of function and activity in the physical and emotional realms, so that instead isolation and fixation set in.

Or we have the reverse phenomenon: the teacher says something and it goes in one ear and out the other! The ego is powerless to hold thoughts. We are often just pleased if children know something, and don't particularly attend to whether their knowledge is fixed or truly alive and absorbed. But we must learn to attend to this. Can children grasp and then release knowledge at various stages of a lesson? Or do they get stuck on certain things? Here too a kind of breathing is needed: absorbing, consolidating, and then releasing, so that one is free again for something new. Where does a child rich in imagination stand in relation to the tendency to compulsive thoughts, when he is unable to forget or let go of his ideas? What does such a child need? How can one help such a child? If we adults have our head full of problems and no longer know how to deal with them, or if our thinking is blocked, we often set ourselves in motion and hope that a change of scenery will help bring movement into our thoughts. Similarly, movement is the remedy for the children described. They need subjects in which a sense of movement can be very consciously practiced; for example, in writing we ensure that the children don't get stuck on single letters but really come into flowing movement.

Singing is also a movement subject! A person who is afraid is also plagued by ideas he can't get rid of. Many people start singing when this happens, and actually feel freer. Singing can be a decisive help to the child rich in imagination: his whole body reverberates with his own activity, his life of thought is unblocked and comes into flow once again.

For the child poor in imagination, who finds it hard to draw up his thoughts, the teacher should expend all her love and care in helping him learn to use his senses. Sense activity aims to help consolidate the life of thought as ideas that can be remembered. The means to do this are for the child to watch how painting is done, careful observation, attentive listening. Instrumental music too, where one has to listen very carefully, is helpful for these children. Rudolf Steiner suggests getting the children to play instruments and sing in the same lesson, alternating between making music themselves and listening to others. By this means the children themselves can have a healing effect on one another, also when some make music (rich in imagination) and the others listen (poor in imagination).

Eurythmy has a special role in treating children both rich and poor in imagination. On the former, who cannot rid themselves of their thoughts, it has a direct and clear effect. It has a decided effect if they move their whole body in running, stepping and hopping. The vowels have a particular effect on these children. The vowels live in the bloodstream and form the organs. When they are practiced in walking and moving they have a calming effect on thoughts rising too strongly out of the organism. They stimulate the growth forces to form organs, and root them there so that they cannot so easily release themselves. In the curative eurythmy course,[17] Steiner describes how the vowels stimulate "selfing" and the consolidation of form. But the children poor in imagination, too, can benefit from eurythmy. For them it is good to practice the consonants, primarily while standing, just with the arms. Consonants help to dissolve rigid forms and to counteract deformities—they "unself."

A eurythmy teacher once gave a lovely example of how she put this suggestion of Steiner's into practice with a high school student who spent hours on homework because he found it hard to remember what had been taught in the lessons. The pupil agreed to join a fairy-tale performance, together with his classmates, which local eurythmists were preparing. These high school students were used as a narrator group, and their main task was to represent consonants while standing. They had to practice this for an hour twice a week, and towards the end extra rehearsals were added, which this pupil attended without complaint. When the teacher asked him one day whether this might be too much for him, he replied: "No, I was really on the ball yesterday after the rehearsal, and I finished my main lesson book." This shows that the consonants, especially when done while standing, can loosen the spirit from the metabolic-limb system, allowing the organs to release impacted forms and find their way into new structures, to re-form themselves in a healthy way, and for growth forces to be more easily released to serve thinking.

Thus we see how self-awareness, which is of such importance in later life, lives between remembering and forgetting, and how the ego is really called upon to stand at the threshold of consciousness and to be master of its sleeping and waking, its remembering and forgetting. This picture—the ego which stands at the threshold and guards its life of soul—can accompany us in every eurythmy and music lesson, and in every other lesson in which one works with these elements.

When we look at the physical size and form of a child with either a large or small head, we are concerned with the imprint of the ego on the physical body. That is why the treatment approach is physical in nature. In the case of the earthly or cosmic child it is not the form aspect but the process that gives rise to this form that is involved. The imprint of the ego here lives in a more functional way, in the etheric. Therapy therefore also lies in the realm of soul and function. Awakening stronger feelings stimulates the growth forces to penetrate the forms: the ego is encouraged by the stimulated astral body to work its way into the etheric-physical constitution. In the case of children either rich or poor in imagination, we focus on the content of consciousness, on how the ego works with what the astral body makes conscious, what lives in sleeping and waking, and what is present in the ego as remembering and forgetting. Here the aim of therapy is thus also to help the child develop his center so that a true inwardness can arise, developing an understanding of the child's 1) Biographical and family anamnesis; and 2) Relationship anamnesis.

Therapy also seeks understanding the child's social situation and position: what place does he occupy in the class? Does he primarily meet with sympathy or antipathy in the family and/or social context? How do individual teachers respond to the child? In other words, in what qualities of human relationship does the child live and have to prove himself and develop? For example, I even once recommended taking a child out of the Waldorf school and sending him to the local elementary school because the relationship network would be more constructive for him there. But in general we need to meet the challenge of shaping the Waldorf school as living context in such a way that relationships can affect the child as constructively as possible. Steiner develops the so-called pedagogical law in lectures 2 and 4 of his curative education course.[18] This highlights the healing or deleterious effect people can have on another—especially the adult on the child. Even though it is common experience that the health of the physical body is largely determined by habits of living, eating, work, and sleep, that is, by qualities of the etheric organism, and that the health and flexibility of the etheric organism depend on how each person feels—whether he has reason primarily to have emotions such as fear, jealousy, anger, hatred, depression, or boredom; or, instead, positive emotions such as joy, confidence, and trust, nevertheless the quality and mode of emotions depends on the capacity of the adult or child to handle his feelings. To realize how strongly a human being can exert a healing or harmful effect on another depending on whether he lives with the question of how he must conduct himself so that the other can feel particularly good, shows the significance of a teacher consciously working with this pedagogical law, or not.

Understanding a Pupil's Specific Intentionality

What are a child's strengths and weaknesses? What is he aiming for? Living with the question: How can I stand by you as you grasp hold of your life's task by helping to create the conditions necessary for this? Living with such a question allows one to have quite different ideas and perceptions in education and therapy than when one doesn't live with such a question.

Anamnesis of the Real Potential for Helping the Child, Both at Home and at School

This issue is often related to the social commitment of the school doctor. For instance, he can collaborate in creating a health working group at the school, with whose help fundraising can perhaps be undertaken to pay for an additional position at the school. Perhaps an additional support teacher could be employed, who has been trained in the most diverse techniques; or the long-desired full-time therapeutic eurythmist. Sometimes all that is needed is one-on-one supervision which can be achieved by offering a practicum at a local teacher training college. It is actually often the parents, and also individual teachers, who show astonishing creativity and willingness to help in such working groups.

Education as Therapy

Rudolf Steiner asked:

> But how can we educate if the human being has, in addition, lost that old, medieval relationship to tradition and memory, as has happened in modern times? Outwardly human beings have lost their trust in tradition, while inwardly they wish to be free beings who face life in an open, unprejudiced way at every moment.[19]

The school doctor needs to stand securely within the historical context of evolution, based on which he can judge what contemporary or cultural phenomena are helpful to child development, and which of them should only be taken up by the young person in late adolescence or even adulthood. Emotional development is currently far more precarious than physical or mental/spiritual. In fact, physical and mental health depend ultimately on the success or failure of healthy emotional development. This perspective should inform our study of Rudolf Steiner's curriculum suggestions.[20]

Participation—if Needed—in Parents' Evenings on Developmental Questions; Developing a Position of Trust among Pupils

Pupils often find it possible to talk to the school doctor about things they dare not discuss with parents or teachers. Their trust in the school doctor grows from the fact that he is usually familiar with both the home and school environment, and so can have the best overview of the pupil's social context. In adolescence, particularly, this position of trust allows the school doctor to give the developmental help through discussion which he was formerly able to give in a more practical, medical sphere during early and later childhood.

CHILD STUDY

Christof Wiechert

In the first years after the founding of the Waldorf School Rudolf Steiner was often a guest in the College of Teachers meeting. If a colleague asked for advice in the meeting, perhaps because he was unable to help a pupil, then Steiner visited the class and observed the child, and then gave his advice in the meeting. Such advice was kept brief, and a child study usually lasted no longer than a few minutes. Here is an example from the meeting on May 26, 1920: [21]

> Several children in 5th grade are discussed, especially E.E.
>
> Teacher: He's not making progress. He's gifted in languages. He's cunning and clever.
>
> Steiner: One needs to occupy and stimulate him now and then, taking as much account of his individuality as possible. Then you would need to vary this, and repeatedly give him specific attention.
>
> Teacher: Shouldn't he attend the support class?
>
> Steiner: Why should he go to the support class, what would he do there? He's a passionate little fellow. It would make a deeper impression on him if you got him to make a pair of shoes. You should get him to do something like hammering in nails and making shoes. Proper boots for someone else. That would be a positive thing for him, a start. He would enjoy making shoe soles, double soles.

Let us form a clear picture of this: the circle of teachers, with Rudolf Steiner in the middle. The teachers ask questions and receive answers. From the group of teachers at the circle's periphery come questions, and from the center comes the answer—and indeed, the wise answer of someone who knows a great deal.

Then the situation changes; Rudolf Steiner is no longer available and the teachers have to manage on their own, are thrown back on their own resources. What does this look like now? Pictorially, there is the circle of teachers and they have questions, for instance about a child. What is at the center now? The question now occupies the focal point, and the periphery has to answer. In the case of a child study, the child and the question occupy the center, while the periphery considers the answer: an inversion.

This process signifies something of great importance. After all, we experience the faculty or college meeting as the soul of the school, as its heart. A heart also tries to learn. We cannot just regard the child study as something necessary for helping a child and his teacher, for it is also, at the same time, a learning opportunity par excellence for the whole faculty. It can become a "college of psychology," in which the teachers continually further their education. Conceiving of this inversion in very real terms can give one cause to ponder: wisdom and help originally flowed from a center to the periphery, which tried to absorb it. But then the question itself became the center, and the periphery has to develop the capacity to respond with wisdom and help. But there are preconditions for achieving this. Practice has shown that these conditions make the process of study and observation easier, and are worth striving for. They lie in the social realm. While the child study itself should not become formalized, it is equally certain that one gain help from observing the following:

1. The child study needs a discussion chairperson. This does not have to be the chair of the faculty meeting. Nor is it necessary for this person to be the class teacher of the child in question. What matters is that the discussion chairperson has the capacity to create the right balance between leading the discussion and allowing it to develop. He should be capable of maintaining this balance. For this the chairperson must be able to intuit the direction the discussion is taking in relation to the child.

2. Rudolf Steiner repeatedly stressed that teachers should avoid becoming specialists. For a child study this means that it is a false route to leave it to the specialists: in other words, not just the teachers who know the child should participate in the discussion, but also those who do not know him. One often finds that people not involved in teaching the child can make valuable suggestions and ask questions which set the direction of discussion. And colleagues who only participate by listening with great interest can also create the right basic mood. It is therefore suggested that all colleagues should participate.

3. In every faculty, some members have gotten further than others in studying anthroposophic knowledge of the human being (*Study of Man*).[22] In every child study there are teachers who know more about the particular child than others. These two categories of teacher are the ones who should practice reticence. If one takes the image of the circle seriously, a colleague can, through enthusiasm for his work, influence the discussion too much in one direction. The important thing is to attempt to form a basis of discussion among the whole circle of teachers.

4. A point about the length of discussion. Some faculties take two meetings for a child study, and some even use three meetings. This is fine, but its success is entirely dependent on the extent to which teachers manage to devote their attention to the child over one (or two) weeks.

Only when this works does it have a point. The reality, however, is usually that it proves difficult, due to circumstances, to carry the picture of a child throughout a whole week. When attempted one often finds that the second meeting after a week has passed has lost sight of the picture, and one has to start over again. It is our view that a child study can actually be undertaken perfectly well at one sitting, over about one and a quarter hours. This requires the practice of presence of mind.

5. It is often asked whether the parents of the child in question should participate in the child study. If the school can reach a point at which parents can join such a discussion, that is good. It really depends on the whole mood in the school. How does the school organism relate to parents? Is there a fundamentally open attitude between those involved? Or is there still some fear of contact? The answer to this question is the deciding factor.

6. But in every case parents should be asked in advance whether they agree to their child being discussed. (The teacher will also usually feel the need to speak to the parents beforehand.)

7. To conclude, here are a few remarks about healthy procedures. What is discussed in the child study should be passed on to the child in the most responsible and circumspect way, as if he himself had been present. A teacher who gives his own emotions free rein to in such a discussion would be better off saying nothing. Then it should be self-evident that what is discussed does not become a topic of conversation a coffee break. The limited period of the child study must be kept sacred. A teaching faculty helps take itself seriously by asking a colleague to record the results of the discussion in writing. Then, when a review is held after a few weeks, and these results (which of course consist of tasks for teachers to carry out) are mentioned, it will be possible to ascertain two things: were the suggestions carried out, and did they have a good effect on the child?

Having examined these characteristic forms, let us now look at the way such a child study develops. It is worth emphasizing again that a child study cannot be formalized. Each child creates the form he needs. A fixed procedure with a predetermined agenda is inimical to the nature of the study.

This work tends to progress through three phases, which we can call: forming a picture, finding the causes, seeking help.

The picture-forming process begins when the class teacher announces in the faculty meeting that she would like to discuss a child because she has a certain question that she is not able to solve on her own. This announcement does not need to take more than five minutes. The school doctor (who may be present) will have seen the child in advance, and the class teacher will have discussed him with his parents.

At the next faculty meeting, the child study begins as the class teacher describes the child as succinctly as possible. It helps to structure the study as a description both of the child's spatial form and of his development over time.

How does the child appear? What would strike us if we could see him? Can we see anything in his shape and form which is specific to this particular child? How has he developed through time? What did he experience in his younger years? How does he behave, and what are his capacities, abilities, and habits? Does he have a characteristic form and manner of movement? And finally, what is the "problem"? The class teacher should complete this presentation within fifteen minutes. Concentration has a refreshing effect. The chair of the meeting then asks each colleague who teaches the child to speak in turn, noting that it is not necessary to repeat anything that has already been said. For instance, if a subject teacher says that she has had the same experience in her lessons, that is sufficient. Then the school doctor can add medical observations, if a case history is already available for the child. For instance, has the child broken a limb, or does he invariably hurt his head? Has he suffered serious illnesses or been hospitalized? It helps to mention the age at which such events occurred. Each speaker tries to keep the picture pure, avoiding opinion or interpretation. This is a task of the faculty of teachers, monitored by the chair of the child-study meeting. Thus a full, rounded picture develops.

While this happens, something remarkable can be noted in the listener. We listen; we try to attend without adding our own view to what is said. We try to listen very specifically, without sympathy or antipathy. But nevertheless we notice a quiet judgment forming. Is what I hear essential for the child being described, or is it of less central importance? Does any detail in the description point to the whole child, or does it just pass him by tangentially? The whole description should highlight the phenomena. But somewhere in us something stirs that makes us clair-audient for the riddle of the child. If a hand, or voice, or stance or gesture is described, it can have this significance, but does not inevitably. Thus we are on the lookout for something symptomatic. This subtle, inner seeking can enormously enhance our interest in what is being said. This is an activity that occurs in listeners, outwardly unnoticed, during the first part of the study. That those listening are as active as the teachers giving presentations is the foundation for the study developing through the strength of the whole community.

The child-study chairperson now has the task of leading the conversation to its next phase. This is not always easy, for people like to stay with the observations and perceptions, which offer something to hold on to. However, it should be expressly stated that this first phase does not need to be complete. The picture does not have to be exhaustive, and endless descriptions actually have a paralyzing effect.

The chair of the study will therefore ask what the presentations and descriptions have to tell us about the child.

Now it will soon become evident that descriptions of the child continue, and that an attempt to answer this question will throw up ever new observations. This is a dead end. The study requires us to use what has already been said, even if something has been left out in the process. Thus we seek the transition to the next phase, and the study chairperson closes the first part of the presentation.

But here, once more, a remarkable inner fact becomes apparent: we suddenly feel lost, having left the safe ground of the sense-perceptible. One enters a sphere that offers little outer security, the sphere of causes. It is important to develop a right feeling for this fact. It does not represent a weakness of the faculty of teachers but marks the transition to a new sphere.

Suppose we are discussing a girl in the second half of fourth grade, who has suddenly grown short-sighted and is therefore wearing glasses. She no longer shows interest in anything. She even appears a little slow-witted, although previously she was always a very lively, cheerful girl. The child-study chairperson repeats his question and the participants seek within themselves to see whether they find anything that points to the question of causes. One person tries and says, perhaps, that we can see here how the ego organism is not properly integrated into the sense sphere, or has somewhat withdrawn from it. Now we are urged to consider this idea. Do we find any further confirmation of this suggestion?

The chairperson now has the particular task of pursuing this idea in discussion without rendering the appearance of another idea impossible. It requires great sensitivity, for only two things can now occur. The direction being pursued either turns out to be correct, or not. If not, someone will open up another line of thought. But how can we tell what is "right?" This requires a subtle sensitivity, a feeling that I am on the right path; or, if not, one feels that one "loses" the child about whom one is speaking. If the discussion becomes abstract, we lose contact with the soul reality that binds the participants. This does not necessarily imply failure. What is more important is that we attend to these subtle processes which only occur within us, and which weave between colleagues as a mood. To put it objectively, does a feeling of evidence arise within the group of participants?

This process of finding the causes can quickly lead us to develop an inkling of the child's essential being, and to grasp it as it now manifests; or a long journey of feeling our way forward can begin. In some cases, we will have to admit that we have not found the way through, and will have to try again in a new child study. This is a possibility and a learning phase that does not have to produce a melancholy response. However, it can also happen that people feel they would like to continue further, since the child's problems are urgent. It is possible to progress from the first step directly into the third. If external circumstances suggest this, it can be tried. However, we must be conscious that the phase of finding the causes has been skipped, and that any suggestions will not necessarily be responsive to the child's actual being.

This process reveals how far a faculty has internalized anthroposophic knowledge of the human being. What work has been done in faculty meetings, and how sure are we in handling this knowledge? This is apparent primarily in how fast or laboriously one gains access to an understanding of the child. Is it a question of temperament, a question of the rhythmic center, or a question of the relationship between the upper and lower poles of the human being? The latter can express itself in shape and form, but also in the mutual relationship between the three soul forces.

Picture-forming, the first step of the child study, primarily takes place in conceptual thinking, while the second step (cause-seeking) occurs in feeling thinking, or thinking feeling, and is far more delicate in nature. The second step may also involve associative psychologizing (for example, the child is so closed off because her aunt is depressive; the girl is so mad about horses because she doesn't get enough love at home).

We move on to the third step, giving help. Once again there is uncertainty in this transition. How can the study advance now? What should follow? The chair of the study can ask how we are going to help the child, or what we are going to do now. There may be a variety of misunderstandings, with some contributions remaining in the previous phase. However, those listening can sense that a different stance is required for the next step. A will aspect is involved, a commitment to the whole child. How could I help this child? What will help here?

Here we must touch on an idea that we will need to develop later. In asking what will help, we need to distinguish whether the problem rests in the sphere of soul and emotions alone, or whether it expresses itself physically too. In the theoretical case of the girl with new eyeglasses referred to above, eye eurythmy therapy, if available, is clearly desirable. Pedagogical help can also be given. For instance, the class teacher can say he will use the first geography main lesson to intensively awaken the interest of the class (including the child in question) in their environment. Interest is, after all, a force through which ego forces descend into the astral body.

Geography is excellent for properly integrating the astral body. Another teacher may conceive the idea of helping in handwork lessons by making things other than just those which have to be made. He or she will ask the children what they would be interested in making. Or the class teacher undertakes to pose to the child (and the class) a riddle each day, but the answer is only to be given the following day. This simple example shows that there is both a more therapeutic measure, in the actual sense of the word, but also a soul remedy initiated by teachers, proceeding from education and, in particular, from the effect of the teaching material on the child. Here lies a great potential to use the teaching material as a healing force (we will return to this theme later). In other words, the first question in this third phase of the study should be: How can we help? Nowadays we tend to call on a specialist to address difficult problems. This may indeed be necessary. But first we must determine what we, as educators, can do.

If several measures have now been found, and brought into proper balance by the faculty group, then the child study can be concluded. The most important facts are recorded, particularly action items.

If it proves possible in a (bigger) school, to carry out a child study at more or less every faculty meeting, after two months one can give it a rest. Then it is good, instead, to use the hour and three quarters to review past child studies. What has been done? What effect has it had? What more needs to be done? This review, after the planned measures have been implemented, is a significant moment for the faculty or college. It shows them how the forces used have taken effect in the right way. It can also show where something is not working. For instance, certain measures may not have been followed through, for various reasons. It can also happen that the child's well-being has improved radically. (It has also often been noticed that the day after a study the child in question seems changed, and shows himself as he would really like to be. This experience later closes off again after a few days, and the child returns to his more familiar behavior.) Whatever the case, it is right to look back and examine the results of what was planned, and this helps to give the child study the seriousness which it needs.

CHILDREN WITH SPECIAL GIFTS

Michaela Glöckler

Statistically, the number of highly-gifted pupils in any given year's group is usually estimated at just above 2%.[23] Among almost 80,000 Waldorf pupils in Germany, over 1800 pupils would fall into this category. In a very few cases, they become "problematic" in the classroom. It also sometimes happens that such pupils leave the Waldorf school because they feel under-challenged, or because their parents believe that their children should receive greater intellectual stimulus. Feelings often get mixed up with this that actually have nothing to do with the professed problem. Such issues can often be connected to the children or parents seeking an elite education. The teacher's difficulty with such students is understandable: teachers naturally want to be "a step ahead" of students, and a "smart alec" sometimes knows a subject better or can do math more quickly, or even highlights a teacher's mistakes.

Wenzel Michael Götte, a Waldorf teacher and teacher trainer at the Stuttgart Waldorf education seminar, discusses this in his book *Hochbegabte und Waldorfschule* (Highly Gifted Pupils and the Waldorf School),[24] which I hope will soon be available in translation. Of his own childhood, Rudolf Steiner writes in his Autobiography[25] that the many questions he carried within him, "made me very lonely as a boy." To be taught by a teacher for whom "teaching was a tedious occupation" also became a "tedious occupation" for this first grader. His father home-schooled him for a while, after an injustice led to a serious altercation with the teacher. After the family moved when his father changed jobs, Rudolf went back to school, and around the age of nine discovered a geometry textbook belonging to a teacher: "I devoured it with enthusiasm. For weeks my soul was filled with congruence, the similarity of triangles, cubes, polygons. I racked my brains with the question of where parallels actually intersect; Pythagoras's theorem enthralled me."[26]

Since highly gifted pupils are rarely easy, but tend to be more individual, also perhaps appearing to be socially difficult, the first task must be to take a clear look at this phenomenon itself. Why is this the case? Highly gifted children think differently, more quickly, have more differentiated or also simpler feelings than average people. They are also often preoccupied with questions and worries which the adult believes they are too young for. But the less a child feels understood, the less at ease he will feel and the more difficult and at odds with the world he will appear. Nowadays teachers don't just have to teach but also work on relationships with pupils. As class teachers for eight years, we accompany the children for longer than many marriages last. Such developments are also something that a teacher needs to consider today.

It is therefore good if teachers also reflect on where professional help might be needed. Such professional help is necessary in a similar way for both gifted pupils and those with learning difficulty, depending on how a personal relationship is established with the child or not.

As school doctor I was repeatedly consulted on questions of destiny in relation to a possible change of school, or part-time attendance at the Waldorf school and parallel to this extra support for highly gifted pupils at the music conservatory or university. Individual cases like this can always be solved if one focuses one's full interest on the child in question to decide whether a child should be removed from his class group and skip one or two grades. Below are suggestions for managing this situation:

- Great importance should be accorded to an age-based class group with its natural age-range of a full year. Why? Because it strengthens pupils' sense of their own age-group, the generation they belong to, and—of particular importance—it counteracts the divergence between physical and mental/emotional maturation processes that are anyway present.

- It is a good idea to share the main lesson period with the rest of the class-group, and then, depending on ability and gift, to leave the group for individual support lessons.

- Special homework can be set which requires more of a pupil, and also gives him an opportunity to show and present to the class something of what he has achieved.

- Within the class, social competency can be practiced if a gifted pupil is shown how to help a less gifted one in completing his work in a way that is helpful to the latter and at the same time strengthens and supports social cohesion.

- One should try to ensure that the gifted pupil has an *integrated* rather than a general special status, so that the harmonious overall maturation of his personality can be supported.

A preventive medical view will also give us another perspective. I know of many cases of people of higher or above-average intelligence who fall prey to degeneration of the central nervous system, including Alzheimer's disease. In the anamnesis of such patients one often finds that they skipped a grade when they were young. Likewise, some studies suggest a link between childhood intelligence and Alzheimer's.[27] The question is whether this reveals an important constitutional connection between childhood incarnation and age-related excarnation.

If one includes anthroposophic study of the human being, with its knowledge of the etheric, one can point to a clear link here: where intelligence is drawn on too early, the etheric organism is not allowed sufficient time to complete its body-focused work of growth and development. Premature, copious demand on the etheric forces to develop various forms of human intelligence is simultaneously connected with release of the etheric organism from its body-bound activity. The more abstract a thought process is, the more it stands in contrast to the organism's activity of growth, development and regeneration. In the Waldorf school, therefore, during the major growth period, creative forms of intelligence are favored such as are cultivated in artistic work, together with nurturing of inner images and imaginative activity. The stronger underlying feeling element here means that such activity unfolds in a physiologically less body-free way than does abstract thinking activity. By proceeding in this way one gives the nervous system a greater opportunity, on the one hand, to mature undisturbed, and on the other this nurtures a creative mode of intelligence. More detailed research is still needed in this field, requiring the collaboration of pediatricians and school doctors with internists and gerontologists. The case of Else Klink[28] was always exemplary for me as an instance of support for a highly gifted pupil at the first Waldorf school while Rudolf Steiner was still alive. It was seen as self-evident that she could begin her eurythmy training from tenth grade onward, after main lesson each day, but she still remained an integrated part of her class. In my experience it is actually sufficient to nurture highly gifted pupils in one or two subjects of their choice, and also to allow the rest of the class group the pleasure of having a highly gifted child in their midst. This can be enormously stimulating and inspiring for a whole class; and, vice versa, can give highly gifted pupils the opportunity to develop ethical and social capacities that are so urgently necessary today alongside intelligence.

THE SCHUBERT REMEDIAL CLASS

Reinoud Engelsman

Schubert's "Supplementary Class": More Modern Than We Thought

In the framework of a working group we studied the question of how to get a structured overall picture of therapeutic pedagogical support in the school. We discovered three basic types of pedagogical support that represent a therapeutic intensification of existing domains:

1. Supplementary instruction for individual pupils (including artistic therapies) is an intensification of the specialist teacher principle

2. Therapeutic eurythmy is an intensification of eurythmy, which of course occupies an important central position in the canon of school subjects

3. The age-overlapping supplementary class is an intensification of the class-teacher principle. (The "programme of supplementary classes" as a school of its own is here left out of consideration, as it is not relevant to us for other reasons.)

Types 1 and 2 exist in our schools and do valuable work. Type 3, however, lies dormant and is little known. We find that the archetype of the supplementary class was established by Rudolf Steiner[29] soon after the founding of the Waldorf School in 1919 and was first led and organized by Karl Schubert. We know of no school today that has one.

What Is a Supplementary Class?

On first glance, an age-overlapping supplementary class is surprising because of its formal middle position between the two poles of individual extra help and of integration in the class of peers. It has something of both approaches: on the one hand "removal" and on the other hand "integration with the class as a society." Children are taken aside for special attention, but not isolated with experts. Rather, we entrust them to the guidance and reponsibility of a teacher who is there only for them. What does this mean? What gestures and relationships are to be seen here?

One criticism of the supplementary class form is the seemingly overbearing figure of an omnipotent teacher who, as an unskilled auxiliary without any specialized training, is supposed to help a large group of children of different ages with a variety of development problems.

Karl Schubert himself is said to have stated, referring to the early days of Waldorf education, "I had to start without having received any previous directives."[30] Was this an approach that actually made do without any programmatic specialist concepts at all? If one follows the history of the origins at that time, the reply must be: yes. But as a matter of fact, significant large-scale projects started up without a concept or specialist-tested competence are by no means unusual or doomed to fail. Every initiative has known a moment of uncertainty.

There are three possible explanations: Rudolf Steiner made a compromise; Karl Schubert was a giant, and his achievement can only be reproduced by another giant; or Schubert's approach is relevant today, and deserves further investigation.

Although the first two possibilities cannot be ruled out, we consider the third to be correct. Why? Because our present times show symptoms which make it clear that *we cannot build on expertise alone*. A very specific supplement is demanded by the conditions of life today.

The Auxiliary Role of the Supplementary Class and Its Current Relevance

In many areas of life, including those of health and education, the complex aspects of the work and the resulting tasks are being experienced as increasingly difficult to handle.

That the attempt has been made to respond to this increasing complexity with an equal increase of treatment scenarios, strategies, differentiations, and specializations, is understandable and to some extent necessary. But at the same time these conditions of life unveil a remarkable "sound barrier," against which ever-increasing expertise eventually becomes powerless. This happens every day in great as well as small matters. The complexities continue to "catch up" with the experts, leaving them behind, and the specialization screw keeps turning in the same direction: more, more....

After being tried for a significant number of years, the "add more" approach to solutions has developed cracks. Cost increases, gradual at first and now dramatic, make these programs unaffordable even in industrialized countries. They have forced us to the insight that other, "leaner" ways must be found. So if we are not to intensify and reinforce externally, then where can we do it?

Today more than ever, interest is focused on approaches that produce a noticeable qualitative enhancement of personal work, because in a proactive way they strengthen one's consciousness in the approach to a task and then concentrate together and implement healthy, life-relevant impulses coming from the individual's own spiritual-human substance. These approaches show up as a characteristic feature of an "essentialization" in acting: a bundling of right ideas and deeds at the right place at the right moment—there is more flow.

The change in focus, to healing through teaching instead of searching for defects, and instead of favoring increasingly costly repair machinery operated by a horde of specialists, to attend to the question of the outer and inner conditions for health, goes in the same direction.

The trial-and-error discovery of this approach, and the anthroposophic approach overall, is like the story of the hare and the tortoise: anthroposophy is already there; essentialization is one of its natural gifts. This is the foundation of its widely practical fruitfulness in all areas of life. What does this approach consist of? It is re-infusing practical work with the living spirit. Anthroposophical knowledge of man increases our watchful readiness to enable our love for our work to find chances to help the child in an appropriate way.

The auxiliary class in the structure of the Waldof school

The common element at work in all Waldorf schools is the gesture mentioned above: that which, as Rudolf Steiner said, cannot be "audited out" of Waldorf pedagogy; it is what comes into existence when teachers are inwardly permeated with a knowledge of the entire human person in the process of becoming.[31] Through this knowledge they are able to neutralize the dents in their own egos and become receptive to the individual riddle of each child and endowed with the perception, imagination, warmheartedness, language, and intuition necessary for Waldorf instruction and education.

This spiritual, inner digestive process is what creates the Waldorf pedagogical strength and capability and is therefore the real reason for the undoubted worldwide success of this method. (The superficial objection that this makes too high demands and requires teachers with special capabilities falls into the trap of a fallacy. Of course here things are no different than anywhere else. A change of direction and level does not at all mean that the expenditure is also increased.)

What is being carved out of this heartwood of the Waldorf pedagogy is the now largely forgotten creation of the "supplementary class" (as it was then called) of the first Waldorf school, as can be clearly seen from the records of that time.

Everything that was developed in the first Waldorf school can be reviewed relatively easily in the light of whether it was a question of a necessary, historically-delimited compromise with the existing conditions, or a pedagogically interesting creation in which Steiner's intentions can be discovered and further developed. As far as the supplementary class is concerned, the latter applies.

Content, form, and character of the supplementary class

As early as 1919, the necessity of a class of this kind was perceived and characterized by the type of pupils it was to serve: pupils with "…weak abilities or developmental disturbances, pathological symptoms, with intellectual or psychological defects."[32]

This applied to children of the second to the eighth classes.

The instruction given, in a form comparable with an age-overlapping village school class, takes up the main instruction time and comprises about 10 to 12 children. After the long school break the children return to their schoolmates of the same age, although in the upper classes some of them no longer attend foreign language instruction. The duration of the supplementary class varies widely, and may last from a few weeks to several years. The main figure is not a specialized expert, but a teacher who out of his/her own strengths seeks and follows new ways in line with the spirit of the pedagogy.[33] The ways come into existence by the very fact of being entered and followed, in the inner dialogue between the encounter with the child's character, studious research, practical subject-related imagination and spiritual inspiration, always on the basis of an attitude that asks: Where is this going?

Every day in the supplementary class, the children experience the full commitment, intensity, love, and dedication of a teacher in his pedagogical supportive work. They are treated and instructed as a class. For the child, this continues until the "cure" is ended. This creates a special atmosphere.

Like his colleagues, the supplementary class teacher has full teaching freedom and orientates his work not only according to the contents of the plan of instruction appropriate to the children's age, but more intensively to the needs he experiences on the part of the child as well as the information he receives from the class teacher, doctor and parents.

EXAMPLES FOR REMEDIAL SUPPORT
Pedagogical-Medical Diagnosis and Medicine

Ingrid Ruhrmann

For the past 30 years children with developmental disorders have been brought to my colleagues and me for consultation. Over the years our team has systematically compiled bases for diagnosis drawn from the work of Rudolf Steiner,[34] and from secondary literature by Walter Holtzapfel,[35] Karl König,[36] and Michaela Glöckler.[37] We have been able to add to their suggestions with our own phenomenological research, giving rise to a differentiated specialist knowledge in these areas:

- The six pedagogical constitution types
- Curative education pictures
- The pathology of basal body senses and resulting deficits of social perception in the higher senses
- Developmental disorders in the areas of motor skills, language and intelligence

When parents approach us, we offer them one to three 90-minute consultations. We send them an anamnesis questionnaire that enables them to recall at leisure their child's specific developmental steps. I start the discussion by asking, "What can I do for you? How can this consultation be useful to you?" Depending on the parents' wishes, we answer questions or begin with a diagnosis:

- Observation of the child
- Examining the drawings he has brought
- Looking at photos
- Referring to the (already read) anamnesis questionnaire
- Questioning the parents about the four areas named above

In simple, pictorial language we explain to the parents our insights into their child. From these insights we jointly develop ideas for changing the child's daily life so as to promote the child's development without too strenuous efforts, and re-establish family harmony. If they want, and if they give permission, we confer with the family physician, kindergarten teacher, or class teacher. We offer parents a weekly telephone conference. Sometimes we also suggest movement, speech, and educational therapy.

Case Study: Jonas, aged 3.5 years, is presented in the kindergarten due to unusually intense separation anxiety. He is very tall for his age, but very thin. His hands and feet are dry and cold. The anamnesis shows that he cried a great deal as an infant, had problems with weaning, and refused other foods.

No shyness with strangers, from the age of 18 months panic tantrums caused by changes to daily rhythm and at meals. The "terrible twos" and saying "I" at 2.5 years did not take place. He only eats bread with one type of cheese, apples, raw carrots and kohlrabi, millet, potatoes and spaghetti without sauce. He only drinks cold water. It takes him one and a half hours to fall asleep: he sleeps like a "tensed bow" with neck excessively stretched. Movement development: premature face-down position in excess stretching, sliding on floor with help of elbows, bear's gait, no crawling, premature walking at 10 months. He often falls over and cannot manage stairs alone yet. He spoke more words than "Mummy" and "Daddy" before walking, and now speaks uninterruptedly in adult-type speech. He is very attached to his mother and follows her everywhere. He is afraid of children of his own age.

Diagnosis Motor development: his irregular development and his sleeping position point to persisting early childhood reflexes. I ask him to crawl as mummy- and baby-dog, and clearly see the reflex pattern of STNR and that of PALMAR in the hands.38

The basal senses: apart from a disorder of the sense of movement and balance resulting from uninhibited reflexes, with consequences for the senses of hearing and speech—he does not listen to his parents—Jonas primarily suffers from an impairment of the sense of life. He is pale, long, and thin (astral body and ego not united with metabolic-limb system), has sleep disorders, fussy eating, a symbiotically close relationship to his mother, fear of children his own age. He looks at me and then away again immediately. Is not shy of strangers, no "terrible twos" accompanied by saying "I"; but instead, panic attacks from one-and-a-half years, and his premature and unusually developed speech show moderate developmental disorder. If it was more severe one would call it autistic.

No symptoms relating to constitution and curative education pictures.

Recommendations: I decide to begin with the sense of life, since this is the reason for the separation anxiety, which is the question the mother came with. In simple images I describe to the mother the context of maturation disorders in her child's behavior. She is rather shocked since, like all mothers, she hopes her child is developing properly, but on the other is relieved that the problems are not to do with educational inability or that her child is a natural tyrant.

Ideas for daily life: the sense of life gives a sense of well-being, so how can we enhance it?

With lavender baths in the evening, together with a short, often-repeated rhythmic story. As the child is going to sleep the mother cleans the bath next door with gentle sounds as calming "sleep music." Vegetables are "secretly" pureed to make a creamy soup, which tastes good! The parents "work" with the child, cooking, gardening, repairing things. Jonas will also learn to play through these shared, purposeful processes.

Follow-up after four weeks: Jonas is now falling asleep within thirty minutes and his mother no longer sits with him. He eats the soup after being initially skeptical. Working together is very enjoyable: the mother speaks rhythmically to accompany these activities, and Jonas has stopped constantly talking at her. His mother will not bring him back to kindergarten until after the holidays. She has now invited a mother and her daughter from the kindergarten group to visit regularly. We are both pleased, and take a further step by treating the persisting reflexes. Using my doll I show the mother Rota-therapy lap exercises. Jonas plays at our feet.

EDUCATIONAL AND MEDICAL ASSESSMENT AND THERAPY

Bernd Ruf

Individual Support and Its Documentation:
The PARZIVAL Schools–Social Learning through Integration into the School Environment[39]

Olivia and Rene attend the PARZIVAL School Center in Karlsruhe along with about 100 other pupils. At the Center are a school for children with behavioral difficulties, a school for children with learning difficulties, and a school for children and adolescents with other special needs.

Case Study: Olivia is tall and slim and has long, dark hair. She has a well-groomed appearance and wears fashionable clothes. She lacks self-esteem and displays a marked desire for recognition as well as a strong need for approval. Olivia appears fearful, very easily hurt and can barely cope with criticism.

Olivia finds it difficult to adhere to rules and agreements. She always puts her own needs first. She seeks to breach boundaries in the way she interacts with others. Her behavior is deliberately provocative—physically and verbally. She does not accept that she makes mistakes. Her awareness of wrongdoing is not very highly developed.

At age 15, Olivia attends eighth grade at the PARZIVAL Schools. She was admitted two years ago on the recommendation of the child and adolescent psychiatric services.

Olivia is her mother's third child, but was taken in by her paternal grandmother shortly after birth due to her mother's inability to cope. She has not had any contact with her mother since then. Her father only took up contact with her in early 2004 when she was admitted to child and adolescent psychiatric services. She had been sent there after an episode of self-harm (massive cuts on the lower arms). Her father is in a new relationship and has recently had a child, triggering a strong jealous reaction in Olivia. He has not been able to look after Olivia to the extent promised. Olivia would like to live with him, but that is not considered feasible by everyone involved.

Since her admission to child and adolescent psychiatric services, Olivia's home situation has deteriorated further. Disputes, mainly with her grandfather, have intensified, finally leading to a marital crisis between the grandparents.

Olivia increasingly seeks to escape the home situation and looks for refuge with gangs of adolescents. She ignores agreements, frequently goes missing and is then sought by the police. Olivia refuses to allow anyone to tell her what to do. The parental influence of the grandparents is waning rapidly. They feel helpless and appear to have reached the limits of their disciplinary possibilities.

Olivia's school performance has been permanently influenced by her persistent personal crises. In her first weeks of attendance at the Parzival Schools she revealed herself to be a conscientious, hard-working pupil, kept attractively designed school books, and finished her tasks on time and satisfactorily. In seventh grade, her attendance at lessons became increasingly irregular. Olivia has a pronounced spelling weakness. The grammar and sentence structure of her texts often contain errors. There are considerable gaps in her knowledge of mathematics. Her strengths lie in the artistic and creative field. Olivia quickly learned the technique of watercolor painting, understood the tasks, and transformed them into successful paintings. Olivia is particularly gifted at drawing.

Olivia's attitude towards learning and work deteriorated during eighth grade. She was distracted very easily. Her concentration is weak, as is her willingness to make an effort. She requires constant attention, intensive support, and constructive help in all her work. Olivia's ability to evaluate herself continues to be inadequate. She often refuses to cooperate altogether.

Olivia is reserved in her social behavior, sometimes with a depressive tendency. She likes to avoid difficulties. Her introversion can quickly transform into noisy rebellion.

Olivia's self-centeredness and hidden aggressive behavior often lead her into conflict situations. She reacts aggressively in meetings held to deal with these conflicts and takes offense. She rarely has insight into her own part in the conflict. She has difficulty in adhering to rules and agreements. Her awareness of rules is not very strongly developed.

Case Study: Rene is 13 years old and attends seventh grade. He was seriously neglected at a very young age. At the age of two-and-a-half he was tied to his bed and forced to watch his younger brother starve to death in the bed beside him. Rene himself was rescued by police and placed in a children's home. For approximately eight years he has been living with a foster family where he receives intensive support.

Rene is of normal size. He looks neat and well-dressed. He has a noticeably angular head with a prominent forehead and sunken cheeks. His overall appearance is angular. He has athletic hips and is a good runner. He often displays insecurity in his fine motor skills. Rene is far-sighted and wears glasses.

Rene was psychiatrically diagnosed with Tourette's Syndrome. He was intermittently prescribed three psychoactive drugs (Ritalin, Tapridex, Moclix). In addition he received ergotherapeutic treatment and speech therapy. Rene suffers from allergies (Paracetamol, house dust, grasses).

Rene was barely able to improve his learning and work during his first six months in school. His motivation was very low, his concentration limited. Individual cognitive work is still impossible except to a very limited degree. He is very easily distracted. His attention span is not appropriate for his age. His persistence is weak, as is his willingness to make an effort. Rene is driven by constant inner unrest. In all his work he requires constant personal attention, intensive support, and constructive help. His slow progress means that he requires a lot of time to complete his tasks. Rene has become more reliable in carrying out his classroom duties. Only in recent months has it been possible for Rene to follow the content of some lessons a little better and with greater concentration. As a result he has participated with greater interest in the progress of the lesson and the conversations.

In terms of emotional and social development, Rene displays a very immature perception of self and others. In conflicts he often fails to recognize his own part and is seldom able to perceive the actual reason for a conflict or its real beginning.

His constant unrest, attention deficit, and poor concentration mean that he finds it difficult to engage in social processes.

Rene has very low self-esteem. He is not yet able to argue his own case. In social groups he behaves like a weathervane. He wants to be part of the group. This also means that he is easily used. In order to impress others he may act provocatively towards teachers and violently against weaker fellow pupils.

In the middle of the school year, Rene developed a tendency towards verbal and sexual molestation of female pupils. This reduced towards the end of the year. Rene finds it difficult to keep to limits, rules and agreements.

As regards academic learning, Rene displays deficits in German in all areas regarding the correct use of language, and above all in spelling. His writing is legible. He can read simple texts reasonably fluently. Text comprehension is sufficient. There is a deficit, on the other hand, in his knowledge of grammar. In mathematics there are considerable gaps in Rene's knowledge of the subject. This applies to all four basic types of calculation (addition, subtraction, multiplication, division) and the multiplication tables. He has no access yet to abstract and complex problem-solving. Rene's musical competence is sufficiently developed. When he succeeds in concentrating on the matter in hand for a short time, he can develop pleasure in singing. But all rhythmical tasks cause him great problems. In sport, Rene shows little team spirit or awareness of the rules in team games.

Rene has failed so far to master the techniques of watercolor painting. He is hardly capable of producing differentiated transitions in black-and-white charcoal drawing. His great interest and special gifts lie in gardening. Here he works well. He has no difficulty in learning basic gardening skills. However, in team work his clowning about often has a de-motivating effect here too.

Since 1999, the PARZIVAL Schools have successfully implemented a special integrative model based on Waldorf education: teaching pupils with so-called behavioral and learning difficulties together as a class.

This is intended to give pupils the opportunity to profit reciprocally from the strengths of the others and to balance their own weaknesses. Children with behavioral difficulties who frequently display challenging behavior in the social and emotional sphere can experience their own social value in helping their fellow pupils with learning difficulties (who often also display a certain motor inaptitude) to solve tasks—tying shoelaces, being able to balance, and so forth. The pupils with learning difficulties, who tend to be quieter and less socially and emotionally volatile, in turn contribute through their character to making lessons more harmonious.

In 2005, another school for children and adolescents with special needs was added to the School Center. The school collaborates with the other schools on a daily basis.

Pupils are offered remedial provision in life skills in classes of 12 to 15 children of roughly the same age. The concept is based on the educational ideas of Rudolf Steiner, involving study of the human being and developmental psychology. The same concept underlies the Waldorf schools.

The curriculum for children and adolescents with differing needs is based on the Waldorf curriculum. The generally familiar subjects requiring cognitive study (such as German, mathematics, science, history) are supplemented with a greater emphasis on musical and artistic subjects (music, painting, sculpture) and crafts and technology (wood- and metalworking, handwork, ecology, technology, gardening) as well as subjects involving movement (sports, eurythmy). The focus is on holistic learning approaches in which the head (cognitive and intellectual sphere), heart (social and emotional sphere), and hands (affective and volitional sphere) are equally developed and supported.

All key cognitive subjects are taught in blocks of 2-4 weeks in so-called main lessons by a class teacher who stays with the class for a nine-year period. The class teacher provides continuity and meets the children's requirements for a person with whom they can develop a relationship over a period of time. The main-lesson form makes it possible to delve deeper into the subject and cultivates motivation, concentration, and perseverance. Subjects requiring regular practice, such as foreign languages (which are taught from first grade), follow the main lesson.

The remedial and therapeutic provisions tailored to the individual needs of the pupils are integrated into the school day. They include above all therapeutic eurythmy (movement therapy), art therapy, music therapy, speech therapy, horseback riding, and other forms of therapy related to the senses and experiential activities.

Working with individual support plans

The gravity of Olivia and Rene's case studies is by no means unusual at the PARZIVAL Schools. What help does Rene require? What stage of development and learning has Olivia reached? What specific provisions should they each receive? In order to facilitate and ensure a support plan that is guided by the needs of the pupil, and in order to ensure that the whole teaching faculty has an awareness of the developmental progress of each pupil, the PARZIVAL Schools, like many other schools, work with support plans as a supplement to the child and class reviews.

Individual support is one of the key educational aspects. The support plans are structured collections of information about the learning development processes of the child. Their objective is to clarify the child's developmental situation and to formulate short-, medium-, and long-term learning and developmental targets using appropriate support measures. The plan starts from the strengths of the child and links specific support needs with aspects of subject teaching. Lessons thus become aids for the development of the child. In addition, support plans include consideration of the proposed duration of the support measures as well as other organizational requirements.

Support plans are intended to help work out individual solutions to individual problems.

Observation as a form of assessment: starting from the strengths of the pupil—self-reflection—evaluating and documenting results

The drafting of individual support plans always requires advance planning. The main use of any assessment for the purpose of developing support measures is to achieve an understanding of the individual character of the child in order to plan educational and therapeutic actions on that basis. That is why one of the basic requirements of support planning is to gather all information which contributes to an understanding of the child: observations by teachers, presentation of development so far, medical and psychological reports, therapeutic and health reports, information from meetings with parents, school reports, and so forth.

A key factor for understanding the child is to gain an insight into the circumstances of his or her life and experience. It is therefore essential for the teacher to know the child's home environment. Home visits and meetings with the parents are important aids in this respect, together with communication between the teacher and child. An assessment of the home environment is essential for the creation of a support plan. Many children with special educational support needs in particular have often undergone a long and frustrating ordeal of failure until they are finally given formal support. Thus building up or rebuilding self-esteem is a central support task. Such an approach should take as its starting point the child's strengths, the things that he or she is particularly good at and likes to do.

Support plans must also begin by determining the child's specific stage of development.

The most important component of this form of assessment is not interpretation, but observation, description, and documentation. These skills are essential for the success of cooperative support planning. Hence teachers must undergo training in precise observation and exact documentation. An initial collection of information about the strengths and weaknesses of a child can be provided by observation reports that describe the behavior of the child in specific situations.

Since there are no objective evaluation procedures that can exclude the impact of the teacher-pupil relationship, it is important to be aware of the relationship between the child's behavior and our own. Ritualized patterns of behavior between teacher and pupil must be exposed and broken through. This is the task of the teacher, and it requires self-reflection. Training in self-reflection is also required to expose our own bias in the observation and description of children.

Assessment of support needs must always be understood as a process. It is not an isolated evaluation of the child by medical, psychological, or special-needs experts, but a process that accompanies the child's development. Hence support plans should undergo evaluation and further development every three months or so. In this context, the responses and reactions of the child to the educational and therapeutic measures should also be included.

Steps for drawing up a support plan

At the PARZIVAL schools, support plans are drawn up every three months for each pupil by the teachers and are recorded in writing. These class reviews to draw up support plans do not, of course, replace the child reviews which are undertaken by the teaching faculty as a whole.

Comprehensive and academically sophisticated models already exist for the creation of support plans. The PARZIVAL Schools use a simplified, seven-stage process.

1. Initial situation/data: Name, birth data, parents, siblings, place of residence, attachment figures, leisure activities, preferences, curriculum vitae, illnesses and disorders, therapies, development in school, class, teacher, school reports.

2. Current situation: Strengths and weaknesses of child.

3. Determination of support requirements, or multiple support requirements as appropriate: Perception/sensory functions, motor functions, cognition/thinking, language/communication, learning and work behavior, emotional development, social development.

4. Determination of specific support needs. Each support requirement can be divided into several specific support needs:

    a. Perception/sensory functions: lower, middle, and upper senses, physical/spatial orientation.

    b. Motor functions: gross and fine motor skills, hand-hand coordination, eye-hand coordination, movement control, posture, physical dexterity, responsiveness, body image.

    c. Cognition/thinking: memory, recall, conceptualization, ability to form abstractions, comprehension of tasks, ability to synthesize information, generalization, problem solving, creativity.

    d. Language/communication: vocabulary, speech ability, language comprehension, writing/reading ability, use of facial expression, gestures, eye contact, nonverbal communication, establishing contact.

    e. Learning/work behavior: motivation, perseverance, concentration, work speed, drive, resilience, independence, attentiveness, attitude, scope and sustainability of interests, curiosity.

    f. Emotional development: self-perception and perception of others, empathy, self-esteem, self-assurance, tolerance of frustration, affect control.

    g. Social development: ability to make contact, ability to cooperate/interact, ability to play, tolerance of frustration, willingness to help, compliance with rules, critical faculties.

5. Support targets: Description of long-, medium-, and short-term targets for the individual support needs.

6. Support measures: Description of measures intended to achieve the targets described. A distinction can be made between teaching and therapeutic measures.

7. Organization requirements: Information about the duration of support, form of work, number of hours per week, support teachers or therapists, room allocation, provision of any work materials.

Following are some aspects of the support plans for the two case studies described above:

Olivia's Support Plan

1. Current situation

    - Strengths: enthusiastic, creative, gifted at drawing, likes to clean.

    - Weaknesses: verbally aggressive, aggressive towards objects, anxious, depressive, scratches, at risk of addiction, disrespectful, disturbed relationship with authority, stays out at night, plays truant, egocentric, threatening, dominating, aware of her power, manipulative, goes to the limit, tendency for total refusal.

2. Determination of support requirements, or multiple support requirements as appropriate

    - Learning and work behavior, emotional development, social development.

3. Determination of specific support needs

    - Learning/work behavior: motivation, drive, attitude.

    - Emotional development: self-perception and perception of others, self-esteem, tolerance of frustration, affective control.

    - Social development: ability to make contact, ability to cooperate/interact, tolerance of frustration, compliance with rules.

4. Support targets

    - Stabilization of personality, building stable self-esteem, dismantling aggression, dismantling anxieties, support of ability to integrate, support of ability to cope with conflict, support of self-perception and perception of others, support of affective stability and control, support of awareness of rules.

    - Integration in class (rootedness), emotional stabilization,

5. Support provisions/organization

    - Special emotional attention in lessons and during breaks, setting of clear limits, consistent adherence to rules and agreements, clearly structured teaching framework.

    - Anger management and counseling in female only group: small group 2x per week; therapeutic eurythmy: individual support 30 minutes 2x per week; music therapy: individual support 30 minutes 2x per week; piano lessons; remedial teaching in small groups in German and mathematics: 1 hour 2x per week.

Olivia's Evaluation

Overall situation has worsened, total refusal in home, school and therapeutic situation. Support measures could not take effect since Olivia rejected all attempts and avoided the home and school environment for months.

Continuation of support plan. Extended support target: reintroduction to school.

Rene's Support Plan

1. Current state

    - Strengths: likes to sing, loves cycling, water and working in the garden, is fast.
    - Weaknesses: no awareness of limits, attention not appropriate for age, limited perseverance, weak concentration, almost no independent cognitive learning, ADHD, Tourette's Syndrome.

2. Determination of support requirements, or multiple support requirements as appropriate

    - Perception/sensory functions, thinking/cognition, learning and work behavior, emotional development, social development.

3. Determination of specific support needs

    - Perception/sensory functions: lower senses.
    - Thinking/cognition: recall, ability to form abstractions, structuring. Learning/work behavior: attention, concentration, resilience, perseverance.
    - Emotional development: self-perception/perception of others, self-assurance, tolerance of frustration.
    - Social development: ability to make contact, ability to cooperate/interact, compliance with rules, setting limits.

4. Support targets

    - Stabilization of personality, building stable self-esteem, support of ability to integrate, support of ability to cope with conflict, support of self-perception and perception of others, support of concentration and perseverance, support of awareness of rules, strengthen awareness of limits, rhythm support.

5. Support provision/organization

    - Setting of clear limits, consistent compliance with rules and agreements, clearly structured teaching framework, help in learning situations in school, working out conflict resolution strategies.

- Therapeutic Measures: individual support 30 minutes 2x per week; music therapy: individual support 30 minutes 2x per week; speech formation: 20 minutes 1x per week; warm baths and massages will be attempted; remedial teaching in small groups in English and mathematics: 1 hour 2x per week; archery: small groups 1 hour 1x per week; gardening: 2 hours 1x per week.

Rene's Evaluation

Clear improvement in overall situation, self-esteem strengthened, perseverance increased, increase in attention and concentration span, reduction of symptoms of Tourette's Syndrome.

Cooperation in support planning as quality management

Teaching children and adolescents who need special educational support requires collaboration among all those involved in the education process. This applies above all in the fields of emotional and social development. If each teacher pursues different aims and has different expectations, and if there are no agreements and no discussion takes place amongst the teaching faculty, the educational effort becomes neutralized and the quality of educational work is reduced. In the long term, a lack of collaboration will lead to social conflict and contribute to a persistent bad atmosphere in the school.

Cooperative support planning, in contrast, can produce transparency and commitment in educational practice. It facilitates cooperation among teaching colleagues and enhances the efficiency of educational work. Against a background of medical and psychological reports, special education reports, and structured observation by teachers, support areas are defined, specific support needs set out, support targets are determined, and support provisions are developed and monitored. The support is documented and evaluated. In this way support plans can become an instrument of quality development and assurance in remedial education.

EOS EXPERIENTIAL EDUCATION

Michael Birnthaler

The EOS experiential education organization is a charitable association based in Freiburg/Breisgau, Germany, for experiential education based on Waldorf ideas. It is a recognized funder of youth support (Freie Jugendhilfe) and youth education (Jugendbildung) bodies.

EOS began with the observation that young people's hunger for images and experiences has never before been so elemental, vehement, and insatiable as it is today. Threshold experiences of the most diverse kinds nowadays seem to be an integral aspect of every adolescent's biography. At EOS, educators are called on to find a response to this widespread contemporary phenomenon.

From the late 1980s, it was primarily educators of children with challenging behavior who discovered that "difficult" adolescents—those who had succumbed to a career of drugs or violence, whom the school system had given up trying to help—could be restored and re-socialized through experiential education.

Since then experiential education has become an international beacon of hope. In a wide variety of professions, from kindergartens, schools, homes, youth support institutions, and colleges, to local governments, industry and businesses, experiential educators are now in great demand as specialists and collaborative partners.

From the perspective of Waldorf education, too, experiential education offers a great, untapped resource which, in our view, is particularly suited to meeting the increasing hunger for hands-on experience among young people.

The latest results of the PISA study,[40] and research into so-called "Indigo children," also reveal the need for a holistic, experiential form of education. EOS believes that experiential education is not simply concerned with maximizing experiences, but rather with cultivating the capacity to feel and experience things. This new approach, based on sensitive and sensitizing experiential education, makes a subtle distinction between having an experience as a kind of possessive gesture, and undergoing it as a living reality.

We chose the name EOS (Greek: goddess of the dawn) in the belief and hope that the potential of experiential education could open developmental opportunities for the young generation.

The Experiential Education Institute (Erlebenspädadgogik-Institut) was founded to research the bases of an innovative spiritual experiential education, and to spread its findings. Here various courses of training and further training in experiential education are offered, with current student numbers standing at over 200.

Alongside this, in February 2006, a 10-week, full-time training in experiential education began (course entry in February, May, July and August). Other activities of the EOS are:

- Holiday camps
- Class trips
- Outdoor activities training, company training, counseling, coaching, "Management by Spirit."

CHAPTER 16

Examples of Spirituality in Science, Art, and Religion

> *Science imbued with life!*
> *Art imbued with life!*
> *Religion imbued with life!*
> *That is education, ultimately,*
> *That is teaching ultimately.*
>
> —RUDOLF STEINER[1]

In an early article on education, Rudolf Steiner stated:

> We do not have the task of conveying certainties and convictions to our younger generation. Instead we should induce them to use their own power of judgment, their own powers of comprehension. They should learn to see the world with open eyes.... Our convictions only apply for us. We teach them to young people in order to say to them: That is how we see the world—now discover how it appears to you. We should awaken capacities, not pass on convictions. Today's youth should not believe in our "truths" but in our personal qualities. They should notice that we are seekers, and we should help them to be seekers too.[2]

What is needed, as stated here, is to awaken capacities—in the spheres of science, art and religion.

It is easy to understand that science requires attentiveness (sensory training), learning to think for oneself, drawing conclusions from observation, experiment, and experience, and gaining insights. In art we call on capacities such as understanding of process, transformation, and experiencing totalities and beauty. In the religious domain, on the other hand, we encounter social qualities such as gratitude, love of our fellow human beings, and responsibility. Even if it is evident that, through the course of child development, religion is a natural gift of early childhood, art a gift of middle-school age, and that the strongest disposition for developing a scientific attitude lies in late adolescence, it is nevertheless clear that at each phase of childhood these three realms require attention and care in order to grow into habits—and thus true capacities—by the end of schooling. To achieve this is the declared aim of Waldorf education, since this is the only way to make the developmental goal of full humanity the basis of education. It is therefore a great challenge for every teacher and educator to work on his own fundamental approach to science, art, and religion. The three articles in this chapter aim to clarify, in ideal terms, what is involved here, and how it can be used.

On Science

An example of methodological interest is in Eugen Kolisko's article below. He demonstrates firstly, the consistent search for the overall context in which a phenomenon exists, and secondly, the comparative method. The more we succeed in demonstrating that a certain phenomenon is a part of a larger whole, or is linked to more complex phenomena, the more pupils can experience its larger sense and purpose. Isolated knowledge, in contrast, easily strikes them as barren and purposeless. Both the work involved in placing a detail in the context of a wider whole or tracing its relationship to this whole, and the comparative mode of observation, offer the most differentiated possibilities for posing questions, and also stimulate pupils to independently develop and pursue the most varied lines of inquiry. This wakens the will for thinking, promotes the autonomous development of ideas, and practices questioning as the source of all scientific discovery.

Kolisko's article on circulation, first published in 1989, retains its relevance today. His findings have been augmented by more detailed and striking examples from human physiology, which prove that the heart does indeed exercise important perceptive functions and is also hormonally active.

Parabase

Joyfully, for many years
The spirit's been diligent, involved
In researching, in discovering
How nature's life is in creating.
And it is the
One eternal
Revealed in huge diversity;
Small the big and big the small,
Everything in its type and mode,
In endless flux yet holding constant;
Shaping and reshaping—and I'm there to wonder and behold.

– J. W. V. GOETHE[3]

THE HEART DOES NOT DRIVE THE BLOOD, BUT THE BLOOD DRIVES THE HEART

Eugen Kolisko[4]

"The heart is a pump that moves the blood." This is taught in all physiology textbooks as an absolute certainty, and every child must learn it today through the popularization of science.

The circulation is a primal phenomenon of life. No living phenomena exist without the flow of fluids. Even a single cell shows this. Currents flow toward the cell walls, where the cell tends to die off. Where the organism has an external boundary, a death process is really at work, and the fresh flow of nutrition has to flow there for it to remain alive. Life is continually prevented death. The stream of fluid replaces what dies off in meeting the external world. In their pseudopodia, amoeba show internal centrifugal and external centripetal flows. The internal currents lead nutrients out of the cell's interior, while the outer currents carry away what has been used. This recalls higher organisms.

This is like a cellular model of the limb circulation in higher animals and the human being. The plant too shows sap flows of all kinds. The stonewort (Chara) has been cited from time immemorial as a wonderful instance of fluid circulation. There is no apparent propulsion or driving force creating this circulation. Many transitional stages lead from here to the ingenious sap circulation in trees. It is the same primal phenomenon of life, continually enhanced. Basically, fluid circulations are merely the expression of the plant's polar self-differentiation. What grows more strongly also requires a means of sap supply. Growth and sap flow are inseparable. The mere fact that all life is linked with nutrition and respiration leads to the development of a flow of nutrition and its attraction to and absorption by the parts of the organism that continually die off as they function. What has been used up is led away, and oxygen and nutrition are sucked in. This also already embodies the primal phenomenon of the circulation rhythm. Life is a continual self-renewal of the organism, and thus the flow of sap is a primal phenomenon of life.

Based on this view let us examine the development of blood circulation in animals. Circulation precedes the formation of the heart. First, in polyps (coelenterates) the intestine is at the same time both nutrition and circulation system and distributes nutrients. Here we have a gastro-vascular system: in other words the parts of the body suck directly on the intestine to obtain the nutrients for their function. Then, when a bodily cavity forms, the blood circulates in the polyp without any specialized blood channels. The flow of nutrition moves between the parenchyma composing it. Island-shaped static parts are encircled by moving ones. Thus circulation precedes cell-wall formation. The cell wall develops around the living flow of fluids. The more that the streaming parts become distinct from static ones, the more do these latter form walls. In the lymph vessel system too, which remains at a primitive level, such indiscriminate flow is still decisive. For the white blood cells, the blood vessel wall represents no boundary, and they migrate through it without problem.

The annelids (Annelida) possess a secondary bodily cavity that suppresses the primary one, which remains as an autonomous system of vessels. Here one has a blood tube encompassing the intestine, and a back and stomach vessel. Later the blood tube surrounding the intestine disappears again, leaving only individual blood vessel annulae, or rings that surround the intestine and connect back and stomach vessels. This looks like a magnet surrounded by wire. Now all vessel walls are originally contractile tissue, but individual vessel parts are more strongly developed. In most annelids, therefore, the back vessel as a whole is contractile. In earthworms the annulae between the main vessels are especially so, whereas in the lancelet fish, the forerunner of vertebrates, the stomach vessel can be contracted as a whole.

One sees, therefore, that heart-type structures arise through the contracting of all the rhythmically contractile substance composing the circulation system walls. Originally the whole circulation system is a heart. It only appears as such, however, if it can fully focus its forces in a single location.

The development of the nervous system determines where, initially, pulsating and metamorphosing parts arise. In worms and segmented creatures, the blood circulates in the reverse way to lancelets and vertebrates. The former have their "heart," or rather the most strongly contracting vessel area, on their backs, while the latter have it on their stomach-side. Why? Worms and segmented creatures have their nervous system on the front, whereas vertebrates possess a spinal cord. The nervous system is the mediator of consciousness, but it is also the bearer of death. Where there is greater consciousness there is less life or vitality. With increasing consciousness in the evolutionary sequence of animals, the power of regeneration diminishes.

The nerve substance itself is least capable of regeneration compared with all other animal tissue. That is why the flow of fluids is directed toward the nervous system. This flow always passes from life toward death. If the nervous system is situated in the stomach region, the blood must stream from the back; if it is situated toward the back, the blood flows the other way. In the tunicates one finds a remarkable transitional state between these two. The blood flows in alternate directions, forward and then backward. Here the stomach-centered nervous system is still pronounced, but at the same time one finds an incipient spinal system. Thus we see an experiment undertaken by nature itself: the circulation arises from the original polarity of life and is not driven by mechanical forces.

The fact that the circulation develops as a balance between two polarities is also shown in embryology. Vitellus circulation is present before one can discern any heart or even differentiated vessel development. The nervous system is the first thing to develop in the embryo, distinguishing itself from the nourishing vitellus. A circulation starts between the polarities of nervous system and the metabolic foundation of the vitellus. The stream of nutrition follows the form of the embryo as it arises from the womb of life. Here too there is circulation which precedes the heart. The heart only develops later in the circling blood.

The presence of the embryo's three blastodermic layers also points in the same direction. From the outer blastodermic layer develops the nerve-sense system and the skin, while from the inner layer the intestinal system develops. The middle layer which forms between the two is where blood and the circulatory system develop. Thus the circulation system arises as a balance between the poles of consciousness (nervous system) and metabolic processes. The human organization is a product of this developing polarity. What we see in miniature in the cell, that the flow of life streams from the living to the dying, is also apparent in the larger scale, in the complex totality of the human organism. This is the "One eternal revealed in huge diversity."[5]

But a solely mechanistic concept is also inadequate if we observe the fully-formed circulation system. The attempt to understand blood movement in purely hydrodynamic terms fails. After endless fruitless trials it is now admitted that a law such as that posited by the French physicist Poiseuille about resistance in the capillaries does not apply to the bodies of animals and humans. The capillary flow is autonomous. Its rapidity depends on the intensity of the life process in tissues, not on their narrowness or breadth. The arteries too, quite apart from their tonus, show active pulsation phenomena. This is apparent from the active streams in the arteries, the independent movements of developed arteries, the relationship of the umbilical arteries in the embryo, the continuation of the circulation for some time after the heart has stopped, and the emptying of the arteries that accompanies this, together with many other phenomena. There is an independent flow in the veins. This is clear from the venous hearts of some animals, the impossibility of explaining venous flow by means of the heart systole and thorax aspiration, particularly in veins in the lower extremities. The tonus of the blood vessels is not just a kind of highly developed, elastic tension but an active, rhythmic collaboration with blood circulation. Based on numerous subtle observations drawn from medical practice of the normal function of the vascular system and changes to it, we know that the extracardial part of the vascular system must be seen as playing a role equally important as that of the heart.[6]

Every function of an organ makes blood flow toward it. And the more intensive the function becomes, the more strongly does the supply-flow mechanism develop, and the more compressed and rhythmically flexible does the vessel wall become. The organ's function sucks blood toward it. The organ generates the circulation's driving forces, rather than the vessel walls, which themselves only arise as mechanism to aid organ function. What does it mean to say that organ function gives rise to circulation? It means that the totality of life functions, the life body, causes blood to flow. The active parts of the life body draw blood toward them. Every organ also includes its blood supply as integral to it. Its development is at the same time followed by the forming of a rhythmically pulsing channel for the flow of nutrients. The blood is autonomous in its motion. It can never be thought of as resting, as though it were only subsequently impelled by some driving force. It is in primal movement. The more organs are differentiated and develop through polarity, the more complex the circulation has to become and the more important is the complexity of the vessel wall musculature.

This leads us back to the significance of evolving organ development for the circulation. What distinguishes the animal from the plant? In the plant, every organ is leaf. In other words, all organs are really of equal value. Each resembles the whole plant. Everything is leaf, which is also why every organ of the plant can give rise to the whole plant. Here the power of regeneration is particularly pronounced. In the animal, every organ becomes a part of the whole. Each organ lacks something of the whole. And it is precisely a real organ because it is not the whole. But what has happened to the missing part, the lack of possibility to be the whole, the lack of resemblance to the whole? Instead of this we see in animals the development of interior feeling experience. What the animal lacks in forces of external growth and structure appears as internal life of feeling. This gives rise in the animal to differentiation into the poles of nervous and metabolic systems, with the circulation providing equilibrium between the two. The organs of the animal point to an equally diverse differentiation in feeling life. The soul is not separate from the organs but makes use of them to become conscious. Thus organ development and soul development are one and the same. A particular development in any organ system is simultaneously linked to a particular development of soul functions. The more a nervous system crystallizes out, the more something resembling conceptualization can arise from primal inner soul experiences. But the metabolic system also differentiates at the same time, along with a more subtle development of will life. Between these two, the circulation develops and must become ever more complex in order to mediate between the poles of consciousness and will. The most highly evolved circulation is at the same time the expression of the most highly developed life of soul. Here the blood is harmoniously drawn upon by all parts, giving rise to the miraculous structure of the heart as ever more refined focus and collaboration of all peripheral organs. The heart can only be understood from the perspective of the periphery, and never the blood circulation from the center, from the heart. Just as the heart hypertrophies if an organ sucks in too much blood during intensive physical exertion, so it has developed out of and through the periphery, not just in its extreme but also in its normal formation.

It is therefore hardly astonishing to find that all soul experience in the human being, particularly the life of feelings, is intimately connected with the movements of the blood. Joy, pain, anger, fear, shame are all linked to particular motions of the blood. Through these physical processes of circulation our "I" comes to awareness of feeling processes. Similarly, ideas and imaginations affect the blood circulation. If we move our limbs, the blood flows toward them. If we exert our thinking, the blood flows toward the brain. If we imagine a lemon, our salivary glands function and blood is sucked toward them. In other words, every conceptual preoccupation with an organ area makes the blood flow toward that organ. Our soul lives in the organs, and from simple observation of these phenomena one can say that our soul drives our blood. Feelings, and awareness of particular organ areas, are always connected with the circulation.

In the evolutionary sequence, organ development is the same as soul development, which shows that the increasing refinement of the soul is what makes the circulation ever more complex. We usually say that soul life is accentuated the more the nervous system develops. But in fact the nervous system only manifests the degree of development of the part of soul life oriented to the senses and conceptual life, while the other organs show that of the rest of soul life. Overall organ development is the expression of soul development. Apart from their purely physiological significance, as described by modern science, the organs also have mental and emotional significance. As the organs develop, soul forces are freed and live on in them. The circulation is the linking context, the rhythmic balance between organs of the metabolic and nerve-sense systems, and thus also between the contrasting soul forces of thinking and will. In the human being the soul manifests as the true moving force of the blood. It is the soul that makes blood flow in the body. In the motions of the blood, when we feel fear, joy, and other soul expressions of the "I," it is apparent how this "I" experiences itself in the blood's circulation. In the rest of the world of organisms, the soul aspect conceals itself behind the organs, between which the circulation develops. In the human being this soul aspect becomes manifest, as the movement of the blood gives expression to our deepest inwardness.

The heart can only be understood through the mutual interactions of the whole periphery. We need only examine the effect that the development of the lung has on the heart's development. The lengthwise subdivision of the heart is solely a result of lung development. The more that air alone is breathed, the more the heart divides. Likewise, the division into two chambers can be seen as an expression of the developing polarity of above and below. This division first appears in cyclostomes, where blood and lymph channels divide and the head starts to evolve. Above and below become distinct. And when, from the lungs, air has penetrated circulation, once blood is arterialized, the right and left sides of the heart divide. It would be a task in itself to demonstrate this link between the start of lung breathing's effect on circulation and soul development. At any rate, here too it is apparent that the structuring of the periphery simultaneously gives rise to the central heart as the greatest artistic creation of the organism. All organs have fashioned it together. The more that organs develop in polarity the more clearly does the heart develop in the center to rhythmically balance this polarity. Initially polarity is lacking. In the single-cell organism, in the undifferentiated mass of the fertilized egg-cell, it is not yet pronounced. But then it arises and with it simultaneously the first rhythmic movement of equilibrium. In the human being, the contrast between organ systems has advanced the furthest, and here there appears the most wonderful structure and function of the heart organism.

Anyone who says that the heart drives the blood like a pump fails to see that this so-called pump itself arises from the blood. The concept of a pump is redundant the moment the pump itself is seen as a creation of the fluid moving through it. This kind of thinking is like asserting that if a person runs to help another when the latter cries out, it is not the cry for help which drives him, but his legs. Of course one can see it in those terms, but what is needed is to understand how such a cry for help can work right down into the legs. And in the case of the heart we have to realize that its apparently mechanical functioning is produced through a polarity of phenomena: that, in fact, the evolution of the soul, which continually shapes the organism to be an ever more subtle instrument bringing it to consciousness, expresses itself in the evolution of the circulation.

All densification of the cell walls is simply the result of enhanced organ function and organ differentiation. Just as in the case of heart hypertrophy, when the enhanced function at the periphery gives rise to a stronger "pump" in the heart, so the whole heart can be seen to have developed from the periphery through the increasing complexity of the blood flow. The whole vascular system arose in the same way that enhanced function gives rise to capillaries and thickens arterial walls. The real driving force is the spirit-soul element, which ultimately can only come to consciousness through differentiated, polar organ development.

There was a time—in fact when the circulation of the blood was first discovered—when people applied mechanical concepts to the human organism with a certain inevitability. People wanted to understand everything, including the human being, in mechanical terms, for the machine can be understood. One has insight into the law governing its creation. Mechanical concepts of the organism were needed in order for people to emancipate themselves from traditional medicine's increasingly confused ideas. Today, the human organism can once more be understood as a bearer of the soul and spirit. The soul-numbing doctrine of the heart as pump must be replaced by the truth: *the blood, and in fact the soul, drives the heart.*

Experiences with Modeling, Speech, Eurythmy, and Methodology

MODELING

Hella Loewe

Report by Hella Loewe about her experiences with basic modeling forms in the first three school years.[7]

Alongside form-drawing and painting, I also regularly modeled with the children in the first three grades. The background to this was as follows.

In the summer of 1986, I took on a first-grade class for the second time, at Kräherwald Waldorf School. The class had 36 children. Every first-grade teacher knows that it is not easy for the children, even if they have come up through kindergarten, to adapt to the big new school community in which new demands are placed on them. It quickly became apparent that diverse gifts and a variety of cultural and national influences, languages, and religions had met in this new class. This multicultural mix gave rise to tangible and perceptible social tensions, leading in some children to marked aggression. Other children suffered serious physical injuries as a result, not to mention emotional distress. The behavior of children not yet able to interact socially made it difficult, sometimes impossible, to work properly in the first part of main lesson (between 8:00 and 9:45am), which focuses on whole-class activities involving rhythmic movement, speaking, and singing. During playground breaks too, extremely critical situations often developed. Normal educational measures did not help sufficiently. I could not and did not want to remain responsible for this situation for any length of time. The question therefore became increasingly urgent for me of how to transform into purposeful activity this accumulated aggression expressing itself through the children's hands in pushing, hitting, tormenting, and throttling others. This was no doubt not just an expression of childish exuberance but rather of fears and insecurities.

The following idea came to me as an answer to this question:

I wanted to put a compact, earthy material into the children's hands for them to work on—earth, clay. I wanted to model with them and also with the whole class. Why modeling particularly? I was later asked. Since I myself had often enjoyed clay modeling I knew the beneficial, liberating effect which creating modeled forms can have on the person doing it. I therefore believed that it would be very healing for the children with behavior difficulties to release their accumulated aggression and anxiety into the modeling material, into the pleasantly tactile clay. I also counted on it having a positive effect on children if they were allowed to grasp something fully and with both hands, thus learning to sensitize their inner palms. Such controlled will activity, I hoped, would help the whole class. I also believed that the modeling exercises should be artistic and therapeutic ones if they were to have the right effect.

After making this decision, my sense of responsibility toward the curriculum and my colleagues made me ask: Why? Modeling with clay in first grade was—as far as I knew—not usual. Some class teachers had children model small figures in wax during Advent. Modeling of basic, non-representational forms in clay was however acknowledged by very few teachers as a part of the artistic curriculum, and scarcely practiced. Against this background I was very grateful to the faculty of Kräherwald Waldorf School for granting me the freedom to pursue this unorthodox activity with the children in the first three grades. The faculty accompanied and questioned my work—primarily in the initial phase—with critical and at the same time supportive interest.

I told an experienced lecturer at the Stuttgart seminar for Waldorf education of my decision. Prior to working there, she had taught pupils of all ages. It is thanks to her initiative that soon after I started modeling with the children, a small group of colleagues was willing to meet to collaborate on an educational research project devoted to modeling work in the first three school years. This group included two other tutors at the Stuttgart college who, like the lecturer mentioned above, worked in the field of sculpture. All three encouraged me to do what I felt was right for these children in my care and what life was now asking—regardless of what was considered usual. Due to pressures of time, this working group, which also initially included three class teachers from other Waldorf schools, was able to meet on only a few occasions during the three years. Nevertheless, our intensive shared effort pioneered a methodological path for modeling basic forms with children in the lower grades that can be considered to accord with Rudolf Steiner's indications. At each meeting of the group we reviewed the practical educational experiences I had had with the children in my class and took account of them in seeking appropriate forms. In this process, simple forms were developed that could mold themselves smoothly into the children's hands. Due to the children's age, we avoided all sharp-edged, pointed shapes or those with cavities and enclosed, interior spaces. Well-rounded and at the same time clearly formed shapes were the result. Relief-type forms and forms built up from a solid base were excluded.

We also started searching for comments by Steiner about modeling with this age, and gradually we discovered important indications. In this way the foundation of this sequence of forms was developed, showing how steps can be taken based on insight into the human constitution. In the following years I independently developed a selection of forms, still following the principles discovered in the working group. This sequence may serve interested teachers and educators, and possibly also therapists and parents, as a stimulus for their own work.

Let me also briefly report on the class which had motivated this educational research: by maintaining the weekly painting day as well, wherever possible, artistic and pictorial work was intensified during the fall and winter months through regular modeling. The children also practiced form drawing in three- to four-week blocks. This had an extraordinarily harmonizing effect on the whole class. Over time, the particularly aggressive children found their way more and more into this consistent and controlled will activity of modeling, increasingly learning to harness their own wills.

The Artistic Process in Therapy. Ruth is fourteen years old and was referred to child psychiatry due to depression. Her mother died when she was nine. Since then she has been living with her father, brother, and grandmother, the latter being her main caregiver. When Ruth was thirteen her father married a woman he had known for some time, whom Ruth likes. Six months after the marriage Ruth began to withdraw from friends, school, and all activities outside the home. She became less and less motivated. Her general practice physician prescribed antidepressants, which made her feel still worse. Finally her parents brought her to a child psychiatric ward.

Apart from medical treatment, she also took part in hospital tuition, receiving eurythmy and painting therapy. Over a period of three months she painted every day. Initially her downcast eyes, slumped shoulders, aimless gait, and delayed reactions expressed heaviness. Whenever I collected her for painting therapy it seemed that the unexpressed plea for me to "lead her" was emanating from her. Because she was scared of yellow and red, I let her paint in just blue to begin with. Only gradually was she able to extend the shading of blue into neighboring green and mauve, carefully lightening it to sky-blue before adding yellow, and at last creating a luminous white central motif, a stork.

After this, for a period of three weeks, she devoted herself to the motif of a tree changing through the seasons. The uprightness of the tree seemed to impact her own uprightness, something one could even perceive in her posture. Her attention was also drawn to the forms of trees, their surroundings and changes. In the last weeks of her psychiatric stay, she was preoccupied with "the different stages of human life." The veil technique of watercolor painting was one she had already practiced when painting trees. I helped her with her difficulties in forming the shapes and proportions of the human figure by preparing small sketches. During this time conversations developed about various different human interests, about movements and activities, and about moods at different stages of life.

First she painted a rosy infant lying on a spring-like, sunny meadow. On the second sheet she painted two children, a girl and a boy. "It's better to play with two," she said. The color mood and the hopping children expressed cheerfulness and lightness. From the third picture onward she decided to orient the sheet lengthwise. She used the tree motif which was familiar to her from the previous sequence, painting two children climbing on the tree and picking cherries. The fourth picture showed a teenage girl and boy walking through a hilly landscape.

The landscape's colors conjure a fresh morning mood. The boy points in the direction they are walking. The fifth picture portrayed a man and a woman. The man is walking ahead. Both figures are distinguished through intense red against the green background. In the background are two pointed mountains with white peaks, behind which an orange sun is setting. As she was painting she said: "I want to have high mountains here, because they are both at the summit of their lives!" Where light and brightness dominate in the first pictures, in this picture the polarity of red (enhancement of light and dark) and green (the connection between light and dark) are accentuated, giving tension to the color mood. The color intensity she chose radiates strength. The sixth picture portrayed an older couple turned toward each other, on a brown field. The background is formed by a sequence of green trees, over whose tops the sunset shines. Her commentary to this is that "They have reaped what they sowed."

By now she had come to create her pictures quite independently and with joyful involvement. In the last picture one sees two old men walking along a lakeshore as twilight comes on. In this picture one does not see the heavens directly, but only reflected in the lake. The light illumines the earth beneath the autumnal trees. When I asked her why the figures in this picture were both men, she replied: "When you're old it doesn't matter whether you're a man or a woman!" Her last two pictures stood out in particular for their warm earth tones and richly nuanced darkness.

Review of Painting Sessions. Ruth's special ability lay in creating diverse colors, in the play of light and dark, and the relationship between stages of human life and the surrounding landscape. This spoke of a rich and differentiated soul life.

The forms of the figures and their proportions were still difficult for her to master, demonstrating her difficulty with growing into and taking hold of her own physical body. Considering the human being at different stages of life helped her to inwardly evaluate and integrate outer perceptions in the creative artistic process. Growing into one's own figure and form becomes a living symbol in the seventh-grade Waldorf school activity of sewing a dress. In language arts and eurythmy lessons the human being's soul gesture is considered in wish, wonder, and surprise. These soul expressions are also to be found in the gestures of Ruth's human figures. After being discharged from hospital she transferred from her old school to the Waldorf school, developing particular enthusiasm in the eighth-grade play, where the roles allowed her to give full, gestural expression both to her richness of soul and her efforts to enter fully into the human form.

SPEECH

Barbara Deanjean-von Stryk[8]

*To one who understands the sense of speech
The world unveils
Its image form.*

*To one who listens to the soul of speech
The world unfolds
Its true being.*

*To one who lives in the spirit depths of speech
The world gives freely
Wisdom's strength.*

*To one who lovingly can dwell on speech
Speech will accord
Its inner might.*

*So I will turn my heart and mind
Toward the soul
And spirit of words.*

*In love for them
I will then feel myself
Complete and whole.*

—RUDOLF STEINER[9]

Do we really know what we do when we speak and imprint our thoughts, feelings and will impulses upon the air as sound and form? Language is more than a mere communication medium, it can be an expression of our whole human nature. If we immerse ourselves consciously and with full sensitivity in the process of word formation, if we seek to regain a direct experience of our speech, we can come to a new awareness of ourselves. In language and speech, secrets are concealed which are closely linked with riddles of the human being and the world.

Contemporary civilization suffers from an impoverishment of speech and speech disorders. But if the human being finds no means of expressing his soul through speech, only two routes remain open to him: he can withdraw into himself and shut himself off in his own world of thoughts, or he can try to communicate his feelings to the world, possibly by violent means. Autism of the soul and chaos can ensue where speech no longer mediates between soul and soul.

Human speech can only be exemplified by a human "I" present in the speech process. Acquisition of language depends on the "I" or ego dwelling amongst other egos. To the extent to which the heard and spoken word is replaced by media, it loses its ego-stimulating forces of equilibrium; instead of ensouling, the human being experiences automation of his thinking, feeling, and will habits.

But it is not just the soul that can find in the rightly spoken word its proper mode of expression. Speech processes work as it were inward, giving physiological shape and, through breath transformed by speech, enlivening all the body's organs. Because the body is thoroughly sculpted by language in this way, the precondition for harmonious, individual development is provided. We can thus exert a beneficial or a harmful effect on our body, soul, and spirit organism, depending on how we use language. This gives rise to a responsibility that goes beyond our own individual destiny and affects the whole of humanity.

It is extraordinarily important to encompass living speech processes in conceptual terms and to find the right words for the nature of the Word. Language is so fluid and flexible that we cannot fully grasp it with our normal thinking. The processes belonging to it have to be dynamically grasped if we are to gain a sense of their vitality.

This book[10] thus aims less to enrich the reader's knowledge than to deepen his sensitivity to language and his power of experiencing it. But it also offers a basis for insight and understanding so that phenomena of human expression in speech can be penetrated with awareness.

We cannot speak about language without speaking about the human being, for the one determines the other. The interconnections between language and human being can be discerned right into physical functions. For this reason, I have tried to view the various speech processes and impulses from the perspective of a spiritual-scientific understanding of the human being. "One can only perceive material existence by becoming familiar with the specific workings of spirit in material existence." Processes that are extremely complex for a layperson to grasp can be absorbed more easily if one grasps and dynamically experiences their gesture. The examples that follow suggest a path that can lead us out of the cul-de-sac of speech distortion and impoverishment. Behind the many words that we unthinkingly use each day stands the Word, which can unfold its healing, artistic, spiritual forces if we are prepared to unite ourselves with it in the right way.

We can approach the true nature of the Word in various ways. Before we are ready to take hold of, work on, and change our speech, we can first create a foundation of understanding about the relationship between human being and language. Religious, philosophical, or spiritual-scientific texts on this theme can help us to reflect on language and speech and generate a mood of receptivity leading to further questioning and a more comprehensive search. We may be astonished to discover how many significant figures from ancient times through to the modern era have been preoccupied with processes of speech and breathing and how much knowledge there is to be acquired in this realm. Plato, for instance, develops a very vivid, sculptural, and colorful doctrine of speech sounds. He has Socrates say:

> We should experience how much God himself is the true originator of these forms, of poetry and its spoken recitation. But God uses human beings, artists, as instruments, so as to voice himself through them and make himself audible.[11]

Our personal experience of and with language can pick up on such descriptions. By allowing speech processes to resonate in our feeling we create the precondition for opening the heart to a theme that affects each and every one of us.

Without a new kind of hearing, a renewal of speaking is not possible. We can practice and awaken such hearkening if we repeatedly enliven in ourselves the question of the speaking human being. In our own speech, or that of another, we instinctively experience pleasure or discomfort. We can trace this further inwardly, making ourselves aware of the voice's resonance, placing, and quality, noticing whether it strikes us as flowing or stumbling, living or fixed, whether it moves us and takes us with it, or leaves us wholly uninvolved, whether it is well-shaped and structured, or unclear and blurred. To perceive this more distinctly we must learn to listen through the content of what is said and to discern how someone is speaking (see Chapter 1, "Education: A Pathway of Silent Healing"). Head consciousness must fall partially asleep for heart consciousness to awaken. If we then perceive the creative power and tone colors of the other soul as an artistic act, we meet the speaking person in a most inward way, even if we just overhear what he is saying for a moment.

It is harder to do this in relation to our own speech, for every artistic process is disturbed when we reflect on it. We can therefore only retrospectively eavesdrop on our speech and ask how what we just said sounded: what is the tonal form we experience in the reverberation of our words, what images and moods arise in the soul when we experience ourselves resonating in the echo of our speech? We can then try to discover whether our voice sounds piping, croaking, or rumbling, whether we are repeatedly forced to whisper due to hoarseness, or whether we start spluttering through speaking too quickly and grow tired. What modes of speech creep in unawares which we developed as a habit at some point and now use involuntarily? Do we speak because we simply cannot be silent or because we have something important to communicate? Is speaking easy for us, or do we experience the transition from inward thought and feeling to word as a painful threshold each time? With loving humor we can then also imitate ourselves, for instance intentionally accentuating our too high and nervous head voice, and then for a while playfully experimenting with the deeper tones, to see how they feel.

Once we have practiced listening to the after-echo of our speech, we can augment this by trying to hear our words in advance. In daily life this is rarely possible, but gradually we may be able to educate ourselves to inwardly hear the first phrase we wish to speak after a pause in the conversation, in as well-formed and resonating a way as possible, before we make it audible for the other. Through such exercises, breath and speech will grow calmer and more ordered, and we can begin to feel directly responsible for a process that otherwise takes place in a habitual way. A new social power develops in us if we learn through practice to listen receptively, rather than continually seeking to push ourselves forward through our own speech.

The chalice which received the blood of the Crucified One and the spear which wounded Him are the content of the Grail mysteries. In them we can experience archetypal pictures of hearing and speaking. Through the ear we receive the voice of the person speaking, and perceive his ego through listening. Like the spear, though, the word can either wound or heal, depending on whether it is spoken from our lower nature or, led from above, overcomes materiality. Hearing and speaking must live in equilibrium so that a social breathing process develops. Hearing in advance, attending in full listening, and hearkening to the after-echo are fundamental preconditions for a harmonious speech process that strives to unfold both in an individual human being and in a human community.

In every true act of hearing, the soul opens as though in a mood of questioning, and this can lead to the decision not only to approach one's own speech with sensitive perception but also to work at it. We can experience how difficult it is to penetrate our own habits if we try to banish a word or inappropriate turn of phrase from our habitual speech. It can take days before we even notice the word occurring in our speech, and later we may sometimes catch the word in the act of slipping out of our mouth. It may take weeks before we become able to guard the threshold of the mouth and keep back the words that we wish not to say. This is the start of a long road of practice through small, perhaps disappointingly slow steps. The processes and sequences we need to master before we can learn to rule our words are of significant dimensions, corresponding to a reining in of our egotism.

Another means of approaching speech with both insight and feeling is to rediscover for ourselves the real meaning of a concept that has grown empty of life and soul. We have already learned to feel our way out of the word. If one feels one's way back into a word such as "interest" and discovers its Latin derivation of "inter" (between, among) and "esse" (to be) then we can gain a strong sense of interest as a way of dwelling among things or phenomena, of being wholly with and alongside them. Likewise, in the word "mundane" we can feel the full weight and import of earthly things (mundus = world) rather than just the sense of something banal. We can learn to feel in the word "importance" something that we carry right into ("import" into) ourselves, and in the word "courage" a quality that is closely connected with the heart (coeur).

Just as we become more sensitive to speech sounds and syllable gestures, we can gradually experience the fact that even small prefixes (such as pre-, re-, in-, or ex-) express something essential and significant.

Premeditate, reawake, intend, and express all acquire coloring, gestures, and shades of meaning through these apparently insignificant prefixes that distinguish them from the verb they unite with.

Our experience of language becomes richer when we begin to hearken to the inner gesture of the thought contained in the sound.

If one wishes to unite oneself still more profoundly with language, one can try to awaken the concept of an inner pictorial quality. A saying, an excerpt from a poem, or a passage of literary prose are suitable for this. First one can read the words or say them quietly to oneself, and reflect on the content. Worlds can open up if then, in a second perusal, each word is experienced as picture and we begin to move within these pictures and from picture to picture. A much-used grace by Christian Morgenstern could then be deepened and enlivened in the following way:

Before speaking	**Speaking**
Inwardly bend down, seeing the earth or a part of a field and approaching this:	Earth
Entering into the plant kingdom And seeing how this grows out of the earth:	Who gave to us this food
Expanding upward to the sun, experiencing its radiance, warmth, and light:	Sun
Experiencing how the plants rise up and grow toward the sun, producing leaves, flower, and fruit:	Who made it ripe and good
Now bringing to the sun the warmth and gratitude of human beings:	Dear sun,
Now turning back toward the earth and encompassing it in love:	Dear earth
Seeing both planetary bodies vividly before one's gaze and conjuring our intimate ties with and gratitude to them:	By you we live, Our loving thanks to you we give.

EURYTHMY

Ulrike Wendt, Helga Daniel

The interview reproduced below, on eurythmy as a Waldorf school subject, was conducted by Ulrike Wendt, tutor at the Stuttgart Eurythmeum, and Helga Daniel, tutor for the eurythmy training course in The Hague, Holland.[12]

Question: Why does the Waldorf school include eurythmy in the basic curriculum?

After four years of research into pedagogical eurythmy in grades one to four, a Dutch colleague remarked: "For the Waldorf curriculum eurythmy is like salt in the soup." This hits the nail on the head as far as eurythmy's educational mission is concerned. Eurythmy develops a pupil's capacity for concentration and will to learn, and the artistry involved in it supports learning capacity in all other subjects.

Question: How is this actually achieved? What are the tasks and aims of teaching eurythmy?

Speech and music are deeply innate capacities in the human being. In eurythmy they are the foundation of movement. Each tone and speech sound corresponds to a certain movement. For instance, if a "K" sound is spoken, the corresponding movement must be performed at the same time. This requires great concentration of pupils, to really move what is heard. It is similar to playing the violin, when one has to hear precisely whether the note is "clean." Something similar applies to the gestures of tones, intervals, harmonies, and all other elements in music and language. On the one hand the pupil has to listen very attentively, and on the other he must control his gestures so that he can perform them at precisely the right moment.

Question: Are only tones and speech sounds realized in music? Speech and music also have many other expressive possibilities surely!

The same applies to rhythm and dynamics in music and speech. In this case it is the legs that are activated. They move faster or slower, always led by what one hears! Thus two different activities have to be carried out simultaneously: the coordination of legs and arms and their impulse for movement derived from the music or speech sound that is heard. The limb activity must occur at the same time as a perception. This dual activity requires one to turn inwards and grow still on the one hand—i.e., enormous concentration; and on the other to be active in full presence of mind. This can only succeed if the pupil really knows the text or the music and has an inward connection with it, i.e. is always a fraction ahead so as to move at the proper, simultaneous moment.

Only then does one get the sense that it is "right." By practicing hundreds of poems and pieces of music throughout their school days, pupils develop a personal connection with text and music. They develop an inner stylistic sense and a capacity for judging whether something is authentic.

Question: In class, how does an individual's performance relate to the whole group?

Well, we do not just focus on individual solo activities. The structures of language and music are also reflected in the various group formations. The pupils move together, and each is responsible for a different aspect of the whole. For instance in a piece of music the top and bottom parts can be divided, or the different instruments can be allocated. The whole only succeeds if all do the right thing at the right moment, and for this it is necessary for the group to have an overview of its movement. Here one is practicing overview and social competency!

In addition, a pupil in a eurythmy class, as in other classes, also finds that he develops new capacities through constant practice. Such experiences awaken enjoyment in learning and in mastering ever new areas of ability.

Question: So more is involved here than movement training?

Eurythmy educates children and adolescents in general human skills, above and beyond the learning of spatial forms and movement sequences, giving them the capacities which they need in all other subjects and also later in life: concentration, learning to listen, precise perception, will to learn, capacity to learn, stylistic sense, sense of truth, sympathy, coordination of legs and arms, presence of mind, quickness in acting, overview of whole situations, social competency. All these skills in the domains of cognition, emotion, and action are called on equally through movement, and thus cultivated and educated.

It is self-evident that giving children these living experiences requires great educational skill, and sensitivity toward children, adolescents, and eurythmy itself.

Question: How are these goals differentiated at different ages?

In kindergarten and elementary school, we work a great deal with children's capacity for imitation. The children live in movement stories. By connecting the inner images of a story with movement stimulated by language, a great diversity of differentiation is achieved.

In middle school, the children know and are able to perform a great deal of the movement material. Here play is central and its varying use. A subtle capacity for distinguishing the appropriateness of each respective movement element, connected with great dexterity, enhances joy in movement and trains pupils' general artistic sensitivity.

In high school, pupils have the opportunity to grasp the inner logic of eurythmy movement and to develop their own artistic projects from this understanding.

Question: Have investigations been carried out into the effectiveness of eurythmy lessons?

As far as I am aware, the only knowledge we have is based on practical experience. However, a masters degree for eurythmists is soon to start, in which this could be one of the many themes. If there is a eurythmist who would like to embark on such research, a research result will eventually be forthcoming.

Question: Not all pupils love eurythmy. What is necessary to establish it as an accepted subject?

Eurythmy teachers themselves and the faculty play the biggest role here. If a faculty is fully aware of the educational task and potential of eurythmy, pupils experience it as an integral part of a Waldorf education. If the eurythmy teacher is both a eurythmy artist and also an educational artist, and if he knows how to involve pupils in eurythmy in age-appropriate ways, pupils will accept this subject as they do every other. Some of them will love it, others just go along with it, or have no inclination for it, just as things are at school.

But since they can be profoundly touched, inwardly, by eurythmy, it can also no doubt be the hardest subject for them. There's no opportunity to cheat or hide. They stand there without any mask in front of their classmates and the teacher, so it's quite understandable that they might try to withdraw from it in some way. But those who allow themselves to be touched by it will realize clearly that eurythmy has something to do with them as human beings—but they don't speak of such things. They keep it to themselves.

Question: What relationship exists between eurythmy at the Waldorf school and the presence of artistic eurythmy in the world? What can professional performances mean for pupils?

The most important thing for pupils is that eurythmy teachers continue to develop artistically and demonstrate what they have achieved to pupils, for instance at seasonal festivals. "At least she can do what she asks of us." If the pupils then get to see a professional eurythmy performance, and witness the difference between this and the efforts of their own teachers, the eurythmy dimension deepens for them, and they can have a real encounter with art.

METHODOLOGY

Rudolf Steiner[13]

How can we understand the etheric body? This requires a much better preparation than is usual for understanding the human being today. We understand the etheric body when we enter the shaping process, when we know how a curve or angle grows from inner forces. We cannot understand the etheric body in terms of ordinary natural laws, but through our experience of the hand—the spirit permeated hand. Thus, there should be no teacher training without activities in the areas of modeling or sculpture, an activity that arises from the inner human being. When this element is absent, it is much more harmful to education than not knowing the capital city of Romania or Turkey, or the name of some mountain; those things can always be researched in a dictionary. It is not at all necessary to know the masses of matter required for exams; what is the harm in referring to a dictionary? However, no dictionary can give us the flexibility, the capable knowledge, and knowing capacity necessary to understand the etheric body, because the etheric body does not arise according to natural laws; it permeates the human being in the activity of shaping.

And we shall never understand the astral body simply by knowing Guy-Lussac's law or the laws of acoustics and optics. The astral body is not accessible to such abstract, empirical laws; what lives and weaves within it cannot be perceived by such methods. If we have an inner understanding, however, of the intervals of the third or the fifth, for example—an inner musical experience of the scale that depends on inner musical perception and not on acoustics—then we experience what lives in the astral human being.

The astral body is not natural history, natural science, or physics; it is music. This is true to the extent that, in the forming activity within the human organism, it is possible to trace how the astral body has a musical formative effect in the human being. This formative activity flows from the center between the shoulder blades, first into the tonic of the scale; as it flows on into the second, it builds the upper arm, and into the third, the lower arm.

When we come to the third, we arrive at the difference between major and minor; we find two bones in the lower arm—not just one—the radius and the ulna, which represent minor and major. One who studies the outer human organization, insofar as it depends on the astral body, must approach physiology not as a physicist, but as a musician. We must recognize the inner, formative music within the human organism.

No matter how you trace the course of the nerves in the human organism, you will never understand what it means. But when you follow the course of the nerves musically—understanding the musical relationships (everything is audible here, though not physically)—and when you perceive with spiritual musical perception how these nerves run from the limbs towards the spine and then turn upward and continue toward the brain, you experience the most wonderful musical instrument, which is the human being, built by the astral body and played by the I-being.

As we ascend from there, we learn how the human being forms speech through understanding the inner configuration of speech—something that is no longer learned in our advanced civilization; it has discarded everything intuitive. Through the structure of speech, we recognize the I-being itself if we understand what happens when a person speaks a sound "ah" or "ee"—how in "ah" there is wonder and in "ee" there is consolidation of the inner being; and if we learn how the speech element shoots, as it were, into the inner structure; and if we learn to perceive a work inwardly, not just saying for example, that a rolling ball is "rolling" but understand what moves inwardly like a rolling ball when one says "rolling." We learn through inner perception—a perception really informed by the spirit of speech—to recognize what is active in speech.

These days information about the human organism must come from physiologists and anatomists, and information about what lives in language comes from philologists. There is no relationship, however, between what they can say to each other. It is necessary to look for an inner spiritual connection; we must recognize that a genius of speech lives and works in language, a genius of speech that can be investigated. When we study the genius of speech, we recognize the human I-being.

We have now made eurythmy part of our Waldorf education. What are we doing with eurythmy? We divide it into tone eurythmy and speech eurythmy. In tone eurythmy, we evoke in the child movements that correspond to the form of the astral body; in speech eurythmy, we evoke movements that correspond to the child's I-being. We thus work consciously to develop the soul by bringing physical elements into play in tone eurythmy; and we work consciously to develop the spirit aspect by activating the corresponding physical elements in speech eurythmy.

Such activity, however, only arises from a complete understanding of the human organization. Those who think they can get close to the human being through external physiology and experimental psychology (which is really another kind of physiology) would not recognize the difference between beating on a wooden tray and making music in trying to evoke a certain mood in someone. Similarly, knowledge must not remain stuck in abstract, logical rules, but rise to view human life as more than grasping lifeless nature—the living that has died—or thinking of the living in a lifeless way. When we rise from abstract principles to formative qualities and understand how every natural law molds itself sculpturally, we come to understand the human etheric body.

When we begin to "hear" (in an inner, spiritual sense) the cosmic rhythm expressing itself in that most wonderful musical instrument that the astral body makes of the human being, we come to understand the astral nature of the human being.

What we must become aware of may be expressed this way: First, we come to know the physical body in an abstract, logical sense. Then we turn to the sculptural formative activity with intuitive cognition and begin to understand the etheric body. Third, as a physiologist, one becomes a musician and views the human being the way one would look at a musical instrument—an organ or violin—where one sees music realized. Thus, we understand the astral human being. And when we come to know the genius of speech as it works creatively in words, not merely connecting it with words through the external memory—we gain knowledge of the human I-being.

These days we would become a laughingstock if in the name of university reform—medical studies, for example—we said that such knowledge must arise from the study of sculpture, music, and speech. People would say: Sure, but how long would such training take? It certainly lasts long enough without these things. Nevertheless, the training would in fact be shorter, since its length today is due primarily to the fact that people don't move beyond abstract, logical, empirical sense perception. It's true that they begin by studying the physical body, but this cannot be understood by those methods. There is no end to it. One can study all kinds of things throughout life—there's no end to it—whereas study has its own inner limits when it is organically built up as a study of the organism in body, soul, and spirit.

The point is not to map out a new chapter with the help of anthroposophy, adding to what we already have. Indeed, we can be satisfied with what ordinary science offers; we are not opposed to that. We are grateful to science in the sense that we are grateful to the violin maker for providing a violin. What we need in our culture is to get hold of all of this modern culture and permeate it with soul and permeate it with spirit, just as human beings themselves are permeated with soul and spirit. The artistic must not be allowed to exist in civilization as a pleasant luxury next to serious life, a luxury we consider an indulgence, even though we may have a spiritual approach to life in other ways. The artistic element must be made to permeate the world and the human being as a divine spiritual harmony of law.

We must understand how, in facing the world, we first approach it with logical concepts and ideas. The being of the universe, however, gives human nature something that emanates from the cosmic formative activity working down from the spheres, just as earthly gravity works up from the central point of the earth. And cosmic music, working from the periphery, is also a part of this. Just as the shaping activity works from above, and physical activity works from below through gravity, so cosmic music works in the movements of the starry constellations at the periphery.

The principle that really gives *humanity* to the human being was divined in ancient time when words were spoken—words such as "In the beginning was the Word, and the Word was with God, and the Word was God." That Cosmic Word, Cosmic Speech, is the principle that also permeates the human being, and that being becomes the I-being. In order to educate, we must acquire knowledge of the human being from knowledge of the cosmos, and learn to shape it artistically.

RELIGIOUS QUALITIES IN EDUCATION

Elisabeth von Kügelgen

In an eleventh grade Religion lesson I observed, a student asked: "Why do we have to have religion, couldn't we do ethics?"

"Why ethics?" asked the teacher. "What do you mean by ethics?"

This was met by silence.

"What is ethics?" the teacher repeated.

The student answered, "No idea."

The word "ethics" is intriguing because one does not actually know what it means: it is the unknown. The decision to call our Religion lessons "Life Skills" was met with deep satisfaction. But why does the word "religion" has a negative sound for us, why does it seem so loaded?

All kinds of associations come up when we think of the word "religion." Applied to history and modern times it makes us think of wars, intolerance, coercion, moralization, commandments, church, fundamentalism, "old stuff," absence of spiritual freedom, and much more.

Today the term religion evokes mostly negative connotations. If we go back to its Latin root, *religio*, the focus shifts: *religio* means to tie together, to search for a connection, to create a relationship, order, law that is the basis of everything and connects everything; to appreciate, respect, care for or reconnect, to nurture. In medieval times the word was used in this way. Entering into a relationship can mean coercion, but it can also mean to make a connection with something, to bond, to discover and initiate connections—then it becomes simply a healthy way to live our everyday life. In order to be able to connect with a cause or with a person you need to have or to establish an interest, love, trust. Each learning experience and each friendship relies on this. Order creates clarity, security, reliability. Entering into a relationship means taking on responsibility. Relationships need to be fostered, need to be renewed again and again, they need space to grow, otherwise they go to sleep. They need constant new activity. *Religio* in this sense is the essence of our humanity.

To be prepared to enter into a relationship means to be open, to develop devotion, love, respect, to be able to experience gratitude. A relationship always involves giving and taking on both sides. This is also true for our relationship with the divine; and there, just as anywhere else, we are more easily prepared to take (or ask) than to give. If we understand the word religion as I just illustrated it, we realize that this is what we call social awareness nowadays, these are social virtues. Instead of talking about "fostering religious qualities" we could ask: what makes a child, or what makes me as an adult, capable of entering into a relationship, capable of social behavior? How do we acquire these archetypal gestures of social interaction?

Coldness in the social realm reflects a world that has become insecure, that is without religion, a world where a request is met by a demand: what's in it for me?

How do we teach social skills? The small child does not respond to admonitions and commands. What does the child bring with him? A newborn baby does not think, speak, or walk; it is powerless, helpless, exposed and open to everything. We can call this powerlessness, but we can also call it total devotion. The child accepts everything that comes from us, without defense, at the same time full of expectation, trusting and open, he is all perception. He brings something else with him: the ability to imitate! The child's openness is not passive. Without the example of others, we do not learn anything: for walking upright, for speaking, and for thinking we need the example of another person. This kind of imitation is pure will, zest for activity; in it lives the absolute will to become human; to embark on a journey. The child is a will being, everything becomes movement. The child imitates, practices everything; everything he looks at becomes example, everything is taken hold of. It is this will gesture of the child, combined with his great openness and devotion to his environment, that leads Rudolf Steiner to speak of a state that anthroposophic medicine refers to as a "bodily religion"[14] in which the child lives—he is all devotion, searching for a relationship with his whole being! The child needs an environment that allows him to imitate as much as possible. There should be enough that is meaningful and worth absorbing and imitating, there should be people who strive to become worthy of being imitated—in their thoughts, feelings, gestures, actions. The child takes everything in unfiltered—sound, color, our presence—and he absorbs it. This means that all his experiences become part of what forms his body and what fills his soul. The small child's relationship to the world lives entirely in his senses, in his eyes, ears, movements. Thought and reflection do not come into it. Thoughts and feelings are realities just like tables and chairs. Everything becomes physical movement: if the child is happy he will express it with joyful sounds and movements. Body and soul are always active together. Everything the child sees and hears becomes impulse for movement, seizes hold of his body, of his entire will being. Truth, untruth, hatred, love—everything is absorbed by body and soul with the same degree of devotion. This means that the child's sense of language will be corrupted if adults speak to him in baby talk. If everything around him is worth imitating, beautiful, and meaningful, it gives the child health and security. Rhythmic repetition, things that come again and again, awaken a feeling of security and trust in the child. This is why children love repetition. What the child experiences in his environment will become part of his inner being. Speaking about the moral and social education of the child, Rudolf Steiner draws our attention to three virtues that underlie all religious-social behavior: gratitude, love, and a sense of duty (or respect for the actions of others and for one's own work).[15] They emerge out of each other and form a threefoldness which we can assign as an underlying mood to the first three seven-year periods and to kindergarten, elementary, and high school as three leading stars, towards which all teaching should be directed.

We should appeal to the will for gratitude during the first phase, the will to love during the second and the will to work, the love for working, during the third. Rudolf Steiner also points out that they develop out of each other as a matter of course. These phases are also present in our later lives, in our relationship to the world, to other people, to our work, to the divine; they necessitate each other.

The first phase stretches beyond the seventh year into school life up to fourth grade (Rubicon): If what the child imitates and experiences is worth being grateful for, gratitude streams toward us from the child. This can only happen, however, if we allow the child to experience that we are grateful, too, and that we can also express this. That we are grateful for the sun, his light, the warmth, the beauty of a flower, a kind word, our daily bread, grateful and happy. Saying grace before a meal, for example, only makes sense if we are truly grateful. Then the child will feel our own gratitude. If we just speak a verse because there are children sitting at the table, then they will not like to say grace anymore from the age of nine, because we have taught them that saying grace or praying before eating is something 'little kids do'. They will imitate us and try to leave saying grace and praying behind as soon as possible, so that they appear older. 'Why are we doing this?' Answer: 'Because I am grateful to God'! Not: 'Because others are starving' or anything like that; because then one would not need to be grateful anymore once everybody has everything they need. We should avoid attaching conditions to gratitude!

In this respect we can learn a lot from fairy tales. Here, gratitude plays an important part, simply helping others and giving. We don't have a right to expect something or to have somebody around who is there for us, helps us and works for us, but gratitude goes together with giving freely, with friendliness, a good heart, helpfulness that does not serve a purpose. Example: Mother Holle by the Brothers Grimm. A quick look at the stages: practical help (taking the bread out of the oven, shaking the apple tree), the gratitude is expressed in the reward. The shower of gold at the end 'because you were so friendly and diligent' comes as a surprise. And in the fairy tale gold does not just signify money! Free gifts and acceptance are part of gratitude with no strings attached. The lazy sister sets off with the purpose of getting the reward. She does not take the bread out and does not shake the apples from the tree and she gets nothing in return. Reluctantly, she shakes the bedding for three days and waits for her reward. She does not take in her environment, is lazy, thinks only of getting it over with, and wants to go back when no reward is forthcoming. She gets covered in pitch. Carelessly she walks along without seeing nature, ignores the work, does not want to be thanked but wants money, the reward. It is the intellect speaking: I am friendly, I help, so I must get a present. If you are nice you get something in return: this is purely utilitarian thinking. We find this as a theme also in "Pennies from Heaven" or "The Three Little Men in the Wood" - it lives in many fairy tales. The "I do something in order to get something" attitude is the death of gratitude, of free giving and taking in social interaction. The child senses this: it has to come from the heart, just like that, out of freedom, "for the love of God" as the saying goes. In first grade, the mood of the fairy tale reigns, in the religion lessons as well as in all other lessons. Through our gratitude and our ability to be cheerful we enter into a relationship with the world, with people, with God—out of freedom. We should not constantly admonish the child, but allow him to experience life! Saying "thank you" because one has to go against the nature of gratitude. Maybe we will become aware ourselves that a day is full of gifts and wonder and not just full of stress. Immersed in this mood, the child in second grade learns about nature and the world through the pedagogical story: plant stories, animal stories etc. The flower is grateful for shade, rain, earth and sun, and for the stars at night; the animal lives from the plant and helps people. All these things still speak to the child and help him relate to the world around him. Stars, moss, stones, the night, the brook—the world speaks through their being to the child. Everything has its place, its time, its particular task, its meaning, everything is ordered by deep wisdom, even the processes of wilting and dying. The child understands their language, learns to love them, to see them—feels more and more at home, safe, belonging to nature and to the world. Thankfulness, joy, sympathy, reverence, respect, love—these are the threads that weave this relationship, that give the child a home and an instinctive feeling of trust in his existence.

Further examples: the spider that weaves a web across the entrance to the cave in order to protect the Holy Family from their pursuers on their flight to Egypt, because they think: nobody can be in this cave, otherwise the spider's web would not be there. Suddenly spiders are no longer horrible. The first flowers under a thick blanket of snow announce the coming spring—hope, anticipation. The frost gives the sloe-berry its sweetness so that its juice can bring us strength and health to get through the winter. The child learns to love and respect nature, and responds with a universal feeling of gratitude and trust. He experiences the world as a huge, living organism, to which we belong, with which we are connected, and which we can help or harm. There is something in the world that carries me, that gives itself to me, that looks after me even if I feel miserable at times!

Out of this gratitude, love grows in the child. Gratitude lies at the root of love for nature, love for other people, love of God. This universal gratitude is the basis of any true religious feeling. Rudolf Steiner captured this mood in the so-called morning verse that he gave for first to fourth grades. The whole class speaks this verse every morning at the beginning of main lesson and the fundamental motives for all the lessons of the day resound.

From the age of nine or ten, the relationship of the child to the world undergoes a drastic change. He sees the world as separate from himself, more naked, from the outside, he becomes more fearful but at the same time more himself. The loneliness and fear that the child experiences now are necessary. He has to live through them. What carries him now is the love, the trust in the adult. She is now also seen more from a distance, her leadership, her being there, however, becomes more important. What Rudolf Steiner calls loved authority can never be demanded from a child. But the teacher becomes a loved authority if she can give the child the support, the feeling of being held, the guidance that he needs now. During this stage it is important and right that the child learns through love for the teacher, trusting in her guidance and in the tasks she sets for him. The tasks should be clear and meaningful. If the adult has a loving relationship with the children, if her work, her duties and her tasks are done out of love and devotion, then the children will follow her instructions and their activities will be inspired by her love for the work. They want to do it well and beautifully. The firmness of the instructions awakens a feeling of trust in the guidance which the child cannot find in himself yet. Reassurance is important! 'You did that beautifully. You really made a good effort' or 'I know you can do it even better, even more beautifully.' Encouragement from the adult to whom the child looks up. Working together is important. The child wants to be seen. The teacher must also notice when the child did not make enough of an effort. The children can easily see through unjustified praise. This loving trust awakens the ability to form relationships: love also forgives inadequacies. If we ourselves have role models, if we look up to something that is bigger than we are, if we make an effort, then the child will learn to love these ideals within us and he will also learn to accept our weaknesses without being disappointed. All moral impulses are rooted in love. If I love something it is valuable to me for its own sake!

This will be the mood that underlies the plant and animal studies in middle school. The cow no longer speaks. But the cow is also not just there to give me milk and meat, to be useful. Otherwise it would be sufficient to treat it so that it can fulfil this purpose. We will describe the nature of an animal, the environment that it needs and with which it has a relationship. With living beings the child can sympathize and suffer. He marvels at the things the cow is capable of: this incredible calmness, patience, endurance. It is all metabolism, rhythm, repetition. How the grass is transformed through the chewing of the cud in the seven stomachs of the cow: a calm will. It is the same will that enables us to achieve transformation. To inspire the child to live, to love, to suffer with nature and with people in the world, to evoke a feeling of wonder at the wisdom that lives in nature; out of this feeling of wonder grows interest, a loving interest, in the course of an event. And it is enlivening to experience what one learns oneself! I had a lively experience of this once when I went for a walk with my nephew. We had just accomplished the ascent and were about to embark on the long journey back. The boy was tired and became grumpy and miserable. "Are we nearly there yet? I can't walk anymore!" Looking down from the height we saw some cows on a meadow just beneath us. "We will stop there and have a rest." Having an aim in sight helped. As soon as we got there he threw himself on the ground. When he lifted his head, his interest was caught by a cow chewing the cud. Suddenly the little chap jumped up into the air calling out joyfully: 'Did you see that? I saw it! I saw it! Exactly what Mr. S (the class teacher) told us about." He had happened to witness the moment when the cow brought up the ball of grass in order to chew it again. All tiredness was forgotten. An hour of descent was saved. In great detail he told me what he had learned about the cow in school. And it was true! He had seen it with his own eyes! The recognition, the interest made all tiredness vanish.

By nature we tend to become capable of love towards puberty. The natural development helps us. This ability to love can and should, however, extend to include the whole world and everybody in it and become love of nature, love of others, love of God. If not, it will be restricted to the physical body and turn into one-sided sexuality and self-love. We should teach about history, the sciences, discoveries, inventions, if possible in connection with biographical stories, starting from the human being or the natural phenomena. This speaks to the feeling and takes hold of it, then thinking ensues.

Universal love for others is a necessary prerequisite for the ability to respect the dignity of the human being. Every person is an enriching experience because he is different. The gratitude and deep trust in the unity and support of the divine world of the Father, of which I am a part and which carries and keeps my humanity, out of which I and all things have come, is joined by a love for the world, for the relationships and friendships between us. We learn that there are crises, pain, obstacles that we can overcome, that help us grow and learn. The feeling that every human being has his destiny and that people can help each other is something that should now be brought to the young person in all its richness. Then it will begin to dawn on him that the highest form of love for others is the love of Christ for the human being. HE is present in this love for others, HE is the source of it and HE accompanies the human beings and the earth in their destiny. To know that love can bring sacrifices, can forgive, renounce, can give and strengthen, even carry! This leads us to trust that our life is meaningful, trust in the future and in divine providence. We find these motives as part of the youth service that Rudolf Steiner gave for the free Christian religion lessons, just as we find the motives that were described for the lower school as part of the children's service.

With puberty the young person becomes aware of his destiny and his own future, because puberty provides the physical basis for human love and human future (the young child lives in a timeless realm). Sharing somebody else's suffering or joy now involves different feeling qualities compared to an earlier age. We could say that the young child lives in activity with the other person, the adolescent during the second seven-year period lives in feeling with the other person; and in high school the world wants to be understood, the foundation for unprejudiced judgment should be established. Through thinking we learn, understand, and make connections. And to act out of understanding means to act out of oneself, out of the cause, out of an impulse. The young person learns, in a new way, to perceive what people are doing in their world of work. Life goes together with tasks, aims, work: the respect for other people's work and love and responsibility for one's own undertakings. Rudolf Steiner calls this third stage "love for work" (Werkliebe)[16] and this needs to be fostered and developed. The authority of the adult recedes; the young person should develop trust in his own thinking and judgment. Aim: the ability to act out of insight, out of acquired knowledge. The students perceive very clearly the impulses behind our actions. The strongest impulse for self-directed action grows out of genuine ideals, led by objectives which arise purely from the spiritual, and which I want to realize in the world. Ideals have to be presented in picture form, through stories, for the young child to take hold of them; the older pupil experiences them in 'real' biographies, in real people. They will live on in the feeling life, in the search for ideals. The older student and the adult person can raise an ideal up to the realm of pure soul and spirit. If one has ideals, if one can experience ideals, one lives religiously, i.e. in the future! Ideals describe the aim of all human evolution, of becoming human. They lead us beyond ourselves and they carry within them the power of transformation: they take hold of our will. If an ideal lives in us it will give us strength, it will give us wings—it carries the power of realization, the belief that this can 'move mountains'. If ideals are alive in us, we do not need commandments. If devotion has been fostered in the child and has become interest and love, then he can continue to learn throughout life out of interest and love, i.e. freely and out of himself—for the sake of a cause or a person. It allows him to take on responsibility, helps him find his place in society. These three fundamental gestures which I have talked about have their source—religiously speaking—in the divine Father, the divine Son and the divine Spirit. In education they appear as forces that make us human, in gratitude, devotion, reverence, wonder, love, trust, respect, love for work, responsibility, conscience—all of these should penetrate our teaching methods, in different, age- appropriate ways. These gestures are at their purest when fostered and practiced in religious activity where they are directed to the divine. They will then live in our everyday life as social skills toward other people, toward the world and toward work, and give meaning and confidence to our lives. This is why, in Steiner schools, we try to make sure that these qualities are an inherent part of our teaching methods, that they are fostered in age-relevant ways. As such they should complement intellectual-scientific, artistic-enlivening, creative lesson structure and content. These qualities are totally independent of any religious confession, but they are deeply human and humanizing.

The child moves from doing to understanding, the adult from understanding to doing. What the connection between science, art and religion and the educational practice consists of, and what it is that forms the foundation for a fully rounded education system that can strengthen the child, was described by Rudolf Steiner in a speech at the opening of the first Waldorf School: "Science that comes alive! Art that comes alive! Religion that comes alive!—in the end this is education."[17]

The teacher must re-engender this life within herself again and again. She has to learn, search and transform herself repeatedly. In a very early essay on education Rudolf Steiner wrote:

> ....It is not our task to provide adolescents with traditional beliefs. We have to ensure that they use their own powers of comprehension. They should learn to look into the world with open eyes.... Our beliefs are for ourselves only. We can share them with young people in order to show them that this is how we see the world: you have to look and find out how it presents itself to you. We have to awaken abilities, not pass on beliefs. The young people should not believe in our "truths" but in our personality. They should see that we are seekers. And we should direct them towards the path of the seekers.[18]

The awakening of abilities is our main objective: in the scientific, the artistic, and the religious sphere.

This is why Rudolf Steiner introduced free religion lessons for all those pupils who did not receive denominational religion lessons. His reasons were not philosophical but purely educational:

> One has to strive to develop all human potential. In the end this is the more abstract form of the educational point of view. We speak from this point of view when we say that, based on the knowledge of the human being which forms the foundation of this education, the child is born religious, that during the first seven years of his life even his body is religious. Therefore, if we replaced religious education with mere ethics, it would be as though we prevented a physical limb, such as a leg, from forming because we were of the opinion that a human being needs to develop everything but not the legs. To leave out what is essentially part of the human organization may spring from fanaticism but can never be the result of pedagogy. Insofar as we are following pedagogical laws here, we can say that religious education is a real necessity.[19]

This religious disposition is part of our humanity and therefore belongs to Steiner education everywhere in the world, in all cultures. Rudolf Steiner frequently talked about the fact that anthroposophy, being a science, never wants to be religion, never wants to appear as giving rise to a religion. But it gives us the laws of humanity, the study of the human being as a basis for education, a comprehensive description of the human being in spirit, soul, and body, and therefore it is able to bring to life again what has become tradition, what has possibly become rigid, and to show us the way to a spiritual understanding of the world that is appropriate for our times. Addressing the relationship between anthroposophy and religion Rudolf Steiner said in London:

> Thus anthroposophical science will be able to let religious life spring up in the human soul again....it can contribute to human evolution the recovery of a sense of the religious in all that exists, and help human beings find a new appreciation of Christianity. Anthroposophy will not form sects, but serve already existing religions and re-enliven Christianity. It not only seeks to preserve ancient religiousness and move it forward, but aims at a resurrection of religious life, which has suffered rather too much from modern civilization. Anthroposophy, therefore, wishes to be a messenger of love, to awaken and resurrect mankind's inner sense of religion.[20]

What has been said is therefore valid for all education everywhere in the world, just as Steiner education is becoming part of all cultures on all continents.

CHAPTER 17

Questions of Today

Introduction

It is often asked—How does anthroposophic medicine view allergies? Or—what does Waldorf education say to early schooling, or to football? As valid as these questions are, it is certainly important to attempt an answer from the best of one's knowledge and judgment. It is equally important to show a way for people to answer these questions for themselves. Begin by observing the problem and then work on the anthroposophic study of man. It is out of this approach that the following articles are written.

The following table shows the integration of the four sheaths, as found in the notebooks of Rudolf Steiner.[1] We place it here as a reference for the rest of the chapter.

The ego body gives in the	*physical*	=	*form*
	etheric	=	*inner movement*
	astral	=	*inner life*
	spirit	=	*ensoulment*
The astral body gives in the	*physical*	=	*movement*
	etheric	=	*desire*
	astral	=	*feeling*
	spirit	=	*thinking*
The etheric body gives in the	*physical*	=	*self-experience*
	etheric	=	*self-knowledge*
	astral	=	*self-preservation*
	spirit	=	*memory*
The physical body gives in the	*physical*	=	*egoity = being in oneself*
	etheric	=	*image/idea*
	astral	=	*sensing, feeling*
	spirit	=	*perception*

THE CHILD AND TECHNOLOGY

Michaela Glöckler[2]

Technology and the multimedia culture enthuse and preoccupy adults and therefore also children.

Developmentally friendly engagement with this electronic world can succeed if we understand the importance of technology for human development.

Beginning with the Industrial Revolution in eighteenth-century England, the change from handcrafts to machine production took place. This was driven by the development of the steam engine, followed by generations of internal combustion engines. With the large-scale technological use of electricity and domestic electricity supplies, machines that were growing ever smaller and easier to use were augmented by a wealth of measuring instruments. It is hard to conceive the speed with which the use of electricity spread across the globe. The electric light bulb, invented by Heinrich Goebel in 1854 and further developed by Thomas Edison, did not become commercially available until 1879. The invention of cinematography and the carbon microphone took place within the same period.

After the Second World War, the third great technological revolution began. Machines were developed which could take over intelligent tasks: information and computer systems. Thus human will and labor have been replaced at physical, soul, and spiritual levels, a threefold technological revolution, giving rise to mass unemployment. This is accompanied not just by poverty but by nearly epidemic alienation, resignation, and depression. Millions of people feel that they no longer play a useful role in society.

The problem which arose in the wake of technological development is the confrontation with the aim and direction of one's own will, the way to handle one's own capacities. Work always signifies the development of skills and sensory experience linked to this. Thus a golden rule for dealing with technology in education is this: Accomplish work oneself to the fullest extent possible before handing it over to the machine. Just as in the course of history, human work was only gradually replaced by machines, so it is also necessary that children and adolescents themselves first become acquainted with the various realms of human work and skill, and learn to develop these before they allow technology to relieve them of these tasks. Creative capacity is paralyzed if one expects everything of the machine and little of oneself.

Lack of gratitude and a demanding attitude is also fostered if one has never developed a sense of how much personal effort is spared by machines.

Children must understand that hot water flowing from a tap and light appearing at the touch of a button does not happen by itself. Arrange holidays on an isolated farm, or go camping, or travel to a place without modern facilities, where laundry is still done by hand, where water is heated over a fire, to help them appreciate the blessings of technological achievements.

Allow your child to first learn to sing, paint, model, dance, and act, before the whole world of images, colors, and tones in media overwhelms him with impressions and threatens to paralyze his own creativity.

At school, calculators should only be introduced once skills in basic arithmetic, and in particular mental arithmetic, have been developed. Why should the computer be used and become the pupils' constant companion before they have learned to know and appreciate the work which it replaces and before they even know how it actually functions?

It is important to demonstrate a relationship with energy and technology that reminds the child that resources are not limitless, and that technology should be used only where it is really needed and purposeful.

Nature, the human being, and the social environment must not be confused with machines.

Technology involves perfection and optimization. Defects are repaired, models that have become obsolete are disposed of. If we superimpose conduct developed in relationship to technology on the human being and nature, problems arise. These grow still worse if children and adults spend many hours of very personal interaction with their computer or their smart phone. The qualities which people often miss in personal encounter—full attention, interest for the reactions, questions, and concerns of the other—are devoted to the computer with a dismaying naturalness. The more that soul interaction of this type is nurtured with machines, which react as one expects them to, or which, after one has undertaken the necessary corrections, meet one's expectations, the stronger does this reinforce conduct that fails to cope in relation to other human beings and in particular in relation to nature. The latter do not respond in a predetermined schema, but out of the conditions governing their own life and development.

Human community requires the capacity to also accept mistakes and mistaken behavior, even if we cannot swiftly remedy them, but have to first learn to live with them. Openness to new learning processes, to new and unexpected developments, is what is needed. Living in close proximity with technology unconsciously promotes greater distance in our relationship to the surrounding world. It is therefore scarcely surprising if our interactions with other people, at the so-called relationship level, function less and less.

In his books *Cuckoo's Egg*, *The Cyber Wasteland*, and *High Tech Heretic*, astronomer and computer security expert Clifford Stoll[3] has argued for proper handling of computers in adolescence and adulthood, and against their use in kindergarten, elementary school, and at home. At this age of life, the development and nurturing of human relationships should be accorded the highest priority. At home, calm, peace, reflection, and warmth should reign—qualities we do not associate with home computer use.

Comparing the development of creative potential in the human being with technological development, one is struck by remarkable parallels. Werner Schäfer, an enthusiastic beat musician active in the 60s, noted at the beginning of the 70s that something was "no longer quite right" with him: his attention was drawn to this by disorders of the inner life of meditative thought and reflection, and the dulling of perceptive capacity for social interactions and nature. His wide-ranging analysis of the effect of media on human beings included a summary, given below, of the compensation one needs in terms of inner, creative activity if one is going to safely use various technical media.[4]

TECHNOLOGY	NECESSARY COMPENSATION THROUGH INNER WORK
Photography	Creating of active, pictorial and vivid perceptions and schooling of the senses, culture of remembrance, "spirit remembrance."
Images	The same but now illumined by spiritual meaning. Rudolf Steiner's lectures on the first Goetheanum with slides, or his lectures on art (GA 292) point in this direction.
Silent film	Michaelic experience of space and time. Mastery of authentic, objective imagination.
"Time-loop," films played backwards	Mastery of the astral capacity of vision which runs "backwards" (cause follows effect) and can be trained for instance in the evening "daily review" exercise.
Film with sound, TV	Mastery of genuine, objective inspirations.
The Internet	Mastery of genuine, objective intuitions (at all levels).
"Backward masking" (words and melodies imported backwards into a recording)	Clear, precise imaginative reversal of melodies and words as habitual ability, that can be accomplished at any time. This only works, however, if they are audible, which is almost invariably avoided with backward masking. They are integrated below the level of audibility and thus become subliminal effects, smuggled directly into the physical subconscious and unfolding their effects there, without passing through awareness.
Computer	Mastery both of living and also body-free thinking based on a fully mature individuality, one capable of heart-imbued social spirituality.

THE CHILD AND TELEVISION, COMPUTER GAMES, AND COMICS

Michaela Glöckler[5]

Inadequate Vision and Disintegration of Sensory Activity

While watching TV the eyes are locked on the screen while the pictures on the screen are moving. The child sits with muscles rigid, entranced by a flood of flickering visual impressions. The immobility of the eyes conveys itself to all the body's muscles. This way of seeing is abnormal, as normally when one looks at something the eye muscles are in constant movement scanning the object of vision. Moreover, the colors and proportions do not correspond to reality, and what is actually three-dimensional is reduced to two dimensions. Only two senses are communicating with one another: eye and ear, while all other senses are hardly stimulated, promoting the disintegration of their functions. It is as if the whole body, not just the area around the eyes, were set in plaster. In eye clinics this phenomenon is used therapeutically. A few hours of television are prescribed for patients who had eye surgery because it is the only way to keep the eye muscles still. A muscle that has been operated on needs to be kept still to support the healing process. But what happens if countless children between the ages of three and twelve are watching television for four to six hours daily? If a child sleeps on average eight hours and one deducts the time for meals and school, a twelve-year-old child is left with about six hours for free play and movement, activities that foster child development. Even if we only assume the lower figure of two hours of television a child would have spent a whole year "in plaster" by the time she reaches age twelve.

Stimulating the Central Nervous System for Passive Reception

The brain does not process impressions from watching television in the same way that it processes ordinary visual impressions. For the latter, the eyes are constantly moving and observing while all the senses are engaged in taking in the subtlest color nuances of real objects. The flood of information that comes from television far exceeds the child's ability to independently process it. The child takes in incoherent fragments and is totally unable to make a connection between the pictures he sees and the words he hears. The brain is stimulated to perform fragmentary and associative thought processes; this affects the fine nerve connections in the brain that are still developing. The child's brain develops into an instrument suitable for these kinds of thought processes rather than for active, creative thinking.

Cultivation of Aggression and Restlessness

After watching television, which goes together with an unnatural immobility, an equally unnatural surge of restlessness often ensues. The fact that children are often unmotivated, bored, restless, or aggressive after watching television is not necessarily related to the content of the program. It has to do with forced immobility in front of the screen.

Other Symptoms and Experiences

Children who watch television regularly[6]

- Meet other people with less respect and distance;
- Find it difficult to establish personal contact;
- Tend to "pull faces" and avoid direct eye contact;
- Often give stereotypical or superficial answers and lack deep interest in things;
- Read less and prefer pictorial presentations like comics and non-books;
- Hardly ever actively work through what they have seen or read;
- Lack concentration.

Some lasting effects of prolonged television exposure may include the following.

- The tendency toward alcohol and drug abuse increases as children become used to receiving passive stimulation of soul and spirit—just by pressing a button, so to speak.
- Will development is undermined because children are sitting in front of the screen without moving instead of being active and imitating the surrounding world.
- Language development has been shown to be considerably delayed.

From parents, we often hear the following objections:

- These are children's programs and all the other children watch them. My child should not be excluded.
- There is nothing I can do about it—television belongs to everyday family life. I also need some peace sometimes so that I can get on with my own things.
- Surely there would not be television in school, devices for children, and children's programs if they were all that harmful?
- It is still better if my child watches TV at home than somewhere else.
- One has to know what is going on in the world, and children need to be able to feel that they are a part of it.

Our response is that children's programs usually have fantastic, unrealistic contents with caricature-like images that are forced upon the child's soul. This development of an unrealistic, illusory world should be restricted to the minimum and replaced by inner imaginative pictures such as those that arise when children have stories and folk tales read to them.

The toy industry targets children with clever advertising. In the United States, computer games for babies are already on the market. For this reason, it is more important than ever that adults think about their and their children's consumer attitudes and strengthen their own resolve. Their children will be grateful in later life that they have been brought up to be active and have developed a healthy self-confidence; that they have learned to use media when they want and need to, rather than from habit; and that their soul life is not completely taken up by caricatures and the pseudo-experiences of virtual reality.

Television-Free Children Are Popular Playmates

Which child is more likely to develop independence: the one who does not want to be different from others and always wants to be "cool," or the one who has the courage to say: "We don't watch TV at my house, we play?" Children who have been brought up without television and video are popular playmates. They often get invited to play by other parents so that their own children don't watch so much television.

- Maybe the neighbor would welcome the idea of sending his children to you to play and will happily agree to look after the children on another day, also without letting them watch TV.

- What can children possibly miss if, instead of getting to know nature, human beings, and social life as caricatures and from animated films, they meet them through direct experience or from stories, which they can mentally illustrate with their own pictures and thoughts? Playing, moving around, listening to folk tales are activities that awaken abilities in children that will benefit them for the rest of their lives.

- Consider who is financing and supporting the entertainment industry—at the cost of the children.

- Television-free children are healthier.[7]

Media Education

How do children learn to deal with television as the archetype of audiovisual media? If parents do allow television, the most important thing is that, to start with, they watch together with their children. This is the only way to make sure that the TV is switched on and off consciously. It is also important that parents choose with the children what to watch, when, and for how long; this example teaches children to deal responsibly with the medium. What has been watched can then be discussed, and the content can be reviewed and reflected on. Parents of older children should know what their children are watching and should encourage them to talk about it, because they might still need help with processing what they have seen.

After puberty the situation is different. If adolescents have had enough other stimuli up to then, they will not be overly fascinated by television and will have developed into moderate, autonomous TV users.

Parents should keep media devices in a room that is not easily accessible to the children. Children can and do accept that certain things are only for grown-ups.

While many believe that it is best to accept things as they are and to live with them, and to intervene only when things become extreme, this attitude is not helpful for the child. It covers up the real problem, and negative habits and their consequences will just continue.

Help from America[8]

One can only hope that the books, lectures and workshops of the American science and technology critic Clifford Stoll will initiate such a widespread movement for a more humane approach to the multimedia culture. We would like to quote some of his disturbing statements directly:

> The computer changes the ecology of the classroom. Predictably, kids love the new computers and the kindergarten increasingly looks and sounds like a video arcade. Meanwhile, the machine becomes the center of attention, pushing aside clay, crayon, and teacher.... Somehow, computers are supposed to be 'good' because they're interactive and non-commercial. Television is "bad" because it's passive and commercial. Videotapes, on the whole, are "good" because they don't have commercials. I'll bet that to a child, there's not much difference. All provide big, colorful cathode-ray tubes. All show their favorite characters in fast-paced animated clips. All deliver long stretches of mental excitement with minimal muscular activity. Suppose we want to encourage attention deficit syndrome. I can't think of a better way than to point youngsters at fast animated video clips. Give 'em electronic games with races, spaceship dogfights, shoot-'em-ups, and lots of explosive noises, garish colors, and disconnected information coming from diverse sources. Give them post-modern hyper-linked media rather than simple storytelling. Encourage them to write programs with computerized Turtle Graphics rather than touching a real turtle. In short, lock them in an electronic classroom. Doubtless, multimedia systems provide visually stimulating images. Almost every children's software product is labelled "exciting." But lack of excitement simply isn't a genuine problem for kids. If anything, they're exposed to too many animated screens, with TV, videos, and Nintendo. Show me the computer program that encourages quiet reflection.... Plenty of computer programs have strong educational content with minimal computer glitz. Yet the medium broadcasts a powerful message: We're training the youngest children to explore through the computer rather than with their hands, feet, and imagination.... I can hardly think of a less appropriate place to put computers than kindergartens and pre-schools. Think of the things a three-year-old most needs: love, affection, personal attention, human warmth, and mainly, care. Four- and five-year-olds need to develop human skills... how to get along with others. They should be playing with things, not images.... Then, too, calculators and computers trivialize mistakes. When he gets a wrong answer, a student will typically dismiss the mistake with "Oh, I just pressed the wrong button!" rather than recognizing that he went about solving

a problem the wrong way. Good algebra teachers demand that students show their work to see whether a mistake's due to calculation or misunderstanding. You got a good grade if you took a good path to the answer but made a mistake in calculation. Students were graded on the method, not just the final answer. But when a calculator's in use, there's no trail of reasoning and no telling why a mistake occurred, so the instructor can't tell the difference.... What's the effect of using computers in math education? Over the past fifteen years, colleges have seen an astounding growth in remedial math classes. Pre-algebra, once the mainstay of seventh and eighth graders, has become a common college class. Indeed, two thirds of college math enrolment is in courses which are ordinarily high school classes.... In the 1930s rural electrification was supposed to save the family farm. After three decades of extensive promotion and wire stringing, all the farms were wired. So where's that family farm today? Gone.

In the 1950s, television was promoted as a boon for education. It would bring the finest educators into the classrooms and homes of even the poorest families. That genuinely happened, thanks to governmental subsidies to broadcast stations and extensive grants for educational programming.

What happened to the great educational boon that was supposed to follow? Promoters in the early 1980s glibly stated that communications satellites would encourage global unity through world-wide television. Unity through MTV, perhaps.... We naturally perceive other cultures the easy way: by watching them on TV or glimpsing them through a porthole of the Internet. This conveys images, not understanding. Rather than shrinking our globe, this shallow electronic information system makes foreign cultures more distant.... Social skills. Strength of character. Trust. Determination. Perseverance. Not traits downloadable from a Web site. Quite the opposite: Every hour that you spend with your brain in cyberspace marks sixty minutes you aren't sharpening those skills that our world so desperately needs. The best way to create a community of loners is for each of us to escape into the welcoming arms of the Internet.[9]

Computer Games Are Not Harmless Either

If one observes children who are playing computer games, it is obvious that their physical development is neglected in the same way as when they are watching television. The mouse replaces the remote control in this case. Minimal movements of wrist and index finger cannot bring about whole body movements (playing sports, horsing around, jumping, wrestling).

If a ten-year-old girl can manage to tickle a dragon in a desert, the inventors of the game glorify this as a "creative idea." Most computer games are about sports, wars, science fiction, manhunts, car chases. They all have in common that the encounter with people and the world is reduced to action and reaction; actions and creativity are only possible within the boundaries that are predetermined by the program. What positive learning experiences can be the outcome? Alertness and ability to respond are, no doubt, fostered, but with what kind of contents? Is it meaningful to practice these skills in an extraterrestrial attack on planet earth or while hunting down a criminal? The child or adolescent is caught in a distorted world of illusions that has little in common with the real world. Arrogance, cynicism, joy in manipulating, and in making fun of others are provoked. Intelligent response is mobilized in a one-sided way and associated with certain visual events, whereas imaginative and creative intelligence that is not fixed on prefabricated pictures and that arises from the child's inner life is not cultivated. On the contrary, it is suppressed because it cannot thrive in an environment of emotional distance, cynicism, cruelty, and tension. To develop an inner life requires moments of silence, listening, and reflection.

Comics and the World of Pictures

Comics influence the child's mental pictures. The pictures that children draw in the waiting room while one has a conversation about them with the mother are often shockingly stereotypical and poor: clouds with outlines, well-known grimaces and patterns without any particular originality. These children are unable to create their own inner pictures even when they listen to a fairy tale. Prefabricated caricatures have taken their place. Why are children so fascinated by these picture series, often long before they can understand the writing in the speech bubbles? Because their own thinking is not ready for abstract, picture-free content, but it is a picture-thinking that is saturated with the pictures they take in. This is why they are attracted to pictures and why they always look for the pictures first in any book they open. In the same way they are attracted by the colors and strong outlines of comic books. The problem is that these pictures do not leave the soul as free as other sense perceptions. On the contrary, they confine the imagination because of their narrow delineation and strong suggestive power.

An adult can distance himself from comic-book and television images with the help of his abstract thinking. A child is not able to do this. Such images paralyze and weigh down the child's imaginative and emotional development. What makes things worse is that morally valuable ideas are often attached to these caricatures, which means that the child will always associate ideals and pure concepts with these images.

Why Are Animated Films So Popular?

If we ask adolescents what they like about them they say things like: "It's so nice and relaxing" or "It's so silly that it makes me laugh" or "It is obviously unrealistic but still really cool." The fascination has, however, deeper causes. Contemporary designers, artists, and writers are more or less consciously looking for answers to fundamental developmental questions.

If one looks at the storyline and content of animated films and comic books, three areas seem to be particularly popular:

- Hidden wishes, fantasies and fears, longing for self-knowledge
- Cruelty, destructiveness, irony, cynicism
- Animal or animal-like heroes who chase, outwit, destroy, attack each other or help and love each other

It is as if the not-yet-humanized instinctual nature of the human being is lifted to consciousness in a kind of caricatured self-image. What is called the double in psychology is being instinctively sought here: the meeting with the lower self and the search for ways of dealing with it consciously. A reality that is not sense-based is brought into picture form: the movement, language, color, and proportions of the pictures do not correspond to reality as we know it through our senses. And the heroes are often extraterrestrial beings who have been sent to earth from a known or unknown planet. The subconscious longing of humanity to cross the threshold of the spiritual world and to leave the physical world behind creates a caricature of itself so that, at least in this way, people can become aware of this other dimension.

THE CHILD AND DRUGS

Michaela Glöckler[10]

Why do adults, youngsters, and even increasing numbers of children[11] use drugs? How is it possible that people take substances which are known to be harmful and life-shortening? Children and adolescents are often led to drug abuse out of curiosity or through peer pressure; they might not want to lose a friend or feel excluded from a group. But nowadays they also frequently describe motives similar to those we encounter in adults of all ages:

- Escape from a world that has become uncomfortable; from a home where conflicts and misunderstanding are the rule; from worries and problems at school or at work.
- Fear of failure—in a relationship, at work, at school.
- A longing for warmth, light, joy, harmony, for the closeness and protection of a community that can provide what one has been deprived of during childhood and adolescence; but also a longing for spiritual experiences.
- Curiosity to experience something extraordinary, dangerous, adventurous; the wish to "really get something out of life."

Behind all these longings, hopes, and wishes—which are as natural as life itself—stands the drive for identity, inner security, and fulfillment. It is hard to imagine anyone not having this drive. The question we are faced with is how education can develop the forces of soul and spirit in such a way that these longings and desires can find fulfilment through inner activity and self-development rather than through the passive self-stimulation of drug abuse.

We would like to give a clear picture here of how much the drug problem has become part of our modern lifestyle, since—due to emancipation and isolation—the young child is already confronted with his own self and loneliness. The side effects of this can become unbearable unless a strategy is found to counteract them. The drug problem challenges the twenty-first century education to find this strategy. As a first step we need to understand the effects of different drugs, and then we can ask how the same kind of experiences can be brought about in a healthy way, through the right education and upbringing.

Alcohol

Expected effects and experiences: feeling part of a community, being able to talk together in a relaxed way, leaving all worries behind, enjoying oneself and switching off, finding comfort in loneliness.

Some harmful consequences: brain damage, sleeping disorders, sweating, nerve paralysis, pancreatic and liver diseases, birth defects.

Nicotine

Expected effects and experiences: improved concentration, relaxation, creating a distance, being able to make a new start, having a really short break to wake up properly, avoiding nervous eating and drinking which would result in taking in unnecessary calories, having a nice social time and interesting conversations, needing less sleep, staying awake longer.

Some harmful consequences: heart problems, headache, respiratory diseases, increased cancer risk, lack of circulation in the limbs, reduced sperm viability, birth defects.

Opioids

Expected effects and experiences: deep calmness, relaxed and warm sleep despite pain and worries, out-of-body experience, experiencing oneself as a hovering, not weighed down by thoughts, being at one with the surrounding light, color, and beings; finding eternal peace and sleep, darkness, extinction of consciousness; being "in paradise," experiencing oneself in an after-death-like spiritual world, euphoric joy and blissful happiness, experience of being transported from the constrictions of everyday life.

Some harmful consequences: weakened digestive system, inhibited sexual functions, muscular spasms, pale skin, weight loss, stiff joints and limbs, ultimate destruction of all bodily functions and forces, hepatitis.

Cannabis (marijuana and hashish)

Expected effects and experiences: relativization of reality, standing above everyday habits, duties, restrictions, stress, and frustration, feeling "high," laughing at everything, feeling good, experiencing thoughts, feelings, perceptions as well as space and time in a new and different way. Many experiences seem more elemental, separated from their usual context, in a new light, isolated or bizarrely enlarged. Conscious experience of the dream state between waking and sleeping.

Some harmful consequences: impaired ability to drive, reduced concentration, problems with learning, reduced sperm count, irregular menstrual cycle, developmental disorders in the unborn child, weakened immune system, lack of motivation.

Hallucinogens

Expected effects and experiences: out-of-body experiences, colorful visions and hallucinations, experience of light and warmth, panoramic view of own biography, experiences, and memories from the long distant past, being totally in oneself and at the same time out of oneself in another world.

Some harmful consequences: temporary psychosis, delusions, kidney and liver damage, unreliable sense impressions, flashbacks.

Cocaine and Amphetamines

Expected effects and experiences: experiencing oneself as strong and able, and above all as extraordinarily clear-thinking and intelligent, longing for spiritually demanding activity and excitement, for being extremely special, tremendous self-esteem and feeling of superiority over others, euphoria, feeling of unlimited physical power, ability to overcome fatigue, being awake and strong.

Some harmful consequences: irritability, restlessness, feeling rushed, headache, rapid heartbeat, paranoia, sleeplessness, stomach cramps, dizziness.

Ecstasy and Designer Drugs

Expected effects and experiences: changed feeling life, being able to open up and show feelings, fearlessness, more open to conversation and relationships, experiencing intuitively how others are feeling, disinhibition, showing one's true feelings, feeling uninhibited and direct.

Some harmful consequences: disorientation, hallucinations, anxiety, depression, exhaustion, sleeplessness, palpitations.

All drugs carry the risks of premature aging, disturbed ego-function, and disrupted self-control in body, soul, and spirit.

Prevention and Therapy

In Place of the Self: How Drugs Work,[12] by Dutch drug therapist and psychologist Ron Dunselman, describes the different effects drugs have on body, soul, and spirit. It is a fact that drugs substitute for the ego: I don't have to be active at all: the drug provides certain experiences without me having to do anything. Pharmaceutical psychotherapy struggles with the same problems: It is much easier to take a sleeping pill or a tranquilizer than to learn, for example, how to pray, how to find inner tranquility through a meditative life, how to rediscover the spiritual in nature, how to experience one's own thoughts and feelings as more colorful and real. It is so much easier to swallow tablets that provide the feeling of being protected or happy than to do the exercises that are necessary for self-development and that help to establish an inner stability and strength for coping with life. On the other hand, it is astonishing to see how much hardship some people can endure and how hard they work on themselves while others turn to drugs because they feel that they cannot bear their lot any longer.

The approaches to prevention and therapy described below can only be effective if a genuine human contact with the addicted person can be established. The human being can resist any temptation if he does it for his own good or out of love for another person, if he strives to put his ego in control of his thinking, feeling, and willing. The best helpers and therapists in these situations are certainly those who at some point in their lives came close to taking drugs, or even took drugs for a time but managed to get away from them. Without effective intervention, drug abuse and addiction will lead to illness and to an increasing loss of inner activity and ego strength. Lack of motivation and will, emotional exhaustion, and disordered thinking are signs of this.

Disorientation, doubts, and hatred directed toward a world that seems unfair and evil, as well as existential fear and worries, are on the increase throughout the world—even in children and adolescents. It is therefore not surprising that one in every three to five people in the world drinks alcohol, and one in every ten to fifteen people is in danger of giving in to some inner or outer pressure and turning to drugs.[13] At a time when traditional social pressures and religious traditions are less influential, yet new inner forces and personal autonomy have not been adequately developed, a crisis situation seems unavoidable. But instead of accepting this situation, we would advocate that all possible efforts be made to put the active human ego back in its place, freed from drug use, so that it can support the development of the self and of the environment.

Children and adolescents who experiment with drugs or alcohol are often more sensitive than others. They cannot cope with the hardship of their everyday life. They try to avoid problems, or try to solve them forcibly. It is difficult for them to face their problems and deal with them day by day. This is why no therapy can be successful unless the person concerned makes an enormous individual effort and has supportive surroundings. We can here only hint at the most important elements of a preventive education:

- Give the possibility to be self-active, to be dependent on oneself.
- Breastfeeding instead of bottle-feeding.
- A genuine interest in the developmental stages of the child.
- Nurturing the senses.
- Establishing good habits in daily life, including regular mealtimes.
- Avoiding sweets between meals.
- Setting boundaries, finding the middle way between strictness and giving in so that the child can feel secure.
- Strengthening the imagination by telling fairy tales and reading meaningful stories, legends, and biographies.
- Protecting the child from passively consuming prefabricated images.
- Spiritual and undogmatic religious upbringing.

EDUCATIONAL TASKS FOR ADOLESCENTS

Christof Wiechert

The first Waldorf school initiated a clear movement towards coeducation as early as 1919. This fact is easily forgotten and easy to ignore now that coeducation is the norm.

But Waldorf schools have gone one step further in a different direction in setting standards here: boys learn traditionally feminine skills, such as how to knit, to sew a shirt, and in the upper classes we see them on the stage performing eurythmy alongside the young ladies in dress, including veils, irrespective of gender.

In the meantime, education in general has absorbed a great deal from Waldorf schools: main lessons, foreign languages in the lower grades, an emphasis on art and artistic activities, senior essays, practicums, and so forth. But what has so far not been copied is the transfer of traditionally female activities into male activities. This step is difficult to follow.

Coeducation in Waldorf schools means not only that the girls do what the boys do, but also that conversely the boys join in what the girls do.

Can it be that the message of this approach is that the sexes have polarized too far? Are the differences becoming too great? Are the sexes no longer complementing one another? Has a chasm arisen between them, are there unbridgeable differences instead of the union of the polarities? And does this accord with a developmental spirit that takes the human being into account? If we consider the fact that 8 out of 10 crimes are as a rule perpetrated by male adolescents or men,[14] then we can see that coeducation has not yet been as successful as it might be.

I would go as far as to assert that the whole of the education system is still too one-sidedly male-oriented despite the general introduction of coeducation. In school, pupils encounter any amount of "macho," after all: fun, wicked, gross, cool, fucking good are simply the expressions used by adolescents themselves. School makes its own contribution with performance-oriented teaching, intensive courses, examinations, learning-oriented environments, time-frames with exhaustive calculability of required results; in short, the citadels of rationalism and efficiency serve the forward-looking male spirit. Anyone who cannot cope with this is in difficulties because this is just the start of a rationale of neuro-educational exploitation of young people. Male thinking in its purest form.

The impossibility of reforming the education system shows how sclerotic these structures are. And change goes precisely in the direction which we should avoid; the aim should be not to consolidate what is there already, not more checks, greater emphasis on performance, more supervision, but instead we need to learn to be guided by the child and his strengths and needs.

The colder this climate becomes, the more heated will be the response. Such a heated response to an educational bureaucracy which has no concern for the human being has different aspects, in my view. Violence is one aspect, right-wing extremism another. Right-wing extremism is also a product of our educational habits resulting from a predominant selection procedure which itself also displays fascistic roots. A third aspect is leisure activities that lack any quality of balance: either we give ourselves over entirely to the party and disco scene or we become LAN networked computer zombies—a dominantly male form of culture. You'll scarcely ever find a girl at a LAN party![15] The only bridge between these contrasts is alcohol. This scenario is illuminated by an omnipresent economic sector which continually anticipates what young people might want next.

It is a miracle that children and adolescents are as normal as they appear to be. But are they really? Or are we losing our yardstick of what is normal?

In these inner and outer landscapes adolescents grow to maturity, then start their own families. Rudolf Steiner speaks of earth-readiness, indicating that there is more at stake than simply the ability to procreate. He characterizes earthly maturity as the possession of a genuine love of the world, from out of oneself without external instruction or reason. In Rudolf Steiner's opinion, the capacity for sexual love is part of a general capacity for love in relation to the world. In order to allow this capacity for love to develop in a healthy way, education must introduce adolescents entering puberty to the world in such a way that their main interest is the world and not themselves. Too much self-centeredness in puberty should be avoided. If it occurs in boys, Steiner says, it will lead to the thrill of power and eroticism. In young women, by contrast, it produces isolation from the world and an introverted interest in their own person.

In the 1920s, Steiner wrote that the main task of education during puberty is to ensure a proper balance between inner and outer; "facing the world" versus "focusing on one's self." The enthusiasm for the subject being taught is seen as a bridge. The strong relationship to learning produces a balance between inner and outer world. For Steiner, puberty was something to which attention had to be paid, rather than a problem. Hence his two lectures on this subject are called "Educational Questions during Puberty," *not* "Educational Problems during Puberty."[16]

Today, reaching earthly maturity or earth-readiness is often (though not always) associated with problems which the pupil has to face and in which the school plays an important role.

What can Steiner's approach achieve today? What is the significance of inner and outer experience at puberty? What does ability to love the world mean? The perception of the child begins to change. The twelve-year-old looks at something with a general, indeed, almost objective interest, it rouses his curiosity but remains free of the soul's emotional experience. That is well demonstrated in the way adolescents approach hobbies. The stamp collector is completely immersed in his special interest. He possesses a great deal of detailed knowledge, can give a well-informed opinion on the rarity and value of a stamp. Something in his soul has driven him to engage in this hobby, but mostly he will not know himself what it is. He only knows that he wants to do it and it gives him satisfaction to the extent that he can know that of himself. But anyone watching him will see that he is not fully immersed in it, something remains outside. It looks like preliminary practice. The soul seeks selected objects in order to unite with them chastely in a defined space but with a high degree of specialist skill and knowledge. In girls we can study this first devotion to the world within a restricted framework if, for example, they fall in love with horses and riding. They immerse themselves in a small, clear area of the world on a trial basis, but they do so with all the intensity at their disposal. And yet they are not completely engaged, they observe themselves. And it is surprising to see how such immersion dies after a few years. There is no mourning at its passing, the enthusiasm has gone and they smile to themselves at the memory.

At puberty, the situation is completely different. Distance from the object not only disappears, but nothing is undertaken or experienced that is not driven by his own wants—be it homework for a "dumb" or "cool" teacher, be it maintaining friendships, or the experience of awakening sexuality. Eroticism and embarrassment become burningly relevant in a completely new way. The radius of experience broadens powerfully. The soul passes through terrifying depths and dizzying heights. Aggressive and vulnerable at the same time, adolescents rush from one experience to the next. Everyone around the adolescent experiences this intensity too, depending on temperament.

The adolescent must find his way in an inner world that demands two things: in one part of the soul it seeks ideals, love, and devotion, and therefore also a desire to follow which comes to expression as identification. In another part of the soul, the inner world has to deal with erotic and sexual love. This conflict was more of an inner one in earlier times which did not take place in the public sphere. Today it screams at every passer-by from the rooftops: a big part of human existence consists of the worship of sex. The question surfaces of a right relationship between the two. It becomes a dilemma for many.

Steiner once characterized it in the following way. He was speaking about the relationship between the head and body, and that this was originally different, and adds:

> But this has created a very curious situation.... the situation has been created that human beings are an image of the gods precisely in the organs which are normally called the organs of their lower nature. The only thing is that this image of the gods has been spoiled in the way that human beings are on earth. Precisely the higher element in human beings, what should be spiritual from the cosmos, precisely this element has become their lower nature. Please remember that this is an important secret of human nature. The lower human nature has become as it is through the luciferic influence; it should actually be the higher human nature. That is the contradiction in the nature of the human being. It is something that provides the solution for innumerable riddles of the cosmos and life if it is understood in the correct way.[17]

Let us try to understand it in the correct way. Can we use these thoughts as the basis of our disposition in our conduct as teachers? Can we experience that the most holy and profane elements can exist in close proximity, in our own life, too, and that education in this context means adopting a sensitive approach towards adolescents? Do we still know the nature of this sensitivity as an educational tool for adolescents?

Are we prepared to consider how we ourselves are involved in this matter or how we were involved in our youth? Can that be a help in dealing with young people? If we do so, we not only acquire the necessary respect for how young people express themselves, we also acquire the strength and honesty not simply to respond to our young friends with dislike and reproof. We do not need to rely solely on avoidance or prevention; we can also support them. Perhaps we recognize in them something from our own youth?

In a Christian Community summer camp, the parents noticed the uninhibited way that boys and girls related to one another. When the minister in charge was asked about this, he responded: "If they're going to do it, they might as well do it here rather than elsewhere." A wise statement. The young people directly concerned and those involved with them experience this time as a miniature cosmic process with which we adults are also familiar and which we ourselves have passed through.

"Understanding" has become a trite word. Is it not better to "love" these "suffering" adolescents?

Unobtrusively, but with all the greater intensity in accordance with Steiner's motto that the difference between teachers and other people is that teachers can love more?

It is hard to escape the impression that educators (both parents and teachers) often respond to puberty with a fearful attitude. Fear is always a bad counselor. How often does fearful helplessness lead to adults taking the wrong measures?

If the school, parents, and teachers can keep a young person engaged in the subjects taught of his own volition, that is generally sufficient to get him through this period. But such voluntary engagement with school subjects places the greatest demands on teachers specifically at a time when it is commonly said that teaching in the upper school should be more neutral or sober as pupils are now capable of making their own judgments. Precisely the opposite is the case. Lessons do not call for sobriety but the most intensive struggle to keep the interest of pupils. Every teacher knows that precisely these years are a roller-coaster ride.

Rudolf Steiner gives some advice in this respect in the last lecture of *The Foundations of Human Experience* (*Study of Man*) when he says that the years between age 12 and 15 is dependent to a high degree on the imaginative accommodation of the teachers, on the imaginative capacities of teachers.[18] Specifically at this age! We can build on that and say that the whole way in which we deal with this age must be inventive, free, and without fear, seeing the pupil as a developing human being and not as someone there merely to supply work. The latter approach would, indeed, be more appropriate for ages 5 and 6, since the work performed at that time is still free of the self-referential soul.

A pupil in grade 10 smokes (illicitly) in school. Should we give him the standard punishment or should we be more inventive? Such banal decisions may, under certain circumstances, decide a pupil's future. The standard punishment takes the attitude that you are not actually our pupil but a subject that requires correction. But a teacher who is inventive and requires the pupil to give a botanically exact presentation of the tobacco plant as an exercise addresses the nascent human being in his developmental attitude. Such a "punishment" will be remembered for the rest of one's life with considerable amusement, whereas we will try to erase the standard punishment from our memory as quickly as possible: somehow the latter fails to take account of the nature of the human being.

The following fact is still worthy of note, representing an important path of exercise for the teacher. In his lectures on this subject collected in *Education for Adolescents*,[19] Rudolf Steiner describes with magnificent empathy how the adolescent appears differently on the outside than he is on the inside. Now the question arises, how do I react as a teacher to the adolescent when I meet him? Is the externality apparent in him my sole reference point or do I try to concentrate on what is not apparent?

I have to tell myself always to pose the question, "How does that look from the inside? Is his unacceptably loud, crude attitude not the evidence of inner insecurity or of the actual request for encounter?"

A really challenging student had chosen to make her English teacher's life difficult during lessons. But since the teacher understood this girl in her innermost being, she was always able to prevent a confrontation. When one day she finally did lose her temper, the girl reacted, deeply shocked, and said: "But you know me."

We must be aware of the disparity between outer and inner, particularly with male adolescents. Their loudness is an expression of inner insecurity, because in the developing male the ego combines with the astral body only much later. This means that for long stretches they are without orientation or any foothold. Precisely because of this, the emotions in their soul are the exact opposite of what they demonstrate outwardly.

The opposite is true of girls in puberty; the ego combines easily and at an early stage with the astral body, which means that they present impressive powers of judgment and maturity. They are more likely than boys to appear to be more than what they really are. A power is displayed that can dazzle. But such assurance can, if confronted, also collapse in on itself.

These basic patterns of human development are hidden by society. We therefore have the dual task of interpreting and understanding the young person as he appears, while uncovering the veil of cultural stance to penetrate to the real person. Not an easy task. But all those who love their pupils can do more.

And here we come to the crunch question in education during puberty: Are we able to give these young people love? Can we approach them with a pure, unrestrained, active love for the human being? Of course we can, convention says. But practice shows something different.

It is not easy to call on this ability. If, for example, we recall our own school days and our own teachers, we will see that in elementary school it was all about whether or not the teachers were nice. Competence or authenticity did not yet make a lasting impression. But then in high school, it was knowledge in harmony with authenticity that made a lasting impression. What we remember is the way teachers handled their material, how they were able to let the material work on us, the extent to which they could fill us with enthusiasm. That also determined our relationship with the teacher.

There were teachers with whom one could get up to all kinds of things. It was fun but one had little respect. But there were also teachers with whom one felt that one could get down to business and speak matter-of-factly because they were genuine. In these teachers their personality was completely in harmony with the subject they taught. That had a positive effect, that we could trust them. These encounters become powerful experiences and can give an inner foothold to adolescents in puberty. It is not by chance that the choice of many a university course after school can be traced back to such an encounter with a subject taught by a "beloved" teacher.

Such a quality cannot be characterized simply as the capacity for love. Such an educational effect can only be achieved if the teacher has truly acquired authenticity in his life. And that is a capacity of the ego.

This characterization confirms the central educational law: what emanates from the teacher affects the next lowest element of the human being. An encounter that ignites the soul of the adolescent must therefore come from the sphere of the individuality. If we attempt such an approach, then we do not need school rules that prescribe behavior but discount personal responsibility. If such forms of teacher self-education begin to be realized, then adolescents will also find the way to discuss with their teachers the things that must be discussed in the course of growing into adulthood.

Perhaps we still have a chance to assign to everything connected with sexual awakening the right moment in the pupil's biography through an education that is infused with a profound, active understanding of the human being. One thing appears certain to me: a greater degree of educational artistry is required.

QUESTIONS RELATING TO SEXUALITY AND SEX EDUCATION

Michaela Glöckler

Illumination of life matter can be found in the Waldorf curriculum. However, daily experience shows that despite, and indeed perhaps because of, the omnipresent theme of sexuality and silence around it, questions about sex education continue to be of a burning nature. Therefore we will look at some commonly raised issues.

The play of children in kindergarten is based on what they have picked up at home, including so-called "doctor games"—which one takes care to keep within reasonable bounds. The telling of fairy tales, picked up again in first grade, can incorporate age-appropriate ideas about sexual relationships, depending on the level of questions arising in the class or home situation. In second grade, the legends of the saints provide a wealth of material to show how someone like Francis of Assisi, who squanders his youth with harlots and alcohol or lives a dissipated youth, can nevertheless become a saint. In telling how someone lived before he became a saint, much can be incorporated or accentuated which this or that child may have witnessed at home, thus giving it greater objectivity and a more hopeful orientation. In third grade, as part of the Old Testament stories, the creation of the human being and the differentiation of the sexes is described; and Adam and Eve, and the snake, can be conjured in a more or less detailed way. If children of this age—grades three and four—sometimes ask their parents where they came from, however, they are not really asking for biological sex education but to know whether they are truly their parents' children or not.

Around third and fourth grade, children experience themselves for the first time as separate individuals—Steiner refers to this in the *Study of Man* as the "rubicon"—and not just a part of the family or the circumstances and environment in which, like a fish in water, they have hitherto felt themselves wholly integrated. They suddenly feel that they are, after all, very different from other people, and in consequence cannot really imagine that they didn't enter this family or these circumstances from "elsewhere," or perhaps even that they are a foundling child. On the one hand, a child at this age wants to hear parents tell him that he is truly their child; and on the other, he would feel a profound sense of satisfaction if an adult were suddenly to say: "My dear, I must tell you the truth about where you come from…"

After these more social and spiritual perspectives on the child's origin, the themes in fifth, sixth, and seventh grades surface more in the emotional and interpersonal realms via Greek mythology. The marriages between the gods, between gods and heroes, and among human beings, embedded in a context of wars and re-established peace, play a central role here. All the emotions that can play into relationships between men and women can be addressed here.

Then follows early historical development and the first ethnology main lesson, possibly also accompanied by very characteristic folk dances and songs that often accentuate gendered elements. In grades eight through eleven, the biology main lessons provide a space to examine various aspects of sex education. Cell biology and embryonic development are suitable material for eleventh grade, followed by the evolution of species including birth and development of the child in the first three years. Parents' evenings are held to accompany this, and usually it is suggested that parents deal with the "mechanics" of biological issues at home in private and only involve the teacher or school doctor if the atmosphere at home is unsuitable for tackling these questions.

It is a consequence of the sexualization of our society that sex has become so central to student awareness from an early age. The Waldorf curriculum highlights the spiritual and social aspects of male and female in elementary school, and emphasizes the individual development of the child and the human being regardless of gender. Intensive artistic work and diverse stimulus ensure that the awareness of children and adolescents is neither fixated upon, nor restricted too early to, the sexual realm.

How do we respond properly to accelerated development?

At puberty, demands on young people grow, and puberty is coming ever earlier nowadays. A girl needs her mother to have told her everything of "practical value" before she gets her first menses at the age of around eleven and a half. The same applies to father and son, usually at least a year later. It is therefore necessary that suitable opportunities are found to discuss questions relating to contraception, sexual desire, and love; responsibility and sexual partnership; differences in sexuality, for instance hetero- and homosexuality; sexually transmitted diseases, abuse, pornography, rape; and also abortion and test-tube conception.

The vital thing is how an adult approaches these themes, integrating them with social, emotional, and spiritual aspect. Sex education should never be taught in isolation. Rather, it should become apparent that sexuality and our relationship to it is part of our whole stance toward life, and that it occupies and important place in developmental questions in adolescence and adulthood.

What is the source of sexual attraction's power?

In reflecting on the extraordinary power and fascination of sexuality for human beings, the motif of identity continually surfaces. It is the core concept in marriage crises, couple counseling or in discussions about how to separate in as human and friendly a way as possible when a marriage breaks down. What ultimately makes the imagined or actual separation from the other so painful if we have really loved each other? Or, to put it metaphorically: what wound is bleeding here?

We can approach the mystery of human development in a particularly striking way when engaging with sexuality. Here the experience of our own identity can extend to our sexual partner in a way that makes a breakdown in the relationship seem—at least temporarily—tantamount to loss of identity. However much we may regret the lost relationship, and suffer from it for years perhaps, there is no better way to learn to differentiate and observe the question of identity in its dangerous mix of self-love and love for another than in the wake of a separation consciously worked through.

No one can absorb such a truth initially, of course. It usually takes a longer process of discussion and counseling for the person concerned to come to the point where we can gain this insight ourselves and—in the words of Wagner's Parsifal—heal the wound with the same weapon with which it was made: the power of one's own ego.

What are sexual perversions?

By perversion, we mean something particularly dark and incomprehensible. People today agree that there are no definitive descriptions of "perverse" sexual patterns of conduct. Instead we now experience perversion as any sexual act which is carried out on a partner against his or her wishes. At one end of the scale is a delicate touch or kiss to which the other does not feel able to respond and which makes him or her feel under pressure; and at the other, the worst abuse scenarios, even leading to murder. The question remains, however, why it lies in the very nature of sexuality that these abysses of human misconduct and ungoverned exercise of power over another can surface alongside it. Rudolf Steiner also ascribes these perversions to the hatred toward the "stranger" or "other" and relates the same impulse as part of the tendency to nationalism.

The body-bound astral body works in our desires and passions. In the soul, the astral body lives in polar tension between sympathy and antipathy. It is the bearer of the feeling and emotional life, which is partly body-bound and partly body-free life, and thus also encompasses the forms of musical experience in intervals, and of harmonious/disharmonious relationships between people, things and creatures. In our physical body, the astral body causes movement, attraction and repulsion, tension and relaxation. When its forces work too strongly it can override the ego's leadership where the ego has not been able to develop sufficient autonomy and competency. In this case a human being will be capable of reactions to which he or she feels driven, or which are triggered by environmental particulars.

In the soul realm we encounter a struggle with likes and dislikes, and in the mind and spirit the search for identity and autonomy of action. The less security of identity we have in the realm of spirit, the greater is our longing for safety and stability in the soul and body. The need to find refuge in a group, the longing for recognition, or the fear of exclusion or abandonment can become the triggers of destructive behavior. In nationalism and fanaticism we can find a collective substitute identity that occupies the place of the non-existent or weak personal identity. Every form of ideologically-based group therefore contains the danger of loss of personality and identity. It supports de-individualization and subjection to or dependency on others, replacing the individual ego. Here the opposite developmental process occurs to that described in the first sections of this article as the three ideals which can stimulate the development of our humanity: truth, love, freedom.

Where the ego withdraws or cannot incarnate properly, other powers enter, as if into a vaccuum. Thoughts, feelings and motivations are realities whether we want to believe it or not. The spiritual world's forces and beings extend into the human soul, which is itself the arena of the human spirit's evolution.

How can we understand homosexuality? Is there such a thing as a homosexual destiny?

At puberty, homosexual eroticism and longing appears as a tendency in almost all of us, until the definitive sexual orientation has formed, either hetero- or homosexual. Only after this transitional phase can we see whether a homosexual tendency is consolidating in the long term.

A person's sexual orientation can also change during the course of life. In such cases, the ambivalence of youth remains present in a latent state. A person with a homosexual disposition can later enter into a heterosexual relationship and start a family, but the reverse is also true: after ten or fifteen years of marriage, with one or several children, a separation can take place after which one of the partners will choose a homosexual relationship.

Human relationships are first and foremost constellations of destiny and not primarily a subject for purely constitutional observations. Both constitution and destiny must be seen in their mutual influence or interaction. The human being, unlike the animal, is not instructed by his organs but must himself instruct them. The human being's disposition allows us far greater freedom of relationship with our organism than does that of the animal. As a result we can also have such highly individualized and diverse experiences. If we learn through experience to be more human—more truthful, loving, and free—we will grow ever healthier through the course of life, whether we possesses a homo- or heterosexual disposition.

One can imagine many possible reasons why one's own gender is attractive to oneself while the opposite leaves one cold. There can also be reasons of destiny for a person imbued with a deep abhorrence for either the male or female gender. If a woman, for instance, for political or other reasons, is repeatedly compelled to submit to men against her own will, she may experience this as such crippling humiliation and loss of dignity that she develops a profound distaste for being a woman. Correspondingly one can also imagine a man who has no capacity to conduct himself sexually in a socially acceptable way and harms a woman or women to such an extent that he acquires a deep antipathy toward the male gender. Since, according to Rudolf Steiner, male and female incarnations usually alternate, I can easily imagine that in the next incarnation such an individual will seek out inherited and social conditions that confront him with the life question of homosexuality. We could also inquire here into the karma of compulsory sexual abstinence (e.g. in monasteries or convents), or into other "one-sided" sexual conduct.

As well as physical attraction, however, decisive or changing individual aspects also play an important part: those one loved most dearly in one earthly life may reincarnate in male or female bodies, regardless of which gender they inhabited before. We need to find our way to the people who belong to us through destiny, and to solve, either alone or together, the questions raised by destiny constellations.

What help can we give children and parents who may be deeply affected by the discovery that the child has a homosexual disposition? How would we make this easier for those affected in the context of school—where in the curriculum can we speak about homosexuality?

If this occurs in an understanding educational context, it does not have to be any different from adolescent first discovering a serious sexual inclination toward the opposite sex. This is always a profoundly incisive experience that sometimes feels like a powerful jolt to the adolescent.

The right time to address sexual issues is always when pupils are concerned with the relevant questions. Only then does it make sense to raise these issues, and to do so even if they don't fit into the current curriculum content at all. Sexuality is something so universally human, and extends from the biological through to the soul to the spiritual realm. I would find it difficult to assign it to a particular curricular subject. Basically the whole way we teach must educate pupils about sexual matters. In the way we comment on life processes, describe this or that, in the way that we relate to men and women, to pupils of both sexes—all this is sex education in the very best sense, awakening trust and creating the basis for addressing even awkward—and usually individual—questions.

With regard to the homosexual student and the family having difficulty, these issues are difficult to deal with in brief. Everything stands and falls here on whether there is strong enough interest in the individuality of the child, in the person within the child or adolescent.

Helplessness in the face of homosexual tendencies is due to the fact that one cannot (yet) accept or integrate circumstances of destiny, and one's identification with the body or sexual tendency has not yet been properly established. If the normative idea of "proper women" or "proper men" is more substantial than that of the eternal individuality, of what as human being one wishes to experience and learn in this body and in this sexual orientation, then there will be profound identity problems. It is often not possible to solve these without professional help—and such help is therefore definitely recommended.

What effect might it have on the individual to live as homosexual and, as it were, to be always different from others? What does society gain from integrating the homosexual?

This question you raise of "being different" characterizes something that affects every homosexual in comparison with the heterosexual, through being in the minority. But what does this mean, living in an awareness of belonging to a minority, not fitting in with wider society, having to battle for acceptance of one's mode of life? The positive aspect of such a situation of destiny is surely often that this strengthens awareness of one's own personality, of self-acceptance. How easy it seems, in contrast, to be "normal" and to swim along in the broad current! Belonging to a minority always means that we stick out, invite rejection, have to justify ourselves, and—in order to be accepted—must usually work harder than others. Not only when confrontation has a happy outcome but also in the case of repeated or even long-term failure, this great, additional effort furthers development as part of repeated earthly incarnations. It also takes great courage and real love to live in a loving relationship and to persist when social acceptance is withheld or made difficult. I am therefore always particularly pleased to receive a marriage announcement from a homosexual couple, since I know that years of struggle and anxiety will often have preceded their "coming out."

As far as sexual life is concerned, I often think that this should be people's own private matter, not just for homosexuals but also for heterosexuals. To talk a lot about sexual life or to parade one's lovemaking publicly is something I do not regard as an adult pursuit, but adolescent behavior. In contrast, all human relationships characterized by mutual respect, love and tenderness, whether with or without a sexual basis, have a positive effect on the social milieu. When people unite, forces arise that can benefit others. And thus a stable relationship between homosexual men or women can likewise be an open house for others, or can spark important activities, as much as a marriage between a man and woman can be, or an intact family life. Ultimately everything depends on whether a human relationship is productive and therefore valuable for those around it. And thus human beings have the opportunity not just to produce physical children, but also soul and spirit offspring.

When I see how few children nowadays come from intact families, and how seldom men and women succeed in integrating their sexuality into living together in such a way that long-term life partnerships can arise, I often wonder what feeds the arrogance and self-regard which representatives of the heterosexual way of life so often demonstrate toward homosexuals. Nevertheless, it is certain that homosexuality represents a challenge for society and requires us to develop active tolerance and understanding for the "difference" of others.

Who can a student confide in if the social milieu has a distaste toward homosexuality?

This is an important question. It would be desirable for people such as school doctors and therapists at Waldorf schools to be contacts for such issues; or a particular teacher. But the same applies to sexuality in general. Heterosexually-orientated adolescents also have questions relating to sexuality for which they find insufficient understanding at home or in their social circles. It is of inestimable value if there is a person they trust at school. At the same time, we should acknowledge that there are many adolescents—whether heterosexual or homosexual—who feel strongly that they must take responsibility themselves for their sexuality, and who prefer to find the information they need from life itself or from books rather than from discussions with trusted individuals.

Teacher training courses should definitely highlight ways in which potentially or actually homosexual children can get positive confirmation. The way in which a teacher deals with this theme, either dismissively or in a positive but matter-of-fact way, can sometimes affect a person's whole life.

Do homosexual teachers present a risk in the classroom?

We must not conflate pedophilia with homosexuality. Pedophilia is irreconcilable with the teaching profession—a perversion, as I referred to at the beginning of our discussion. Homosexual teachers present no more risk to their students than heterosexual teachers—heterosexuality is not tantamount to morally perfect and socially exemplary conduct.

As teachers, we must manage our sexual lives responsibly. We must also reckon with the possibility that pupils who sense a teacher's homosexual orientation will address him or her in a certain way, ranging from provocation and curiosity through to pupils who seek advice about their own homosexual tendencies. And naturally it repeatedly arises in the teaching profession that pupils fall in love with their teacher—of whatever sexual orientation—and that the teacher must then respond in an appropriate way to such adolescent passions. This is a fundamental issue beyond homo- or heterosexuality. Whatever draws people to one another, in love and hate, is always deeply rooted in the destiny of those involved, and has to be worked through, has to find healing clarity and also relinquishment of egotistic wishes so that, ultimately, one can nurture the other on his path as far as one is able.

CHAPTER 18

Areas of Collaboration with Parents and Pupils

Stefan Langhammer

> *We have to regard collaboration with parents as the foundation
> for everything we undertake in the Waldorf School…*
>
> —RUDOLF STEINER[1]

Parents and teachers both want the best for "their" children. But what is the best? This is where views often diverge. Is the best what gives children pleasure? Or is it what they really have to work to achieve? Shouldn't one leave children in peace to develop their innate capacities? Or should one instead give them clear forms and structures? Clearly these issues are a point of departure for working with parents. What do I want for my child? And why? Yet working with parents should not mean forcing a point of view on them; instead parents and teachers need to engage in a shared space of experience and understanding. We need to ask how the child can mature—supported by education and school—to become an inwardly free, self-determining human being. What means can we use to support this maturation at various developmental stages? And also: What does this particular child need right now?

Developing an Understanding for Waldorf Education

As long ago as 1923, Rudolf Steiner saw it as a core task to discuss Waldorf education in a way that awakens parents' understanding of what is done at Waldorf schools:

> But what we need above all for our work in the daily life of the school is the understanding of those who are initially most closely involved, and who send their children to us. Without this trust we couldn't do our work at all.…We must develop vigor in expressing our school ideals—inasmuch as we realize that what manifests through Waldorf education has its deep roots in the most important cultural needs of our time and the near future. That is why we must strive to ensure that the things we aim for are expressed fully and clearly to people today, who can bring understanding to meet them.…Thus we try to create a relationship between the school and parents which is not in any way based on submitting to authority. That has no value at all for us. The only thing that has value is what comes to meet us as understanding for our aims and intentions, right down to the smallest details.[2]

Discussions at various levels can help us work toward this understanding. First, there is the great need on the part of parents who have sympathy with the Waldorf school but stand outside it to discover what the real, overarching aim of Waldorf education is. Parents have to want an education that takes its lead from children's development—not least because this education is founded on the interest in such development of those involved. Educational work will not thrive without collaboration. In other words, parents should not simply deliver their child to the Waldorf school; rather, teachers and parents have to embark together on the adventure and educational journey. The more willingly parents do this, the warmer will collaboration be. At this level of teacher-parent encounter, therefore, we need to represent the bases of, and school-specific approach to Steiner education in a way that enables parents to unite their will with it—or not.

One thing that has proven helpful is to offer the school community and interested people lectures and presentations on specific themes of Waldorf education. These can take place during the year, at times that fit with other school demands. Inviting experienced speakers can mean these events are also stimulating for parents already familiar with Waldorf education and for experienced colleagues. It may also be a good idea to draw on school staff for such lectures. If they find the courage—perhaps in twos—to give a 45- to 60-minute presentation, with questions and discussion, this can have many positive side effects. Those attending will not only learn something about Steiner education but also about the particular way it lives in this school. At the same time they can get to know teachers who they may only have heard about previously. And the teachers giving the presentations not only have a welcome motive to articulate in a practical way their own understanding, but also have to activate their social impulses. Such a presentation has to be prepared together. By identifying and questioning what we struggle with daily as teachers, by drawing therefore on a pool of experience, we can respond to the need of many colleagues and contemporaries to gain stimulus for their educational work from the experience of others.

Over and above this, at every parent evening, ongoing discussion is needed about Waldorf education through the grades. This means, primarily, sharing perceptions from both home and school so as to develop an understanding of child development. This is important, firstly, for parents to understand why a particular curriculum content is being taught now, or why a particular skill needs to be acquired. It can also clarify the fact that the class group's current phase is asking for something that is not in the normal curriculum, but is nevertheless needed. Thus a middle-school group that is quick at learning but finds it hard to engage in practical activities, may strike the teacher as needing extra practical work. On the other hand, this understanding is important for educational work in the home. If I recognize that my daughter's indifference is not just a mood but the expression of a prepubescent process of separation, and that the same is happening in a similar way in other families, I can handle it more calmly and with greater and more detached understanding.

Educational questions that weigh on parents' minds because of their daily experiences should be addressed at parent evenings: questions relating to computer use or the child's wish for a mobile phone, brand-name obsession, stealing, or experiments with alcohol. Here, unfortunately, there are two common, but less effective, ways of dealing with such questions: either the teacher talks down to the parents and creates resistance, or she simply hands the problem back to the parents and avoids getting involved. The result of this may be an exchange of views that is lively but ultimately unsatisfying. It can help if teachers and a few parents prepare for the theme to be addressed, such as mobile phones, so they can present the problem from a common, unprejudiced, fact-based standpoint. Work in small groups following on from brief talks can enable parents to share experiences, problems, and questions among themselves. If, at the end of such a parent evening, the main conclusions are presented in the large group, and the main points highlighted again, this will form the basis for a subsequent meeting where an educational approach to the theme can be discussed in a similar way. By this means, attentiveness is stimulated so that in the following weeks the question of educational consistency can live in people, rather than immediately seeking a fixed solution. If it is also possible to air this theme in the faculty meeting in the intervening period, and develop a stance towards it, one can be fairly confident that not only will discussion at the next parent evening gain greater depth, but that this conscious work will give rise to greater focus and will. It has often been observed that a problem is solved not through a solution arrived at intellectually, but that the work of shared perception and understanding itself has an impact on pedagogical measures, and directly helps the children.

The Focus: The Individual Child

Another level of educational discussion between teachers and parents is that relating to the individual child. This discussion represents a developmental opportunity for the child if those involved make efforts to develop a shared understanding. As adults we are familiar with this: a sense of growing wings if another person really understand us, perceives and affirms what we strive for inwardly. A kind of awareness that does not criticize but lovingly observes the humanity growing in one's own soul helps us, more than all criticism, to find our way to ourselves. Teachers and parents should feel themselves called upon to develop such awareness together. Here the starting point is always sharing observations about the child and his surroundings. The more diverse the modes of observation of parents and teachers, and the more interest one devotes to the specific ways the child expresses himself, the more imbued with reality can these observations be. Here it is a help for parents to experience their child in the school context—at the beginning and end of the school day, on the school grounds, or when playing with school friends. Likewise, the teacher can understand the child better if she sees him in his home surroundings. The Waldorf approach of developing education from the child's reality rather than following an abstract theory also prompts us to get to know about the child's home life:

> The spirit of Waldorf education takes account of the whole person in the child. It takes account of the whole human being, but since it does not have the whole person there, having the child only during school hours, and perhaps in a few activities relating to school, it has an intrinsic need to remain in the closest contact with the child's home, where the child spends the rest of his time....

Because the spirit of this schooling does not wish to be one of theory, of abstraction, of rigid, theoretical principle, but of full life and reality, it seeks entry to the reality of the child's home.[3]

It is not just that the child directly experiences the teacher's interest on a home visit and wishes to show himself in the best light, but that the teacher can also immerse herself to some extent in the home atmosphere, and absorb something of the physical, emotional, and spiritual circumstances that accompany the child's daily life. She sees, for instance, the rabbit which is lovingly cared for and proudly shown her, a Harry Potter poster over the child's desk, the washing up that he does as a matter of course after the meal is over, the TV at the end of the bed. Various things in the child's behavior will become immediately clear to the teacher ("Ah, at school too he carries out tasks he is given reliably and with care") or surprise her ("Goodness, the offhand way he speaks to his parents is something I haven't heard at school"). Such observations will provide the starting point for a wealth of conversations, sharing, and asking about what she observes. But one must be very alert to one's own responses: not falling into judging or condemning, but retaining a questioning stance in common with the parents. A TV beside the bed is liable to make a Waldorf teacher's hair stand on end, and it would be easy to come out with one's own categorical view that it really ought to go. But if this reaction doesn't arise naturally from a question from the parents themselves, such an attempt can—perhaps quite justifiably—be seen as an inappropriate intrusion, immediately impairing what would otherwise have been an open exchange. However, simply maneuvering around this critical issue will not get us anywhere either, but just create inner barriers. How can we handle such a situation if, clearly, very different ideas about what is good for the child are meeting head-on?

The parents can also find themselves in conflict with the school. At home, for instance, they may make efforts to ensure that their son overcomes his laziness and achieves his full potential. But at school, the teacher may be happy with essays that last only three sentences, and may let a shoddy main lesson book pass without even marking it or writing a comment on it. It is easy to conclude that the teacher just wants an easy life! The parents would like her to make more effort and set her pupils age-appropriate tasks. Here too, the view that the other person ought to change will seriously hamper constructive dialog. Such a judgment already represents a psychological barrier that renders open-minded discussion impossible.

Any attempt to "educate" an adult is bound to fail. An adult can only educate herself. When, therefore, one discovers judgments in one's own soul, and mistakes their destructiveness for fruitful collaboration, it is good to work on these judgments and try to resolve or dissolve them. One can soon discover, for instance, that an easy life is a one-sided interpretation of the teacher's conduct. It may be simply a sanguine temperament, together with the numerous tasks the teacher has taken on to help with running the school, or a personal situation. And then, perhaps, there were already two main lessons this year that motivated and enthused their son, and that he worked at very diligently. And maybe one can remember main lesson books that did get full and detailed remarks. A premature judgment—even if justified—is like a crystal that isolates itself from its surroundings through clear boundaries; and the response of the person concerned can be easily envisaged, however gently one imposes this judgment on her. If, instead, we manage to dissolve this crystal, the quality of its substance is not lost but can now nurture growth.

In relationship to television, therefore, rather than coming out with one's own, perhaps rather fixed views, it is better to maintain or develop an interested, questioning attitude. Did the child ask for the TV? Which programs does he like to watch? Do the parents limit what he watches? How does the child feel after he's been watching TV? By asking such questions one can easily discover whether the parents also have any questions about the TV in their child's bedroom, or whether they feel somewhat helpless about it, which could then be a starting point for discussing the whole issue further or doing so at the next parent evening. The less this occurs as a purely knee-jerk reaction, without reflection, but instead out of a perception of the other person, the more wholesome such confrontation can be for the whole process of dialog. Being awake and alert in the here and now helps us form the right intuitions about how we can best act in any given situation. In daily life we easily just react, or act with a particular goal in mind, or act ineptly. It can be an enormous help to us if, in a conversation, without judging or condemning, another person helps us become aware of such ineptitude or lack of reflection. Even if this might alarm us initially, or be extremely embarrassing to become aware of something we were unaware of before—there is no way round this for anyone who wants to develop. Failings and inadequacies are developmental potential, opportunities presented by life for self-education. Only a person who doesn't want to change will defend himself against everything that might cast doubt on his behavior, and will instead demand from others the change he himself doesn't embark on.

When necessary, the child study provides another opportunity to intensify developmental discussions. In a child study, observations by that child's teachers and the whole faculty are brought together in certain questions and perspectives. An attempt is made to approach the inner nature of the child and his developmental potential, so as to develop shared educational ideas on this basis. A consequence of the child study is that teachers develop more attentiveness for a particular child. Each teacher will be more alert to and aware of him in daily encounters, as well as in the inner preparation and review of lessons. This can strengthen the teacher's educational presence and capacity for intuition in relation to the child. It has also proven helpful to involve the parents of the child in these studies, as long as a constructive dialog has formed between parents and class teacher. When the parents collaborate, it is possible to give an authentic picture of the child's first seven years and the domestic circumstances surrounding him. Having the parents involved in developing strategies based on the study is a further guarantee that they will be directly aware of the teachers' intentions, and can pursue the same impulses at home.

In a parent evening in 1923, Rudolf Steiner referred to a special kind of dialog—that of reports. A Waldorf school report does not aim to judge the child or assess his achievement; rather, the teachers endeavor to characterize the child's capacities and difficulties in a way that can lead to constructive work with them in future. But nevertheless, the report is still usually one-way traffic: the teacher writes it and the parents read it with more or less good will. Of this Steiner said:

> …the teacher should really be sure that such reports are met with loving interest on the part of the parents. And I believe that if parents could manage to write a brief answer to what the teacher describes in the report, this would be enormously helpful. There is

no point in introducing this as a rule, but if it became a need of the parents to do this it would be hugely important educationally. Such replies will certainly be read with very great attention in our Waldorf school; however, many misunderstandings or mistakes they might contain, they would be far more important to us than a good number of contemporary cultural commentaries by well-known authors. In reading such a reply one would be able to see deeply into what is needed—as a teacher not working out of abstract ideas but from the impulse of our time....

An intense knowledge of the human being would flow from what parents could, in all devotion, tell teachers; and I am not exaggerating if I say that the reply to the report would be almost more important to the teacher than the report is for the child.[4]

This unconventional suggestion once again underlines the point that Waldorf parents are urged to collaborate! Parents do not need to simply listen in silence to the teacher's monologue, but can play a confirming, strengthening part in forming an image of the child, and also modify and question it. This mirroring back by the parents can be a help to the teacher to be more alert both to the child and to himself, and thus to develop greater inner vitality.

Scope for Parents' Initiative

Waldorf school parents are offered many opportunities to collaborate in the educational sphere and at the organizational and administrative level, and to share responsibility in many areas. The help of parents in the class context is indispensable for large-scale projects and class trips. What would the class teacher do without enthusiastic and committed parents by her side during the crafts or building main lessons in third grade? What would the eurythmy teacher do without many helping hands to sew and iron before a festival or performance? What would the class teacher do without supportive, helping parents on an excursion with 35 lively fourth-graders? This collaboration not only enables parents to contribute their own capacities and skills, but also gives them the chance to observe: What is this class community like? What tasks does it present the teacher with? How can I or others help in future? Helping also often leads to shared responsibility. Parents who have actively worked to support the class and have experienced its dynamic will usually be slower to form critical judgments. They will find it easier to respect what is achieved, and to lend a helping hand where difficulties arise. Such support also helps parents to form a community in which each individual develops a willingness to contribute what he or she can to help the whole.

Whether or not this can happen depends, in part, on the class teacher and the faculty. A teacher who wants to do everything herself should not be surprised if parents grow passive and critical. Likewise a colleague who leans all too readily on parents will gradually paralyze parents initiative and waken resistance. Parental initiative has to be nurtured and cultivated, because it comes from the heart. Do the parents feel free to get involved and become co-creators? Is their work properly and individually acknowledged? Is it perceived and valued? Are too many demands sometimes placed on them—as can happen to families with several children in the school? Many parents regard it as a great opportunity to have a hand in shaping their child's school. To avoid this becoming burdensome, a faculty will do well to tell new parents joining the school what is expected of them (for example, regular attendance at parent evenings) and what they can do beyond that.

In every Waldorf school, working groups form for various tasks and responsibilities. These groups may have an advisory function or decision-making powers. For instance, most schools have a buildings group that oversees new construction and maintenance, a group that takes responsibility for the annual school fair, and a parent-teacher group for issues affecting all classes, such as setting up clubs or a school kitchen. If there is a school finance association, work on its executive council will involve important joint work between parent and teacher representatives, which may decisively affect the character of the school. To offer one's services to the school impulse shaped by parents, teachers and pupils and, for instance, to ensure that the school has a sound financial basis, requires skill and social sensitivity. Rather than seeking power, those involved need to act out of a perception of what is needed. In committee work, parents unite with the school in a way that goes beyond their personal concern with their child's development and involves integrative work within or even beyond the school. This starts in a small way if, in conversations with non-Waldorf parents, one suddenly becomes a representative of one's own school or the whole movement. Perhaps someone asks: Why do you send your child to a Waldorf school?

Handling Conflict

Of course, collaboration between teachers and parents does not always run smoothly. And however often one tells oneself that conflicts exist for us to develop through them, in everyday life our emotions, personal stake, or even self-love are often stronger than any such insight. Conflicts between parents and teachers often arise due to different educational perspectives, differing expectations of pupils' achievement, or communication problems. Tensions not dealt with often change levels: what should really be dealt with between adults alone is suddenly foisted onto the child,[5] who must then suffer the tension between his parents and beloved teacher—and may become ill as a result. Just as a positive, affirming relationship between parents and school strengthens the child's health, a tense relationship also leads to physical problems: headaches, fatigue, and all sorts of other symptoms may follow. In contrast, a huge amount can be achieved educationally if differences and interpersonal tensions are overcome with the help of experienced colleagues and parents, allowing new developmental impulses to arise for the adults involved! The child or adolescent then has a direct experience of adults who do not resign themselves but make efforts to overcome their problems. This will be sensed and acknowledged, and can give a young person direction and confidence in life.

A great help here will be to engage in constructive work on open or simmering conflicts, and to find parents and teachers who can be involved in mediating. Here too, trusting collaboration between parent and teacher representatives is desirable—ideally both a male and female representative—so that both parties to the conflict can feel properly perceived and understood. Some parents find it difficult to speak freely to a committee consisting only of teachers. Anyone who has experienced how paralyzing it can be not to find someone to talk problems over with—perhaps because their relationship with the class teacher is fraught, and no one else is there to deal with the problem—will find a committee or delegation like this very helpful. As with other delegations, here too it is important to define task areas, responsibilities, and procedures. Otherwise one may have a discussion partner with much good will and skill but lacking the authority to make a decision.

Parent Collaboration during Various Developmental Phases of the School

Committee and groups are rarely found in very new schools. The founding of a new school is sustained by enthusiasm and great sacrifices. And when one is immersed in such an endeavor, and works together day and night with like-minded people, a pioneering spirit prevails. At this stage differentiation into numerous committees and areas of responsibility would be artificial, and there would not be enough people anyway. Establishment of the high school is often the time when this pioneer stage[6] comes to an end, requiring division of labor (the differentiation stage). Parents and teachers join who are not so closely connected with the school's founding impulse. They therefore have a greater distance from school processes and seek clearer working structures. When high school teachers join the faculty, they are often specialists who have a different perspective on school and teaching than the all-round genius of the class teacher.

These different perspectives have to find common ground, and for this clear forms are needed! And ultimately, a few years after the school is founded, the number of parents and teachers has grown to a stage where, as in a growing organism, structure and allocation of tasks is necessary. With her second class group, a class teacher often succeeds in interrelating teaching content more strongly. Whereas in her first class she will primarily have been striving to give each main lesson block a form that was appropriate to the children, she now has a better overview of the links and relevance of different subjects to each other. She now understands how each lesson relates to the whole curriculum. Likewise, in the school organism it normally takes at least a whole cycle of twelve years for sufficient experience and skill to develop among people at the school so that more far-reaching school goals can be formulated. Awareness focused on accomplishing daily work can now open into a broader vista of the school's future. If it proves possible to formulate the school community's inner direction in a way that allows parents and teachers to unite with it, it will be possible to give work in the various committees a common direction and thus integrate and coordinate them more strongly. A common will orientation in the form of a guiding picture is particularly important in relation to the question of the place occupied in the whole school by state examinations. At this level, nowadays, many anxieties, ideas of prestige and "excellence," and unexamined convention exert an influence, both amongst parents and teachers! Together one should become aware of these tendencies, to prevent them developing an unwelcome life of their own and increasingly determining the school's policies. This development of the school organism will always go hand in hand with efforts to integrate the school into the community's social milieu, its associations, churches, etc. Once again it is the parents who can have a helping and supportive influence here, by using their connections to public life and thus initiating and cultivating active collaboration.

Collaboration with Pupils

In every lesson the teacher collaborates with the pupils. There is no scope here to address the mode of such collaboration at different ages. Instead we will focus on the opportunities for Waldorf pupils' involvement in the three areas of education, school organization, and school management.

What characterizes this age? In the transition from the second to the third seven-year period, the child undergoes fundamental changes. Sexual maturation, the development of secondary sexual characteristics, and the breaking of the voice (in boys). The child has completely arrived on the earth, has descended right into his bones. Linked to this, soul life also changes. The adolescent adheres more and more to causal logic and increasingly relates to a desire to understand the external environment. At the same time, feeling life deepens and grows more sensitive: an inner world is experienced as increasingly differentiated, providing endless subjects for discussion. At this age, experiencing one's own being with a previously unknown depth is common to both sexes. Questions about the meaning of life, of where we have come from and where we are going, or the nature of true friendship are often now experienced with existential intensity. At the same time, adolescents' distance from a sustaining environment becomes greater and not infrequently leads to a marked separation and self-demarcation: a stance in which the imperfections of what has previously been familiar and trusted is "seen through" and mercilessly criticized.

From these few hints it is evident that the transformation of a child into an adolescent must also involve a fundamental change in the pedagogical approach.

Fortunately, this transformation does not occur suddenly but in stages, from around sixth grade onward. Adult authority is increasingly questioned, and it is good if adults do not dogmatically uphold the authority that the child previously granted them as a matter of course. The opposite will result if they do, and the adult will instead offer a broad target for all sorts of attempts to "out" her real personality and get under her skin. For at this age adolescents want to know who you really are, what questions you ask of life, and what you are working to achieve. How do you work with your failings and imperfections? Are they concealed, or can you own up to them and work with them? And how do you deal with it when I get under your skin? The adolescent wants to share in the adult's confrontation with the world and learn from his example how to be true to oneself and grow into oneself more and more. In other words, at this phase of life, when the adolescent's feelings chaotically erupt and become free, the desire also awakens in him to focus this life of soul and direct it toward the world in a self-determining way. This directing, an ego quality, is what the adolescent wishes to learn from the adult—not just as theory but authentically. Not infrequently, this transformation of the educational relationship can lead to serious crises and confrontations both at home and at school. Crises at fifth, sixth, or seventh grade are often connected with missed opportunities for transformation. At this age it is important to involve young people in processes and decisions. This can happen in the planning and realization of a class trip, a presentation to parents, the organization of festivals or seasonal celebrations, the arrangement of the classroom, and so forth. What is vitally important here is that the young person's utterances and self-expression are taken seriously, rather than the adult always "knowing better."

Speaking with the Pupil Rather Than about Him

If a ninth-grader has gotten into trouble, disrupts lessons, or is making little effort, a discussion with him should always give him an opportunity to develop awareness of his own behavior, and to say how this behavior arose. Certainly, the teacher can resort to "consequences", but in doing so he is missing an opportunity. From ninth or tenth grade on, "consequences" should increasingly have the character of an "agreement." A conversation with a pupil should aim to make shared agreements for the future based on an understanding of the situation. These agreements should enable further constructive collaboration to develop. During adolescence, education can become self-education. The educator must continue to ensure that agreements are kept and consequences enforced, but the adolescent will play a substantial role in deciding what the consequence will be.

Sometimes in this kind of discussion with a pupil, things arise that can aid the teacher's self-knowledge. Over-sensitivity on the part of teachers can easily obstruct educationally valuable intuition. As an educator, whether a parent or teacher, it is good to cultivate a sense of humor, which protects us from rigidity and can re-establish a direct human connection in stressful situations. In some Waldorf schools, so-called "parent-teacher-pupil" discussions take place from grade ten onwards. Without waiting for some external necessity, an individual discussion is held with every pupil in the class, in which the parents, the class teacher, and one or two specialist teachers take part. In these discussions the focus is on the pupil's own self-reflection: Where do I stand? What can I do well? Where do I need practice? What tasks do I see for myself in the world? What must I, or do I want to learn in my remaining school days? To become aware of one's own capacities and perspectives for the future can noticeably motivate the pupil's will for learning and work. This applies particularly to pupils at stages where they find it hard to feel enthusiasm for curriculum content, and cannot derive their motivation for work from the content itself. Here self-reflection externally stimulated, and agreement about steps to be taken to attain short- or long-term goals, can have an awakening effect, and bring about a noticeable intensification of focus in learning behavior—although only when this goes beyond mere agreement, to checking that things agreed actually happen.

Taking Educational Responsibility

Responsibility and initiative are particularly addressed and awoken if, as a high school student, one gets the opportunity to teach or work educationally oneself. A ninth-grade class is glad to mentor some first-graders. Each ninth-grader is given a first-grader to help and support in the first few months in this new, overwhelming place: school. At an age when the prime focus is often on oneself, the ninth-grader is called on to be a grownup and to try to see the world through the eyes of a first-grader, so as to help him. It may be the first time that the ninth-grader sees himself as a model and example for younger children, that they imitate him, and that he bears responsibility towards others for his actions. Another way of taking educational responsibility is offered by project days.[7] It has proven effective to have older pupils give a course on the theme of their annual project. For instance, a student who is writing a project on acting can offer a theatre workshop and help rehearse the class play. Another might hold weekly meetings to discuss important aspects of sustainable development in Africa, collecting participants' questions and ideas as stimulus for further work. It can also be extremely beneficial if pupils use their own academic skills to help others. For instance, a competent high school pupil can give a math support course to other pupils. If the subject teacher accompanies this course on the first occasion as mentor, the teaching pupil can also acquire thorough methodological know-how, so that in future the teacher or the math faculty will have tangible help in the form of several such courses. But also other areas not directly related to teaching, such as drumming or dancing, model-building or a foreign language, can, in the context of a project lesson organized by pupils, represent a motivating palette of possibilities in the daily course of school life, as long as they are accompanied by enthusiasm and cheerful experimentation.

The experience of having oneself and one's skills taken seriously—I can do something, and because of this I can help others—and of integrating them into the life process of the school, is psychologically strengthening and creates confidence for life beyond school.

However, the faculty should not exploit this possibility of pupil collaboration. This would happen if, for instance, courses given by pupils were used to replace regular lessons. A pupil will only be able to pass on a limited skill—and only a few of them will be able to structure this in an interesting way over several weeks. A pupil will not be able to work out of an understanding of the developmental phases of childhood, nor have an overview that enables him to handle teaching material so as to stimulate psychological development processes. Specialist subject skill is also likely to be very limited. For this reason, normal lessons should only be given by those who are trained to do so and have the necessary experience—in other words, the teachers. But practice and experimentation sessions are very welcome, in which pupil-pupil learning situations can be tried out alongside normal lessons.

Involving Pupils in School Management

A blackboard just for pupils' concerns? Lockers for pupils so they don't have to carry everything around with them all day? A winter sports day for the whole school? A carnival for the high school? Snacks sold at break times? Who should take care of such issues? Those affected preferably! In many schools, therefore, including public schools, pupils are involved in school administration or management. The class representatives, and others who want to be involved, meet regularly with the teachers responsible and discuss the requests, needs, concerns, and fears of pupils. Let's take, for instance, a request for a common room for leisure times, lessons, or lunch break. If the desire for this is expressed by several pupils it can be discussed in the school co-management group. The group will examine feasibility and the plan can be developed and then presented to the faculty. If agreement is given, realization can be planned, and the room furnished and arranged by volunteers. The school co-management committee is therefore an organ that perceives impulses living within the school and helps them to become reality. This can relate to both educational matters and extra-curricular needs such as organizing a dance or setting up a basketball court. Something is practiced here that is needed in life: developing ideas into plans and then implementing them. This work, helped and supervised by teachers, can also give rise to a strong identification of pupils with their school.

The fundamental intentions of Waldorf education include close collaboration between school, parents, and pupils: with parents because parents and teachers share a common educational task that can be realized only with close collaboration; and with pupils because teaching reaches young people only when they feel that they are being taken seriously and that their deeper questions are recognized and acknowledged.

CHAPTER 19

The College of Teachers as a Working Group Responsible for School Management

Michaela Glöckler

At a Spiritual Level

Any situations where adults work together will succeed or fail depending on whether or not the individual members see themselves as active contributors. No matter what task or position they hold within a company or institution, they must be able to experience themselves spiritually as responsible contributors to the organization. For this to happen, the ideals or tasks of the organization have to be directly accessible to all colleagues so that they can inwardly understand and carry them. This shows clearly what leadership means. Its starting point is the ideal, the idea, the task, the objective, to which a community, institution, or company decides to devote itself. This means that spiritual aims are ultimately what unites everybody, and they mandate an orientation to those who have taken on leading roles. Rather than people themselves, the aims to which people have dedicated their labor gives the direction of leadership. In this sense, labor is not sold but is dedicated to a cause. This dedication needs to be honored. It can really not be paid for. If this kind of consciousness lives in a company, a fraternal mood can awaken that makes it easier for the individual to make his contribution—however great or modest—toward the successful completion of the common task.

In order to support this principle, the institution needs a body or organ where the individual can freely express his opinion about the aims of the organization and where he, at the same time, has the opportunity to hear what other colleagues think about important issues such as work structures. The extent to which he wants to fruitfully integrate his experiences and perceptions into his own field of work depends on his professional interests and abilities. Only if each individual person works on improving his way of promoting the common aim through his work and attitude to colleagues can a working atmosphere be created where one feels free and supported. Envy and criticism have a paralyzing effect and create an atmosphere of suspicion. In a community where people don't work together, criticism can eventually be directed against everything and everybody, and the potential for criticism will grow if personal initiative and entrepreneurial spirit are suppressed. To recognize this and to change one's own attitude, by expecting the best of oneself and by gratefully acknowledging the positive contributions of others, will help the development of one's own social responsibility. One can then become a helpful and creative member of the whole organism.

How many problems that prevent fruitful collaboration arise just because someone expects more from others while demanding more recognition for himself? In a faculty discussion about a problem between teachers and parents, a colleague said: "We could try and develop the imagination to recognize what each of us can contribute towards balancing the weakness of others, so that their strengths can become more apparent." Nothing is more destructive for a school community than a teacher who tries to increase his own popularity with students and parents by speaking negatively about a colleague who is less well-liked.

If parents and students experience the faculty as a constructive community that openly and fairly discusses problems and works on them, they can bring respect and trust towards its educational work. If teachers help and support each other and deal openly with problems with parents and students, the school becomes a place where everybody involved can unfold their potential. Any feeling of social martyrdom ("Look at all I do while others can't even cope with half as much") can be avoided. The individual person can become independent and know what he is willing and able to contribute to the whole. He does what he thinks is the right thing to do, out of his own initiative, without asking what others are doing. He becomes his own master or employer even if, externally, that is the headmaster or the personnel manager. The principle of the hierarchical power pyramid can thus find a healthy way into modern society—at an individual level. The individual does for himself what, in former times, was done by the ruler for himself and for his subjects.

Legal Aspects

What rights does the individual have within the community? What are his duties? Where are emancipation and shared decision-making not only meaningful but necessary, and what kinds of duties emerge as a result? When, for example, will it be necessary to carry out decisions that one was not part of? And when must this not happen? Our sense of justice is kindled whenever we feel equal to others. Where people work together there are, moreover, duties and rights that are based on agreements that are valid for everybody and that are necessary for a smooth and efficient running of the institution. In a school, for example, there should be agreements on how much time is allocated for certain tasks or projects, where and when punctuality is essential, what leadership or social structure a project requires. When are leadership, mandating, or delegating necessary and useful for a task? What kind of control organs for quality and achievement should be in place? The more clearly this is arranged and understood, the better each individual can integrate himself into the process. Every newcomer has the opportunity to look at these agreed-upon working conditions and choose to say yes to the rights and duties that they involve, or choose not to accept them. Solidarity and trust can develop when everybody accepts these rights and duties and has, from time to time and within a working group, the opportunity to consult on and improve them.

At this legal level each individual has an equal part in democratic decision making and this is necessary to the interests of the whole. In order to ensure optimum distribution of work and of money, guidelines are needed that everyone involved has to respect for a fixed period of time.

A particularly important area in need of consent is quality control, which assures that agreed objectives are achieved. There have to be people who are given the mandate and trust to raise objections, to bring up problems for discussion, to receive complaints and refer them to those who are responsible. There have to be socially capable colleagues who have the mandate to talk openly about failings and shortcomings. A dismissal or change of tasks might become necessary as a consequence and can happen, with the utmost understanding for the person in question, but in a sober and professional manner. If this is not possible, the quality and standards of the institution will correspond less and less to its actual aims.

The clearer the rules for these kinds of social processes and the better people are at adhering to them, at correcting themselves or confronting each other if it comes to infringements, the more constructive the work process can be. Continuity and quality foster not only the work process, but also the individual, because he can count on continuous support for his own development within the community. He learns to respect functions and mandates, accepting that mistakes will be made in the course of people learning and improving, and he carries and supports this without questioning or attacking the mandate holder. For an agreed period, this person or group enjoys the confidence, trust, and support of all others, being thus enabled to successfully work on their task. Only if the structures within the organization are transparent and all its members can support how decisions are made and how information is passed on, can they each feel accepted as human beings and therefore commit themselves to these processes. At the legal level, democratic principles can thus find a useful and constructive place within the whole organization.

Personal and Social Aspects[1]

Nothing is as "unfair" as the reality of the social realm. Each person comes with his own talents and challenges, and his particular expectations of himself and of his community. The needs of a community's members are as varied as the range of talents. One person might find his workload just right or too much, be it a full-time teaching post or an office job, while somebody else has more energy than is needed and can pursue several hobbies or take on additional responsibilities at work.

Personal development—and this is true for everybody—happens in challenging situations that arise in the tension between an individual's abilities and the tasks that need completing. One must know one's own capacities. There is a fine line between illness and health that can be easily crossed if work loses its meaning or attraction because it has become mere routine and duty or is done under pressure. In order to work against such tendencies toward illness, one has to show interest in as many colleagues as possible and in their individual potential. A lot is already gained if, while assessing someone else's work, one does not measure it against one's own or other people's achievements, but only measures this particular colleague's achievement against his specific job description, looking at how he has grown into his position and what progress he has made. This is the only way to ensure that the other person feels understood and recognized. And it is, again, an important condition for him to be able to love his work.

If dissatisfaction and criticism arise in relation to someone else's work, the problem has to be addressed directly with the person concerned and must not be talked about with others behind his back and without his knowledge. If I don't have the courage to do this or if I have the impression that the other person could not handle this, the time is not ripe yet to address the problems I have with that person. In this case I should either drop it or refer the question to the colleague or colleagues who have the mandate (and hopefully the ability) to deal with the issue. Supervision and quality assurance find their way into more or less every life situation. It is ideal if they arise in a self-chosen, self-established striving for self-development. It is a definite advantage if supervision can be entrusted to a colleague within the workplace, because this strengthens confidence building among colleagues and ensures continuity in the work. Even if outside help seems more attractive because it promises anonymity and objectivity, experience shows that problems are best solved by those who will live with the consequences of the remedial measures that are put into place.

The most flexible structures are those which an institution develops for its own purpose and which it regularly adjusts to meet changing needs. Constructive collaboration requires individuals to accept justified criticism, while rejecting that which is not justified.

If one is part of an initiative one has to reckon with criticism. Criticism will always be there—but one must make sure it is justified. The challenge lies in determining whether criticism is justified; if it is, one can respond accordingly. Performance and profile of an organization depend on the extent to which its members are helped to contribute to it to the best of their abilities. For this reason a hierarchy of abilities and corresponding distribution of skills are of the greatest importance. It has to be ensured, however, that the power of those in charge is restricted to their particular area of responsibility and that they don't end up with having more weight and influence in other areas as well. If a school, for example, has an acknowledged *spiritus rector*, he has to learn to use his authority to protect others and their abilities rather than undermine them.

All of this is not easy to put into action and to live into. Without the will for self-development and for learning it cannot be achieved. There are always two sources for learning processes, insight and experience: either recognizing deficits and mistakes, or recognizing opportunities and good examples. The mistakes we learn from do not have to be only our own; we can learn from the mistakes of others too. Interestingly, the miracle of recognizing deficits and mistakes can happen. A colleague's mistakes may simply disappear, or he may overcome them, just as our own mistakes disappear once we have worked enough on them and learned our lessons. By experiencing this we can build up a strong confidence in the wisdom of destiny. We realize that life has placed us into the right conditions for our further development. If prevailing structures and other people's power or skills prevent us from realizing our full potential in an organization, we can find aims and tasks for ourselves in a different organization. If such a transition is not possible, we can rededicate ourselves to our organization and its social environment.

All institutions, including self-administered ones like Waldorf schools, need social forms that enable each individual to devote all his initiative to the completion of the common task. They must also make sure that the colleagues who are best suited are entrusted with leadership positions. In this respect one often hears that the most important management tasks must be taken on by a collegial body. But where that happens, sooner or later people start objecting to the number of meetings and the enormous amount of time administration takes up while other work gets neglected. However necessary meetings and working groups might be, they can never replace the good work that an individual can unfold in the service of the whole community. In a school or social therapeutic institution, for example, the parents must be clear about whom they can contact and who is responsible for which decisions and actions. Clearly defined areas of responsibility, flexibility, and the ability to decide and act quickly make it possible to be economical with everybody's time and energy. In this way, meaningful procedures can be discussed together, on the one hand, while on the other a jointly appointed representative can make decisions within his particular mandate without having to repeatedly go through long debates and social processes.

It becomes obvious that the most satisfactory management structure for institutions and enterprises in our time has to be based on the idea of association: the upside-down pyramid. Hierarchical or democratic systems will always lead to conflicts because the first does not do justice to the employees and the latter does not do justice to the work that needs doing.

Threshold Experiences in the Social Realm

Questions of power and leadership affect most people directly in their development, and they often find it difficult to deal with them, both inwardly and outwardly. It helps to keep in mind that the old hierarchical and pyramidal structures of leadership and the democratic principles that are so popular in our times are both forms that require certain personal skills and good regulations in order to function. This is because they both belong entirely to the physical world. This changes when we move on to conscious application of the "associative principle" in a society. Such a step is only possible if the individual is willing to give his labor voluntarily in the interest of the common aim and ideal. In order to achieve this, one has to overcome the same obstacles that one encounters when one approaches the threshold of the spiritual world; one must not just strive to do one's duty with regard to work, employer and colleagues, but also with regard to the spiritual orientation of the institution. Working in the associative context means working voluntarily in the service of the spiritual world towards which one feels responsible.

Such idealistic principles can be misused as a kind of moral imperative, for example when selfless commitment is expected or even demanded from colleagues. This danger can only be averted by applying the principle of crossing the threshold—which is also the basic principle of associative leadership: each individual decides freely for himself. Structures that support the ancient hierarchical systems or those of democracy and shared decision-making can be established, organized, and imposed on people by outer means. All of this, especially if accompanied by moral pressure, is not possible in the associative society. One can put certain structures into place that support associative leadership principles, but any attempts at organizing and imposing would come up against the resistance of all those individuals who have not freely decided to work for these aims. In the associative society, leadership and contribution do not primarily mean that certain social structures are being established and accepted, but that a particular attitude towards work and colleagues is being practiced.

People who have near-death or out-of-body experiences often return to life as changed human beings. Every moment of their life is now precious to them, and they have completely different priorities in their social and working life. They can forget about themselves and look at others with the greatest interest. They have experienced what lies beyond the threshold of death and, in the light of this experience, value their life and its meaning in a new way. The following thought experiment can already change the way we look at life: How would I live this day if I had died already and had the opportunity to come back just for this day? What would I look out for? What would be important? What would I still try to sort out?

Work on the future-oriented associative society begins quietly, unnoticed, within the individual who sees its necessity and is willing to work towards its realization. Independent of outer positions and social or hierarchical power structures, individuals can foster an associative attitude and, in doing so, have a healing effect on the entire social environment.

Even today's global economic and ecological problems and conflicts will begin to solve themselves in unexpected ways, possibly even quite rapidly, if enough human beings take the initiative to embark on the associative social life—no matter what their work or life situation might be. Human beings who choose to follow this path are already working on the cultural transformation that is urgently needed to replace a social system that is based on egotism with a system based on principles of empathy, fraternity, and love for the earth. They develop a spirit of enterprise not just for their professional and personal life, but for the whole of humanity.[2]

CHAPTER 20

The Life and Work of Karl Schubert

Elisabeth von Kügelgen

> *Through the power of the Word raise upright in the physical,*
> *heal in the etheric, forgive in the astral and console in the ego.*
>
> —KARL SCHUBERT[1]

Karl Schubert: Lebensbilder und Aufzeichnungen (Karl Schubert – Life Events and Biographical Notes) by Hans-Jürgen Hanke provided the basis for this contribution on Karl Schubert for the annual meeting of the Anthroposophical Society in Stuttgart on March 16, 2005. Schubert left behind notes on education and curative work that is filled with many valuable and enriching impulses.

> Rudolf Steiner always gave me tasks which I myself felt resistance to. I would have much preferred to do other things. And if I had known that I would one day become a Waldorf teacher, I would have started to prepare myself for this three hundred years beforehand.[3]

These words, which Karl Schubert addressed to two students at the teacher training seminar in 1945-46, show both his profound sense of humor and also a characteristic biographical signature. Rudolf Steiner gave him tasks which he actually would neither have sought out himself, nor could have done, since they did not yet exist: being a curative educator at a Waldorf school, a teacher of nonsectarian religion lessons, and performing nondenominational Sunday services for children whose parents requested them.

When Rudolf Steiner spoke at the March 8, 1920 teacher meeting on of the need for a support class for children with learning difficulty, and stated that Dr. Schubert should take charge of these children during main lesson, Schubert did not yet have any contract of employment with the school, nor did he know that Rudolf Steiner was planning to make him a curative educator. In January 1920, Schubert had sought employment at Emil Molt's factory in Stuttgart, mentioning that, if possible, he would also like to sit in on classes at the Waldorf School. In answer he received a telegram from the Waldorf School, inviting him to an interview together with a request to give a sample lesson (fifth-grade French). So at the beginning of February 1920 Karl Schubert arrived in Stuttgart and found himself in a fifth-grade class with Rudolf Steiner! During this French lesson, Rudolf Steiner let slip a piece of paper which fell to the floor. Karl Schubert rushed to pick it up and in doing so fell his whole length. Rudolf Steiner helped him up and said: "You won't take that as a bad omen I'm sure." The lesson went very well. Rudolf Steiner's presence did not make him feel awkward, but gave a sense of security.[4] Schubert now thought he should become a language teacher, something he was extremely well-qualified for: he spoke fluent English, French, Czech, Russian, ancient Greek, and Latin. Languages just flocked to him. Besides history and philosophy, he had also studied philology.

On April 1, the contract with Emil Molt was signed. It was quite clear that Rudolf Steiner wanted Karl Schubert at the Waldorf School and had a special task in mind for him. Initially, though, Schubert had to take on a seventh grade, continuing with it on into eighth grade up to September 1921. But as early as May 1921, Rudolf Steiner was once more talking about a support class in the teacher meeting, saying: "Dr. Schubert should do this." In the meeting at the beginning of the new school year, on September 11, 1921, he said: "Now we should consider starting the support class again. This is necessary...I would be very pleased, Dr. Schubert, if you would take on this support class."[5]

Thus Karl Schubert became a curative educator, and Stuttgart the starting point for integrative education. When Rudolf Steiner held the curative education course in Dornach in 1924 (at the request of curative educators Siegfried Pickert, Friedrich Löffler, and Albert Strohschein), he naturally brought Karl Schubert to Dornach and treated him as his colleague: he involved Schubert, and passed members' questions on to him, so that he could report from his first-hand experience of special needs children in the support class. This close collaboration with curative educators, including Dr. Ita Wegman from the Medical Section at the Goetheanum in Dornach, was something Schubert continued after Steiner's death, and revived again after the end of the Second World War. No official stenographer had been engaged for Steiner's curative education course. Schubert, who could take perfect shorthand, was allowed to write down what was said. Thus Ita Wegman and Karl Schubert were later able to publish the course. Ita Wegman involved Schubert in conferences and meetings at the Sonnenhof in Arlesheim, and he also accompanied her to England and Holland. A Dutch curative educator said of Schubert: "He made friends, brothers of us." After the war people referred to him in children's homes as the Angelic Wayfarer. He was a welcome guest, and sought to link the curative education movement both physically and in his consciousness too. When Friedrich Löffler asked Rudolf Steiner about the destiny of these children, Steiner replied: "Whenever I arrive in Stuttgart and visit the support class I always tell myself that here work is being done for future earth lives, quite irrespective of what can be achieved now—though this can be a great deal with the right insight and devotion."[6]

Karl Schubert's biography shows how this special curative educational work was deeply rooted in his destiny and nature, and also how a special relationship with Rudolf Steiner was apparent from a young age.

Karl Schubert was Austrian, born in Vienna on November 25, 1889. He was strongly religious as a child, and, though his parents did not belong to any particular denomination, he came into contact with Catholicism through a Czech nursemaid. With his brother he played through the music for the mass, and as a boy developed a powerful singing voice. The changes Schubert underwent between the age of nine and ten (Rudolf Steiner's "Rubicon") affected him deeply. "The being of Christ revealed itself to me," he said.[7]

This experience of the closeness of Christ vanished again, and as he approached puberty he developed a strong interest in technology. Religious doubts surfaced, an alienation from the Church, and this propelled him into a search and questions that led him to Jakob Böhme, Angelus Silesius, and Novalis. At the same time he was giving learning support to a boy with special needs who later attended high school. In 1903, Schubert's father took 14-year-old Karl, with whom he had a strong connection, to a theosophical lecture. Through this circle of theosophists—the family was now living in Klagenfurt—Karl Schubert met the 30-year-old building contractor Guido Ratzmann. In 1906, Ratzmann attended a lecture by Rudolf Steiner in Munich and came back telling others that they really ought to hear this man speak; the group took up studying lectures by Steiner. In November 1908, Rudolf Steiner was invited to give three lectures to this group in Klagenfurt. Guido Ratzmann sent Schubert—then just 19—to the station to collect Marie von Sievers and Rudolf Steiner. For Schubert the lectures opened up new dimensions: Rosicrucianism, the path of self-development, and above all religion. In 1909, he attended another lecture by Rudolf Steiner on the nature of Rosicrucianism and the Rose Cross meditation. Schubert's notes include the following:

> A deep comparative experience of advanced development, and of the moral debt owed towards the innocence of those left behind, can give rise to a sense of humility, or the longing for perfection. This longing for perfection can work in the human being in such a way that he strives to cleanse and purify his nature of passions, and to transform his blood so that it becomes chaste and pure like the red of the rose.[8]

Schubert had found his teacher and now, alongside his academic studies in Vienna and London, he embarked on a course of inner work, pursuing a path of self-development with the utmost discipline. At the same time he struggled earnestly to know the nature of Christ. Karl Schubert was a man of strong will, and fought almost ferociously with the imperfections of the human state. One can find traces of this path in his diary. His time in London brought about a strong inner transformation at age 21. If one rightly interprets these diary entries, Schubert experienced a new closeness to Christ at this time.

Back in Vienna, Schubert completed his studies with a doctorate. The chemist and later founder of the Wala medicines company, Dr. Rudolf Hauschka, relates that Schubert was nicknamed "Spiritual Might" by the student circle to which they both belonged. A few days before he had to leave Vienna in 1915, he met with Rudolf Steiner, who spoke these words of farewell: "Have no fear, I am with you. Think of me. Take *Occult Science* with you."[9] Schubert noted in his diary: "Like a blessing his words and books accompanied me," adding in his own inimitable style: "I never yet made it through *Occult Science*—a bullet wouldn't get through it!" Besides *Occult Science*, he also took with him the Bible and Novalis.

In 1916 Schubert married Helene Nierl, who worked at the first Goetheanum in Dornach during the war. For two years Schubert was a prisoner-of-war in Russia. In his diary we read: "I scarcely manage to complete my inner soul work, since I'm always with comrades who don't care to attend to such things." (September 26, 1915). On November 11, 1915, he wrote:

> May it be granted me, I beg at God's universal throne, to return to my friends, to proclaim to them with trembling voice the new knowledge I have found. The death of Christ on

the cross lights the path for human beings to tread. *In conspectu morti* (in contemplation of death) the human being experiences the greatness of all that his body means on earth. As though he were already dead he looks back on his life. In astonishment, wonder and remorse he experiences the profundity of its meaning. In spiritual love I encompass all in the army who wish to confront me with dissatisfaction and anger. May hatred be transformed through love, and become the seed of future understanding.

The wartime diary ends with the words: "Peace to all beings!"—the same phrase that concludes the last diary entry of his life (December 12, 1948).[10] With his fellow prisoners of war, Schubert rehearsed the Oberufer Christmas plays, which he had known—clearly by heart—since 1910-11. Later, Rudolf Steiner wrote the part of the Tree Singer for him in the *Paradise Play*, rehearsing this role with him, and that of the Star Singer in the *Nativity Play*. This work with Rudolf Steiner on the Christmas plays in Dornach in 1921 led to Schubert taking charge of rehearsals of these plays for many years with the Stuttgart college of teachers. They thus became a firm part of Christmas celebrations in Waldorf schools and curative education homes.

The day after he was released from war imprisonment in 1918,[11] Karl Schubert met Rudolf Steiner in Vienna! The latter went up to him warmly and embraced him. In 1919 Schubert's first son, Michael, was born, and on January 11, 1920, he applied for a job with Emil Molt as described above. Karl Schubert worked with the power of the word as awakening element, but also out of the deep awareness that the Logos, the being of Christ, the goal of humanity's perfection, lives in language as human-shaping force; and both could and must be appealed to in the constitution of the children in need of special care in his support class. Rudolf Steiner drew on Schubert's uncompromising will to heal, and on his power to awaken the being of these children. There was no one in this first college of Waldorf teachers whom Rudolf Steiner praised so fully and exclusively as Schubert, for Steiner trained these first Waldorf teachers lovingly but also strictly. The words recorded by the first eurythmy teacher, Nora von Baditz-Stein, are typical:

> In December 1919 Dr. Steiner appointed me as eurythmy teacher at the Stuttgart school. To my question about what I should do, since I had never before taught children, he answered: "Never adopt a moralizing stance with the children. Just ask yourself always: Is this illness? Is this health? Then the love you need will grow in you." … And Rudolf Steiner also advised me to visit Dr. Schubert's support class: "There you will experience how these sick children are completely out of their bodies; but then Dr. Schubert makes a great noise and the children come back into their bodies. He instructs them in all possible subjects. You will hear how he speaks the first words of the St. John Gospel with a few, shows another how to write letters, does sums with a girl—always using the time when the children's essential being is 'present.'" Smiling he went on: "But after a while you must watch out, for when Dr. Schubert notices that the children are absent again, he makes a far bigger noise even than before—for he is in the right place! Dr. Schubert is really in just the right place, he is made for this work, he does it very, very well. Visit him repeatedly in the class, and you'll get the stimulus you need."[12]

Karl Schubert received no instructions initially for his support work. When at last he asked whether Steiner wasn't going to come and see whether he was doing things right or not, Steiner replied: "What are you asking for? I can see that the children are making progress." Schubert, a little irritated, replied: "But Herr Doctor, you haven't visited the support class yet." Rudolf Steiner answered: "But I can still judge how things are going." When Rudolf Steiner did eventually come, he gave suggestions for waking up sleepy children "in their center" through the use of will exercises. This "waking up in the center" became Schubert's prime work. Rudolf Steiner suggested to Schubert that, in preparing for his teaching, he should form a very detailed picture of the child and all his weaknesses and imperfections; and then of the "star," the being or essence belonging to and approaching the child, as image of the future, as longing for perfection. By bringing these two pictures together inwardly, according to Steiner, one could find the inspiration to do what is needed. This practice of sensing and intuiting became for Schubert an inexhaustible source of imagination and stimulus.

He was willing to sacrifice his considerable intellectual education, that is, to wholly transform and refashion it, to let it pass through his heart and intuiting mind, and re-forge it in the fire of his will. Steiner's repeated references to Schubert's exemplary, blessed, and beneficial work may also be connected with this. During the 1923 educational conference at Ilkley, he also spoke about Schubert's work and described the qualities a person must have to work fruitfully with these children: such work, he said, required character, the right temperament, an extraordinary capacity for love, devotion, willingness for sacrifice and resignation—and Karl Schubert had all that.[13]

The tasks that Steiner gave Karl Schubert included giving lectures and helping run conferences in Germany and abroad. At the same time he often used to specify the lecture title, and often even insist that Karl Schubert give the concluding lecture. At the Christmas Foundation Meeting in 1923-24 in Dornach, for example, Karl Schubert was required to speak on the theme of "Anthroposophy, a Path to Christ." He was one of the first official Goetheanum speakers appointed by Steiner.

Schubert describes as follows his last encounter with Rudolf Steiner when the latter visited his support class in Stuttgart:

> Then he let his love shine out over children and teacher as though in blessing. He told the children how he had first met their teacher in the Austrian mountains many, many years ago, and how he had always wanted him to come to teach at the Waldorf school. These last words bound teacher and pupils together in his love. Then he went, leaving this blessing behind.[14]

The year 1934 brought profound disruption to the school, and to Karl Schubert. The Nazi regime began to issue warnings that the college of teachers included several non-Aryan teachers, including Karl Schubert, whose mother was a Czech Jew. In order to spare the school the shameful torment of having to dismiss him, Schubert offered to resign. But at the same time he asked to be allowed to continue to teach his children without payment, and independently of the school. This was granted, and led to the remarkable situation that the support class and its children were overlooked when the school was closed by the Nazis in 1938. Schubert carried on working, finding new premises in the so-called Lehrs House at 20 Schnellbergstrasse. Parents brought their children to him as inconspicuously as possible, and Schubert lived through the war, continuously risking his own life, on donations and whatever the parents could give him. Schubert carried his life's task like a protected seed through the period of prohibition, a time that brought all other anthroposophic institutions to a standstill. In 1944, the Gestapo ordered Schubert to prepare for transportation, telling him to bring food for a three-day march. Frau Dr. Geraths won him a reprieve with a medical certificate—but the official said that Schubert would still be top of the list for the next transport. Friends took him to Eckwälden, so that Stuttgart was no longer his place of residence. From then on Schubert took the train each day to Stuttgart, to his children in Schnellbergstrasse.

After the war, Stuttgart fell in the US Zone. Because foraging trips to the country were forbidden, checks were carried out on trains. Imagine the scene then on the Saturday before Advent 1945: Karl Schubert is traveling from Eckwälden to Stuttgart, a rucksack full to bursting beside him. An American soldier carrying out checks makes a beeline for him and orders him to open his rucksack. Karl Schubert opens the rucksack and starts taking moss out of it. The soldier waits for food to appear under this supposed cover. But the rucksack is emptied, and beside Schubert is nothing but a great mound of moss. Annoyed, the soldier turns away, and Schubert is allowed to pack it away again. He was traveling to set up the Advent garden for his children. It is from him that the form of the Advent garden comes, and the story of Mary's journey through the stars, and verses and songs such as the one so beloved of children in German-speaking countries: "Über Sternen, über Sonnen" ("Over stars, over suns"). He created all these for the children in his care. Many legends (such as the St. Nicholas story) and rituals marking the course of the seasons, which have since become integral to Waldorf kindergartens, schools, special needs homes, and related institutions, also come from him.

Helene Schumacher tells of his last Advent garden celebration in 1948:

> The adults carried light for those who had died, and also those who were in distress or danger. Dr. Schubert carried the light through all the years for absent children of his class, or people for whom he wanted to do a loving deed. At the last Advent celebration, however, something unheard-of happened. With a loud voice he called out the names of the angels, the archangels, the archai, the names of all the hierarchies, right up to the Holy Trinity, then took the candle in his hand, strode into the brightly illumined garden himself and lit it for the hierarchical powers of the cosmos.[15]

The greatest pain that Karl Schubert ever had to suffer and bear in his life no doubt occurred when the Uhlandshöhe Waldorf School re-opened in October 1945. Schubert asked to be re-admitted to the college of teachers, together with his support class. He was refused! The letter from the school's executive board reflects the concern that this support class might frighten off new parents and funders, and harm the school. However, he would be welcome to rejoin the college of teachers as a religion teacher. Today this strikes us as almost beyond belief. Though deeply hurt, Karl Schubert did not turn away. He gave the religion lessons offered to him, held the Sunday services in the school, and accepted a small fee for doing so. At the same time he continued to teach and care for his special needs children at 20 Schnellbergstrasse. During these first postwar years it was mainly friends from curative education homes in England and Holland who sustained him and his family with food parcels and gifts.

Just back from a lecture trip, early on a Sunday morning on his way to the service in the Waldorf school, Karl Schubert suddenly felt very unwell, and was forced to turn back. Three days later, on February 3, 1949, he died.

But, in collaboration with the association of curative education and social therapy institutions on the one hand, and the Waldorf Schools Federation on the other, his support class grew into the working group of curative education schools. An English friend once said to Walter Johannes Stein after Schubert had departed: "What is it with this Schubert, who is still present even after he's left?" Stein replied: "That is the all-pervading presence of love."[16]

CHAPTER 21

The Life and Work of Eugen Kolisko

Peter Selg[1]

Eugen Kolisko was born in Vienna on March 21, 1893, and he died on November 29, 1939, in London. He was without question one of Rudolf Steiner's most significant pupils and one of the most gifted anthroposophical doctors of his time, acknowledged and held in high esteem by Rudolf Steiner himself.

Eugen's grandfather (a descendant of the famed physician and professor Carl von Rokitansky) and his father, Alexander, were both well-known Viennese doctors and professors. His father was a professor of anatomy, leader of the university medical faculty, morphologist, and medical advisor to the law courts. Rudolf Steiner described him as one of the most courageous doctors in Vienna and commented on his honest and humane handling of the aftermath of the death of Rudolf, Crown Prince of Austria, whose suicide was kept secret by the Austrian Emperor.

Walter Johannes Stein characterized Kolisko as a deeply impressive personality, and he valued his clear scientific knowledge along with his humility and good-natured bearing.

Little is known about his mother, Amelie Kolisko, who was born with the title Baroness Purtscher von Eschenbach. She was a gifted pianist, notably reserved, and it was into this cultivated, aristocratic milieu, steeped in art and culture, that Kolisko found himself, situated in the great city of Vienna with its dynamic present and glorious past. The great curative educator Karl Schubert, who was a few years older than Kolisko and also from Vienna, wrote: "The grandeur of the Austrian spirit was no longer present, but one was still enlivened by its radiance and warmth." Within this atmosphere, Eugen Kolisko grew up and received what can only be called an education fit for a king.

He was a delicate child, prone to illness. He suffered from a chronic, purulent weakness of the joints that called for many operations and finally the loss of his right elbow. The subsequent disfigurement caused people to think him arrogant as he often kept his lamed right hand in his trouser pocket. Only a few of his close friends really understood his deeds and suffering.

Kolisko shone from an early age and soon rose above the average. He learnt tirelessly from his house teacher, a former Benedictine priest, from his brother Fritz, seven years his senior, and also from the Benedictine monks in the "K and K school of Scotland," which he attended from the age of ten. He was respected by his school friends, who for the most part underwent a traditional, orthodox education. After Kolisko's death, Karl Schubert wrote: "One could believe that through such a man the past century was revealed in all its grandeur." However, in his early youth he often experienced Kolisko as awkward, clumsy, and unresponsive to the demands of society and his family's expectations. He lived in the shadow of his older brother, who grew up to become a gifted doctor and lecturer of chemistry at the University of Vienna.

After his first year at the Scottish school he found himself sitting next to Walter Johannes Stein in class. Two years his senior, Stein became his guide into anthroposophy and the work of Rudolf Steiner. From the beginning their friendship was under a special star of destiny. It was marked by two deaths: In 1908 the 17-year-old Stein lost his father, and in 1909, at the age of 15, Kolisko lost his older brother Fritz to cancer. At the time Kolisko wrote in his diary: "Now I am quite alone. I have lost my spiritual father." Walter Johannes Stein was tasked with looking after Kolisko by a classmate of Fritz's who died a few years later in the war. "Now little Eugen is alone, it will be your task to look after him," he wrote. Walter Johannes Stein reported later that he followed this wish and actively sought contact with Kolisko even though it was not always easy! His diary entries of the time tell us that he found him arrogant and unfriendly, his knowledge as "programmed." (Kolisko slavishly followed a self-made work schedule of which he later commented: "It was essentially a sound endeavor but sadly cloaked in vanity.") At the same time the link of destiny between Stein and Kolisko was always inspiring. For example, in 1909 Kolisko made a study of personality development in the family from the first to the fifth child. Stein's response, in keeping with his character, was to test its conclusions by looking at specific examples in the family biographies of Helmholz, Goethe, Heine, von Siemens, Schiller, Bismark, Herder, Wagner, his own family, the school class, and so forth. This led to him disproving Kolisko's thesis. Soon they were studying together, discussing mathematics and physics and even putting forward anthropological observations of passersby on the streets of Vienna. Later, both became excellent teachers, thoroughly knowledgeable in the realm of anthropology.

In October 1911, Kolisko began his study of medicine at the University of Vienna, making a seven-year plan of study. His friend Stein did military service (Kolisko was exempt due to his bad arm). Stein began his studies a year later, taking philosophy, mathematics, and physics, and this was when he first came across anthroposophy, indirectly through Mother Hemine, who gave him Rudolf Steiner's *Occult Science* which he immediately read in his usual impulsive way. Later he wrote about the book: "Here, a world view is presented which is either true or false. If it is true, I must make it 'my own' and if it is false I must fight it vigorously!"

He faced an important life decision at this time and began, earlier than Kolisko, an intense study of anthroposophy, often reading ten hours a day. In January 1913, Stein attended a lecture by Rudolf Steiner. Afterwards, in conversation, Steiner introduced him to the works of Berkeley and John Locke and asked him if he would write a thesis on "Knowledge of the Spirit."

In the summer of 1913, the young Walter Johannes Stein traveled to Munich with great enthusiasm to see Rudolf Steiner's four mystery dramas, which at the time were only for members of the Anthroposophical Society. However, as Rudolf Steiner said: "You can join and then resign again after the performances!" Stein remained a member until he was sadly asked to leave 22 years later.

On his return to Vienna, Stein met Ernst Blumel and Karl Schubert, who were both students of anthroposophy and later taught in the Stuttgart Waldorf School.

In 1913, Eugen Kolisko borrowed some books by Aristotle and Fichte from Stein. The two friends discussed Goethe's *Metamorphosis of Plants* and embarked on a study of Steiner's published works together. Kolisko, who was well versed in both natural and spiritual science, followed in his brother's footsteps by joining the medical department of the university.

In 1914, soon after the opening of the First Goetheanum and the death of Christian Morgenstern, Rudolf Steiner gave a series of lectures in Vienna on "The Inner Nature of Man between Death and a New Birth."[2] Stein, Kolisko, Michael Bauer, and Margareta Morgenstern all attended. So Kolisko became a member of the Anthroposophical Society and Stein was given the task by Steiner to study the connection between Aristotle and Fichte.

At this time, Rudolf Steiner also spoke in Vienna about the new Goetheanum building, which young Stein and his mother visited. The Goetheanum was later christened "The Free High School of Spiritual Science."

In 1914, three months after his first meeting with Steiner, Kolisko wrote to his father, who as noted above headed the medical school at the University of Vienna. Eugen described the collapse of the educational system, saying that most universities had fallen into decadence and were little more than training centers for beaurocrats! Materialistic aims had taken the place of spiritual principles, and the situation was getting steadily worse. He feared that soon the trend towards materialism would become irreversible. Kolisko enclosed a German train schedule with the letter so that his father could attend Rudolf Steiner's lectures! In Steiner, Kolisko said he could sense the potential for a renewal of spiritual life and hopefully the whole education system.

This letter, written at age 21, foretold Kolisko's future life, which was to be filled with suffering and difficulty. Later, in 1920, Kolisko would leave his family and Vienna under great misunderstandings and move to Stuttgart. He was an active member of the medical section at the Goetheanum and helped to build up the School of Spiritual Science in Dornach and also in London during his exile there. "Anyone who attempts to bring about change here will soon realize that he can no longer hold onto or rely upon the old established traditions, conditions which in the past have provided secure foundations. No—he will have to say: That which was, no longer provides an adequate basis for my endeavors. I will have to change it. For without change, humanity cannot progress."[3]

Meanwhile, soon after Kolisko's letter to his father in 1914, the decline of the Austro-Hungarian Empire began, and the First World War broke out. Kolisko tirelessly treated wounded soldiers in the Vienna clinic. Ita Wegman said of him: "He always showed great interest in his fellow men—especially when they were sick!"

Due to his deep human understanding and endless patience, Kolisko was able to help people, and in an atmosphere of selfless giving and care for the wounded soldiers, he first met Lilli who was to become his life's partner. Little is known about her—she came from a working-class background in contrast to

Eugen's privileged upbringing. She was working in the laboratory at the Lazarett Clinic when they met, analysing bacteria, testing blood samples, examining microscopic images of cells. She worked selflessly and with great energy, remaining focused at all times.

The war's end in 1918 brought Eugen's promotion to Doctor of Medicine at the University, followed by the death of his father. Meanwhile, Walter Johannes Stein's activities in Vienna focused on the realization of Rudolf Steiner's radical ideas for a new social order—the Threefold Social Order. He collected signatures for Steiner's "Call to the German People." Karl Schubert said: "It is as if he (Kolisko) has given up his own path of destiny in order to serve the Movement." Step by step Kolisko let go of his own middle-class heritage and moved away from everything which lacked a spiritual, social element. In the summer of 1919, he met Rudolf Steiner to discuss the Threefold Social Order. Then in August the first Waldorf School was opened in Stuttgart. Kolisko described the event as "A festive deed in the course of a New World Order."

Amongst those present at Rudolf Steiner's last course for teachers was Walter Johannes Stein, who remained in the Waldorf School as substitute teacher, librarian, and final member of the original College of Teachers which Steiner appointed: a group of twelve.

After the 1919 Christmas Festival, Eugen wrote to Lilli in Vienna, "The whole school is full of joy. It is vibrant and alive!" Kolisko was able to take part in Rudolf Steiner's science course for the teachers. He spoke of light, color, sound, weight, electricity, and magnetism. Soon after his return to Lilli in Vienna, Kolisko received a letter from Emil Molt, director of the Waldorf Astoria tobacco factory and founder of the school, inviting him to return because a class teacher, Friedrich Oehlschlagel, had gone to America and a substitute was urgently needed. After some deliberation he decided to go. His mother's comment was: "Now you have fallen from Viennese professor to anthroposophical schoolteacher!" In March, Eugen took over grade six at the Waldorf School. He also taught chemistry, anthropology and hygiene. He helped with teacher training, and in October 1921 became the school doctor.

An exciting time followed. It was early spring and on top of his teaching, he attended Rudolf Steiner's lectures on warmth and gave talks himself on chemistry. He wrote to Lilli telling her of a new initiative, an academy that would be linked to the Waldorf School. He also attended Steiner's course for doctors, which began on March 21—his birthday—in Dornach. Kolisko took exact notes of the lectures and sent them every day to Lilli in Vienna so that she could also take part from afar. He was also developing his own style and frequently lectured on chemistry. Friedrich Husemann said after one of these talks: "The impression left was unforgettable. He did not speak in an abstract way but always in pictures, often pausing to find the right image."

During this time Kolisko worked closely with Rudolf Steiner in treating the children. Ingeborg Goyert, who was partially paralyzed, came for an interview to join grade six. She had been home-schooled by Friedrich Hiebel. She later recorded her impressions of the interview: "The afternoon sun shone through the large windows. A beautiful view of the town in the valley could be seen. Dr. Kolisko asked me if I knew anything about chemistry. No, I replied, but I would like to. He then asked me about physics, and I gave the same answer. When it came to Roman history I was able to say that I did know something because Friedrich Hiebel had taught me this. In most other subjects I was pretty much a beginner. I knew little of maths, languages, literature, Goethe. and Schiller—but I was eager to learn! After the interview, Dr Kolisko went to his colleagues in the Waldorf School and said: 'You know, the little one is so keen to learn, I think she should join class nine instead of class six.' They all agreed, so I found myself with my own age group in class nine!"

This event once more revealed Kolisko's great warmth of heart and deep understanding of the being of childhood.

Another event around this time involved a boy with a broken leg. After main lesson, many people came to see the school doctor: mothers with blisters, nervous children, class teachers with questions about their boys and girls, upper-school pupils with difficult life problems—people of all ages. The boy with the broken leg sat with his pet rabbit on his knee and said: "This would only be allowed by a doctor like our Dr. Kolisko!"

However strenuous his teaching had been, he always emerged bright eyed and full of humor, with time for all who wished to see him. You felt as if you were the only one, as if there was no one else waiting. He never hurried and even those who were waiting felt at ease.

Together with his colleague Bettina Mellinger, Kolisko worked to help underprivileged children who were poorly nourished and badly looked after. With great effort he established free meals for more than 120 children a day. Clothing was collected and holiday camps organized. Bettina Mellinger described how Kolisko never showed any fear or concern for danger where these trips were concerned. Whether it was ice-capped mountain glaciers or long sea crossings he had absolute trust that all would go well. He would even become angry should anyone begin to question safety issues. For Kolisko, everything was possible. Problems were to be overcome with courage and humor. His firm belief was always: "Where there's a will, there's a way!"

At any given time he had up to a thousand children in his consciousness, and he gave everything to them. He developed new therapeutic methods and helped to start clinics and communities. He also found work for the unemployed within the school community, built bridges between people, and gave new direction and purpose to many. Such was his social consciousness and humility.

Rudolf Grosse, one of Kolisko's pupils, later said of him:

> In Dr. Kolisko we all experienced such a warm-hearted, tactful and personable teacher that we always looked forward to his lessons. We felt that he really knew us, and because he was also our school doctor, a very special relationship of trust developed between us. So, although he was seen as an important teacher, the children mainly worshipped

him for his warm personality. His Viennese dialect also carried something charming in it, especially for Schwabish and Swiss ears. Strict discipline was not really part of his teaching method. Things often went in a casual way without the lesson suffering. He made a big impression with his large black eyes which seemed to look right through you in an all-seeing gaze. If you asked him a question he would first pause to observe you, like a painter taking in the whole picture before going into detail.

On February 27, 1921, his 60th birthday, Rudolf Steiner spoke in The Hague about the necessity of establishing a worldwide Waldorf school council, to make Waldorf education available to children from all social classes. Friedrich Rittelmeyer published his book, *Vom Lebenswerk Rudolf Steiners* (*Rudolf Steiner's Life Work*).[4] This coincided with the first edition of a new magazine, *Die Drei*. The editor asked Sigismund von Gleich to help, but she directed him at Rudolf Steiner's wish to Ernst Uehli and Eugen Kolisko, who tried to develop the newspaper into a global channel for the free spiritual life.

Kolisko gave countless lectures on anthroposophical topics in the years that followed, taking many different themes to Stuttgart, Dornach, Darmstadt, and The Hague. After his Hague lecture, Rudolf Steiner said: "One cannot underestimate his contribution to the movement. When Kolisko spoke about biology, chemistry, natural science, or the free spiritual life expressed through anthroposophy, one always felt that he spoke from the heart, and that the truth lived in and spoke through him."

On June 11, 1921, Rudolf Steiner addressed the Congress of Vienna, and for Eugen and Lilli this was a very important lecture, for the theme was "Anthroposophy as a Striving for World Christianity."[5] It followed the lecture cycle "Man's Inner Nature between Death and a New Birth," which contained the three Rosicrucian sayings: *Ex Deo Nascisimur / In Christo Morimur / Per Spiritum Sanctum Revivisimus*.

Steiner spoke of the need for anthroposophy to not just approach science but to fully permeate it with knowledge that is filled with the Christ force and is in harmony with the divine hierarchies. Through real examples he showed both doctors and teachers that anthroposophy demands brotherhood in the human social realm. "Anthroposophy can only thrive in the soil of brotherhood—where each is prepared to offer what the other needs." This credo Kolisko always attempted to live by.

There then followed the New Year's Eve, 1923 fire that destroyed Rudolf Steiner's Goetheanum and all the work that had gone into it: work carried out by people from many countries since 1913, work to build a new social order. Eugen and Lilli Kolisko were in the adjacent canteen when the fire broke out. Steiner asked Lilli to set up a first-aid station while Eugen, who joined the firefighters, suddenly disappeared! He only reappeared when the large dome began to collapse. It seemed significant that Eugen, who had been so deeply connected with the Goetheanum, only just managed escape the flames. Later he wrote: "At the moment when the Goetheanum was taken from us, the world had no idea what a tragedy this was. The place which was to nurture the new wisdom of the spirit was lost. The Goetheanum was in its form and structure an unquestionable inspiration to human self-knowledge and the path to higher worlds.... One day the fire will be remembered alongside the greatest of world catastrophes." News of the fire quickly spread to all corners of Switzerland, and so the Goetheanum became a symbol for a great deed of love which was sadly extinguished by a world of hate.

In the early hours of the next morning Lilli asked Steiner if he still intended to lecture that evening. He answered that he did, and in his introduction to the Three Kings Play he said, "The great pain which is felt remains unspoken. The work, fulfilled through the selfless love and devotion of so many friends over the past ten years has been destroyed in one short night."

That night Steiner gave the sixth lecture in the cycle "The Foundations of Natural Science."[6] In the course of the evening he said: "Out of the pain we must find the strength to reach our goal; a goal which finds its foundations deep within the course of human evolution. Now, after the tragedy we must work with even more energy and enthusiasm!"

On January 3, Lilli Kolisko spoke about her experiments in the Glass House. Rudolf Steiner especially wanted the doctors to be aware of these. After the lecture Lilli said:

> I can't remember what I said or whether the doctors who were present were able to concentrate or take anything in at all. Their eyes often turned towards the fire. After the lecture a conversation took place, and I managed to write down Rudolf Steiner's answers to the many questions. When I read them today, they seem wonderful. Indeed his attitude and bearing helped us all through that difficult time to carry out our duties.

The year after the fire, 1923, became for Eugen a year of deep inner contemplation, and at the same time new energy arose in his efforts to help Rudolf Steiner's spiritual research expand. He became intensely involved with the Anthroposophical Society, which in a sense had failed Steiner and was perhaps partly responsible for the fire. On February 25, Kolisko gave a lecture on the state of the Society in the Stuttgart conference for representatives. He said: "We stand with no inner conviction before a world full of enemies. Our own members are unaware of their own inner strength or of how they can best serve the anthroposophical movement." Two days later, Steiner himself spoke about the problems within the Society. He suggested that two societies be formed and so the Free Anthroposophical Society came into being. Kolisko was amongst the few who supported the idea.

The Christmas Conference was for Kolisko an esoteric event of the highest order: the great world-significance of Rudolf Steiner's deed. His personal connection and devotion to the future destiny of the Anthroposophical Society became a clear fact for Kolisko, Willem Zeylmans, and many others.

Steiner lectured in Stuttgart in February, and Kolisko went to him afterwards to thank him for the "immense gift" of the Christmas Conference. Rudolf Steiner valued this gesture of thanks and later spoke with joy about "the greeting from Kolisko which still lives with me today." As Karl Schubert remarked: "Steiner saw Kolisko as an authority to be relied upon. He did not handle him as a student but as someone with an important mission."

Dr. Steiner gave Lilli Kolisko permission to make stenographic recordings of the lessons of the First Class. She went to Dornach every week and then shared the lessons with the teachers in Stuttgart.

In April, Eugen gave some lectures on the connection between education and medicine. He also attended Steiner's second medical course, and in July, he and Lilli were invited to join the small group that participated in the curative education course that Steiner gave in the Schreinerei, Dornach. Finally, in the autumn of 1924, Kolisko attended the performing arts course, the pastoral medicine course, and the karma cycle. On September 15, he wrote to Walter Johannes Stein,

> What we hear and experience is hard to express in words…the Drama Course is like the continuation of the 'Poeticus' of Aristotle…and the Pastoral Medicine course is impossible to value highly enough. Try to read the Faust extract from Lessing. Dr Steiner recited it here during the Drama Course, and when he reached the part where Aristotle appears a special tone entered his voice. He said that Lessing had received a true vision of the karmic relationships involved—you remember how we discussed this last summer?

Stein and Kolisko had already done research together on the question of Rudolf Steiner's own "eternal being" and his karmic link to Ita Wegman. In their past incarnations they were Aristotle and Alexander, the two central figures of the Christmas Conference lectures. Further to this, on September 8, when Steiner recited the Faust fragment from Lessing during his drama course he said: "But who are you? Who am I? Let me consider…I am…I have only just become what I am…And who were you? Wait, wait…am I able to follow the thread backwards…I will try…My name is Aristotle! Yes, that is my name."

Having heard the Karma Lectures[7] of August 21 and 27 September 12, it was clear to Kolisko that the question which he and Steiner had discussed was answered. Just imagine what moved in Kolisko's soul at this time. Ita Wegman said that when Rudolf Steiner gave his great lecture on September 12 concerning the School of Chartres and its link to Plato's teachings, Kolisko was greatly moved. He felt how close he himself stood to Plato's world of ideas, which later came to blossom in Chartres.

After one of Steiner's lectures, Kolisko went to thank him and Steiner took Kolisko's hands, shook them heartily, looked warmly into his eyes and thanked him also. He too was moved.

Later, Kolisko visited Chartres many times. On February 27, 1931, Kolisko gave a talk to mark Rudolf Steiner's seventieth birthday. The title was "Rudolf Steiner, Path-Forger to Anthroposophy." In closing, Kolisko said:

> The task of anthroposophy is to be available for all people. Anthroposophy is not simply a body of knowledge but it is a path to knowledge showing how the spiritual in man can reach the spiritual in the world. It has the possibility to save humanity. It is for the future. Rudolf Steiner, the man who wrote *The Philosophy of Freedom,* was a very great and mighty individuality. His task was to bring anthroposophy to Earth. He built new

communities where all could find a place—he took anthroposophy to all areas of life—this was a necessity for him.

One could say that in his early life Rudolf Steiner must have felt a certain loneliness—he understood the world but was the only one able to see the spiritual dimension behind the physical. He brought anthroposophy to a society that was calling out for it, and at least there were small groups of people who took it up and felt a connection to it. In Steiner's biography we see how he helped man to become a "free being." He was fully connected to modern times and through overcoming materialism he carried a true Christ impulse.

In 1934, Eugen Kolisko decided to leave the Waldorf School. He felt on a soul-level that he was unable to continue. After leaving, he received many moving letters from parents who admired him. Kolisko offered the school Helene von Grunelius to replace him, but they refused, saying that they would not take anyone who had been so closely connected to him! Although he left in a climate of bitterness, as Karl Schubert remarked later: "In looking back at the high point of the Waldorf School, the time when Rudolf Steiner and Eugen Kolisko both worked there—no problems or difficulties can diminish the great work that they both did. Eugen Kolisko gave everything he could and the fruits of his work still live on in the spiritual realm."

From Stuttgart, Kolisko moved to Unterlengenhardt and in 1935, he joined the Burghalde Sanatorium, which was run by Ottilie Matthiessen, Margarete Knecht, and Clarita Berger, who had all helped Kolisko earlier in Stuttgart. Kolisko was happy with the new task "to build up an anthroposophical clinic in a very special place—a place of healing." There followed a time of great activity. Alongside the day-to-day medical duties there were courses, meetings, and seminars for student doctors. One student, Karl Berthold, wrote: "After the lectures we often stayed until after midnight with questions and discussion. I always slept in after these nights but Kolisko would be up at 5:00am, picking flowers and herbs for Lilli to experiment with in her laboratory!"

Kolisko also produced the Christmas plays for the local community: "I go over meadow and field in my attempt to plant spiritual seeds. I speak with the local farmers and village folk to help build a center for anthroposophical medicine here in Unterlengenhardt." In turn, Kolisko was treasured by the locals. They saw how he was prepared to go to remote farms and isolated villages in his work as a doctor. He once stayed two full days and nights to help an elderly woman who had pneumonia. One colleague said: "One learnt a great art from him—to be able to give time to the sick, even when one had no time!" Or from Ita Wegman: "He had the greatest interest in humanity, especially when people were ill. He showed unlimited patience and was really able to help."

Karl Schubert described him as calm, thorough, and always able to lift the spirits of those who approached him. Hans Kuhn wrote: "Kolisko was small and quite humble and with his wonderful eyes he conveyed a great will to help as a doctor. His charming personality made him loved by all."

However, Kolisko's time in Unterlengenhardt did not last very long. For years, friends in England had been asking him to join them in their anthroposophical work, so in the summer of 1936, he emigrated with Lilli and their daughter. Daniel Dunlop was especially keen to have him come, and the political situation in Germany severely limited Kolisko's options. He had also been pushed out of the Anthroposophical Society, which itself was under pressure from the Nazi regime and had been banned in some parts of Germany. There were many good reasons for Kolisko to make a move, so with all the new possibilities in England he said a final farewell to Germany. To Eleanor Merry he said: "I knew that I should come, that I should follow Dunlop in the work to build up a spiritual movement here in England." To this end, Kolisko gave everything he could in the remaining three years of his life. In 1936, he started the School of Spiritual Science in Rudolf Steiner House, London. Young people from all over the world came to hear his lectures on cosmology, anthropology, mineralogy, botany, physics, the arts, and more. Sadly, however, even the English society began to make life difficult for him, complaining that his courses were costing too much to put on. Exasperated, one day Kolisko said: "I will go somewhere new and I will never set foot in this house again!" He felt deeply disappointed and very angry. However, as always, he made valuable connections and helped many people. He even helped some Germans to emigrate to London.

In his Vienna lectures, "Anthroposophy as Mystical Fact," Rudolf Steiner said: "Anthroposophy demands brotherhood—brotherhood is a condition. Anthroposophy can only flourish in the soil of brotherhood, where the one gives the other what he needs…."[8]

In London, Kolisko worked with Eleanor Merry, Dora Krück von Poturzyn, and Karl König, who came to London in 1938. Eugen, who loved music, developed ideas for music therapy with the pianist Walter Rummel who wrote of Kolisko: "After a journey he would not rest but pace up and down the room in order to gather his thoughts. We had a large room for him! He got an idea in one end of the room and developed it as he walked to the other—he so wanted us to receive his ideas and make them our own. His eyes shone, his arms were in the air—he was full of enthusiasm. He carried the mark of someone great." Kolisko and Eleanor Merry did biographical research together, especially taking historical English personalities. They published some of their findings, and enlisted Karl König and Dora Krück in this work.

In spring 1939, Kolisko traveled to America, where he lectured in New York and Boston. He wrote to Walter J. Stein: "While I'm here I will try to visit all the well-known academics." Kolisko was concerned with the question of how to save anthroposophy. Middle Europe seemed to be in decline—what possibilities were there on Anglo-American soil? How could one protect and preserve anthroposophy as a seed for the future?

Kolisko returned to England feeling very low. In August, just before the war broke out, he sat with Karl König in a London pub and talked of his trip to America, of the people he had met, and of the lectures he had given, which were poorly attended. Only with great effort did he manage to lift himself out of the disappointment he felt. He looked tired and ill but he still had ideas and courage for the future. To his wife he said: "If God would still grant me three years, I would break through." She wrote later: "I was surprised by this—why only three years? I thought he still had a lot of time left…." Eugen told Lilli of the plans he had for future books—he wanted to write about her work and about his own research. He planned books about his school doctor activities, about chemistry, anthropology, agriculture, and astronomy. When Lilli asked him, "What if it transpires that even in England it is not possible to build up anthroposophy?" he answered: "Then I shall die." Soon after this, war broke out.

Eugen died a few months later, in November 1939. Some episodes from his last days:

On November 26, three days before his death, Kolisko appeared before his wife, strangely tense yet happy. He said: "Just imagine, last night I dreamt of Dr. Steiner. I had to walk through a long, narrow, dark passage and when I finally came out I saw him standing with his hands stretched towards me. I was so full of joy that I embraced him."

Early on the morning of his death Kolisko threw a bundle of notebooks over to Lilli. "Now I know everything! Now we can start to write the book about agriculture!"—"Do you really know everything?"—"Yes, now everything is clear to me and we can write." On this day, they had planned a trip to the Biology Institute in Bray, but as so often, Kolisko the doctor was detained. There was always a telephone call, a doctor's appointment, a prescription that needed to be written. In the end he took a hurried taxi ride to Paddington Station to meet Dr. Engel. He paused at a newsstand to read about Willem Zeylman's arrival in London while Lilli went ahead to the train. Kolisko collapsed at the newsstand but managed to recover—Lilli had already boarded the train so he got on the next one. He then died in his compartment. Karl König wrote:

> His heart suddenly stopped beating. This happened while he was completely alone, in an environment that could hardly be less cheerful: A dark November night in a London suburb, surrounded by the ghosts of modern technology, alone in a railway carriage. That was the place to which his angel had led him—far away from everything in order to extinguish the last flicker of light from his heart.…At that time a great stillness enveloped the world. Poland had been flattened. England lived in the illusion of the Phoney War and was completely oblivious to the situation on the continent. The Second World War had begun. In this emptiness Eugen Kolisko left the earth.

After Kolisko's death, Karl Schubert said to the pupils of the Stuttgart Waldorf School: "His life's work was like an unfinished symphony. But everything that you learnt from him lives on. Let it come to fruition within you and later when you have achieved something, remember with gratitude the teacher who gave you the impulse. So let our feeling reach out to him like the hands of our souls in greeting! May we accompany him in our thoughts with the hope that one day we will all meet again in soul and spirit, in a realm of love—if it be God's will."

Chapter Notes

Preface

1. See, e.g., *Faculty Meetings with Rudolf Steiner, Volume 2.* (Hudson, New York: Anthroposophic Press, 1998): We are in the fortunate situation of having Dr. Kolisko as the medical member of our faculty, and we should not undertake such therapies without speaking with him first, since a certain understanding of chemical and physiological things is necessary to arrive at the correct opinion. Nevertheless, every teacher needs to develop an eye for such things.

2. See, e.g., Rudolf Steiner, *Hygiene – A Social Problem,* from a lecture in Dornach, April 7, 1920 (GA 314). "For the social question is essentially an educational question, and this in turn a medical question—but only in the sense of a medicine, of a hygiene permeated with Spiritual Science."

Chapter 1

1. Rudolf Steiner, *Course for Young Doctors,* "Young Doctors Course: First circular letter," March 11, 1924.

2. Judy Dunn and Robert Plumin, *Separate Lives: Why Siblings Are So Different* (New York: Basic Books, 1990).

3. See, e.g., Julian Laubenthal et. al., "Cigarette smoke-induced transgenerational alterations in genome stability in cord blood of human F1 offspring," *FASEB Journal*, Volume 26, No. 10, October 2012 (Bethesda, Maryland: Federation of American Societies for Experimental Biology); V. Delaney-Black et. al., "Prenatal alcohol exposure and childhood behavior at age 6 to 7 years: I. dose-response effect," *Pediatrics*, 2001 Aug: 108(2) E34 (Itasca, Illinois: American Academy of Pediatrics); and Sharon Begley, "*Parents' Depression and Stress Leaves Lasting Mark on Children's DNA,*" The Daily Beast, thedailybeast.com/parents-depression-and-stress-leaves-lasting-mark-on-childrens-dna (September 2, 2011).

4. Gunther Opp and Michael Fingerle, editors, *Was Kinder stärkt – Erziehung zwischen Risiko und Resilienz* (Munich-Basel, Germany: Verlag Ernst Reinhardt).

5. Michaela Glöckler and Wolfgang Goebel, *A Guide to Child Health,* 3rd Edition (Edinburgh, UK: Floris Books 2003) at 293.

6. Colleen Cordes and Edward Miller, editors, *Fools' Gold: A Critical Look at Computers in Childhood* (Annapolis, Maryland: The Alliance for Childhood, 2000). See also a full PDF of the publication at drupal6.allianceforchildhood.org/fools_gold.

7. Rudolf Steiner, *The Renewal of Education*, (Great Barrington, Massachusetts: Anthroposophic Press, 2001) at 126; (GA 301).

8. Christoph Lindenberg, *Rudolf Steiner – Eine Biographie,* 2 Bände (Stuttgart, Germany: Verlag Freies Geistesleben, 1997).

9. Martin Buber, *I and Thou* (New York: Continuum International Publishing Group, 1995).

10. Karl-Martin Dietz and Barbara Messmer, editors, *Grenzen ertweitern – Wirklichkeit erfahren* (Stuttgart, Germany: Verlag Freies Geistesleben, 1998) at 254.

11. Rudolf Steiner and Karl Rittersbacher, *Wirkungen der Schule im Lebenslauf: Ein Quellenlesebuch der Pädagogik* (Basel, Germany: Zbinden, 1975).

Chapter 2

1. Michaela Glöckler, *A Healing Education: How can Waldorf education meet the needs of the children* (Fair Oaks, California: Rudolf Steiner College Press, 2003) at 22.

2. Michaela Glöckler, *Education as Preventive Medicine* (Fair Oaks, California: Rudolf Steiner College Press, 2002) at 28-29.

3. Glöckler, *A Healing Education* at 29.

4. Wolfgang Schad, "Gestaltmotive der fossilen Menschenformen" in *Goetheanistische Naturwissenschaft, Bd. 4, Anthropologie,* edited by Wolfgang Schad. (Stuttgart, Germany: Verlag Freies Geistesleben, 1985) at 146.

5. Glöckler, *A Healing Education* at 26.

6. Ibid. at 36.

7. Gerald Hüther and Helmut Bonney, *Die Strukturierung des kindlichen Gehirns durch Erziehing und Sozialisation* (Düsseldorf, Germany: Walter Verlag, 2003).

8. Glöckler, *A Healing Education* at 16-21.

9. Rudolf Steiner and Ita Wegman, *Fundamentals of Therapy – An Extension of the Art of Healing through Spiritual Knowledge* (GA 27); see also *Extending Practical Medicine: Fundamental Principles Based on the Science of the Spirit* (Great Barrington, Massachusetts: SteinerBooks, 1997), a translation of the same text.

10. Michaela Glöckler, editor, *Anthroposophische Arzneitherapie für Ärzte und Apotheker* (Stuttgart, Germany: Wissenschaftliche Verlagsgesellschaft, 2005) at 1-21.

11. Glöckler, *Education as Preventive Medicine* at 39.

Chapter 3

1. Rudolf Steiner, *Human Values in Education,* Lecture 5, July 21, 1924 (GA 310). See, e.g., Rudolf Steiner, *Human Values in Education* (Great Barrington, Massachusetts: SteinerBooks, 2002); wn.rsarchive.org/Lectures/GA310/English/RSP1971/19240721a01.html.

2. Bjerner, B., A. Holm and A. Swensson, "Diurnal variation in mental performance," *Brit. J. Ind. Med.* 12: 103-110 (1955).

3. Gunther Hildebrand, "Chronobiologische Aspekte des Kindes und Jungendalters" in *Bildung und Erziehung,* Volume 47, Issue 4 (December 1994) at 452-456.

4. Ibid. at 433-460.

Chapter 4

1. See, e.g., worldhunger.org/world-hunger-and-poverty-facts-and-statistics/#children1 for recently published facts about child hunger. Since the first publication of this book, facts have changed drastically. Undernourishment was the cause of a cited 3.1 million child deaths in 2011 according to UNICEF, WHO and The World Bank.

2. See, e.g., Rudolf Steiner, *Faculty Meetings With Rudolf Steiner, Volume 1* (Hudson, New York: Anthroposophic Press, 1998).

3. P.A. Puhani and A.M. Weber, "Does the Early Bird Catch the Worm? Study on the effect of school age entry on student performance," *Discussion Paper No. 1827,* October, 2005, Darmstadt University of Technology. See a PDF at tp.iza.org/dp1827.pdf.

4. Ulrich Beck, *Risikogesellschaft* (Frankfurt, Germany: Suhrkamp Verlag, 1986).

5. Gunter Opp and Michael Fingerle, editors, *Was Kinder stärkt – Erziehung zwischen Risiko und Resilienz* (Munich, Germany: Ernst Reinhardt Verlag, 1999).

6. Abrahan H. Maslow, *Motivation and Personality* (New York: Harper & Row, 1970).

7. Ibid.

8. Aaron Antonovsky, *Salutogenese – Zur Entymystifizierung der Gesundheit* (Tübingen, Germany: dgvt-Verlag, 1997).

9. See, e.g., Ann Lloyd, *Just 'Til I Finish This Chapter: Tips, quotes, and practical advice for nurturing young readers* (Springfield, Ohio: *Know More Pub*, 2000) (Education consists of example and love—nothing else).

10. Rudolf Steiner, *The Education of the Child in the Light of Anthroposophy* (GA 34). See, e.g., Rudolf Steiner, *The Education of the Child* (Great Barrington, Massachusetts: SteinerBooks, 1996).

11. Manfred Spitzer, *Vorsicht Bildschirm – Elektronische Medien, Gehirnentwicklung, Geundheit und Gesellschaft* (Stuttgart, Germany: Klett Verlag, 2005). Author's translation.

12. See Steiner, *The Education of the Child in the Light of Anthroposophy;* See also Manfred Spitzer and Gerald Huther, *Bedienungsanleitung für das menschliche* (Göttingen, Germany: Gehirn Vandenhoeck & Ruprecht, 2010).

13. Steiner, *The Education of the Child in the Light of Anthroposophy.*

14. William Stern, *Psychologie der frühen Kindheit bis zum sechsten Lebensjahr,* (Leipzig, Germany: *Quelle und Meyer Verlag,* 1967).

15. Rudolf Steiner, "Reordering of Society: The Fundamental Social Law" (GA 34). See, e.g., Rudolf Steiner, *An Introduction to Waldorf Education and Other Essays* (Jersey City, New Jersey: Start Publishing, 2013).

16. Steiner, *The Education of the Child in the Light of Anthroposophy.*

17. While no transcript of this address exists, Nelson Mandela's position on society's responsibility for children is well-known. See, e.g., *The Nelson Mandela Children's Fund,* "Nelson Mandela Quotes about Children," nelsonmandelachildrensfund.com/news/nelson-mandela-quotes-about-children.

Chapter 5

1. See, e.g., Rudolf Steiner, *Discussions with Teachers,* (Hudson, New York: Anthoposophic Press, 1997).

2. See Jean-Claude Lin et. al., *Die Monatstugenden 2nd Edition* (Stuttgart, Germany: *Verlag Freies Geistesleben,* 2015); Rudolf Steiner, *A Road to Self Knowledge and The Threshold of the Spiritual World* (London: Rudolf Steiner Press, 1975) (GA 16 and 17).

3. "How Can the Destitution of the Soul in Modern Times Be Overcome?", GA 168; see, e.g., Rudolf Steiner, *The Connection Between the Living and the Dead* (Great Barrington, Massachusetts: SteinerBooks, 2017).

4. Rudolf Steiner, *Foundations of Human Experience* (Hudson, New York: Anthroposophic Press, 1996).

5. Ibid.

6. Rudolf Steiner, "Address at the foundation-stone laying of the Waldorf School's new building" in *Rudolf Steiner in the Waldorf School* (Hudson, New York: Anthroposophic Press, 1996).

7. Rudolf Steiner, *At the Gates of the Spiritual World,* GA 17; see also Rudolf Steiner, *A Way of Self-Knowledge* (Hudson, New York: Anthroposophic Press, 1999).

8. Rudolf Steiner, *Knowledge of the Higher Worlds* (GA 10); see also Rudolf Steiner, *How To Know Higher Worlds, A Modern Path of Initiation* (Hudson, New York: Anthroposophic Press, 1994).

9. Rudolf Steiner, *Deeper Insights into Education* (GA 302a); see also Rudolf Steiner, *Deeper Insights into Education* (Forest Row, UK: *Rudolf* Steiner Press, 1982).

10. Steiner, "Requirements for Esoteric Training" in *Knowledge of the Higher Worlds.*

11. The family meeting is part of a system of parenting developed by Gordon Training International. See, e.g., *Gordon Training International's Parenting Effectiveness Training* at gordontraining.com/parent-programs/parent-effectiveness-training-p-e-t/.

12. Bart Maris and Michael Zech, *Sexualkunde in der Waldorfpägodic* (Stuttgart, Germany: Pädagogische Forschungsstelle, 2006).

13. Rainer Maria Rilke, "The Poor Words," see Appendix VI.

14. See, e.g., the work of Kim John Payne, such as "Social Inclusion and the New Rites of Passage" at simplicityparenting.com/social-inclusion-and-the-new-rites-of-passage-2/.

15. Rudolf Steiner, *The Curative Education Course, 2nd and 4th Lectures* (GA 317); see also Rudolf Steiner, *Education for Special Needs: The Curative Education Course* (Forest Row, UK: Rudolf Steiner Press, 2014).

Chapter 6

1. Rudolf Steiner, *Roots of Education* (CW 309) (Hudson, New York: Anthroposophic Press, 1997) at 12-13.

2. Rudolf Steiner, *Renewal of Education* (CW 301) (Forest Row, UK: Fellowship Publications, 1981) at 29.

3. Rudolf Steiner, *Practical Advice to Teachers* (CW 294), (London: Rudolf Steiner Press, 1967), Lecture 3.

4. Rudolf Steiner, *Roots of Education* at 42.

5. Rudolf Steiner, *The Education of the Child* (CW 34) (Hudson, New York: Anthoposophic Press, 1996) at 10.

Chapter 7

1. Rudolf Steiner, *Education and Modern Spiritual Life* (GA 307) (Blauvelt, New York: Garber Communications, Inc., 1989).

2. See Rudolf Steiner, *The Roots of Education* (GA 301) (Hudson, New York: Anthroposophic Press, 1997).

3. Friedrich Rittelmeyer, *Aus mainem Leben* (Stuttgart, Germany: Urachhaus Verlag, 1937). Author's translation. (Editor's note: The book's title in English is *About My Life*; we know of no English translation in print).

4. Rudolf Steiner, *Study of Man* (GA 293) (Forest Row, UK: Rudolf Steiner Press, 2011); see also *Foundations of Human Experience* (Hudson, New York: Anthroposophic Press, 1996).

5. Ibid. at 112. Here is the translation of the quote from *Foundations of Human Experience*, page 112: The more things remain as unconscious habit, the better it is for the development of feeling. The more the child becomes aware of the need to do deeds out of devotion to repetition, because they should and must be done, the more you elevate these to true will impulses. Thus, unconscious repetition cultivates feeling; fully conscious repetition cultivates the will impulse because through it the power of decision increases.

6. Ibid.

7. Rudolf Steiner, *Education and Modern Spiritual Life.*

8. Rudolf Steiner, *Education for Adolescents* (GA 302) (Hudson, New York: Anthroposophic Press, 1996).

9. Ibid.

10. See Steiner, *Education and Modern Spiritual Life* (Garber Communications, Inc.).

11. See ibid. at 56.

12. Ibid.

13. Ibid. "These things strongly affect the moral life, whereas the neglect of geography results in an aversion to loving one's fellow beings. Even a superficial observation will confirm this. The connections are there, even if they are not noticed. Today's unhappy cultural phenomena are the effects of such follies."

14. Ibid. at 154. "The remarkable thing is that arithmetic and geometry affect both the physical-etheric and the astral and ego. Arithmetic and geometry are really like a chameleon; by their very nature they harmonize with every part of man's being."

15. Ibid. at 159. "…for it only has a significance here in physical space. Whereas to divide a unity into its members has an inner meaning which can continue to vibrate in the etheric body, even when we are not there."

16. See Steiner, *Foundations of Human Experience* at 107. "If people work physically, they move their limbs. That means they swim totally immersed in the spirit. This is not the spirit dammed up in that person, it is the spirit outside."

17. See ibid. at 216. "We cannot work with the spirit-soul unless we work inwardly with our body. When we work physically, the spirit-soul within us at most participates by providing us with the thoughts to give direction to our walking or to orient us. However, the spirit-soul outside us does take part. We always work in the spirit of the cosmos. We always connect ourselves with cosmic spirit when we work physically. Physical work is spiritual; mental work is a human bodily function. We must comprehend and understand that physical work is spiritual and that mental work is human activity. When we work physically, we are engulfed by the spirit. When we work mentally, matter is active and excited within us."

18. See Steiner, *Education for Adolescents* (Anthroposophic Press) at 65.

19. Rittelmeyer, *Aus mainem Leben.*

20. Rudolf Steiner, *Social Basis for Primary and Secondary Education*, (GA 192) Lecture 1, May 11, 1919. See, e.g., wn.rsarchive.org/GA/GA0192/19190511p01.html.

21. *Knowledge of Higher Worlds* has been translated more recently as *How to Know Higher Worlds* (Hudson, New York: Anthroposophic Press, 1994).

Chapter 8

1. Louis Locher-Ernst, *Mathematik als Vorschule zur Geist-Erkenntnis* (Dornach, Switzerland: Verlag am Goetheanum, 1973). Author's translation.

2. Compare Ernst Bindel, *Pyramiden als Zeugen Vergangener Mysterlenweisheit* (Stuttgart, Germany: Verlag Freies Geistesleben, 1966).

3. Walther Bühler, *Das Pentagramm und der goldene Schnitt als Schöpfungsprinzip*, (Stuttgart, Germany: Verlag Freies Geistesleben, 2001).

4. Louis Locher, *Urphanomene Der Geometrie* (Zurich, Switzerland: Orell Fussli, 1937).

5. See Louis Locher, *Space and Counterspace* (Hudson, New York: Association of Waldorf Schools of North America, 2003) at 271.

6. Dietrich Boie, *Mistel und Krebs* (Stuttgart, Germany: Verlag Freies Geistesleben, 1979).

7. See ibid., citing Rudolf Steiner, "What can the Art of Healing Gain through Spiritual Science?" (GA 319), July 24, 1924. See, e.g., wn.rsarchive.org/Lectures/GA319/English/APC1928/19240724p02.html. Author's translation.

8. See Felix *Sigel, Schuld ist die Sonne* (Leipzig, Germany: New Trinity Media Ltd., 2013). Author's translation.

9. Editor's note: In the 17th century, the mathematicians Paucelot, Reye, and von Staudt, to some extent independently of each other, discovered and researched these laws. For further exploration of Paracelsus, see, e.g.: Hugh Crone, *Paracelsus: the man who defied medicine* (Melbourne, Australia: Albarello Press, 2004).

10. See Hermann Poppelbaum (Jochen Bockemühl, ed.), "The Concept and Action of the Etheric Body" in *Toward a Phenomenology of the Etheric World* I(Spring Valley, New York: Anthroposophic Press, 1985) at 232.

11. Rudolf Steiner, *Autobiography* (Great Barrington, Massachusetts: Anthroposophic Press, 2005).

Chapter 9

1. See, e.g., Frank Woolever, editor, *Gandhi's List of Social Sins* (Pittsburgh, Pennsylvania: Dorrance Publishing, 2011).

2. Rudolf Steiner, *Knowledge of the Higher Worlds* (GA 10); see, e.g., Rudolf Steiner, *How To Know Higher Worlds, A Modern Path of Initiation* (Hudson, New York: Anthroposophic Press, 1994).

3. Ibid.

4. Ibid.

5. Ibid.

6. Ibid.

7. Ibid.

8. Ibid.

9. Ibid.

10. Ibid.

Chapter 10

1. Rudolf Steiner, "Towards the Deepening of Waldorf Education" (Dornach, Switzerland: The Pedagogical Section of the School of Spiritual Science at the Goetheanum, 1991), translated by Roland Everett, near the beginning of the lecture.

2. Ibid.

3. Rudolf Steiner, *Foundations of Human Experience* (GA 293) (Hudson, New York: Anthroposophic Press, 1996), Lecture 1.

4. Ibid.

5. Rudolf Steiner, "How do I find the Christ?" in *Death as Life Transformation* (GA 182).

6. Rudolf Steiner, *Knowledge of the Higher Worlds* (GA 10) and *A Way to Self Knowledge* (GA 12).

7. See, e.g., Rudolf Steiner, *A Road to Self-Knowledge* (London: G.P. Putnam's Sons, 1918).

8. Stefan Leber, *Kommentar zu Rudolf Steiners Vorträgen über Allgemeine Menschenkunde als Grundlage der Pädagogik* (Stuttgart, Germany: Verlag Freies Geistesleben, 2002), *Band 1: Der seelische Gesichtspunkt,* at 362. Author's translation.

9. Steiner, *Foundations of Human Experience,* Lecture 3.

10. See, e.g., Kenneth L. Caneva, *Robert Mayer and the Conservation of Energy* (Princeton, New Jersey: Princeton University Press, 1993).

11. Hartwig Schiller, editor, *Konferenzgestaltung* (Stuttgart, Germany: Verlag Freies Geistesleben, 2000); Heinz Zimmermann. *Sprechen, Hören, Zuhören, Verstehen in Erkenntnis und Entscheidungsprozessen* (Stuttgart, Germany: Verlag Freies Geistesleben, 1997).

12. Rudolf Steiner, *Kingdom of Childhood* (GA 311), Lecture 7.

13. Rudolf Steiner, *Deeper Insights into Education* (GA 302a), Lecture 3.

14. Steiner, *The Foundations of Human Experience,* Lecture 1.

15. Ibid., Lecture 14. See also Steiner, *Foundations of Human Experience* (Anthroposophic Press) at 228.

16. See old note 13; See also Rudolf Steiner, *Conferences with the Teachers of the Waldorf School in Stuttgart,* Volume 3, (West Midlands, United Kingdom: Steiner School Fellowship Publications, 1986).

Chapter 11

1. See, e.g., Rudolf Steiner, *Foundations of Human Experience* (Hudson, New York: Anthroposophic Press, 1996), Lecture 1 (August 21, 1919).

2. Rudolf Steiner, *Deeper Insights into Education: The Waldorf Approach* (Forest Row, United Kingdom: Rudolf Steiner Press, 1983).

3. Steiner, Rudolf: *Mantrische Sprücher Band II* GA 268

Chapter 12

1. See Rudolf Steiner, *Foundations of Human Experience* (Hudson, New York: Anthroposophic Press, 1996) at 27. "A need for imagination, a sense for truth and a feeling for responsibility—these are the three forces that constitute the nerves of pedagogy. Those who would take up education should write this as their motto: Enliven imagination, Stand for truth, Feel responsibility."

2. See Rudolf Steiner, *Discussions with Teachers* (Hudson, New York: Anthoposophic Press, 1997) at 14. In his closing words to these discussions, Steiner "lays upon the hearts" of the teachers to keep steadfastly to four principles: The teacher must be a person of initiative in everything that is done, great or small. The teacher should be one who is interested in the being of the whole world and of humanity. The teacher must be one who never makes a compromise in heart or mind with what is untrue. The teacher must never get stale or grow sour.

3. See generally Steiner's discussion of art, science, and religion in *Foundations of Human Experience*.

4. See *Theosophy,* (Hudson, New York: Anthroposophic Press, 1994), in an addendum to Chapter 1.

5. Steiner, *Theosophy.*

6. See *Anthroposophical Leading Thoughts,* "Ninth letter to members" (GA 26) at wn.rsarchive.org/GA/GA0026/English/RSP1973/GA026_c09.html. "When man seeks freedom without inclining towards egoism—when freedom becomes for him pure love for the action which is to be performed—then it is possible for him to approach Michael."

Chapter 13

1. See, e.g., Charles Dickens, *The Haunted Man* (Philadelphia, Pennsylvania: Samuel A Dalton, 1955). "Lord, keep my memory green."

2. See Rudolf Steiner, "Overcoming Nervousness" (GA 143) in *Anthroposophy in Everyday Life* (Hudson, New York: Anthroposophic Press, 1995).

Chapter 14

1. See, *Kingdom of Childhood,* (Hudson, New York: Anthroposophic Press, 1995) "Nothing is more useful and fruitful in teaching than to give the children something in picture form between the seventh and eighth years, and later, perhaps in the fourteenth and fifteenth years, to come back to it again in some way or other. Just for this reason we try to let the children in the Waldorf School remain as long as possible with one teacher."

2. Rudolf Steiner, *Foundations of Human Experience* (Hudson, New York: Anthroposophic Press, 1996). "This is why it is so important that you have the same children during all of the school years, and why it is so idiotic that children have a different teacher every year."

3. Ibid. at Lecture 14, September 5, 1919. "Thus, just as the soul-teeth appear as a capacity to learn to read and write, an activity of imagination and a permeation of inner warmth announces what the soul develops toward the end of elementary school at the age of twelve to fifteen years. You must emphasize particularly anything that depends on the soul's capacity to fill things with inner love, that is, everything expressed by imagination. You must appeal to the power of imagination, particularly in the final years of elementary school. We are more justified in requiring the seven-year-old child to develop intellectuality through reading and writing than we are in neglecting to bring imagination continually into the power of judgment that slowly approaches at the age of twelve. We must teach everything children have to learn in those years by

stimulating their imagination… In these years we must always take care that, as teachers, we create what goes from us to the children in an exciting way so that it gives rise to imagination. Teachers must inwardly and livingly preserve the subject material; they must fill it with imagination. This is not possible unless we fill it with feeling will. In later years, this often has a strange effect. What we must emphasize, and what is particularly important toward the end of elementary school, is community life, the harmonious life, between teacher and children."

Chapter 15

1. Rudolf Steiner, "Hygiene – a Social Problem" (GA 314), April 7, 1920. See, e.g., wn.rsarchive.org/Lectures/19200407p01.html.

2. See ibid. The cited translation differs slightly from the text, keeping the same meaning, beginning at "One domain of life in particular will be healthily influenced by such a knowledge of human nature—I refer to the domain of education" and ending at "For the social question is essentially an educational question, and this in turn a medical question—but only in the sense of a medicine, of a hygiene permeated with Spiritual Science."

3. See Götte Wenzel, editor, *Hochbegabte und Waldorfschule* (Stuttgart, Germany: Verlag Freies Geistesleben, 2005) and Michaela Glöckler, *Begabung und Behinderung* (Stuttgart, Germany: Verlag Freies Geistesleben, 1997).

4. See Michaela Glöckler, *Gesundheit und Schule,* (Dornach, Switzerland: Verlag am Goetheanum, 1998). The first published report on a 20 year work.

5. See *Die medizinisch-pädagogische Konferenz* at mpkonferenz.wordpress.com. For more information, contact the Konferenz at med-paed-konferenz@gmx.net.

6. See Rudolf Steiner, *Faculty Meetings with Rudolf Steiner,* Volume 2 (GA 300b, February 6, 1923) (Hudson, New York: Anthroposophic Press, 1998) at Lecture 9.

7. Rudolf Steiner, *Education for Adolescents* (Hudson, New York: Anthroposophic Press, 1996).

8. See, e.g., Michaela Gloeckler, "Constitutional Types in School Age Children" in *Anthro-Med Library* at anthromed.org/library/2019/1/13/constitutional-types-in-school-age-children.

9. Steiner, *Faculty Meetings with Rudolf Steiner,* Volume 2 at Lecture 9.

10. See ibid. at 536. "If a child shows too little capacity for synthetic imagining, that is, for constructive imagining where the child cannot properly picture things, if he or she is a little barbarian in art, something common in today's children, that is a symptom that the metabolic-limb system is not in order."

11. See ibid. at 537. "Godly powers allow it to be warm in summer and cold in winter. Those are spiritual activities accomplished by divine powers through material means."

12. See ibid. at 542. "In order to have healthy children in school, teachers must know how to overcome themselves. You should actually attempt to keep your private self out of the class. Instead, you should picture the material you want to present during a given class. In that way, you will become the material, and what you are as the material will have an extraordinarily enlivening effect upon the entire class. teachers should feel that when they are not feeling well, they should, at least when they are teaching, overcome their ill feeling as far as possible. That will have a very favorable effect upon the children. In such a situation, teachers should believe that teaching is health-giving for themselves. They should think to themselves that while teaching, they can move away from being morose and toward becoming lively."

13. See Steiner, *Education for Adolescents.*

14. Ibid.

15. Ibid.

16. Ibid.

17. See, e.g., Rudolf Steiner, *Eurythmy Therapy* (GA 315) (Forest Row, United Kingdom: Rudolf Steiner Press, 2009).

18. See ibid.

19. Rudolf Steiner, *Education* (GA 307, August 7, 1923), see wn.rsarchive.org/GA/GA0307/19230807p01.html, Lecture III, "Greek Education and the Middle Ages." "How shall we educate now that man, in addition to that, has in the modern age lost even the old mediaeval connection with tradition? Outwardly man has lost his faith in tradition. Inwardly he strives to be a free being, one who at every moment shall confront life unhampered."

20. A.E. Karl Stockmeyer, *Angaben Rudolf Steiners für den Waldorfschulunterricht* (Stuttgart, Germany: Pädagogische Forschungsstelle, 2017).

21. See Rudolf Steiner, *Faculty Meetings with Rudolf Steiner,* Volume 1 (GA 300a) (Hudson, New York: Anthroposophic Press, 1998) at Lecture of Thursday, May 26, 1921.

22. See Steiner, *Foundations of Human Experience* (Hudson, New York: Anthroposophic Press, 1996).

23. See, e.g., Paula Spencer, "Is your kid really gifted?" cnn.com/2008/HEALTH/family/08/27/gifted.kids, stating that by various estimates, 2 to 5% of children are gifted.

24. Wenzel Götte, *Hochbegabte und Waldorfschule* (Stuttgart, Germany: Verlag Freies Geistesleben, 2005).

25. Rudolf Steiner, *Autobiography: Chapters in the Course of My Life* (Great Barrington, Massachusetts: SteinerBooks, 2006).

26. Ibid at page 22. "I plunged into it with enthusiasm, and for weeks my soul was completely filled with the congruence, the similarity of triangles, quadrilaterals and polygons. I racked my brains over the question of where parallel lines actually intersect; the theorem of Pythagoras fascinated me."

27. Arehart-Treichel, J: *Childhood Intelligence Linked to Alzheimer's Risk.* Psychiatric News, January 19, 2001 Vol. 36, No.2

28. The eurhythmist Else Klink is well-known in Germany. For an introduction, see, e.g., Henry Barnes, *Into the Heart's Land* (Great Barrington, Massachusetts: SteinerBooks, 2005). See also a wealth of references to German publications at the Wikipedia page devoted to her, en.wikipedia.org/wiki/Else_Klink.

29. See, e.g., Steiner, *Faculty Meetings with Rudolf Steiner,* Volumes 1 and 2.

30. While this quote is unpublished, it has rung true since the days of early Waldorf education and still resonates.

31. The author attributes this approach to Heinz Zimmerman of Dornach, Switzerland. See Heinz Zimmermann, *Speaking, Listening, Understanding* (Hudson, New York: Lindisfarne Press, 1996).

32. See Steiner, *Faculty Meetings with Rudolf Steiner,* Volume 2. "We need to make the remedial class not only for those who are intellectually weak, but also for those who are morally weak."

33. For the foregoing, the author cites an unnamed documentary by French director P. Peterson.

34. Steiner, *Education for Special Needs.*

35. Walter Holtzapfel, *Im Kraftfeld der Organe* (Dornach, Switzerland: Verlag am Goetheanum, 2004).

36. Karl König, *Sinnesentwicklung und Leiberfahrung* (Stuttgart, Germany, Verlag Freies Geistesleben, 2019).

37. Michaela Glöckler, *Das Schulkind* (Dornach, Switzerland: Verlag am Goetheanum, 2004).

38. Editor's note: This is a good basic introduction to retained reflexes, including the ones mentioned here. STNR is symmetrical tonic neck reflex and PALMAR is actual Palmar—as in the babies reflex to grasp. See generally Sally Goddard Blythe, *The Well Balanced Child* (Stroud, United Kingdom: Hawthorn Press, 2014).

39. For a general idea of the Parzival schools, see, e.g., parzival-zentrum.de. See also Bernd Ruf, *Educating Traumatized Children: Waldorf Education in Crisis Intervention* (Great Barrington, Massachusetts: Lindisfarne Books, 2013).

40. Program for International Student Assessment (PISA). For the 2015 study, which was the most recent at the time of this publication, see nces.ed.gov/surveys/pisa/pisa2015/index.asp.

Chapter 16

1. Rudolf Steiner, *Gesammelte Aufsätze zur Kultur – und Zeitgeschichte 1887-1901* (Basel, Switzerland: Rudolf Steiner Verlag, 1989) at 233f. (Author's translation.)

2. Rudolf Steiner, "Speech at the opening of the Independent Waldorf School," September 7, 1919 (GA 298); see, e.g., *Rudolf Steiner in the Waldorf School: Lectures and Addresses to Children* (Hudson, New York: Anthroposophic Press, 1996).

3. Goethe, "Parabase"; see, e.g., Goethe, *Goethe's Poems* (Vancouver, Canada: Ronsdale Press, 2015).

4. See, e.g., Angelica Overstolz, *Dokumentation anthroposophisch-medizinischer Bücher* (Dornach, Switzerland: Verlag am Goetheanum, 2001).

5. See, e.g., Goethe, *Goethe's Conception of the World* (Somerset, United Kingdom: Anthroposophical Publishing Company, 1928) (discussing Rousseau). "His relation to plant lovers and connoisseurs, specially to the Duchess of Portland, may have widened his penetrating sight, and a spirit such as his, which felt called to prescribe law and order to nations, was forced to suppose that in the immeasurable kingdom of plants no such great diversity of forms could appear without a basic law, be it ever so concealed, which brings them back collectively to a Unity… He gradually found the courage to extend to all kingdoms of Nature, to her whole realm, his ideas concerning the manner in which, playing as it were with one basic form, she produces life in all its diversity."

6. William Harvey first famously described the circulation of the blood in 1628. See, e.g., William Harvey, *The Circulation of the Blood and Other Writings* (New York: Everyman's Library, 1963); see also, e.g., Allan Chapman, "A giant leap for mankind: William Harvey reveals the circulation of the blood" in *History Extra*, historyextra.com/period/stuart/william-harvey-reveals-the-circulation-of-the-blood/. "[Harvey knew] that the veins had stepladder valves in them, which…helped the blood get back to the heart, completing the circuit."

7. See also Hella Lowe, *Elementares plastisches Gestalten* (Stuttgart, Germany: NWWP Verlag, 2014).

8. From Barbara Deanjean-von Stryk, *Sprich, dass ich dich sehe* (Stuttgart, Germany: Verlag Freies Geistesleben, 1996).

9. Rudolf Steiner, *The Genius of Language* (Hudson, New York: Anthroposophic Press, 1995), *Translated by Hans and Ruth Pusch.*

10. Deanjean-von Stryk, *Sprich, dass ich dich sehe.*

11. Plato, author's translation. See similar passages in Plato's *Ion,* (Whitefish, Montana: Kessinger Publishing LLC, 2010), e.g. "Had he learned by rules of art, he would have known how to speak not of one theme only, but of all; and therefore God takes away the minds of poets, and uses them as his ministers, as he also uses diviners and holy prophets, in order that we who hear them may know them to be speaking not of themselves who utter these priceless words in a state of unconsciousness, but that God himself is the speaker, and that through them he is conversing with us"; "For in this way, the God would seem to indicate to us and not allow us to doubt that these beautiful poems are not human, or the work of man, but divine and the work of God; and that the poets are only the interpreters of the Gods by whom they are severally possessed."

12. First published in a special issue of the Stuttgart Waldorf School newsletter, *Haussmannstrasse,* Stuttgart, Germany, March 2006.

13. Rudolf Steiner, *The Essentials of Education* (GA 308) (Great Barrington, Massachusetts: Anthroposophic Press, 1997), Lecture 3, April 10, 1924.

14. See, e.g., Rainer Patzlaff et al., *The Child from Birth to Three in Waldorf Education and Child Care* (Spring Valley, New York: Waldorf Early Childhood Association of North America 2011) at 20.

15. See, e.g., Rudolf Steiner, *The Child's Changing Consciousness* (GA 306) (Hudson, New York: Anthroposophic Press, 1996) Lecture 6, April 20, 1923.

16. See ibid. at Lecture 6, April 20, 1923.

17. Rudolf Steiner, "Speech by Rudolf Steiner at the opening of the Independent Waldorf School" (GA 298), in *Rudolf Steiner in the Waldorf School* (Hudson, New York: Anthroposophic Press, 1996), delivered September 7, 1919.

18. Rudolf Steiner, *Gesammelte Aufsätze zur Kultur und Zeitgeschichte* (GA 298) (Dornach, Switzerland: Rudolf Steiner Verlag, 1989), author's translation.

19. Steiner, *The Child's Changing Consciousness,* Lecture 6, April 20, 1923.

20. Rudolf Steiner, *The Sun Mystery and the Mystery of Death and Reincarnation* (GA 211) (Great Barrington, Massachusetts: SteinerBooks, 2006), Chapter 10: "Perceiving the Christ through Anthroposophy".

Chapter 17

1. Rudolf Steiner, *The Essentials of Education* (GA 308) (London: Anthroposophical Publishing Co., 1926), Lecture of April 10, 1924.

2. Michaela Glöckler and Wolfgang Göbel, *A Guide to Child Health* (Edinburgh, United Kingdom: Floris Books, 2013) at 403.

3. Clifford Stoll, *Cuckoo's Nest* (New York: Pocket Books, 1990); *High Tech Heretic: Why Computers Don't Belong in the Classroom and Other Reflections by a Computer Contrarian* (New York: Doubleday, 1999); *Silicon Snake Oil: Second Thoughts on the Information Highway* (New York: Doubleday, 1996).

4. Per Clifford Stoll in *Silicon Snake Oil,* contact Werner Schäfer by mail at Veitlahn 28, DE-95336 Mainleus, Germany. He is happy to send out information relating to his work on the danger to higher human development of inappropriate use of technology.

5. Glöckler and Göbel, *A Guide to Child Health* at 403.

6. See ibid. at 417.

7. See ibid. at 418.

8. Stoll, *High Tech Heretic.*

9. See ibid. at 144. Editor's note: while references to "video tapes," "Turtle Graphics," and so on are no longer current, Mr. Stoll's concerns continue to resonate.

10. Michaela Glöckler and Wolfgang Göbel, *A Guide to Child Health* (Edinburgh, United Kingdom: Floris Books, 2013) at 397.

11. See, e.g., "Monitoring the Future Survey: High School and Youth Trends" at *The National Institute on Drug Abuse*, drugabuse.gov/publications/drugfacts/monitoring-future-survey-high-school-youth-trends, revised December 2018, which shows drug use levels for youth holding steady (except vaping).

12. Ron Dunselman, *In Place of the Self: How Drugs Work* (Gloucestershire, United Kingdom: Hawthorn Press, 1995).

13. The World Health Organization measured the proportion of alcohol users worldwide as potentially higher than one to three in five, see *Global Status Report on Alcohol and Health*, (Geneva, Switzerland: The World Health Organization, 2011), who.int/substance_abuse/publications/global_alcohol_report/msbgsruprofiles.pdf at 12-14, on abstention. The World Health Organization reports further on alcohol and substance use and abuse on an ongoing basis here: *who.int/substance_abuse/facts/en/*.

14. See, e.g., ucr.fbi.gov/crime-in-the.u.s/2015/crime-in-the.u.s.-2015/tables/table-42, compiling data from the FBI, not specifying adolescent perpetrators in particular, but showing that about 80% of violent crimes are committed by men.

15. LAN: Local area network. At a LAN party, guests play multiplayer computer games on a networked system.

16. For Steiner's discussion of the topic see, e.g., *Education for Adolescents,* (Great Barrington, Massachusetts: SteinerBooks, 1996).

17. While Steiner's teachings on the subject have been published and translated frequently, this translation from a German text or lecture was unavailable in English at the time of WECAN's publication.

18. See, e.g., Rudolf Steiner, *Foundations of Human Experience* (Hudson, New York: Anthroposophic Press, 1996), Lecture 14 (September 5, 1919). "Thus, just as the soul-teeth appear as a capacity to learn to read and write, an activity of imagination and a permeation of inner warmth announces what the soul develops toward the end of elementary school at the age of twelve to fifteen years. You must emphasize particularly anything that depends on the soul's capacity to fill things with inner love, that is, everything expressed by imagination. You must appeal to the power of imagination, particularly in the final years of elementary school."

19. Steiner, *Education for Adolescents.*

Chapter 18

1. See Rudolf Steiner, *Rudolf Steiner in the Waldorf School* (Hudson, New York: Anthroposophic Press, 1996) at 122. "The reason for this is that I really believe that this understanding, this working together of the parents with the teachers and others involved in the leadership of the school is something extraordinarily necessary and significant," May 9, 1922.

2. See ibid. at 191-192, June 22, 1923. "For that we need, not recognition—I do not want to say that because an idea that derives as strongly as ours does from the challenges of the present and the future must be self-

contained in the strength of its effectiveness and not count on recognition—but understanding; above all, the understanding of those on whom so much depends, of those who entrust their children to this school. Without this understanding, we cannot carry out our work at all... We must gain leverage for the ideals of our school, and this happens when people see that what comes to light through the idea of the Waldorf School is very deeply rooted in the most important cultural demands of the present and the near future. Therefore, we must strive to present our intentions to our contemporaries in a clearly understandable form, in a form that can engender understanding... Thus, we would like first and foremost to establish a relationship between the school and the parents that does not rest on faith in authority. That is of no value for us. The only thing that is of value is having our intentions received with understanding right down into the details."

3. See ibid. at 219, 225. "The spirit of Waldorf education takes into account the whole human being in a child. But because it takes the whole human being into account without actually having the whole human being—it only has the child during school hours and perhaps for a short time before and after—it must experience an inner need to be in the closest possible contact with the parents, with the home in which the child spends the rest of his or her time"; "This school with its spirit wants to be, not a school of theories, abstractions, and inflexible theoretical principles, but one full of life and reality. That is why it tries to find its way into the reality of the parents' home."

4. See ibid., at 190, 198. "Secondly, the teacher should actually be able to know that such reports spark loving interest at home, and I believe that if parents would manage to write a brief response to to what the teacher wrote in that report, it would be an incredible help. It would make no sense to institute it is as a requirement, but it is extremely important from an educational standpoint if parents begin to feel the need to do this. Such notes are read with extreme attentiveness here in the Waldorf School. Even if they were full of mistakes, they would be much more important to us than many currently acknowledged accounts of modern culture. They would permit is to take a deep look into what we need if we are to teach, not out of abstract ideas, but our of the impulse of our times"; "A powerful human understanding would flow in what the parents could communicate to the teacher in a devoted way, and I do not exaggerate at all when I say that a response to a report card would almost be more important for the teacher than the report itself is for the child."

5. See Michael Harslem, *Wie Arbeiten Eltern und Lehrer zusammen?* (Stuttgart, Germany: Verlag Freies Geistesleben, 1999) at 63f.

6. See Bernard Lievegoed, *The Developing Organization* (London: Tavistock Publications, 1973).

7. See Peter Elsen, "Neuland wagen!" in *Erziheungskunst,* June 2005.

Chapter 19

1. See Rudolf Steiner, *Social Future* (GA 332a), Lecture 5, October 29, 1919.

2. See also Michaela Glöckler, *Macht in der Zwischenmenschlichen Beziehung,* (Stuttgart, Germany: Johannes Mayer Verlag, 2010).

Chapter 20

1. See Hans-Jürgen Hanke, *Karl Schubert: Lebensbilder und Aufzeichnungen* (Dornach, Switzerland: Philosophisch-Anthroposophischer Verlag am Goetheanum, 2004), author's translation.

2. See ibid.

3. Ibid at 174.

4. Ibid. at 44.

5. See ibid.; see also Rudolf Steiner, *Faculty Meetings with Rudolf Steiner* (Hudson, New York: Anthroposophic Press, 1998) at 252.

6. See Peter Selg, *Der Engel über dem Lauenstein* (Dornach, Switzerland: Verlag am Goetheanum, 2004).

7. Hanke, *Karl Schubert: Lebensbilder und Aufzeichnungen* at 42.

8. Ibid. at 31.

9. Ibid. at 36.

10. Ibid. at 37.

11. Ibid. at 125.

12. Ibid.

13. See Rudolf Steiner, "Gegenwärtiges Geistesleben und Erziehung" (GA 307), August 16, 1923.

14. Hanke, *Karl Schubert: Lebensbilder und Aufzeichnungen* at 27.

15. Ibid. at 199.

16. Ibid. at 164.

Chapter 21

1. From Peter Selg, *Anfänge anthroposophischer Heilkunst* (Dornach, Switzerland: Philos.-Anthroposophischer Verlag am Goetheanum, 2000).

2. Rudolf Steiner, *The Inner Nature of Man* (GA 153) (Forest Row, United Kingdom: Rudolf Steiner Press, 2013), April, 1914. See also Lecture 1 at wn.rsarchive.org/Lectures/GA153/English/APC1928/19140409p01.html.

3. Editor's note: this passage has been revised from the original to account for the shift in the narrative from 1914, at the outbreak of World War I, to 1920 and back again.

4. Friedrich Rittelmeyer, *Vom Lebenswerk Rudolf Steiners* (London: FB&C Limited, 2018).

5. Editor's note: While there is no published lecture from Vienna dated June 11, 1921, this could be a reference to a lecture on the same theme as "Anthroposophy and Christianity" given July 13, 1914 in Norrköping. Germany (GA 155). See, e.g., wn.rsarchive.org/Lectures/19140713a01.html.

6. See, e.g., Rudolf Steiner, *The Origins of Natural Science* (GA 326) (Spring Valley, New York: Anthroposophic Press, 1985), Lecture VI, January 1, 1923. Editor's note: The translated publication does not contain this quote about the fire, which may have been omitted as an aside to the central themes of the lectures.

7. See, e.g., *Karmic Relationships: Esoteric Studies,* Volume VIII (GA 240) August 21, 1924 at wn.rsarchive.org/Lectures/GA240/English/RSP1975/Karm08_index.html; August 27, 1924 at wn.rsarchive.org/Lectures/GA240/English/RSP1975/19240827p01.html; and *Karmic Relationships: Esoteric Studies*, Volume IV (GA 238) September 12, 1924 at wn.rsarchive.org/Lectures/GA240/English/RSP1975/19240827p01.html.

8. Editor's note: This is another instance in which published English translations do not contain the quoted text, probably because the full lecture departed from the lecture's central themes.

APPENDIX I

Promoting Health Through Education
A research initiative by the IPSUM Institute

Report on the project
'School entry and health development'

Political background and research situation

Triggered by the PISA studies carried out by the OECD, a series of education reforms were introduced in Germany which are aimed, on the one hand, at **speeding up** school education (G8 model) and, on the other hand, at **earlier entry** by bringing forward the statutory age when children have to enter school. The German federal state that has gone furthest in this direction is Berlin, where children have had to enter school at the age of 5 ½ since 2004 without the opportunity of any postponement. A study by Prognos AG in Basel in 2003, commissioned by the Bavarian Business Association, even went as far as to demand that children should enter school at four years of age, and in 2004 experts from the Friedrich Ebert Foundation called for school attendance from age three.

To justify such demands, the enormous willingness and ability to learn of three- to five-year-olds is cited—along with purely economic reasons—which would otherwise be wasted because the 'window of opportunity' for learning would allegedly quickly close again (an argument which in this form no longer accords with the latest research).

What is left out of consideration here is the question as to whether children are given such a great head start in their overall development through earlier school entry that they are still capable of considerably better performance 10 years later than children who entered school at a later age. And, above all, does restricting childhood in this way through earlier school entry remain without consequences on the **development of health**, on the vitality and creativity of growing children?

The effects on health have not so far been studied. But the question whether earlier school entry leads to better educational attainment was already debated in the 1970s and it is remarkable that researchers have not been able to provide evidence for long-term benefits either then or now, whereas they found clear indications of a negative effect:

Bellenberg, for example, noted in 1999 that children who had entered school at an earlier age were at significantly increased risk of having to repeat years rather than being given a learning advantage. In 2005, *Puhani* demonstrated on the basis of the IGLU primary school reading study with a sample of 6,600 fourth-year pupils that students who entered school at a later age produced significantly better test results than those who entered at an earlier age. Furthermore, the analysis of 182,676 data records of pupils in Hesse who had started school in the years from 1997-1999 showed 'that the school entry age exercises a significant influence on the type of school attended subsequently (e.g. *Gymnasium* [for more academically gifted pupils])'.

'In the light of such results the benefit of a policy of increasingly early school entry appears questionable,' Puhani says in summary, quoting the result of a small survey of 25 school heads in Hesse of whom most complained about 'the lack of readiness for school among very young first grade pupils, particularly with regard to concentration and the ability to overcome frustration and to organize themselves'.

Nevertheless, the research situation is not altogether clear because, in contrast to Puhani, Fertig and Kluve, in their study based on data from the 1960s and 1970s, which also appeared in 2005, do not see any clear connection between school entry age and the subsequent education path. The question whether or not there is an 'appropriate school age' which is generally applicable is answered in the negative by most academics today (Kammermeyer 2001). Research is currently focusing on the question of the conditions which are required to enable children to manage the transitions from home to kindergarten to school. Various approaches of transition research, such as the eco-psychological approach and the contextual system model, view the child as embedded in a reciprocal relationship with his environment and its conditions, but also refer to specific physical, cognitive, social and motivational resources which the child requires to successfully make such transitions; such 'resources' show clear analogies to the current definition of 'school readiness'.

The connection between physical development and the ability to cope in school is something on which school authorities, schools and kindergarten facilities continue to base their daily practice. Health authorities and pediatricians have for years referred with particular emphasis to the increase in motor deficiencies (e.g. in catching a ball, balancing, walking backwards, standing on one leg) in their complaints about the bad state of health of pupils starting out in first year; in so doing, they assume that it is only the maturing of the motor abilities which creates the basis for successful concentration and learning ability in school. One question remains unanswered: is this development subject to age-specific laws or is it so individual that the school entry age should vary from child to child?

The question of sustainability

If the intellectual ability of a child were seen as the sole criterion for judging the age when he should start school, it would be consistent to send children even at the age of three or four as appropriate instead of at 5½ or 6. The political trend in Germany is currently moving in this direction, even if only in a preliminary way, and not without opposition. In the meantime, **UNESCO** declared the start of a world decade of *'Education for Sustainable Development'* in 2005 and from this perspective we should ask the question:

- Does the child who enters school considerably earlier than is traditionally the case and whose learning initially appears to be far ahead of children starting at a later age, maintain this lead years later (e.g. in fourth or eighth grade)?

A second question needs to be added from a Waldorf education perspective:

- Does the child entering school at an earlier age still possess a sufficient degree of **health**, or is the early intellectual lead gained at the cost of later resilience and achievement, mental stability, spiritual presence, and vitality?

That these questions require serious investigation is borne out by many practical observations as well as by the research undertaken by Rudolf Steiner, the founder of Waldorf education, who expressly referred to the **connection between health and education**. It was his groundbreaking discovery that the forces which enable schoolchildren to structure their thinking, to engage in abstraction and the formation of ideas, are the same forces which have previously worked to structure the physical organization, the development and differentiation of the organs: the forces of learning are the forces of growth and development which have been released and which after working on the physical body are then available in metamorphosed form for the soul and spiritual developmental processes. That is one of Steiner's key statements, combined with a warning that these forces should not be used for conscious cognitive and intellectual processes at too early an age; if that does happen, they can no longer work on the physical organization of the body, possibly leading to sustained weakening of the constitution and performance of the child which may only become evident many years later.

Specific educational practice in Waldorf schools was developed by Rudolf Steiner in accordance with this principle and it is standard practice in Waldorf schools today that during the medical examination on entering school, particular attention is paid to the characteristics indicating the release of such physical developmental forces: they include the change of teeth and physical changes, particular motor and sensory activities, speech and cognitive abilities as well as the psycho-social level of development. Decades of experience and data now available in relation to the development of Waldorf pupils speaks for the success of this practice. But *evidence* of the importance of the appropriate school entrance age which would meet current academic standards has not so far been provided by Waldorf education.

Unresolved questions for Waldorf education

The IPSUM Institute wishes to fill this gap and sees all the more reason for doing so in that the current health situation in early childhood gives cause for great concern, as does the health situation of German pupils, which some experts already described as a disaster. The time has come to make the connection between education and the development of health the subject of academic research. The question as to whether or not the age when children enter school plays a significant role in their further development is an appropriate starting point. In this context Waldorf education also faces unresolved questions which require urgent clarification:

- Is child development still the same as in Rudolf Steiner's day?
- As part of rapidly increasing individualization does the age when children enter school not have to be individually determined?
- How does Waldorf education today handle the problem of dissociation (separation of intellectual, physical and social development)?
- Is the concept of 'school readiness' as argued by the Waldorf schools still appropriate nowadays?
- Can the assumed weakening effect of entering school at too early an age be evidenced at all? And if yes: is it permanent or can it be compensated over the years through the therapeutic effect of Waldorf education?
- Do Waldorf schools have appropriate forms of teaching to promote sustained health even if legally required to have a lower school-entry age?
- Does the developmental and health situation ascertained at Waldorf schools differ significantly from other types of school?

Planning of research phases

The IPSUM research project does not claim to answer the questions posed. Its sole purpose and wish is to create a basis for reaching a view through initial academic investigation of two questions relating to German Waldorf schools:

1. Is the individual stage of development of a child as determined by medical examination on school entry of significance for the long-term development of the child's health and performance?

2. If it turns out that the achievement of a certain developmental maturity before school entry favors subsequent positive development, or, indeed, is a condition for it: when do children as a rule reach that developmental maturity? Does it occur at a particular age (with corresponding individual spread) or does such maturity occur absolutely individually?

The following methodological stages are planned for the study of these questions (cf. the following organigram, Tab. 1):

a) During the *school-entry medical examination,* the level of physical, motor, sensory, etc. development of individual children is determined in a cross-sectional study, with focus on the issue of **school readiness** as understood by Waldorf education in the sense described above (release of the forces of physical development). Data is collected by the schools' individual admission bodies via standardized examination procedures.

b) In order to be able to assess later health and performance development, data about the **state of health** of the children must be collected at the time of the *school-entry medical examination* via validated questionnaires for parents, and through anamnesis questions in the admission medical examination.

- When the children have reached *fourth grade*, their state of health, resilience and performance, mental stability and presence of mind should be investigated. Data is collected using the validated questionnaires already used in the admission medical examination, supplemented by interviews with the teachers.

- The data acquired through survey must be combined with the data from survey b) in order to be able to qualitatively evaluate the state of health and development after four years.

- In a last stage, the development which has been determined can be combined with the data from survey a). Given a sufficient number of cases, there should be a statistically secure answer to research question 2 posed above.

Not yet planned but in prospect is a subsequent comparison of the data from Waldorf pupils with the corresponding data from non-Waldorf pupils.

SCHOOL ENTRY MEDICAL EXAMINATION • 4TH GRADE FOLLOW-UP MEDICAL EXAMINATION

shows level of

shows level of

| a) development | b) health | health |

➔ How have the children developed in terms of their health?

≠ Is there a connection between the initial status and the subsequent state of health?

Tab. 1: *'Age of school entry and health development' research project—sequence of research steps*

The most important results in summary

In order to gain a more differentiated picture at which age level the tested parameters achieve their maximum value for the first time in more than half the children, the data was ordered into six quarterly steps, starting with age category 5 ½ - 5 ¾ and finishing with category 6 ¾ to 7 years old. In addition, a seventh group was formed for all children under 5 ½ years old.

The following tables show—separately for boys and girls—the studied parameters by age level. The letter **M** marks the age level for each parameter at which the determined *MEDIAN*[4] *reaches the expected maximum* **for the first time**. A more detailed analysis of the data, which cannot be shown here, shows that in the subsequent age level the median does not as a rule ever again fall below the maximum reached.

Tab. 2: *Maximum values of the items surveyed in the age categories for girls (M = first occurrence of maximum)*

GIRLS Age:	<= 5.5 years	5.51–5.75	5.76–6.0	6.01–6.25	6.26–6.5	6.51–6.75	6.76–7.0
Physical change			M				
Change of teeth			M				
Motor skills:							
Hopping on one leg		M					
Jumping sideways, back and forth		M					
Tight-rope walk backwards			M				
Serial finger-thumb opposition				M			
Rapid hand turning			M				
Sensory and cognitive skills:							
Copying the beat of a rhythm			M				
Speaking a sequence of syllables	(M)						
Completing a shape						M	
Grasping a form	(M)						
Optical isolation		M					
Copying the drawing of a Maltese cross				M			
Copying the drawing of a fish				M			
TOTAL	(2)	3	5	3		1	

© IPSUM-Institut Stuttgart 2006

[4] *Statistics describes a value as a 'Median' (central value) if it lies in the middle of all observed values. At most half of all values are less than it and half of all values are greater than it. The median should not be confused with the 'average value' which represents the arithmetical average of all measured values calculated from the total of all measured values divided by their number.*

Tab. 3: *Maximum values of the items surveyed in the age categories for boys (M = first occurrence of maximum)*

BOYS Age:	<= 5.5 years	5.51–5.75	5.76–6.0	6.01–6.25	6.26–6.5	6.51–6.75	6.76–7.0
Physical change				M			
Change of teeth				M			
Motor skills:							
Hopping on one leg						M	
Jumping sideways, back and forth		(M)					
Tight-rope walk backwards				M			
Serial finger-thumb opposition							M
Rapid hand turning				M			
Sensory and cognitive skills:							
Copying the beat of a rhythm						M	
Speaking a sequence of syllables		(M)					
Completing a shape						M	
Grasping a form			M				
Optical isolation			M				
Copying the drawing of a Maltese cross					M		
Copying the drawing of a fish				M			
TOTAL		(2)	2	5		4	1

© IPSUM-Institut Stuttgart 2006

Analysis of results

The results in the youngest age category in either table cannot be considered in the analysis because it groups children aged from 4 ¾ to 5 ½ (i.e. in three quarters) and no reliable statement as to the age when the maximum is reached for the first time can be made on the basis of the small number of cases. It may be that the tasks set were too easy to identify an age-related improvement. If we look at the remaining results in the age category from 5 ½, the following picture emerges:

1. The time when the maximums are reached for the first time are not broadly distributed but accumulate noticeably in specific age categories: with the girls the peak lies in the last quarter *before* the sixth birthday, with the boys the two peaks are in the first and last quarter *after* the sixth birthday.

2. Whereas the girls have reached the maximum with 6 ¼ years—after just 9 months—in respect of all parameters, there are two maximum phases for the boys (a sign of greater

dissociation?): the first and more pronounced one comprises the 6 months between 5 ¾ and 6 ¼ years, the second lies between 6 ½ and 7 years. The achievement of the developmental maximums does not just occur ¼ year later in the boys than in the girls, but also extends over a significantly longer period of time. This is particularly noticeable in hopping on one leg in which the girls achieve their maximum a whole year before the boys.

3. The conclusion of the physical changes and of the change of teeth, previously seen as classic physical symptoms of readiness for school, coincide in both genders with the phase of greatest accumulation of maximums, thus occurring simultaneously with the peak of skills development.

Tab. 4: Summary: Accumulation of maximums achieved in the age categories for girls and boys

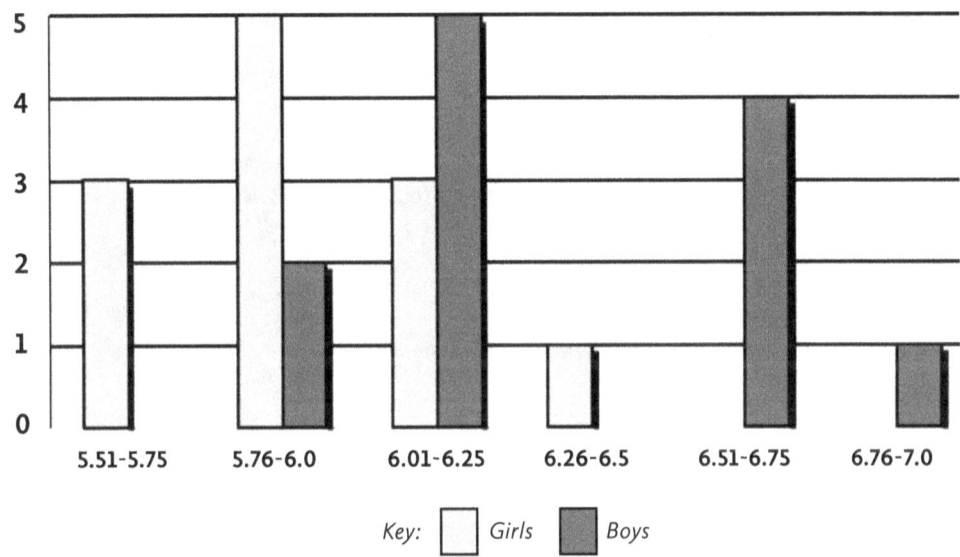

© IPSUM-Institut Stuttgart 2006

Interpretation of the results

A cross-sectional study like the present one does not allow for any statements to be made about individual development because only a single snapshot was taken for each child which recorded the state of development on the given day. But since the age range of the studied children covers a good two years and the findings can be age-related to the day, the data do allow for statements to be made about **the age from which** the full development of individual characteristics and abilities can be expected in the majority of children.

The analysis has shown that the parameters investigated do not reach their respective maximum spread across many age categories but in a very specific, relatively narrow time corridor which comprises nine months in the girls and two six-month phases in the boys. Such a noticeable accumulation suggests the conclusion that the maturing of the abilities at issue does not take place on an exclusively individual basis but that it is dependent to a high degree on age and gender.

If this result is confirmed by the subsequent school-entry medical examinations, we would be entitled to conclude: **The full maturity of important motor, sensory and cognitive abilities cannot be expected in girls before the first half-year of their seventh year of age and in boys before the end of the seventh year of age.** That does not preclude in any way that individuals may reach their peak earlier, but is a clear argument against a general lowering of the school entrance age.

When children are required to go to school as early as 5 ½ years of age, as is the practice in Berlin, then this age lies before the culmination phase determined by us. This means that cognitive and intellectual demands are made of the children before many different basic motor and sensory skill can enter their mature phase. If we assume that sensory and motor maturity is a prerequisite for sustained learning and concentration abilities in school, then premature admission to school can mean overtaxing the forces of the child—unless lessons are structured completely differently from the way that is traditionally the case.

The report was drawn up: Doris Boeddecker, Rainer Patzlaff, Martina Schmidt

IPSUM—Institut für Pädagogik, Sinnes- und Medienökologie, Libanonstraße 3, 70184 Stuttgart Tel. (0711) 24 88 – 210 Fax: -211 e-mail: office@ipsum-institut.de

The research team currently comprises:
- *Dr. Rainer Patzlaff, Waldorf teacher, Institute director*
- *Martina Schmidt, school doctor at the Frankfurt/M Waldorf school.*
- *Doris Boeddecker MPH, health scientist*
- *Dr. Claudia McKeen MD, school doctor, lecturer*
- *Dr. Jan Vagedes MD, pediatrician at the Filderklinik, Tübingen University*
- *Uwe Buermann, Waldorf teacher, computer specialist*

Advisors:
- *Dr. Hanns Ackermann, bio-mathematician, Frankfurt / Main University Clinic*
- *Dr. Christian Heckmann MD, private lecturer, Witten-Herdecke University*
- *Dr. Michael Urschitz, MD pediatrician, epidemiologist, Tübingen University*
- *Uwe Zickmann, statistician, Frankfurt/M University.*

Quoted references:

Fertig, Michael / Kluve, Jochen: The Effect of Age at School Entry on Educational Attainment in Germany.
RWI Discussion Papers No. 27, Rheinisch-Westfälisches Institut für Wirtschaftsforschung, Essen 2005 Griebel, Wilfried/ Niesel, Renate:Transitionen. Fähigkeitvon Kindern in Tageseinrichtungenfördern, Veränderungen erfolgreich zu bewältigen. Beiträge zur Bildungsqualität, hrsg. Wassilios E. Fthenakis, Weinheim und Basel 2004

Kammermeyer, Gisela: Schulfähigkeit und Schuleingangsdiagnostik. In W. Einsiedler, M. Götz, H. Hacker, J. Kahlert, R. W. Keck & U. Sandfuchs (ed.), Handbuch Grundschulpädagogik und Grundschuldidaktik. Bad Heilbrunn: Klinkhardt, 2001, p. 253-263.

Puhani, Patrick A. / Weber, Andrea M.: Does the Early Bird Catch the Worm? Instrumental Variable Estimates of Educational Effects of Age of School Entry in Germany. IZA Discussion Paper No. 1827, Forschungsinstitut zur Zukunft der Arbeit, Bonn, October 2005

APPENDIX II

Research Provides Evidence of Steiner Education's Salutogenic Effects

a) Steiner pupils are healthier

New cross-national research on child health, Cornelis Boogerd[1]

Recent health research shows evidence that children who have an anthroposophic upbringing, live in anthroposophic surroundings and/or attend Steiner schools are healthier than children who go to mainstream state (public) schools. They suffer less frequently from infectious illnesses. The Dutch teacher Cornelis Boogerd explains the research results and looks at possible reasons for these results.

Allergies, eczema, and asthma have been on the increase in the last forty years. Children in particular often suffer from inexplicable infections, viruses and skin allergies. Scientists have been studying this for a long time, but have as yet found no definite explanations.

One recent study tried to find out if there are differences that could have to do with the surroundings in which these children grow up. Research institutes in five Western European countries (Germany, Sweden, the Netherlands, Switzerland and Austria) joined forces and examined around 6,630 children. Two thirds of these children grew up in an anthroposophic context, one third have an ordinary upbringing. The parents had to fill in extensive questionnaires and collect dust from floors and beds. The children underwent different kinds of blood tests.

The research showed that there are 20 to 30% less hay fever and eczema sufferers among anthroposophically raised children than among other school children. With allergies the difference was 32 to 39 percent, whereas with asthma there was no significant difference.

These results naturally raised the question about the cause of the differences, since the answer could provide indications about the origin and treatment of these illnesses. For this reason the lifestyle of the families was also included as a research factor. 40 percent of the Steiner pupils, for example, had never taken antibiotics, contrasted with only 15% of mainstream pupils. For anti-inflammatory allopathica, such as Paracetamol, the figures were 43 as opposed to 8 percent of the children who had never taken any. A quarter of the Steiner pupils had been immunized against measles, mumps and rubella (German measles), as opposed to three quarters of the state-school pupils. A third of the Steiner pupils had actually had measles as opposed to a tenth of the state-school pupils. The differences were most marked in Germany, the Netherlands and in Sweden, but less so in Austria. Eating habits also tended to be different: three quarters of Steiner children eat organic food, but only one quarter of the regular pupils.

Cautious confirmation

The researchers as well as other commentators see these results as a cautious confirmation of the anthroposophic view that infectious childhood diseases help to build up the immune system. This is why parents are more reluctant to give their children antibiotics or fever-reducing medicines. In a sterile environment the immune system cannot be strengthened in the same way. This view is supported by the fact that children who live in the country build up a stronger immune system than city children even though they are exposed to more bacteria.

Organic food also strengthens the body's own resistance. This should obviously not be taken as an invitation to lower hygiene standards. Immunization does, however, prevent children having to fight common childhood illnesses, and thus hinders them from becoming stronger in the process.

Apart from these physically verifiable differences there are also other, educational influences that are physically not so noticeable but still have their effects. Babies and small children in particular need peaceful surroundings, regular rhythms and a healthy diet. Too many chemical additives in the food cause restlessness and aggression. One particularly controversial additive is Aspartame which many so called health products contain instead of sugar.

The excessive impressions, mostly from the media, that children have to process nowadays also undermine the healthy development of the immune system, not only because they can lead to violent behaviour or psychological damage, but also because children cannot really establish an inner relationship to the soulless images that are provided. They cannot process them properly which means they continue to resonate inside them and come to expression in allergies, aggression and hyperactivity.

Parents create culture

This research again shows that the seeds of a new culture are planted within the family. The small conscious decisions that are made here can create culture. This is not about making dogmatic statements and categorically banning all media exposure. It is about adjusting the pedagogical approach to the age of the child. What is important is that parents understand how nutrition, medicines or media affect the children and themselves.

When, as parents, are we weak and enslaved? Parents who come to a clear understanding of this can judge for themselves what they can, and are, willing to be responsible for.

b) Does the school-entry age affect pupil performance?

In Waldorf education it is seen as important that children only start school at the age of seven and that six-year-olds have, for an additional year, the opportunity to be the 'big ones' in kindergarten. A study on the effect of the school-entry age on pupil performance conducted by Professor Dr. Patrick A. Puhani and economist Andrea M. Weber of Darmstadt Technical University in Germany (*Does the Early Bird Catch the Worm? Instrumental Variable Estimates of Educational Effects of Age of School Entry in Germany*. October 2005. IZA Discussion Paper No. 1827) proves that a later school-entry age does indeed affect pupil achievement in a positive way.

Children who start school at the age of seven rather than six benefit from long-term advantages. The greater maturity of the older first grade children results in advanced reading comprehension at the end of elementary school which means that the children are more likely to move on to schools that lead to university entrance qualifications. In the light of these research results the value of an education policy that advocates an ever earlier school start, without taking children's different developmental stages into account, seems questionable.

The research project evaluated extensive pupil data containing information on the age of school entry. It takes into account that the age for entering school can depend on pupil abilities that are directly related to later achievements. It can be assumed, for example, that children who start school later are often considered less capable by their parents and teachers. A simple comparison between children who entered school at different ages would neglect the fact that these children would show achievement differences independently of the actual effect of their school-entry age. The statistical ('econometric') methods used in this study offer an answer to the question about the effect of a later school-entry age without relying on such an unjustified comparison.

Among other things the study draws on data from an elementary school reading survey (*ICLU*) that was carried out in Germany in 2001, in order to determine the effect of the school-entry age on the results of that reading comprehension test. The random tests on approximately 6,600 fourth grade pupils show that children who entered school later clearly achieved better results than those who started school at an earlier age. These results are confirmed by the evaluation of data that contain information on all pupils taught in schools in the German state of Hesse during the school year 2004/2005. Random tests on a total of 182,676 children who entered school between 1997 and 1999 show that the school-entry age has significant influence on what type of school the children attend later on (schools leading to university entry qualification, for instance).

The effects that were measured relate to school-entry regulations that depend on the birth month of the child which means that, in the same grade, the children who are born in the fall or winter are older than those born in the earlier months of the year.

The plausibility of these results is also supported by a small survey carried out among 25 head teachers

in the German federal state of Hesse. Most of the interviewees deplored the lack of school maturity of very young first grade pupils, especially as far as the ability to concentrate, overcome frustration, and self-motivation is concerned. The complete study can be downloaded free from
http://ideas.repec.org/p/iza/izadps/dp1827.html.

c) Reports from the PARSIFAL research project

i. Allergic disease and sensitization in Waldorf Steiner pupils / Results of the PARSIFAL project

A study conducted by Helen Flöistrup et al. (*Allergic disease and sensitization in Steiner school children*. Flöistrup H, Swartz J, Bergström A, Alm JS, Scheynius A, van Hage M, Waser M, Braun-Fahrländer C, Schram-Bijkerk D, Huber M, Zutavern A, von Mutius E, Üblagger E, Riedler J, Michaels KB, Pershagen G, the PARSIFAL Study Group. The Journal of Allergy and Clinical Immunology, January 2006. Vol. 117, Issue 1, Pages 59-66) looked at disease incidence in relationship to allergy incidence in Steiner pupils. The following is a short summary of its outcome.

An anthroposophic lifestyle usually means that antibiotics and immunizations are used less frequently. A previous Swedish study showed that Steiner pupils (who often have an anthroposophic lifestyle) are at a lower risk of suffering from atopic eczema. Particular safe-guarding factors could, however, not be identified. The aim was to look at factors that might contribute to the lower allergy risk in Steiner pupils. A multi-center cross-section test was conducted on 6,630 children between the ages of 5 and 13 (4606 Steiner pupils, 2,024 children from other schools) from five different European countries. The incidence rate of the various tested variables was shown to be lower in Steiner pupils than in the comparison group. In general, statistically significant lower risks of rhino-conjunctivitis, atopic eczema, and atopic sensitization (allergen-specific IgE ≥ 0.35kU/L) were found with some heterogeneity between the different countries. Medically confirmed diagnoses show that children who had been given antibiotics during the first year of their life were at a higher risk of contracting rhino-conjunctivitis, asthma, and atopic eczema. Children who had been immunized against measles, mumps, and chicken pox showed a higher risk of rhino-conjunctivitis, while the measles immunization was associated with a lower risk of IgE-based eczema. Certain characteristics of an anthroposophic lifestyle such as the restricted use of antibiotics and antipyretics are associated with a reduced risk of allergic diseases (J Allergy Clin Immunol 2006; 117: 59-66).

ii. Parsifal-Study: Are Steiner children healthier?

On January 11, 2006 the following notice appeared in the most widely read German medical journal: 'Das Deutsche Ärzteblatt'
(http://www.aerzteblatt.de/v4/news/news.asp?id=22669):

Can an anthroposophic lifestyle prevent allergies? *Restricted use of antibiotics and antipyretics against infections, and rejection of immunization, are said to protect anthroposophically raised children from allergies. A multinational cross-section study in the Journal of Allergy & Clinical Immunology (2006; 117: 59-66), however, only partly confirms this assumption.*

The study on 'Prevention of Allergy-Risk Factors for Sensitization Related to Farming and Anthroposophic Lifestyle (PARSIFAL)' is the most extensive empirical study so far conducted on the influence of an anthroposophic lifestyle on the frequency of allergies. It will attract attention from its numerous followers and critics alike. For this study the parents of 4,606 children from Steiner schools or similar institutions, aged five to 13 years, were questioned. The comparison group consisted of 2,024 children from mainstream schools in the same area. The questionnaire that was used had been validated in the 'International Study of Asthma and Allergies in Childhood'. A blood test was carried out for a sub-group of 28% of the children in order to determine the concentration of the 'allergic' IgE antibodies.

The analysis confirms the wide-ranging differences in lifestyle between anthroposophic parents and their non-anthroposophic neighbours. The adults in Steiner families smoke less and not at all during pregnancy. The parents are better educated, nearly twice as many have a university degree. It is interesting that the study also showed a slightly higher incidence of allergic diseases in anthroposophic parents. A cross-section study has to take these differences into account, which can quite easily be done by statistical means.

The differences that are, however, most noticeable are those in fundamentally anthroposophic areas of concern, and they could have an influence on the allergy incidence. Anthroposophic parents avoid the use of antibiotics if their children suffer from infections. Helen Flöistrup and her group of researchers from the Karolinska Institute in Stockholm indeed show that the frequent use of antibiotics in non-Steiner children leads, according to the parents, to nearly double the number of cases of medically diagnosed rhino-conjunctivitis (Odds Ratio OR 1.97; 95 percent confidence interval 1.26-3.08). Asthma (OR 2.79; 2.03-3.83) and atopic eczema (OR 1.63; 1.22-2.17) are evidently diagnosed more frequently as well when antibiotics are used.

Even though the author goes on to comment critically on the significance of the results, he cannot help acknowledging that, although the frequency of asthma among parents of Steiner pupils is higher, the incidence of diagnosed diseases among the pupils is lower compared to mainstream pupils. This is in itself a highly astonishing and unexpected result.

d) Positive influence of anthroposophic lifestyle on the intestinal flora of children

An anthroposophic lifestyle also affects the bowel flora as the following study shows: Anthroposophic Lifestyle and Intestinal Flora of Children. Alm JS, Swartz J, Bjorksten B, Engstrand L, Engstrom J, Kuhn I, Lilja G, Mollby R, Norin E, Pershagen G, Reinders C, Wreiber K, Schneynius. Pediatr Allergy Immunol. 2002 Dec; 13(6): 402-11. This is a summary of the outcome of this study:

It is assumed that intestinal flora affects the development of the immune system. A nutrition that includes vegetables naturally fermented through lactobacilli, and restricted use of antibiotics, antipyretics and immunization are typical for an anthroposophic lifestyle. The aim of this study was to examine the intestinal flora of children in relation to certain characteristics of an anthroposophic lifestyle.

69 anthroposophically raised children under the age of two, and 59 traditionally brought up children of comparable age, were clinically examined and their parents were asked to fill in questionnaires. Stool examinations were conducted, bacteria identified on the basis of their biochemical properties and the characteristics of the intestinal microflora (MACs) were determined. The number of the colony-forming units (CFU) per gram of feces was significantly higher for enterococci and lactobacilli in children who had never been treated with antibiotics. The number of enterococci was also significantly higher in breastfed and vegetarian children. The lactobacillus diversity (Simpson's Diversity Index) identified on the basis of their biochemical characteristics was higher in babies born at home than in those born in hospitals ($p<0.01$). Some MACs were related to specific lifestyle data and babies that grew up in an anthroposophic context showed a higher proportion of acetic acid and less propionic acid in their feces compared to children in the control group.

In conclusion it can be said that factors that have to do with an anthroposophic lifestyle determine the character of intestinal flora in small children. These differences could have contributed to the lower incidence rate of atopic diseases in children from anthroposophic families.

Studies of this kind that compare certain lifestyles are only the beginning of a development which will hopefully lead to further important discoveries in future years.

There are a number of potential research projects:

- Longitudinal case documentations that show development and progress from school entry to school leaving. Even if it is not really possible to compare one child with another, as each child is unique, it is still interesting to observe how children of the same age and with comparable problems and illnesses change in one way or another during their school life, depending on school system and educational opportunities.
- Research on particular questions such as the menarche in girls from Steiner schools as compared to girls from other schools. Hanno Matthiolus, MD, pursued this question in the 1970s (Matthiolus, H;

Schuh, Chr: "The influence of education on the acceleration of human development using the example of the menarche," published in the German Steiner education journal *Beiträge zu einer Erweiterung der Heilkunst,* 1977, issue 4, p. 129-140). He found out that Waldorf education prevents the accelerated development that leads to incongruence of physical and mental maturity, and that it therefore supports slower and more harmonious maturation.

- Surveys on success and health in later life. Some research has been done in this area and is being done at present. For more information contact the German research institute for Steiner education: Pädagogische Forschungsstelle beim Bund der Freien Waldorfschulen: Wagenburgstrasse 6, DE-70184 Stuttgart. www.waldorfschule.info/forschung.de

APPENDIX III

Research in Rhythm: Two Examples

a) School stress

The Johanneum Research Institute (Franz-Pichler-Strasse 30, AT-8130 Weiz) in collaboration with the Institute for Physiology at Karl Franzens University in Graz/Austria and the 'Institut für Begleitforschung' [Institute for Accompanying Research] in Würzburg/Germany conducted research on the effect that stress and the ability to recuperate have on the autonomous equilibrium and psychology of pupils of different ages.

Point of departure

School stress is not just a slogan. For many pupils it is everyday reality. Teachers as well as pupils are exposed to much more difficult and complex situations today than even a few years ago. Pressure to perform, problematic social situations and information overload are on the increase while little is done to secure the wellbeing and recuperation of those who are affected by all these factors. For the 'School Stress' study, an entirely new approach was applied to find out more about school stress: how does stress affect the chronobiology of the human organism, in particular, the sensitive organism of the growing child? A junior high school in the Austrian district capital of Weiz (Realschule III) offered to participate actively in a physiological and psychological examination lasting several months.

Project realization

A total of 76 pupils from four grades, aged between 10 and 15, voluntarily and very actively took part in the research, with the permission of their parents. In order to establish their daily rhythms their heart frequency and heart frequency variability were recorded over many days. The pupils even took their own morning measurements of these parameters, lying down and standing up, so that the long-term effects could be monitored. Special stress measurements were, finally, carried out with a polygraphic measuring system that is used in space medicine. The aim of the research was, on the one hand, to record the basic stress levels that pupils are exposed to during various typical school situations such as standard lessons, project work and class tests, but, on the other hand also to observe changes that occurred in the pupils during puberty.

Despite fears that the tasks might be too challenging for the pupils, the project turned out to be very successful.

Basically all pupils were able to carry out physiological and psychological measurements correctly and the quality of the data was definitely up to scientific standard. When the research was completed a comprehensive and well-attended exhibition was set up in the school's assembly hall, to inform parents and pupils about the research results. In individual sessions advice was given on how the situation could be improved depending on the results.

Outcome

The long-term measurements showed long wave rhythms for numerous physiological parameters and for the pupils' general condition. Before and during class tests there was often a measurable increase in the heart rate and the vegetative balance shifted toward achievement orientation.

The day measurements showed clear differences between the age groups that also included psychological changes. While for the 10 to 11 year olds the vegetative nerve system was still recuperation-oriented, for older students, especially during puberty it became achievement-oriented, showing typical signs of psychological strain. Pupils in puberty were clearly under more stress than those of lower grades, which also manifested in the reduced amplitude of the day readings.

An innovative procedure for monitoring body rhythms developed by the Institute for Non-invasive Diagnostics showed a clear reduction of diverse rhythms for some students with an irregular lifestyle. Late night computer games in particular as well as television clearly influenced the rhythms in comparison to pupils with a regular lifestyle.

Information about the so called AutoChrone Image technique and the methods it uses can be obtained from Heart Balance AG, Postbus 733, NL-2700 AS Zoetermeer, Holland. One hopes that with this new measuring system more insight can be gained into factors that ensure pupil health.

b) Why life oscillates – from a topographical towards a functional chronobiology

(extracted article from Cancer Causes Control (2006) 17: 591-599 – see Appendix VIII for full article)

APPENDIX IV

The Color Scheme in Steiner Waldorf Schools

The following information is taken from a comprehensive brochure published by the Robert Kaller Studio (Max-Brandes-Str. 23, 44229 Dortmund/ Germany; www.kallerkunst.de) which can also be directly ordered from there. We welcome the opportunity to draw attention to this important initiative for color design in Steiner Schools.

'Man is the measure of all things'

During the past centuries and millennia utensils and buildings were designed with the 'human dimension and proportion' in mind. The measurements of the human body determined size and scope of furniture, rooms, windows and doors, steps, handles etc.

Their effect on the human being was immediate and all past building styles are based on the 'golden section', the 'harmonious measurement' as a universal law, which also governs the proportions of plants, animals and human beings. Johannes Kepler discovered the same laws even in the orbits of the planets. Finding an appropriate color scheme was an integral part of the building process. (Researchers have recently found evidence of interior color design in Egyptian and Greek temples, which architects previously regarded as purely functional buildings.) Architecture and design should ideally represent a functional image of life processes and serve people's needs. Children are much more susceptible to moods and colors than adults. In the child's soul, movement usually proceeds from the external world to the interior one which means that the mood that surrounds the child influences the way he acts. Quality of color design lies in the art of using 'indirect means'. Each age group has its particular fundamental soul mood. The color design should resonate with inner developments.

The color scheme in a school has to be appropriate for the function of each room. The atmosphere of a teachers' meeting room is different from that of a music room or a workshop. Similarly, each subject that is taught has its own characteristic mood. Physics lessons are essentially different from art lessons. It is the task of the color designer to ensure that the identity of each subject is reflected in the chosen color. A teacher might have to teach *against* a mood in a room however well his lessons are prepared. The school should therefore have a color scheme that takes into account the pupils' developmental stage, the identity of particular subjects taught in a room, the entity and characteristic nature of the school and its existing architecture.

The basic polarity of the color circle differentiates between active and passive colors. The active colors include crimson, red to orange, yellow and green. These are all colors that we experience as coming toward us. They represent the light-filled, warm aspect of color sensation and at the same time the side that stimulates feelings and soul life. The passive range includes green, turquoise, blue to violet. These colors seem to move away from us. They form the dark, cold side of the color circle that enhances concentration and is calming; it is related to our thinking and understanding. Green is the balancing, vegetative middle; crimson an image of integration and dynamic.

The similarity to the cycle of the year is obvious: The light-related colors of spring and summer seize our soul life and have an invigorating effect on the vegetative nerve system. The winter months with their lack of light reduce our vitality, but enhance our thinking.

We need to develop a new science of building that is based on knowledge of the human being. Only the study of how we experience space, color, and design will enable us to develop an art of building and designing that is truly meaningful.

It has been shown that many so-called school-related illnesses stem from visual injury to the organism. By improving the visual design of the classroom alone (balance of light-dark contrasts, improved lighting and color schemes) 65% of visual disorders (refractive disorders), 40% of all chronic infections (throat, nose, ear circulation) and 47% of symptoms of malnourishment and growth disturbances could be cured. The research leader, Dr B. Harmon, estimates furthermore that 50% of jaw-closure problems are due to bad posture that is caused by a non-organic field of vision.

Because of their own inner soul constitution, all individuals have their own color space with color tones that shape their identity. The general laws at work in the colors themselves, however, goes beyond subjective color experience. The color designer needs to be able to develop design criteria not according to his own personal color experience but according to place, people, function, room shape, and light conditions, using the effect which the individual colors have on the soul.

APPENDIX V

Addresses and References

Steiner Education

- Pedagogical Section at the Goetheanum, Postfach, CH-4143 Dornach, Switzerland. www.paedagogik-goetheanum.ch

- Pädagogische Forschungsstelle beim Bund der Freien Waldorfschulen: Wagenburgstrasse 6, DE-70184 Stuttgart, Germany. www.waldorfschule.info/forschung.de

- Pädagogische Forschungsstelle beim Bund der Freien Waldorfschulen: Abt. Kassel, Brabanter Strasse 45, DE-34131 Kassel, Germany. www.lehrerseminar-forschung.de

- IPSUM Institut, Libanonstr. 3, DE-70184 Stuttgart, Germany. Dr. Rainer Patzlaff

- The Research Institute for Waldorf Education: P.O. Box 307, Wilton, US-NH 03086 www.waldorfresearchinstitute@earthlink.net

- Ipf Initiative für Praxisforschung: Allmendstrasse 75, CH-4500 Solothurn, Switzerland. www.ipf-ipr.net

- Centre for Creative Education McGregor House: 4 Victoria Road, Plumstead 7800, ZA-Cape Town, South Africa

- Internationale Assoiziation für Waldorpädagogic in Mittelund Osteuropaundweiteröstlichen Ländern e.V. (IAO): www.iao-waldorf.de

Training centers: The website www.waldorfschule.de has up-to-date lists of schools and training centers worldwide. Information on part-time courses can be obtained from the national associations.

- Internationale Vereinigung der Waldorfkindergärten e.V.: www.waldorfkindergarten.org

- Contacts: www.waldorfschule.de

- EOS-Erlebnispädagogik: Erlebnispädagogik-Institut, Villa Mez, Wildbachweg 11, DE-79117 Freiburg, Germany. www.eos-ep.de

- The Association of Waldorf Schools of North America (AWSNA): www.waldorfeducation.org/awsna

- The Waldorf Early Childhood Association of North America (WECAN): www.waldorfearlychildhood.org

Anthroposophic medicine

- Medical Section at the Goetheanum and International Coordination of Anthroposophic
- Medicine / IKAM: Goetheanum, Postfach, CH-4143 Dornach, Switzerland. www.medsektion-goetheanum.ch
- Institut für angewandete Erkenntnistheorie und medizinische Methodologie (IFAEMM e.V.): Dr. med. Helmut Kiene, Schauinslandstrasse 6, DE – 79189 Bad Krozingen, Germany.
- Berlin/Havelhöhe research institute: Dr. med. Harald Matthes, Kladower Damm 221, DE – 14089 Berlin, Germany. www.fih-berlin.de
- Luis Bolt-Institut (research institute): Hoofdstraat 24, NL - 3972 LA Driebergen, Holland.

Training:

- Gesellschaft Anthroposophischer Ärzte in Deutschland e.V., Roggenstr. 82, DE–70794 Filderstadt, Germany. www.anthroposophischeaerzte.de
- International Postgraduate Medical Training: Medical Section at the Goetheanum: Goetheanum, Postfach, CH-4143 Dornach, Switzerland (am@medsektion-goetheanum.ch);

Legal questions: Internationale Vereinigung Anthroposophischer Ärztegesellschaften / IVAA, Roggenstr. 82, DE–70794 Filderstadt, Germany. http://www.ivaa.info

Literature:
Primary source:
Rudolf Steiner: Text//Lecture series

A Theory of Knowledge Implicit in Goethe's World Concept, Rudolf Steiner Press, London 1968

An Outline of Esoteric Science, Anthroposophic Press, New York, USA 1972

Anthroposophical Spiritual Science and Medical Therapy, GA 313, Mercury Press, Spring Valley, New York

Course for Young Doctors, GA 316, Mercury Press, Spring Valley, New York 1994

Curative Education, GA 317, Rudolf Steiner Press, Great Britain 1972

Curative Eurythmy, GA 315

How To Know Higher Worlds: A Modern Path of Initiation, Anthroposophic Press Hudson, New York, USA 1994

Intuitive Thinking as a Spiritual Path: A Philosophy of Freedom, GA 4, Anthroposophic Press, Hudson, New York, USA 1995

Occult Science, GA 13, Anthroposophic Press, New York, USA 1972

Spiritual Science and Medicine, GA 312

Steiner and Wegman – Extending Practical Medicine, GA 27, Rudolf Steiner Press, London 1996

Study of Man, GA 293

The Education of the Child and *Early Lectures on Education,* Anthroposophic Press Hudson, New York, USA 1996

Recommended reading in addition to the above:

Albonico HU et al: F*ebrile Infectious Childhood Diseases in the History of Cancer and Matched Controls,* Med Hypotheses 1996; 51: 315-20

Alm JS, Swartz J et al: *Atopy in Children of Families with an Anthroposophic Lifestyle,* Lancet 1999; 353: 1485-88

Armstrong, A; Casement, Ch. *The Child and the Machine. How Computers May Put Our Children's Education at Risk.* Key Porter Books 1998

Baumgartner S, Heusser P, *Methodological Standards and Problems in Preclinical Homeopathic Potency Research,* Forch Komplementaermedizin 1998; 5: 27-32

Bettermen H et al: *Effects of Speech Therapy with Poetry on Heart Rate Rhythmicity and Cardiorespiratory Coordination,* International Journal of Cardiology 2002; 84: 77-88

Bie G. van der (ED): *Foundations of Anthroposophical Medicine: A Training Manual,* FlorisBooks 2003

Bolk's Companions: *Embryology, Biochemistry, Anatomy, Physiology.* Please order from Louis Bolk Institute, Hoofstraat 24, NL 3972 LA Dreibergen, Tel+31 343 523860 Fax: +31 343 515611, email: g.vd.bie@louisbolk.nl Cysarz D et al: Oscillations of Heart Rate and Respiration Synchronize During Poetry Recitation,. Am J Physiol Heart Circ Physiol 2004; 10.1152/ajpheart.01131.2003

Evans M, Rodger I: *Anthroposophical Medicine, Healing for Body, Soul and Spirit,* Floris Books, Edinburgh Great Britain 2000

Fool's Gold (research on the impact of media on children's health) and 'All work and no play" (about the disappearance of play) can be accessed either via the website www.allianceforchildhood or via amazon.com

Geraets, Truss, *The Healing Power of Eurythmy,* Diametro Verlag, Arlesheim 2006

Glöckler, Michaela, *A Healing Education, How can Waldorf Education Meet the Needs of Children?* Rudolf Steiner College Press, Fair Oaks, USA 2000

Glöckler, Michaela, *A Guide to Child Health,* Floris Books Edinburgh 2003

Glöckler, Michaela, *Anthroposophische Arzneitherapie für Aerzte und Apotheker, Wissenschaftliche*

Verlagsgesellschaft mgH. Stuttgart 2005 ISBN 3-8047-2102-8

Grossarth-Maticek R et al: *Use of Iscador, an Extract of European Mistletoe (viscum album) in Cancer Treatment: Prospective Non-Randomised and Randomised Matched-Pair Studies Nested Within a Cohort Study,* Alternative Therapies in Health and Medicine 2001, 7(3): 57-78

Heusser, Peter: *Criteria for Assessing Benefit with Complementary Medical Methods,*
See www.goetheanum-medizin.ch

Heusser, Peter: Problems of Trial Designs with Randomisation, Blinding and Placebo,
See www.goetheanum-medizin.ch

Holdrege C: *Genetics & the Manipulation of Life: The Forgotten Factor of Context,* Hudson New York USA 1996

Husemann F, Wolff O: *The Anthroposophical Approach to Medicine,* Vol. 2 (out of print) Vol 3 published in Anthroposophic Press, Hudson NY, USA 1982/1987/2003
Download www.goetheanum-medizin.ch
Kirchner-Bockholt M: *Foundations of Curative Eurythmy,* Floris Books 2004

Large, M: *Set Free Childhood,* Hawthorn Press 2003

M. Gloeckler, *A Healing Education,* Rudolf Steiner College Press 2000

Rawson, M; Rose, M: *Ready to Learn,* Hawthorn Press 2003

Ritchie J et al: *A Model of Integrated Primary Care: Anthroposophic Medicine,* Queen Mary University of London 2001

Schoorel, E: *The First Seven Years, Physiology of Childhood.* Rudolf Steiner College Press 2004

Schwartz, E: *The Millenial Child,* Anthroposopic Press 1999

Van Bentheim, T: *Home Nursing for Carers,* Floris Books Edinburgh 2006

Wickens, K et al: *Antibiotic Use in Early Childhood and the Development of Asthma*, 1999; 29: 766-77

Journals:

Circular Letter – Pedagogical Section www.paedegogik-goetheanum.ch

Gateways published by Waldorf Early Childhood Association of North America
www.waldorfearlychildhood.org

Paideia. Published by the Steiner Waldorf Schools Fellowship, paideia@waldorf.compulink.co.uk

Research Bulletin Published by the Research Institute for Waldorf Education
www.waldorfresearchinstitute.org.

Steiner Education Published by the Steiner Waldorf Schools Fellowship info@steinerschoolbooks.com.

Waldorf Science Newsletter Editors David Mitchell & John Petering, davidm@awsna.org

World wide web Newsletter Medical Section www.goetheanum-medizin.ch

APPENDIX VI

"The Poor Words"

by Rainer Maria Rilke

Die armen Worte

Die armen Worte, die im Alltag darben,
die unscheinbaren Worte, lieb ich so.
Aus meinen Festen schenk ich ihnen Farben,
da lächeln sie und werden langsam froh.

Ihr Wesen, das sie bang in sich bezwangen,
erneut sich deutlich, dass es jeder sieht;
sie sind noch niemals im Gesang gegangen
und schauernd schreiten sie in meinem Lied.

The Poor Words

The poor words, who starve in the everyday,
The unnoticed words — I love them so.
I give them colors from my festivals,
And they smile and grow slowly glad.

Their essence, which they fearfully withheld,
Regains its clear form, that all may see;
They've never entered the singing before,
And they step with awe into my song.

RAINER MARIA RILKE, 6.11.1897, BERLIN-WILMERSDORF

APPENDIX VII

Medical and Pedagogical Sections at the Goetheanum

The Medical and Pedagogical Sections belong to the ten sections of the School for Spiritual Science at the Goetheanum in Dornach/ Switzerland which work nationally and internationally on three levels:

- Research, development, and training in their particular subject and profession.
- Coordination of different activities and methods and responsibility for legal recognition of new developments.
- Cultivation of cooperation among the sections and also among representatives of their discipline in the academic field, and representatives of cultural, political, and social life.

An essential concern of their work is the separation of religious and spiritual questions from the 'purely personal and private sphere' and from the division of weeks and months into Sundays and weekdays. These questions have to become culturally creative principles. We usually see priests and religious teachers as performing their work in the 'service of God'. We don't expect this of bankers, economists, farmers, lawyers, teachers or doctors. But what if their work is also a form of divine service? Do people consider which spirit, which intention they are serving in their daily work? Which cultural trends are they supporting? Do people ask themselves if they really want to serve the masters they are serving? What would happen if people served society, not only because it earns them a living, but because they do it out of their hearts and because they wish to serve others? The task is to bring spirituality into everyday life and to make working life fruitful in scientific, artistic, economic, and social fields. A spiritual quest, meditative work, not only means that individuals progress on their path of inner development. It also enables them to base their lives on the results of this inner work, and to make a productive contribution to mankind's further development. The School of Spiritual Science, Pedagogical and Medical Sections included, is committed to this task.

APPENDIX VIII

Cancer Causes Control (2006) 17:591–599 DOI 10.1007/s10552-006-0015-9
ORIGINAL PAPER

Why Life Oscillates: From a Topographical Towards a Functional Chronobiology

Maximilian Moser · Matthias Frühwirth · Reiner Penter · Robert Winker

©Springer 2006

> M. Moser
> Humanomed Centre Althofen, Moorweg 30, A-9330, Althofen, Austria
> e-mail: max.moser@meduni-graz.at Tel.:+43-4262-2071-552
> Fax:+43-4262-2071-501
>
> M.Frühwirth • M.Moser
> Institute of Non-Invasive Diagnosis, Joanneum Research, Franz-Pichler Straße 30, A-8160, Weiz, Austria
>
> M. Moser
> Institute for Systems Physiology, Medical University Graz, Harrachgasse 21/5, A-8010, Graz, Austria
>
> R. Penter
> Klinikum Weisser Hirsch, Heinrich Cotta Str. 12, D-01324, Dresden, Germany
>
> R. Winker
> Division of Occupational Medicine, Medical University of Vienna, Währinger Gürtel 18–20, 1090, Vienna, Austria

Abstract Chronobiology has identified a multitude of rhythms within our body as well as within each living cell. Some of these rhythms, such as the circadian and circannual, interact with our environment, while others run on their own, but are often coupled to the circadian or to other body rhythms. Recent evidence shows that these rhythms might be more important for our health than expected: Disturbance of the circadian rhythms by jet lag or shift work not only evokes autonomic disturbances but also increases the incidence of cancer, as shown in this issue of Cancer Causes and Control. The occurrence of rhythms in the organism obviously bears several advantages: (1) It increases organismic stability by calibrating the system's characteristics: Regulation curves in time and space are crucial for controlling physiological long-term stability. To determine its properties continuously the system varies its parameters slightly over several time scales at different frequencies—akin to what our body does, e.g. in heart-rate variability. (2) Tuning and synchronization of rhythms saves energy: It was Huygens who observed that clocks on a wall tend to synchronize their beats. It turned out later that synchronization is a very common phenomenon observed in bodies' rhythms and can be found, for example, when we relax or sleep. At such times energy consumption is minimal, our body working most efficiently. (3) Temporal compartmentalization allows polar events to occur in the same space unit: there are polarities in the universe of our body, which cannot happen simultaneously. Systole and diastole, inspiration and expiration, work and relaxation, wakefulness and sleep, reductive and oxidative states cannot be performed efficiently at the same time and place. Temporal compartmentalization is probably the most efficient way to mediate between these polarities. Chronobiology and chronomedicine are opening a new and very exciting understanding of our bodies' regulation. The biological time and its oscillations gain more attention and importance as these interrelations are understood.

Keywords Chronotherapy · Chronomedicine · Chronamins · Circadian rhythms · Health

During eons, organismic life has been exposed to various cosmic rhythms. These rhythms consequently have found their ways into the organismic coordination as well as into the human genome. Hormone centers like the suprachiasmatic nuclei or the pituitary are involved in circadian regulation as well as several genes of the clock, cryptochrome and period families [1]. Although in the past most emphasis has been put on the circadian cycle resulting from the variation of light during each day it is but one of the many rhythms observed in living organisms as well as in every cell of our body. The biological significance of these now internalized rhythms are obvious and help to anticipate the needs of life: The ergotropic functions of fight and flight are separated into the day, the trophotropic digestion, immune system function, and regeneration into the resting period, which in human beings is the night. Additionally, the change of heart-rate, hormone levels, and electrolytes, to mention just a few parameters changing during the circadian cycle, exposes the internal sensors to different systemic levels recalibrating them and facilitating their auto-regulative work.

The symphonic orchestra of our body

Besides the circadian rhythm, chronobiology observes a notable amount of different rhythms at all organismic levels and over several orders of time scale magnitude [2–4]. The rhythmic orchestra investigated up to now ranges from milliseconds of a nerve discharge to the annual rhythms of hibernation (Fig. 1). Even longer cycles of seven years can be found, for example, in the biography of celebrities like Goethe, who used to change the lady he adored with such clear periodicity. Recent investigations give hints that the different rhythms are interconnected, at least in healthy subjects, by phase-coupling [5], synchronization [6–8], or mutual modulation [2, 9], and that the different rhythms cooperate like a symphonic orchestra from plants [10] to man. The resulting time network might be a background for organismic regulation, which is a most important precondition for the maintenance of normal development and health. Consequently, there is now increasing evidence that the destruction of the biological rhythms and their synchronization results in the loss of health. Concerning the special case of cancer, this issue of "Cancer Causes and Control" tries to summarize the most recent findings in the context of rhythm disturbances.

The circadian rhythm itself is the organismic response to the daily turn of the earth around its axis and becomes synchronized during the first weeks of human life [11]. Children exposed to a light cycle program displayed improved growth and circadian entrainment compared to continuous dim or bright light [12, 13]. The terrestrial movement around the sun results in the geological year and is responded to by a circannual cycle in organisms living under its influence. The period of the lunar cycle is possibly found today in the female menstrual cycle, although only some studies find a significant connection [14–16], most likely due to the light pollution present in urban societies, thus obscuring the lunar influence. In many traditional societies social life during the year was organized in synchronicity with the lunar cycle [17]. In response to external influences, all of these cycles have been internalized into organisms. Complicated neuronal integrators and genetic control utilizing at least eight genes are present to coordinate, for example, the circadian rhythms [18].

It seems favourable for the organism to orchestrate its functions in synchrony with external conductors like cosmic rhythms as well as among each other. This is the case in the circadian rhythms, which are synchronized with the external day and night by "zeitgebers" [19], of which light [18, 20], feeding [7], and temperature are the most important. The onset of light in the morning triggers a couple of reactions, which turn down the immune system, the readiness to sleep, and the production of growth hormone and melatonin [18], and on the other hand, turn up heart-rate, vigilance, the secretion of epinephrine and other hormones necessary for wakeful activities. It is easily understandable that this has to be done in a synchronized and coordinated way, otherwise the resulting chaos would neither allow for a vigilant day nor a restful sleep.

Shorter cycles than the circadian rhythms do not depend on cosmic events, although some authors claim a connection between body rhythms and solar events [21], some of which may have ultradian cycles. One of the most prominent cycles of short duration is the heart rhythm, which is modulated by and can be used to display a couple of other body cycles. It is easily obtained non-invasively from a 24-hour Holter ECG and has therefore gained attention to create an overview about rhythms present in a subject [22–24]. Information about the sympathico-vagal balance is also contained in the rhythms of heart-rate variability, thus giving access to the state of the autonomic nervous system, which is important for the coordination of different body functions. The heart-rate itself is synchronized to several other cycles, as for example the respiratory cycle, the blood pressure rhythm, and the rhythm of peripheral circulation. This synchronization is especially strong during rest and relaxation, and is not present if subjects are under increased stress and strain—these conditions do not allow for tuning, and consequently spend more metabolic energy than a well-tuned sleep.

The orchestration of the rhythmic system obviously has a horizontal and vertical aspect, as shown in Figs. 1 and 2: Horizontally, rhythms like the circadian conduct the sequences necessary for the daily activities at the time they are needed (Fig. 2a, b). This corresponds to the sequence of themes in a symphony. The temporal compartmentalization arising from this gesture permits oxidative and reductive reactions to run undisturbed alongside of each other within the same spatial compartment. In yeast cells this has been investigated recently [25], and becomes most pronounced under nutrient-restricted conditions (Fig. 2). Interestingly, this condition not only improves the rhythmicity but has also been implicated in prolonging life [26, 27], which might shed light on the connection between rhythmicity and health.

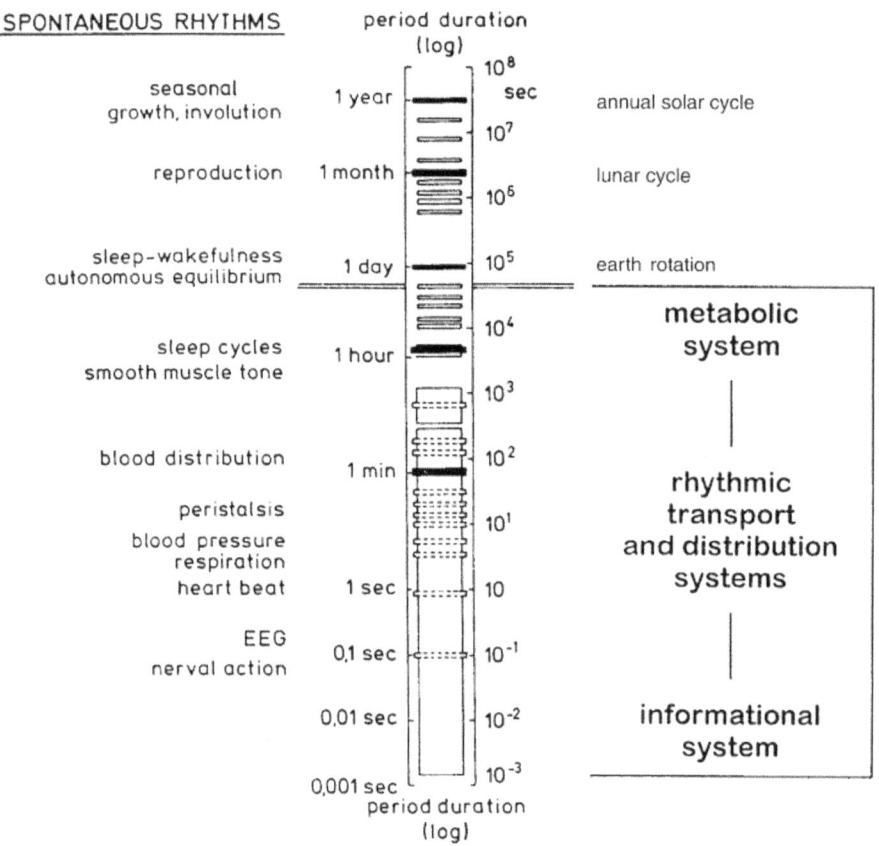

Fig. 1 Spectrum of biological rhythms identified in the human organism (modified after 2). Whereas circa- and infradian long-term rhythms help to anticipate the influences of the earth's movement around its axis and around the sun (circannual rhythm), the faster ultradian rhythms organize the interplay between different organ systems. There is a horizontal orchestration of body functions comparable to the themes of a symphony and a vertical orchestration comparable to the rhythmic interaction between different instruments in a music ensemble

Vertically (Fig. 1), rhythms like heartbeat and respiration coordinate with each other to "give me five" (slap hands) every 4 or so cycles. In an orchestra, this would correspond to the rhythmic interaction present between different instruments during the play—e.g., to the relation of the violins to the slow contrabass. The coordination can be a phase-coupling, a mutual modulation or a synchronization [5, 8]. The "hand slapping" obviously saves energy—it was Huygens who noted that clocks would synchronize their beats if mounted on the same wall [28], indicating that the synchronized state is the one with lower energy.

Rhythmic gene regulation is also important for normal embryonic development [29]. During development time structures in gene expression and cell division are translated into spatial shape, which makes precise timing most crucial to obtain the precise shape of the developing structures [30]. It appears reasonable, therefore, that abnormal development found in cancer cells might be connected to disturbances of rhythms. This is, in fact, the case across several time scales as one might expect if the different rhythms are interconnected and networked. Many of these disturbances are referenced in other papers of this issue, so only less popular findings are reported here.

Rhythm disturbances in cancer

Circadian scale rhythms have been found to be disturbed in cancer patients concerning heart-rate and heart-rate variability [31, 32]. Sleep quality is extremely reduced in cancer patients [33], a fact which hints at a disturbed circadian system [34]. In a study performed on cancer patients compared to healthy subjects we found an impaired circadian rhythm depending on the severity of the disease: Patients with isolated and surgically removed isolated tumours show little differences compared to the healthy controls, whereas subjects bearing metastatic tumours had a decreased circadian amplitude of heart-rate. The worst circadian amplitude of heart-rate was found in chachectic patients who did not show any night time reduction of their very high basal heart-rate (Fig. 3a).

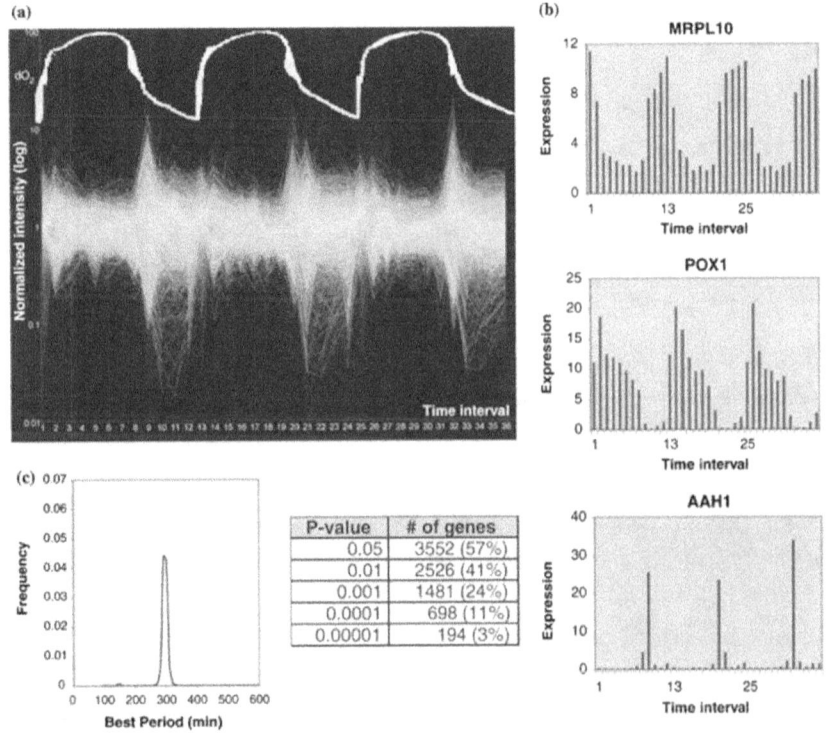

Fig. 2 (a–c) Orchestration of the yeast genome under nutrient-restricted conditions. Genes are activated periodically during the metabolic cycle, which lasts approximately 300 min (a, c) in the yeast. Genes more active in the reductive phase are dyed red, genes active in other phases blue. The cell cycle displays a temporal compartmentalization, in which reductive phases of amino acid and ribosome synthesis alternate with fatty acid oxidation. (b) Between these phases cell division and mitochondria biogenesis occurs (Reprinted with permission from [25], Copyright 2005 AAAS)

Using indicators of autonomic nervous system tone derived from heart-rate variability we could show that even more pronounced differences in the circadian amplitude between healthy subjects and cancer patients could be found, demonstrating the possible diagnostic value of data derived from the heart-rate variability (Fig. 3b–d). It was especially the circadian profile of the sympathetically mediated low frequency heart-rate variability around 0.1 Hz which was able to differentiate between healthy subjects and all cancer patient groups (Fig. 3c).

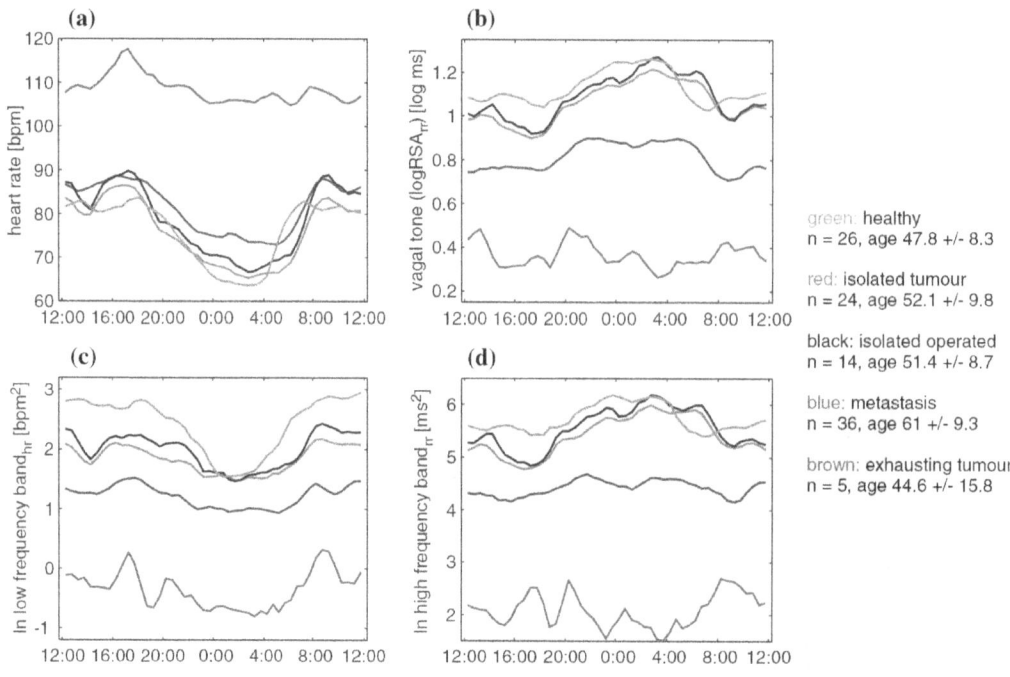

Fig. 3 (a–d) Circadian profile (CIP) of heart-rate (a) and autonomic tone derived from heart-rate variability (b–d) in a group of healthy subjects (controls, green), patients with isolated (red) and surgically removed (black) tumours, metastatic tumours (blue) and cachexia (brown). CIP of heart-rate (a) does not separate the groups except for the cachectic patients whereas a good separation can be achieved by analyzing the CIP of sympathetic tone (c) derived from low frequency variability of heart-rate. Over all, a reduction of the CIP amplitude can be observed as well as decreased sympathetic heart-rate variability (c) in all patient groups compared to the controls, especially during daytime

Disturbances of biological rhythms can also be found in cancer cells and vessels supporting cancer tissue. Cancer cells divide rather slowly, as their metabolism is limited until they connect to the circulation. The vascularization that makes cancer tissue really harmful for the organism takes the form of these sprouting from normal vessels, and is evoked by angiogenetic hormones secreted by certain cancer cells. These new vessels lack normal development and appear disorganized and chaotic compared to normal vessels [35, 36]. Due to the fast development smooth muscle cells in the vascular wall of these vessels are missing, so that they do not respond to the circadian profile of the hormones regulating normal vessel diameter. As there is no temporal restriction to growth, the connected cancer cells grow faster than normal cells. In addition, chaotic behaviour results in the circadian temperature profile of these cancer tissues [35, 37, 38]. Therefore cancer tissues seem to separate their rhythms from those of the remaining organism. This resulting desynchonization weakens the circadian oscillation and decreases the amplitude of the circadian profile in cancer patients, as seen in Fig. 3. As early as the 1980s, Bartsch and co-workers found a disturbed melatonin excretion in breast cancer patients that was not synchronized with the circadian rhythm compared to the synchronized patterns of controls [39]. The circadian clock, representing the most intensively investigated rhythm, is increasingly recognized as an important tumor suppressor [40].

Ultradian rhythms

Ultradian body rhythms oscillate faster than daily but are usually phase-coupled to the circadian rhythm in healthy subjects. Examples are the "basal rest and activity cycle" (BRAC), which controls deep and rapid eye movement phases of our sleep in an approximately 90 min pattern. These rhythms are phase-coupled to the circadian rhythms in healthy subjects, which means that their ups and downs appear approximately each day at the same time.

Self-calibration of control circuits in the human body

Short-period rhythms are present in the human circulation, and permit the study of the possible benefits of oscillating parameters establishing homeodynamic [41] equilibria in the body. Blood pressure control has been studied as early as the 1930s: the blood pressure loop was disconnected under experimental conditions and a dependence between blood pressure and heart-rate was found (Fig. 4).

Increasing the pressure in the carotid sinus (which is responsible for sensing the blood pressure value) lead to a compensatory reduction of heart-rate in a classical experiment performed by Koch [42] via vagal pathways. Along the range of different pressures a sigmoidal shape of the resulting regulation curve was found. Interestingly the steepest part or point of inflection of this regulation curve is located almost exactly where the normal systolic blood pressure can be found, at around 120 mm Hg. As physiological sensors adapt to a steady signal, the blood pressure regulation would probably shift and become unstable after a while if no variation in pressure would occur. A slight variation of heart-rate (known as heart-rate variability today) found in healthy subjects prevents this adaptation by a resulting continuous variability of blood pressure. As a consequence the blood pressure regulation gets the necessary feedback to recalibrate by the amount of pressure change achieved by a certain increase or decrease of heartrate. So the small oscillations present in the organism support the self-calibration of the organismic functions.

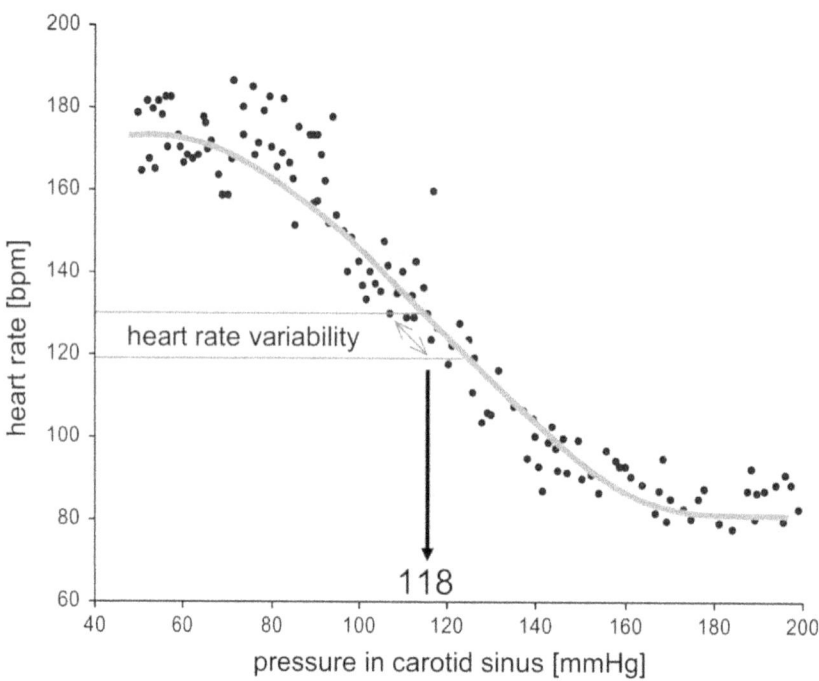

Fig.4 Example of a physiological feedback loop seeking its normal value close to the point of inflection of the system characteristics: The relation between blood pressure in the carotid sinus and heart-rate. Heart-rate variability very likely acts as a search parameter, varying continuously to search for the optimal position on the regulation curve. Regulation is most sensitive at the point of inflection, which also represents the "normal" value of systolic blood pressure (adapted from [42])

Obviously, blood pressure in this framework is not controlled by a single neuron or group of neurons, which know: "Normal systolic blood pressure should be 120 mm Hg". It is rather the result of a perhaps "democratically" obtained regulation curve which integrates all relevant parameters, such as the elastic properties of vessels, blood volume, blood viscosity and peripheral resistance. At the inflection point the strongest interconnection between heart-rate and blood pressure can be found, making regulation around this value most sensitive, and hence, stable for the circulation. Opting for stability in such a crucial supply, it is not surprising that the organism selects this turning point to be the normal value of blood pressure under resting conditions.

It is not yet known whether such curves exist for hormonal parameters as well, but it seems very likely that other control loops are maintained in a similar fashion. This could mean that different oscillations also act as search functions seeking points of inflection in our organismic regulation. It seems remarkable that recent work in that context has connected the decline of the dynamic range of environmental cues to observed biological dysfunctions, like insulin insensitivity and metabolic diseases [43]. A dynamic system lacking variability is more likely to lose its calibration points. On the other hand this knowledge could help provide therapies based on "Chronamins" [44] and life-style approaches, providing dynamic environmental cues [32, 43]. In musical instruments, too, long-term stability of sound is achieved by playing, i.e. vibrating the instrument for a period of time. This stable state may also be mimicked by vibrating the instrument artificially[45].

Space and time in our body

Nowadays we are taking part in various scientific revolutions, one of which might be based on the results of modern chronobiology. Like Andrea Vesalius, who so beautifully described the spatial aspects of our body, giving access to the anatomical shape of our muscles and bones[46], chronobiology is now dismantling the secrets of our hidden time shape (Figs. 5, 6). This is also interesting from a philosophical point of view as science gains access to something that is less a physical matter, not a chemical substance, not its concentration, not energy and not even space—it is time and its biological structure. In a way we are discovering what could be called an anatomy and a histology of time represented in the different rhythms acting in our body and the symphonic orchestra playing the tune of our life.

This has consequences for an understanding of health and its maintenance. For example, as early as the 1930s, the extract of the pineal gland was used as a remedy against cancer with varying success [48]. Even today melatonin contained in the pineal gland is considered to be helpful against certain tumours. The question as to whether a simple high melatonin level is beneficial or a whether special timing of the melatonin application is necessary to improve the organismic resistance to cancer has not yet been clearly answered. There is, however, strong evidence that sleep quality improvement and beneficial immunological effects of melatonin [49] are only present if melatonin is administered in the evening [50]. Many new achievements of applied chronobiology, such as the application of medication in a timed fashion, give us an inkling that the future medical profession will utilize the human rhythms increasingly to support their therapies [51]. Playing in harmony with the body's orchestra is obviously not only more graceful and charming, but more effective than just playing loudly.

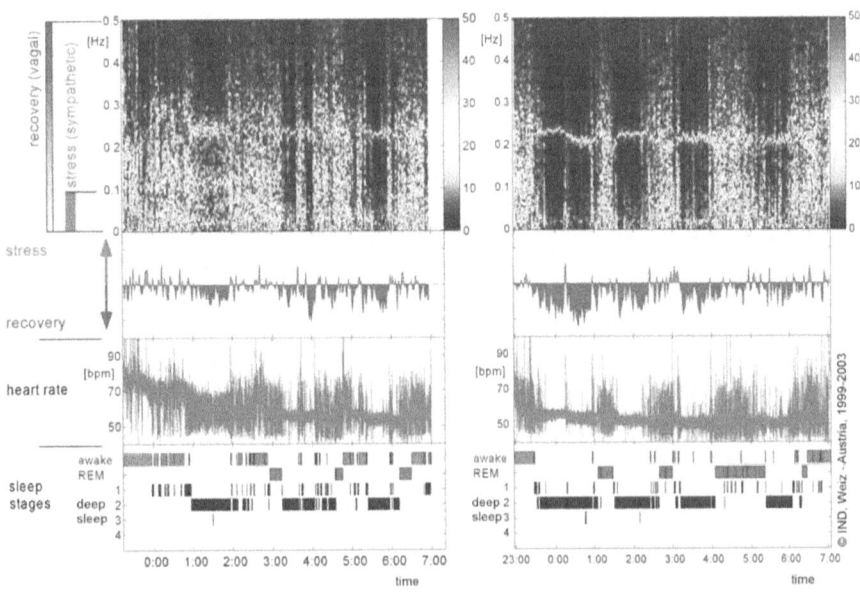

Fig. 5 (a, b) Body rhythms obtained by spectrogram analysis of heart-rate during sleep. The pattern of different rhythms defines whether the subject had slept badly (a, first night in a sleep laboratory) or well (b, second night in a sleep laboratory). It could be observed that good sleep is a process defined by a higher level of order. If this order is disturbed, e.g. by shift work or an unusual environment, the recuperatory effect of sleep is reduced [47]

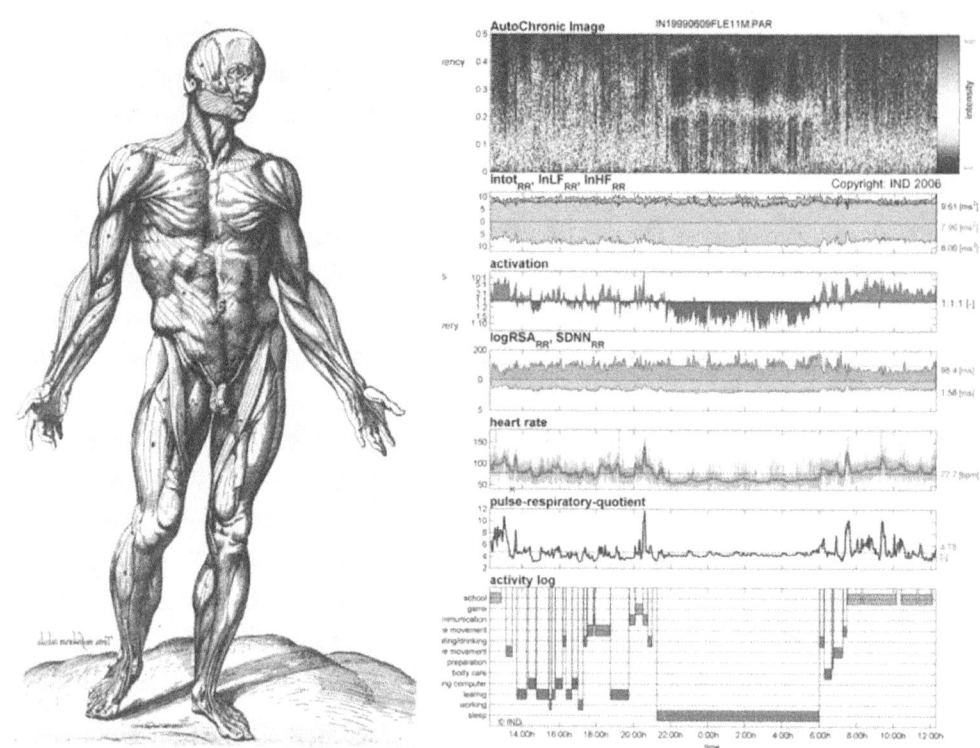

Fig. 6 (a, b) Physical anatomy of the human body is well known since the work of Andrea Vesalius (a). Medical science has only recently become aware of the complex patterns of body rhythms accessible e.g. by spectrogram analysis of long-term heart-rate recordings. Body rhythms display distinct times of chaos (mainly during the day) and order (during well slept nights). They are orchestrated horizontally e.g., by the circadian clock, which conducts the temporal order of different organs as well as vertically, by the rhythmic interaction of parameters like respiration and circulation. These become visible in the 4:1 integer ratio of the pulse-respiration quotient (b, green line) achieved during sleep and during periods of rest. (Left figure from [46])

Acknowledgement We would like to thank David Auerbach (Graz, Austria), Rainier Dierdorf (Arlesheim, Switzerland), Wolfgang Mädeland Henry Puff (Althofen, Austria) for helpful discussions and support in the translation of the manuscript.

References

1. Gillette MU, Sejnowski TJ (2005) *Biological clocks coordinately keep life on time.* Science 309: 1196–1198

2. Hildebrandt G, Moser M, Lehofer M. (1998) *Chronobiology and Chronomedicine – Biologic Rhythms Medical Consequences* (in German). Hippokrates, Stuttgart

3. Winfree A (2000) *The Geometry of Biological Time.* Springer, New York

4. Strogatz S (2003) *Sync: The Emerging Science of Spontaneous Order.* Hyperion, New York

5. Moser M, Lehofer M, Hildebrandt G, Voica M, Egner S, Kenner T (1995) *Phase- and frequency-coordination of cardiac and respiratory function.* Biol Rhythm Res 26: 100–111

6. Zhou T, Chen L, Aihara K (2005) *Molecular communication through stochastic synchronisation induced by extracellular fluctuations.* Phys Rev Lett 95: 178103

7. Challet E, Caldelas I, Graff C, Pevet P (2003) *Synchronization of the molecular clockwork by light- and food-related cues in mammals.* Biol Chem 384: 711–719

8. Cysarz D, von Bonin D, Lackner H, Heusser P, Moser M, Bettermann H (2004) *Oscillations of heart rate and respiration synchronize during poetry recitation.* Am J Physiol Heart Circ Physiol 287: H579–H587

9. Hrushesky WJ, Fader D, Schmitt O, Gilbertsen V (1984) *The respiratory sinus arrhythmia: a measure of cardiac age.* Science 224: 1001–1004

10. Harmer SL, Hogenesch JB, Straume M et al. (2000) *Orchestrated transcription of key pathways in Arabidopsis by the circadian clock.* Science 290: 2110–2113

11. Rivkees SA (2003) *Developing circadian rhythmicity in infants.* Pediatrics 112: 373–381

12. Rivkees SA, Mayes L, Jacobs H, Gross I (2004) *Rest-activity patterns of premature infants are regulated by cycled lighting.* Pediatrics 113: 833–839

13. Brandon DH, Holditch-Davis D, Belyea M (2002) *Preterm infants born at less than 31 weeks' gestation have improved growth in cycled light compared with continuous near darkness.* J Pediatr 140: 192–199

14. Cutler WB (1980) *Lunar and menstrual phase locking.* Am J Obstet Gynecol 137: 834–839

15. Cutler WB, Schleidt WM, Friedmann E, Preti G, Stine R (1987) *Lunar influences on the reproductive cycle in women.* Hum Biol 59: 959–972

16. Law SP (1986) *The regulation of menstrual cycle and its relationship to the moon.* Acta Obstet Gynecol Scand 65: 45–48

17. Endres K-P, Schad W (1997) *Lunar Biology* (in German). S. Hirzel Verlag, Stuttgart

18. Edery I (2000) *Circadian rhythms in a nutshell.* Physiol Genomics 3: 59–74

19. Klerman EB, Rimmer DW, Dijk DJ, Kronauer RE, Rizzo JF, 3rd, Czeisler CA (1998) *Non-photic entrainment of the human circadian pacemaker.* Am J Physiol 274: R991–R996

20. Zeitzer JM, Khalsa SB, Boivin DB et al. (2005) *Temporal dynamics of late-night photic stimulation of the human circadian timing system.* Am J Physiol Regul Integr Comp Physiol 289: R839–R834

21. Watanabe Y, Cornelissen G, Halberg F, Otsuka K, Ohkawa SI (2001) *Associations by signatures and coherences between the human circulation and helio- and geomagnetic activity.* Biomed Pharmaco Ther 55 (Suppl1): 76s–83s

22. Moser M, Lehofer M, Sedminek A et al. (1994) *Heart rate variability as a prognostic tool in cardiology. A contribution to the problem from a theoretical point of view.* Circulation 90: 1078–1082

23. Moser M, Lehofer M, Hoehn-Saric R et al. (1998) *Increased heart rate in depressed subjects in spite of unchanged autonomic balance?* J Affect Disord 48: 115–124

24. Moser M, Frühwirth M, Lackner H et al. (2000) *Baufit–Stress on the building site—made visible by the heartbeat.* AUVA-Report (Vienna) 38: 55–70

25. Tu BP, Kudlicki A, Rowicka M, McKnight SL (2005) *Logic of the yeast metabolic cycle: temporal compartmentalization of cellular processes.* Science 310: 1152–1158

26. Masoro EJ (2003) *Subfield history: caloric restriction, slowing aging, and extending life.* Sci Aging Knowledge Environ 2003 (8): RE2

27. Piper MD, Mair W, Partridge L (2005) *Counting the calories: the role of specific nutrients in extension of life span by food restriction.* J Gerontol A Biol Sci Med Sci 60: 549–555

28. Huygens C (1673) *Horoloquium Oscilatorium.* Parisiis

29. Pourquie O (2003) *The segmentation clock: converting embryonic time into spatial pattern.* Science 301: 328–330

30. Duboule D (2003) *Time for chronomics?* Science 301: 277

31. Bettermann H, Kroz M, Girke M, Heckmann C (2001) *Heart rate dynamics and cardiorespiratory coordination in diabetic and breast cancer patients.* Clin Physiol 21: 411–420

32. Moser M, Schaumberger K, Frühwirth M, Penter R (2005) *Chronomedicine and the new importance of time in cancer diagnosis and therapy* (in German). Promed 1 (2): 16–23

33. O'Donnell JF (2004) *Insomnia in cancer patients.* Clin Cornerstone 6 (Suppl 1D): S6–S14

34. Lavie P (2001) *Sleep-wake as a biological rhythm.* Annu Rev Psychol 52: 277–303

35. Keith LG, Oleszczuk JJ, Laguens M (2001) *Circadian rhythm chaos: a new breast cancer marker.* Int J Fertil Womens Med 46: 238–247

36. Jain RK (2003) *Molecular regulation of vessel maturation,* NatMed 9: 685–693

37. Simpson HW (1996) Sir James Young Simpson Memorial Lecture 1995. *Breast cancer prevention: a pathologist's approach.* JR Coll Surg Edinb 41: 359–370

38. Salhab M, Al Sarakbi W, Mokbel K (2005) *The evolving role of the dynamic thermal analysis in the early detection of breast cancer.* Int Semin Surg Oncol 2: 8–13

39. Bartsch C, Bartsch H, Jain AK, Laumas KR, Wetterberg L (1981) *Urinary melatonin levels in human breast cancer patients.* J Neural Transm 52: 281–294

40. Fu L, Lee CC (2003) *The circadian clock: pacemaker and tumor suppressor.* Nat Rev Cancer 3: 350–361

41. Lloyd D, Aon MA, Cortassa S (2001) *Why homeodynamics, not homeostasis?* Scientific World Journal 1: 133–145

42. Koch E (1931) *The reflectory self-control of circulation* (in German). Steinkopff, Dresden

43. Yun AJ, Bazar KA, Gerber A, Lee PY, Daniel SM (2005) *The dynamic range of biologic functions and variation of many environmental cues may be declining in the modern age: implications for diseases and therapeutics.* Med Hypotheses 65: 173–178

44. Moser M, Schaumberger K, Schernhammer ES, Stevens RG (2006) *Cancer and rhythm.* Cancer Causes Control 17: 483–487

45. www.klangoptimierung.de/en/

46. Vesalius A (1543) *Decorporishumanifabrica,* Basileae

47. Spiegel K, Leproult R, Van Cauter E (1999) *Impact of sleep debt on metabolic and endocrine function.* Lancet 354: 1435–1439

48. Bartsch C, Bartsch H (2006) *The anti-tumour activity of pineal melatonin and cancer enhancing life styles in industrialized societies.* Cancer Causes and Control, this volume

49. Cardinali DP, Brusco LI, Cutrera RA, Castrillon P, Esquifino AI (1999) *Melatonin as a time-meaningful signal in circadian organization of immune response.* Biol Signals Recept 8: 41–48

50. Cardinali DP, Brusco LI, Lloret SP, Furio AM (2002) *Melatonin in sleep disorders and jet-lag.* Neuroendocrinol Lett 23 (Suppl 1): 9–13

51. Mormont MC, Levi F (2003) *Cancer chronotherapy: principles, applications, and perspectives.* Cancer 97: 155–169

ABOUT THE KOLISKO CONFERENCES

Eugen Kolisko (1893-1939) was an Austrian physician who specialized in preventative medicine and worked closely with Rudolf Steiner, becoming the school doctor at the first Waldorf School in Stuttgart, Germany. His practice took into account children's developmental processes in body, soul and spirit. His legacy encourages the collaboration of teachers, doctors, therapists, and parents to support the healthy development of each child.

Over the last few decades, the Kolisko conferences have sought to bring together the pedagogical and therapeutic tools found within Waldorf education. In 2006, for the first time, there were nine such conferences held worldwide in Hyderabad, India; Taipei-Taichung, Taiwan; Cape Town, South Africa; Manila, Philippines; Krym, Ukraine; Sydney, Australia; Guanajuato, Mexico; Järna, Sweden; and Paris, France.

This compilation arose from the 2006 Kolisko conference lectures, spanning topics that include meditation for teachers, projective geometry, children's exposure to technology, how to approach sex education, physiology and its connection to education, and more.

Kolisko conferences also took place in 1992 (Austria), 1994 (UK), 1998 (USA), and 2002 (Finland), often with over 1,000 participants taking part.

In Hawai'i, 2010, the Kolisko conference theme was "Reading the needs of children and understanding the stages of human development—birth to age 21."

In Taiwan, 2013, the Kolisko conference theme was "Shaping a sense of community: From blood family to world family."

In 2015, a Kolisko conference was held in Malaysia, focusing on individual health and community well-being.

In Hawai'i, 2018, the Kolisko conference theme was "Truth, Beauty, and Goodness: the future of education, healing arts, and health care."

> *"Let us make this work, which started as a deep philosophical insight and valuable inspiration for humanity, into a daily practice."*
>
> – MICHAELA GLÖCKLER, "Welcome to the Hawai'i International Kolisko Conference 2018"

www.ingramcontent.com/pod-product-compliance
Lightning Source LLC
Chambersburg PA
CBHW081718100526
44591CB00016B/2413